CASE STUDIES IN BUSINESS, SOCIETY, AND ETHICS

Fourth Edition

CASE STUDIES IN BUSINESS, SOCIETY, AND ETHICS

Edited by

Tom L. Beauchamp
Georgetown University

Prentice Hall, Upper Saddle River, New Jersey 07458

Library of Congress Cataloging-in-Publication Data

Case studies in business, society, and ethics / edited by TOM L.
    BEAUCHAMP.—4th ed.
    p. cm.
    Includes index.
    ISBN 0-13-398512-1
    1. Industries—Social aspects—United States—Case studies.
2. Industrial policy—United States—Case studies. 3. Trade
regulation—United States—Case studies. I. Beauchamp, Tom L.
HD60.5.U5B38   1998
658.4'08'0973—dc21   97-25144

Acquisitions editor: *Angela Stone*
Production editor: *Edie Riker*
Cover design: *Bruce Kenselaar*
Buyer: *Tricia Kenny*
Marketing manager: *Jennifer Weinberg*
Editorial assistant: *Elizabeth Del Colliano*

This book was set in 10/12 New Baskerville by East End Publishing Services
and it was printed and bound by Courier Companies, Inc. The cover was
printed by Phoenix Color Corp.

© 1998, 1993, 1989, by Prentice-Hall, Inc.
Simon & Schuster / A Viacom Company
Upper Saddle River, New Jersey 07458

Printed in the United States of America

10   9   8   7   6   5   4   3   2   1

ISBN   0-13-398512-1

Prentice-Hall International (UK) Limited, *London*
Prentice-Hall of Australia Pty. Limited, *Sydney*
Prentice-Hall Canada Inc., *Toronto*
Prentice-Hall Hispanoamericana, S.A., *Mexico*
Prentice-Hall of India Private Limited, *New Delhi*
Prentice-Hall of Japan, Inc., *Tokyo*
Simon & Schuster Asia Pte. Ltd., *Singapore*
Editora Prentice-Hall do Brasil, Ltda., *Rio de Janeiro*

For Zachary,
Young Entrepreneur

CONTENTS

EXPANDED CONTENTS

This alternative listing of cases is an expansion of the basic Contents. It is offered as a guide for teachers and students. It should be especially useful for teachers who plan a large segment of a course around a restricted range of topics. For example, a teacher who devotes a major part of a course to the topic of business and government can easily locate the large number of cases relevant to this subject. (The headings in the basic Contents are unchanged, but a larger set of cases is included under most headings.)

Chapter 3   THE ENVIRONMENT   93

Chapter 4   THE SOCIETY   139

Chapter 5   THE GOVERNMENT   201

Public Policy and Corporate Responsibility

Benefits for Private Corporations and Citizens

The Ban on Insider Trading

Chapter 6   THE MULTINATIONAL   250

PREFACE

The 35 cases in this volume share a focus on ethical and social issues surrounding business. Over 90 percent of the cases have undergone revisions in this fourth edition. These changes range from minor updates to complete rewritings.

The objective of this volume is to make students aware of situations that require moral reflection, judgment, and decision, while revealing the complexities that often surround moral choices and the formation of public policies. The book has not been produced to create a platform for moralistic criticism of the behavior of individual persons, corporations, or governmental agencies that play leading roles in the cases. Some cases contain dramatic instances of professional irresponsibility, but it should not be inferred that their purpose is to teach what ought not to be done or that conduct in the profession under discussion generally follows this pattern. Irresponsible actions are occasionally featured because more can sometimes be learned from wrongful than from rightful behavior. However, learning through the study of wrongful or negligent behavior is not the primary orientation of this volume. The focus is generally on circumstances in which hard choices must be made under complex conditions of uncertainty or disagreement. More is to be learned from reasoning under circumstances of controversy, personal quandary, and incompleteness of information than from paradigmatic cases of irresponsibility.

The length and structure of the cases also deserve comment. Many cases that now circulate in the general literature of business, society, and ethics are either too short to contain enough detail for discussion or contain such a vast body of data that discussion is retarded by the particulars and their connections. Most of us encounter severe limitations on the amount of information we can study and remember about any sequence of events; and too much information often makes it difficult to find the essence of the problem. Accordingly, most cases in this book conform to the model of tidy cases that come to the essence of the matter without a massive body of descriptions and data.

However, any experienced executive and any experienced teacher will rightly insist that the situations under which decisions are made in business are multifarious, perplexing, and short on relevant information. Executives see real-life cases as too intricate for short summary presentation. This point of view has its merits. Every student should appreciate that cases almost always contain many details beyond the mentioned facts. This is so even when cases are described at book length—as, for example, the Love Canal and Reserve Mining cases reported in this volume have been studied.

I have tried to write cases that contain sufficient detail to facilitate discussion in the classroom without becoming mired in detail. Cases of this length also make it possible to produce a book with a variety of issues at an affordable cost to students.

Many teachers of the subject matter found in this book prefer cases that take an "inside" view of a corporation or institution under investigation in the case. They want to examine the decisions managers must make and the strategies they follow on the firing line. I endorse this form of pedagogy, and several cases in this book are so oriented. However, this approach incorporates only one profitable form of case and style of case study. An *outside* look at corporate activities is sometimes the only perspective obtainable. Moreover, it can be the best approach to cases that involve public policy. A variety of approaches to case writing is therefore used in this book, some taking the inside look, some the outside perspective, and some using a mixture of perspectives.

Some teachers and students like to see questions at the end of each case, in the belief that these questions focus reading and discussion on particular features of the cases. I believe this practice is an editorial disservice rather than a service. A teacher may profitably circulate questions in a class, but the problem with this approach in a text is twofold: (1) Teachers teach the cases with very different approaches, purposes, and problems; and (2) students can easily be impeded in their own thinking by being channeled in a particular direction. For these reasons, no questions or aids other than general introductions to chapters accompany the cases in this volume.

Virtually all cases in this book report actual rather than hypothetical events. That is, they are based on authentic incidents that occurred in a circumstance of business or during the development of public policy. Corporations involved are usually identified by their correct names. However, in several cases confidential material was used or full documentation of some claims was impossible; in these cases, names, dates, and locations have been changed, and no identification of the corporations and persons originally involved is present. In a few of these cases some hypothetical elements have been added to highlight the problem and focus the reader's understanding of the situation. In two instances a composite case was created from several actual cases by combining various features of the cases.

ACKNOWLEDGMENTS

A talented research staff has assisted me for several years in the collecting and writing of these cases, and I have in turn been generously supported through previous editions of the book by several grants. Support came initially from the Exxon Educational Foundation and the Landegger Program in International Business Diplomacy at Georgetown University. The Kennedy Institute of Ethics also supported this work. Through the institute, work on new cases in the third edition was supported in part by BRSG SO7 RR 07136-18-20 grants awarded by the National Center for Research Resources, National Institutes of Health. I also acknowledge the support provided by the Kennedy Institute's library and information retrieval systems, which kept me in touch with the most important literature and repeatedly reduced the burdens of library research. Mary Coutts deserves a special acknowledgment for this work.

Research on the cases in this volume has been undertaken by Jeff Greene, Kier Olsen, John Cuddihy, Ari Paparo, Katie Marshall, Nicole Herb, David Parver, Katy Cancro, Jennifer Givens, Brian Tauscher, Jeffrey Kahn, Kelley MacDougall, Anna Pinedo, R. Jay Wallace, Martha Elliott, Nancy Blanpied, William Pitt, Barbara Humes, Louisa W. Peat O'Neil, Andrew Rowan, Linda Kern, Cathleen Kaveny, and Sara Finnerty Kelly. Ted Moran and John Kline of the Landegger Program steered me in a number of important directions. Helpful criticisms and constructive suggestions in various editions have been made by Ed Epstein, Ruth Faden, Norman Bowie, Tom Donaldson, Theodore Purcell, Carl Kaufman, Lisa Newton, Robert Cooke, William H. Hay, Thomas L. Carson, Archie B. Carroll, George Lodge, Henry W. Tulloch, Vivian Weil, Michael Hooker, Deborah G. Johnson, David P. Boyd, Richard E. Wokutch, Burton Leiser, Homer B. Sewell, Stephen Klaidman, and John H. Bubar. Some useful and substantive suggestions for improving the Introduction were made by Terry Pinkard, Ruth Faden, Judith Areen, and Alexander Capron. Michael Pritchard, William Griffith, Artegal Camburn, and John Modschiedler all reviewed a previous edition and made suggestions for improvements.

A number of corporations discussed in the cases in this volume also provided vital materials and criticisms. A couple threatened lawsuits, but most were extraordinarily kind and patient. I am pleased to be able to name the following sources and constructive critics: Cathy Hughto-Delzer of New York State Electric and Gas; Tom Behan of IBM; James E. Sanderson of Cyprus Minerals Co. (Reserve Mining Co.); Carol Rozek of Barr Laboratories, Inc.; Kathy S. Bartlett of Burroughs Wellcome Co.; Karen J. Megaffee, Canandaigua Wine Co.; Carol A. Boyd of Procter and Gamble; James M. Green of Hooker Chemical; Robert Jeffrey of AT&T; Kathryn Ribbey of Ruder Finn & Rotman; Thomas J. Moore of Tampax; Robert M. Palmer of Polaroid; Aracelia Garcia-Vila of Warner Lambert; John T. Sant of McDonnell Douglas; Frank Tomlinson of McDonnell Douglas; Craig Shulstad of General Mills; Susan K. Hartt of Kellogg Cereals; Carl Kaufman and Bruce W. Karrh of Du Pont; Martha Beauchamp of the American Petroleum Institute; Tom McCollough of Abbott/Ross Industries; J. Lee Bailey of the Cleveland Electric Illuminating Co.; Pat Conry of Johnson Controls; and Roger Shelley of Revlon.

I was also aided by several persons in organizations other than corporations, including a number of officials at federal agencies in Washington. I express gratitude in particular to William Laynor of the National Transportation and Safety Board; Janet Marie-Boetani of Centers for Disease Control; Steven Klitzman of the FCC; Curtis W. Edwards of the Public Health Service; Alan Mills of the American Cancer Society; Jerome Seidenfeld of the AMA; John Renner of the Consumer Health Information Research Institute; Penny Holland of the FDA; James P. Ficaretta of the Bureau of Alcohol, Tobacco, and Firearms; Patricia Taylor of the Center for Science in the Public Interest (CSPI); Joseph Wright of the Children's National Medical Center; Rose Ann Soloway of the American Association of Poison Control Centers; Peggy Charron of Action for Children's Television (ACT); Robert B. Choate of the Council on Children, Media, and Merchandising (CCMM); and unknown sources of the Coalition for Environmental-Energy Balance. Several lawyers and media representatives enabled me to obtain (with permission) confidential papers from corporations. I regret that I am not at liberty to mention these lawyers, media representatives, and corporations by name.

I appreciate the suggestions of the most recent Prentice Hall reviewers: John Modschiedler, College of Dupage; Richard L. Wilson, Loyala College of Maryland; and Jonathan P. West, University of Miami.

T. L. B.
Washington, DC

INTRODUCTION:
THE USES OF CASES

The cases collected in this volume emerge from the intersection of professional practice in business, economics, law, and government. The cases can be profitably explored from each of these disciplinary perspectives. The purpose of this Introduction is to investigate how perspectives in these disciplines affect our understanding of the problems embodied in a case, the nature and history of case methods, different types of case analysis, pitfalls in case analysis, and reservations about the "facts" as presented in cases.

DIFFERENT PERSPECTIVES ON THE STUDY OF CASES

Many students and teachers who benefit from the study of cases agree that cases help to focus and dramatize problems and, at the same time, to identify problems in real-life situations. Beyond this point of initial agreement, however, orientations and styles of case analysis are diverse and plentiful. Different disciplines direct a reader to identify different elements in the cases as problematic and deserving of analysis. This pluralism of approaches occurs in the broad territory of "business, society, and ethics" as a result of two distinct, though not incompatible, orientations: (1) the perspective of *ethics* and (2) the perspective of *business.*

The ethics orientation ("business ethics") consists in the analysis of cases using categories such as justice, utility, rights, and trustworthiness. Cases about reverse discrimination in hiring, for example, are studied in light of theories of justice and social utility and principles such as equal opportunity. In this paradigm, a consideration of moral decisions, quandaries, and virtues is fundamental to a proper understanding of the case. Ethical theories may not be studied and may not be called on for the analysis of each case, but these theories often play a role in the ethical analysis.

The business orientation tends to categorize its endeavor as "business and society" and analyzes cases in terms of various relationships between business and industry, on the one hand, and government and society, on the other. Cases about environmental pollution, for example, are studied by detailing empirical facts about pollution and disease and by examining social processes that have diminished the scope of decision making in business and have created new responsibilities through government requirements. The economic aspects of pollution control are central to this approach. The responses of corporations to changing legal and regulatory situations as well as the importance of skillful management are often heavily emphasized in this paradigm, as are the considerations of what has been and may become public policy. Tax policies and the economic consequences of proposed public policies may be studied in detail and are likely to be viewed as central to the analysis of cases. Ethical principles and other staples of moral philosophy may not be mentioned at all, just as those who examine cases with an ethical interest may ignore questions of good and bad management.

These different orientations are not mutually exclusive, nor is one orientation preferable to another. A more constructive approach is to acknowledge that cases invite multiple forms of productive analysis, and that increased complexity increases the possibilities for different forms of analysis.

THE CASE METHOD IN LAW

Just as different *perspectives* on cases prompt us to look for different ingredients, different *strategies* for analyzing cases yield different outcomes. The oldest and most extensive body of thought on strategies for analyzing cases (apart from religious traditions) is found in law, where the case method has long been a staple of legal training and where case law establishes precedents of evidence and justification. It is instructive to look first to the history of legal case analysis, which has had a deep impact on the case method in business.

The birth of the case method in law occurred shortly after 1870 when Christopher Columbus Langdell became dean of the law school at Harvard. Upon his installation he immediately revolutionized previous academic standards and teaching techniques by introducing the case method. He intended this method to replace the prevailing textbooks and lecture methods, which he condemned as promoting rote learning and worthless acumen for passing examinations. Langdell's idea was to use casebooks rather than textbooks for the entire law school curriculum. The casebooks were comprised of cases selected, edited, and arranged to impart to the student the pervasive meanings of legal terms, as well as the rules and principles of law.

This approach used a Socratic manner of teaching to reveal how concepts, rules, and principles are found in the legal reasoning of judges, as exhibited in the cases. The skillful teacher presumably could extract the embedded nuggets that are the fundamental principles of law, much as a skillful biographer extracts the true principles of a person's reasoning by studying his or her considered decisions over a lifetime.

Langdell was not a disenchanted teacher who disliked conventional methods of lecturing. Rather, he had theoretical reasons for his reforms. In his view the law was no perfunctory profession that any clerk could learn by boning up on textbook wisdom. Langdell believed that the law is a science that rests on an inductive method modeled on the scientific method of the natural sciences. Teachers and students develop hypotheses in their dissection of cases and arrive at principles just as any scientist does. In law, he argued, one extracts from cases a select body of principles that frame the English common law.[1] Although the many particulars in cases vary and their judicial conclusions sometimes conflict, the principles of judicial reasoning remain constant. Also, one could utilize this method to study exactly how far a principle extends. In the process the student acquires a facility and sophistication in moving from particular circumstances to generalizations and back.

Langdell's innovation horrified Harvard students, and they skipped classes in massive numbers. They disliked both criticism by dialectical questioning and the preparation required for every class. There was also a faculty revolt, and the school's enrollment slipped noticeably. But in the end Langdell was victorious. The method was adopted and spread quickly to other echelons of American legal education. Eventually every American law school of renown succumbed in some measure to the new case method. This outcome was unfortunate because there were many unexamined problems and pretentious claims in the Langdell vision, especially the odd notion of making the law a science and reducing its essence to a few abstract principles. This vision tended to suppress such integral aspects of law as legislation, the politics of legislation, particular historical circumstances, jurisdictional variations, and legal practice.

There were, however, good reasons why this method, with appropriate modifications, ultimately prevailed in American law schools. By making analysis of case law a basic component of legal education, teachers have a powerful tool for generalizing from cases. Spanning the tangled web of details in particular cases are principles and fundamental doctrines. Moreover, training in the case method sharpens skills of legal reasoning, including both legal analysis and legal synthesis. One can dissect a case and then construct an improved way of treating similar cases. In the thrust-and-parry classroom setting, teacher and student think through a case and its rights and wrongs. A student no longer simply memorizes a section of a textbook that transmits general wisdom about the right answer. The method prepares the student for the practice of law, not for theoretical wisdom about it.

The case method was the soul of American legal education from roughly 1880 until 1910, and leading legal texts and practices today provide evidence that its legacy endures. However, since 1910 the case method has been less grandiosely conceived than during the Langdell era. Its minor decline, in retrospect, was inevitable.[2] The principles did not prove to be as uniform across courts or time as had at first been thought, because precedent cases revealed incompatible and sometimes rival legal theories. The method was also isolationist in the context of the modern university: It made law a specialty without connections to other professions and undercut interdisciplinary investigation.

Ultimately the theory of law as a science waned and suffered a natural death. However, it left as its substantial legacy not only the extensive use of legal casebooks but also an allied belief in the importance of case analysis and synthesis in legal training. Its enduring value probably rests in the way it teaches students to distinguish the nature of principles and evidence at work in one case as opposed to another. By examining cases students learn which courts are considered adept at legal reasoning, how to assemble facts, and where the weight of the evidence lies. They can then transfer that weight elsewhere in new cases. It is widely (although not uniformly)[3] agreed that this type of study offers substantial benefits in the training of lawyers, whatever its pitfalls and shortcomings.

THE CASE METHOD IN BUSINESS SCHOOLS

Historical Development.   When the case method at the Harvard Law School enjoyed its peak of influence, it spawned a new infant across campus at the Harvard Business School, which opened its doors in 1908. The first dean of the school, Edwin F. Gay, decided that courses on commercial law would use only the case method, whereas other courses would use it in conjunction with lectures and reports. Dean Gay stated that "the example of the Harvard Law School," greatly prized in academic business circles, was responsible for this decision.[4] Cases and reports were introduced gradually into business policy and marketing courses. Because the faculty was acclimated to lecturing, Gay had to push hard for more extensive use of the case system, although he never used the method in his own economic history courses.

The method began to flourish throughout the curriculum under Dean Wallace B. Donham, who assumed the office in 1919. His training in law proved instrumental, as the following account by a later dean of the business school, Donald K. David, makes clear:

> Dean Donham's training in the law and his own wide business experience gave him the conviction that the case method was the sound approach for instruction. . . . Dean Donham recognized that the development of the case system for teaching business would be a slow and expensive process. The law schools had the decisions of the courts, the medical schools had hospital cases and clinical records, and the scientific schools had their laboratories and records of experiments. In contrast, there were nowhere any records of the process of making business decisions. Therefore the development of the case system in the Business School had to take the slow and hard way; . . . those who gathered cases had to go out to the businesses themselves to record the actual situations.[5]

Following Langdell's example, Donham pushed his faculty to develop casebooks for courses. Faculty began to collect materials for cases through systematic and comprehensive searches and from sources in government, business research, and journalism. Although these searches were at first limited to industrial management, the school pursued and persuaded people in different areas of business to provide accounts of their practices and experiences. This pursuit was called *fieldwork* and was done on field trips.[6] There was no attempt to present either good or bad, successful or unsuccessful practices. Rather, the intent was to present the typical and significant problems faced by business administrators. During the period from 1920 to 1940, over $2 million was spent on case development. Dean Donham had achieved the same level of commitment to the case method as had Langdell.

It was never anticipated, however, that the case method in business schools would be a science, or that the cases would be treated in a uniform way. The more typical view has emphasized a broad, common sense perspective:

> The case method is so varied, so diverse, so adaptable to the nature of the individual course and to the personality of the individual instructor, that no single person can portray it accurately. Indeed, the only discernible common thread . . . is the emphasis on student participation in the educational process . . . —assessing the facts, making the analysis, weighing the considerations, and reaching a decision.[7]

Under this model, the cases collected for courses are chosen with two criteria in mind: (1) The case requires reflection and decision making under circumstances of complexity, and (2) the case will incite vigorous classroom discussion. As the first criterion suggests, cases that involve dilemmas are preferred. As both the first and second suggest, a case that promotes recounting of information rather than reflective involvement is unacceptable. Accordingly, the presuppositions of business school professors often stand in sharp contrast to those of law professors. Cases in business are not used primarily to illustrate principles or rules. The fundamental idea is to develop a capacity to grasp problems and reason effectively toward their solutions.

The innovations required for a case-based curriculum generated controversy and sometimes outright hostility at the business school. At stake was the future of two clashing educational philosophies. On one hand were those who believed in distilling wisdom and facts through lecturing. When done well, lecturing can be a highly efficient way of transmitting valuable material to students, who feel comfortable with the controllable facts and safe orientation such a system provides. On the other hand, according to a different ideal of learning, education is a medium that affords the student an understanding of an environment, usually one under constant change and innovation, in which decisions must be made. To adapt a distinction of Gilbert Ryle's, the difference in training and educational philosophy is rooted in the distinction between knowing *that* and knowing *how*.[8] The purpose of the case method in business has long been to train students in how to think and act in complex and shifting business environments. The pioneers who pushed hardest for the case method knew that facts and general principles were sacrificed in order to sharpen the capacities for thought and decision making. Thus, one might know nothing about probability theory but a great deal about how to think under circumstances of probable outcomes.

The Essence of the Case Method.   Despite the previously noted warnings about diversity in approaches to cases, there is a certain essence to the technique of the case method as practiced in business schools. This is accurately recounted in a classic article on the case method by Charles I. Gragg:

> A case typically is a record of a business issue which *actually* has been faced by business executives, together with surrounding facts, opinions, and prejudices upon which executive decisions had to depend. These real and particularized cases are presented to students for considered analysis, open discussion, and final decision as to the type of actions which should be taken. Day by day the number of individual business situations thus brought before the students grows and forms a backlog for observing coherent patterns and drawing out general principles. In other words, students are not given theories or hypotheses to criticize. Rather, they are given specific facts, the raw materials, out of which decisions have to be reached in life and from which they can realistically and usefully draw conclusions. . . .
>
> There is no single, demonstrable right answer to a business problem. For the student or businessman it cannot be a matter of peeking in the back of books to see if he has arrived at the right solution. . . .
>
> The instructor's role is . . . to provoke argumentative thinking, to guide discussion, . . . and if he chooses, to take a final position on the viewpoints which have been threshed out before him. . . . But *authoritarian* use of the cases perverts the unique characteristics of the system. The opportunity which this system provides the students of reaching responsible judgments on the basis of an original analysis of the facts is sacrificed.[9]

One conviction underlying this pedagogical viewpoint is that students have typically been trained in universities as if they were immature children. The lecture-based university is based on the premise that students are unable to think until they have been given a thought apparatus. They are ill-equipped to make decisions because they lack basic facts and principles. Decision making is considered an adult function into which students will gradually grow, upon first learning accepted theories and techniques. Those who initiated the case method believed this assumption about student abilities and training to be entirely false. As they saw it, a school of business administration has as one of its premiere functions "to achieve the transition from what may be described as a childlike dependence on parents and teachers to a state of what may be called dependable self-reliance."[10] The case method was envisioned as the cornerstone of this shift and advance in pedagogy. Many of its practitioners still hold this view.

No assumption is made in this method that there is a right answer to any problem that is presented, but only that there are more or less successful ways of handling problems. Understanding argument and analysis takes priority over understanding substantive theories. These forms of understanding need not be seen as antagonistic or competitive, but the case method in business places a premium on a problem-based form of analysis rather than on theoretical analysis. The student confronts a body of facts and data that cannot be handled except by thinking through problems and solutions. Just as a medical student must learn not only to diagnose a patient's problem but also to exert a clinical judgment about its alleviation, a student who properly uses the case method not only must understand a problem situation in business, but also must construct a recommendation for its resolution. If, by previous systems of education, a student has become accustomed to passive understanding rather than active judging, the role of the case method is to nullify this conception and to teach habits of active engagement.

However, the entire business community has never been convinced that this method should be the sole mode of instruction. Many believe that business is too diverse and requires detailed knowledge unobtainable from case studies alone. For example, CBS decided to sell its ownership of Fawcett Books and the Popular Library. It had not done well in the mass market paperback book industry with these subsidiaries. Interestingly, when it came time to assign blame for failure, the case method received much of the criticism. "Fawcett and Popular were ruined by Harvard MBAs," said Patrick O'Connor, who had moved from Fawcett to Pinnacle Books. He added, "Book publishing is a unique business; it can't be done with case studies."[11]

TWO CONCEPTS OF THE CASE METHOD

The analysis to this point suggests a critical difference between case analysis in law and business. Cases in law are based on the reasoning of judges. A court's reasoned opinion is the *form* of the case, the facts the mere *matter*. In any attempt to extract evidence or other useful parallels from the case, the facts alone are sterile and substitutable. But in business, the cases have no such form. There is no reasoned opinion or precedent case to be studied for its controlling principles and weight of evidence. The cases themselves are nothing but the facts of the case. Any reasoned opinion is an additional overlay; one cannot expect from a study of the facts that principles can be generalized. There are no principles or predictability because there is no set reasoning and no common law. To this extent legal methods are peculiar to law and cannot be transferred to other professional school contexts.

Thus there are at least two concepts of the case method, both deriving historically from Langdell. Let us call these two methods the problem-based case method and the authority-based case method. The former is the governing ideal in business, although it is also used by teachers of ethics. This method focuses critical thinking on a problem. It stimulates reflection on appropriate actions and policies, and the problems provoke decision making on both personal and social levels. In using this method there is (usually) no ultimate authority, and disagreements are expected to abound without final resolution.

The authority-based case method contrasts noticeably. Here the facts of the case are purely instrumental; the judge's reasoning about the facts is the central feature. Students learn how judges think, and they must master this thinking—not the social or moral problems presented by the case. The problem-based method can be used to examine these same cases. However, to employ a problem-based approach is to abandon the authority-based approach. In the latter, predictability in transferring the reasoning from one case to another is a virtue, because what one seeks to learn in using the authority-based method is what will happen in the courts.

THE CASE METHOD IN PHILOSOPHY AND ETHICS

The philosopher R. B. Perry once tendered the following reflection on education in the humanities:

> [I]n subjects such as philosophy and literature, in which it is likewise respectable to entertain different opinions, teachers hesitate to teach their students how to choose among them, and hesitate themselves to choose.
>
> But thought is applied to action through *decision*. Giving students ideas without enabling them to draw conclusions is like giving them sharpened tools without teaching them what to do with them.[12]

Perry's perspective has become influential but not dominant in philosophy. Until recently, this perspective had never been connected to the case method or to professional practice in fields such as business. The field of philosophy is oriented toward a problem-based approach to learning, but the idea of honing the ability to make decisions through case analysis has not traditionally been a part of the curriculum. There has been far less discussion paralleling that in law and business as to whether case-based teaching more adequately prepares a student for judgment and practice than conventional textbook, lecture, and seminar approaches.

This hiatus is modestly surprising. Socrates, the first great philosopher, practiced some aspects of the case method with consummate skill. He taught ethical theory by using a method in which he served as a kind of midwife by eliciting from the student reflection, insight, understanding, and both theoretical and practical judgment. He never lectured about ethics, but rather engaged the student in a dialogue that often eventuated in discovery and mutual decision making. His method started with a profession of ignorance (not a parading of theory) and proceeded to pointed questions that eventuated in proposed principles or universal definitions. He tested the latter by hypotheses, then modified and tested them further until theoretical insight into principles or definitions was achieved. Modifications specifically involved repeated appeals to cases, which, although short, were constantly used in shaping his conclusions.

Another tradition in the use of cases dates from Aristotle, who discussed the role of practical wisdom and practical judgment in directing human activities. The goal of ethics, he maintained, is to engage in practical reasoning. He depicted a person of practical wisdom as one who envisions what should be done in particular circumstances, using a capacity he thought distinguishable from intellectual abstraction and cleverness. Centuries later Immanuel Kant discussed the study of cases and examples in sharpening a student's capacity for practical judgment. Kant did not rely as centrally as Aristotle on the person of good practical judgment, but Kant did maintain that the study of case examples is an effective means of training students in practical decision making.

The case method has also had an interesting history in philosophical and theological traditions now commonly referred to as casuistry. This tradition is skeptical of rules and principles: One can make actual moral judgments of agents and actions only when one has an intimate understanding of particular situations and a history of similar cases. Apart from an acquaintance with both a situation and a case history—such as case histories in the courts that contain authoritative decisions—one is in no position to resolve moral problems. Until there is a case history rich enough that a cultural unit is able to agree that it is normatively adequate, moral reasoning cannot be applied to new cases within that cultural unit.[13] Just as the courts could not function without case law, we could not be moral reasoners without a similar case history that for us is authoritative.[14]

The methods of Socrates, Aristotle, and Kant have long served as routine components of a philosophical education. Recently in philosophy there has been some stirring of interest in the use of case studies and some revival of interest in casuistry as a constructive ethical theory. Philosophers now insist that we must address moral and social problems through both abstract, theoretical thinking and concrete decision making based on attention to particulars. Some have maintained that "case studies are employed most effectively when they can readily be used to draw out broader ethical principles and moral rules . . . [so as] to draw the attention of students to the common elements in a variety of cases, and to the implicit problems of ethical theory to which they may point."[15] The analogy to some legal uses of the case method is apparent in this comment. But, as in the case of law, it is difficult to implement this goal.

Possibly the best use of cases in both philosophy and business is not as a *source* of generalizations, but rather as a *test* of generalizations. By this criterion, cases help to sharpen and refine theoretical claims, especially by highlighting the uses, inadequacies, and limitations of theories. Cases illustrate the application of fundamental ethical notions, rather than act as a medium from which they can be extracted. Cases illustrate principles at work and exhibit how informed judgments are expressed. Case analysis, then, brings a general principle, proposal, or procedure under scrutiny to see how well it applies to one or more particular circumstances. A related maneuver is the use of cases as counterexamples to proposed principles or policies.

A somewhat grander vision of case analysis is found in John Rawls's proposal that in developing a normative ethical theory, it is appropriate to start with the broadest set of our considered moral judgments about a subject such as justice and then erect principles that reflect our judgments. These principles can then be pruned and adjusted by testing cases against them. Suppose, for example, that we select some problems of deceptive advertising and a corporation's failure to be environmentally responsibile for examination. Some widely accepted principles of right action might be construed, as Rawls puts it, "provisionally as fixed points," but also as "liable to revision."[16] Paradigm cases of what we all agree are right courses of action might be listed and examined, and we could then undertake a search for principles consistent with our judgments about these paradigm cases. These principles could be tested by reference to other paradigm cases, and other considered judgments found in similar cases, to see if they yield counterintuitive or conflicting results. The purpose of this process is to bring ethical theories and principles into a coherent unity with our considered judgments about particular cases. That is, general ethical principles and particular judgments could be brought into equilibrium. Presumably, the more complex and far-reaching the cases that force revisions, the richer the resultant theory will be. From this perspective, moral thinking resembles other forms of theorizing: Hypotheses must be tested, discarded, or modified through experimental thinking.

The point of a more theoretical orientation to cases is that the case method in business can become an unrewarding exposure to the unreflective prejudices of others unless defined and shaped by some moral framework. As valuable as cases are, they do not transmit moral understanding through a recounting of facts. Training in case analysis succeeds only when supplemented by ethical theory.

HARD CASES: THE PROBLEM OF DILEMMAS

We have noted that the purpose of case examination may not be to extract general principles, but to establish a forum for testing the authority or weight of principles when they conflict. Such testing can be highly illuminating when a dilemma arises and a hard choice must be made. Despite the saying "hard cases make bad law," bad law need not arise from legal dilemmas, and hard choices need not entail tragic choices. Such cases can improve and clarify the application of principles in law and in other fields. Because this volume contains many cases with dilemmas, the nature of dilemmas and their analysis merits further discussion.

To begin, it is misleading to assume that the only dilemmas in these cases are moral and social ones. Many involve personal dilemmas. For example, a person may be confronted with moral reasons for performing acts that may not be in the person's self-interest. Whistle-blowing cases often have this character, as an engineer named Dan Applegate discovers in the DC-10 case in Chapter 1. In such dilemmas two or more conflicting but reasonable judgments can often be made, as anyone who makes hard choices—be they managerial, moral, or personal—will understand.

As we reflect on disagreements, we may be increasingly tempted to declare them irresolvable dilemmas. Even if rational deliberation plays a pivotal role, reason alone is usually insufficient to resolve dilemmas. Intractable social controversies seem present in many cases. Nevertheless, we should not be consumed by potential intractability. Many apparent dilemmas are partially resolvable, and many cases can be studied with an eye to ways in which dilemmas can be avoided. Many of dilemmas found in this volume could have been avoided or minimized through more skillful management. For example, good management has probably not been present when persons face agonizing dilemmas about whether to blow the whistle on corporate wrongdoing. Studying these cases to determine which steps management could have taken can be beneficial, as can reflecting on procedures that might have deflected or defused a problem. For example, as many cases about conflict of interest illustrate, many problems arise because a manager fails to consult with others or because no peer or employee review committee exists.

Often we need to examine cases in terms of alternative strategies and actions. Usually such a rich array of alternatives is available that it is not feasible to reach agreement on a single best solution. Such agreement need not be the purpose of case analysis. Learning how to spot and manage problems is at least as important.

In ethics as elsewhere, reasonable and informed persons often hold conflicting opinions concerning actions that should be performed and their justifying principles. They can disagree spiritedly over the proper interpretation of cases, and nowhere will they disagree more than in dilemmatic cases. Often such argument changes our beliefs. Cases shock intuition and alter belief. Disagreements, then, may turn into discussions concerning why some beliefs and principles ought to be reevaluated and readjusted.

"THE 'FACTS' OF THE CASE"

The majority of cases in this volume are entirely factual, and most use actual names rather than fictitious ones. What is reported about the role of IBM's management in handling its employees or about Kellogg Cereals in advertising its product are presumably the facts of the case. It is prudent, however, to have reservations about this notion. Events at IBM or Kellogg may not have transpired exactly as reported here, for several reasons.

First, analysis of the notion of a fact has proved to be an elusive task. A fact is typically analyzed as an empirically confirmable or falsifiable statement that describes some event or object. These factual statements are either true or false. A value, by contrast, is an evaluative statement or judgment concerning what is or is not good, right, or virtuous. Evaluative statements appraise and assess events, whereas factual statements describe some concrete aspect of the event and do not appraise or assess. Unfortunately, this ideal of the neutrality of facts often dissipates at the level of personal reports of facts. In criminal trials, for example, eyewitnesses report the facts differently, but often not because of biases or prior opinions. Similarly, journalists often provide substantially different accounts of a press conference or an athletic event. And scientists operate with different theories that guide them to see the facts differently.

Second, the facts as presented are always selected for a purpose. From an infinity of events in a given day, the nightly national news is condensed to less than 30 minutes. Such selectivity does not itself entail a distorting bias. Selection is necessary and may be an intelligent and revealing structuring of an otherwise massive array of events and relationships. The Love Canal case in this volume is an example of a case that requires careful historical selection of data due to the immense amount of accumulated information. Moreover, one cannot assemble a complete set of facts. Whole volumes have been written on some of the cases in this text, and yet these volumes omit many aspects of what occurred. On the other hand, selectivity and sheer lack of available information can introduce bias in the writing of cases. The cases in this volume have been carefully scrutinized to minimize the problem of bias, but the cautious reader should remember the likelihood that different individuals will describe and evaluate circumstances in different terms.

This reminder is particularly applicable when companies and individuals are named. The picture of management at McDonnell Douglas, for example, is not favorable in the DC-10 case, but we lack many facts about what transpired at that company over a multiyear period. What is emphasized in these descriptions may be deemphasized or even ignored in other accounts. There is no neutral mirror of history. Human actors can do no more than interpret the actions of others, without escaping the possibility of bias or incompleteness that such interpretation necessarily entails. A useful rule of thumb is to try to set aside the identities of individuals and companies while *assuming* that the facts are correct. One can then more easily criticize decisions and strategies, rather than individuals or corporate groups.

Third, in cases such as those presented in this volume, corporations have often been treated harshly by journalists who first present the facts of the case to the public. As a result, corporations have become leery of opening their offices to journalists. At present there is something of a cold war between the two groups. Journalists tend to view corporations as inherently secretive and as presenting facts with a lack of objectivity. Management, in turn, often regards journalists as biased and sensationalistic distorters of the truth. They view reporters as unqualified for the range of issues their newspapers commission them to study; and they remind us that a single reporter may be assigned to cover such diverse matters as new products, embezzlement schemes, plant relocations, labor relations, securities, investments, price hikes, company growth, salaries, and profits.

This is not the place to arbitrate their dispute, but it is pertinent to note that the press is frequently a major source of information about the facts of the case. The reports of journalists alone are rarely used in this volume, and attempts to incorporate divergent views of corporate officials have been maximized if press reports have been used. However, the use of investigative journalism in researching and writing cases is a common practice and provides one more reason to place some distance between the facts of the case and the actual circumstances from which they arose. "The facts as reported" or "the facts as they have thus far emerged" are more apt descriptions.

There is a final reason to exercise caution about the facts of the case. Those who study such cases invariably want more facts. They believe that if only more facts were known, dilemmas and uncertainties would disappear. A temptation is to doctor the case by adding hypothetical facts, usually prefaced by someone saying, "But what if . . . ?" These retreats to new or different facts are understandable reactions, but it is best to suppress them in the analysis and discussion of the cases in this volume, which have been selected because they present difficult problems. Part of the process of case analysis is to confront the problems as presented, not to alter the circumstances or shelve the problems on grounds of insufficient facts. Moreover, presenting more facts may not waive the problem; it may only increase the situation's complexity, which in turn compounds the challenges inherent in case analysis.

This position does not imply that it is never useful to modify the conditions and then think through problems under new conditions. To the contrary, this method can be valuable, and skillful teachers use it with success. Furthermore, these warnings are not intended to discredit the careful reader who looks for pertinent missing facts. One should sleuth for missing facts as well as for facts subject to alternative description. However, persons in business must make decisions every day on the basis of incomplete and uncertain information, and the reader should study cases under similar conditions of uncertainty. To do otherwise would be to distort "the 'facts' of the case."

NOTES

1. Langdell's first casebook, *Contracts*, is treated in Lawrence M. Friedman, *A History of American Law* (New York: Simon & Schuster, 1973), pp. 531f. The general account of the case method in this section is indebted to this source, and also to G. Edward White, *Tort Law in America: An Intellectual History* (New York: Oxford University Press, 1980).
2. See White, *Tort Law in America,* esp. pp. 154ff.
3. For a sharp criticism of the method and its milieu in the training of lawyers, see the "Report of the Dean" of the Maryland Law School, Michael J. Kelly, *The Scandal of American Legal Education* (Baltimore: University of Maryland School of Law, 1979).
4. Melvin T. Copeland, "The Genesis of the Case Method in Business Instruction," in M. P. McNair, ed. *The Case Method at the Harvard Business School* (New York: McGraw-Hill, 1954), p. 25.
5. Donald K. David, "Foreword," in McNair, ed., *The Case Method,* p. 11.
6. Copeland, "The Genesis of the Case Method," in McNair, ed., *The Case Method,* p. 32.
7. McNair, "Editor's Preface," in McNair, ed., *The Case Method,* p. 11.
8. Gilbert Ryle, "Knowing How and Knowing That," *Proceedings of the Aristotelian Society* 46 (1945–1946), pp. 1–16.

9. Charles I. Gragg, "Because Wisdom Can't Be Told," as reprinted in McNair, ed. *The Case Method*, pp. 6–7, 11–13 (italics added).

10. *Ibid.*, p. 8.

11. John F. Berry, "CBS Decides It Wants Out of the Paperback Business," *The Washington Post*, February 7, 1982, pp. G1, G4.

12. R. B. Perry, *The Citizen Decides: A Guide to Responsible Thinking in Time of Crisis* (Bloomington: Indiana University Press, 1951), Chapter 6.

13. See Albert R. Jonsen and Stephen Toulmin, *The Abuse of Casuistry: A History of Moral Reasoning* (Berkeley: University of California Press, 1988). This casuistical tradition was prominent among Jesuits in the seventeenth century when it came under attack by Blaise Pascal in his *Provincial Letters*. The negative characterization of casuistry found in contemporary ethics dates from Pascal's attack.

14. John Arras, "Principles and Particularity: The Role of Cases in Bioethics," *Indiana Law Journal* 69 (1994), pp. 983–1014.

15. Daniel Callahan and Sissela Bok, *The Teaching of Ethics in Higher Education* (Hastings-on-Hudson, NY: Hastings Center, 1980), p. 69.

16. John Rawls, *A Theory of Justice* (Cambridge, MA: Harvard University Press, 1971), pp. 20f.

Chapter One

THE EMPLOYEE

INTRODUCTION

The dominant model of the employer-employee relationship has long been that of management and labor. This model gives the balance of power to management. An employee must be loyal, obey orders of superiors, and keep confidential information secret, unless some overriding moral wrong or illegal act is a factor.

A body of law known as the *law of agency* that governs corporations has special significance for the employer-employee relationship. This law, fashioned largely from legal precedent, specifies an employee's obligations of loyalty and obedience, and usually has served to protect corporations. For example, corporate executives and lawyers owe their allegiance and have a legal duty to the corporation, *not* to stockholders, the public, or other employees. In some influential cases employee disloyalty to a corporation or its interests has been considered "private treason."

Recently, this model of the employer-employee relationship has been under scrutiny and revision. Some have asserted that employees possess rights to privacy, due process, security, information about workplace hazards, whistle-blowing, and grievance procedures and that these rights should be respected. Considerable ferment now exists over the nature and strength of these claims. Some corporations have accepted the challenge and have invested heavily in plans to increase worker participation, including reconceptualizing conventional corporate practice to give employees more say about their jobs and benefits. Corporations have established explicit standards for hiring, firing, merit evaluation, retirement, grievance proceedings, and participative management by workers. One such policy under discussion is the case of "Peer Review at Shamrock-Diamond Corporation," which involves peer review of complaints against management.

Even those policies designed to protect and advance the rights of employees allow management to retain important rights against the disloyal and even the feckless employee. For example, the right to protect critical business interests and investments is an important employer right. Employees sometimes function as spies, use company resources for private gain, and retain confidential information when moving from one firm to another. Because employers have a right to protect intellectual property, and employees a right to accept new positions, the protection of trade secrets, for example, has become a difficult problem, as illustrated in this chapter by the "Venture Capital for Rubbernex" case. This case invites reflection on the fact that, under law, an employee can plan a new competitive venture while still employed, and while observing his or her future competitor's secrets. The employee can do so without breaching any obligation to the employer, even though the employee may leave with a wealth of experience in and knowledge about the competitor's processes, products, research, and financial matters.

The traditional rule in law and industry is that an employer is entitled to retain proprietary information for purposes of competition. However, some have begun to closely examine the weights of these competing interests. A few courts have adopted what might be called a *balancing model* of protection, under which the employee's interest in mobility and opportunity is weighed against the employer's right to determine the scope of protection afforded to confidential and proprietary information. These courts have attempted to weigh a public policy favoring protection of trade secrets against a competing public policy favoring employee interests in using the skills and knowledge acquired in a field in order to earn a livelihood. Trade secrets have also been criticized because they allow corporations to shield information from the public about harmful products.

Another current issue about employee rights raised in this chapter is "Du Pont's Policy of Excluding Women from the Workplace," which discusses the increased protection for workers in hazardous environments. Employers have long known of the risks posed by flimsy scaffolding, exposed saw blades, careless dynamiting, and thousands of similar workplace dangers and have taken precautions to minimize these hazards. However, a largely unprecedented situation now prevails—namely, we are beginning to understand the dangers of various toxic agents and airborne dangers in the work environment, and yet we do not have enough information to assess the seriousness of the threat. This problem raises questions about the nature of a safe workplace and the notion of acceptable risk.

Although it is clear that workplaces cannot be guaranteed safe, what constitutes an adequate precaution? Should a company treat employees paternalistically and protect them against their decisions to assume risks? And how much information is adequate to allow employees to protect themselves against, and assess the dangers of, their workplace? This last question plays a central role in the Du Pont case, which focuses on how a corporation may legitimately protect women of childbearing capacity from exposure to toxic chemicals that might seriously harm a fetus. Because the law does not allow corporations to ban fertile women from these environments, the question aris-es whether a fetal protection policy can be implemented that does not dis-criminate against female employees.

Another series of issues concerns conflicts among the roles or obliga-tions an employee must assume. One well-known issue is whistle-blowing; here, the central question is whether employees ought to alert the proper authori-ties about corporate wrongdoing. Although a whistle-blower may believe that his or her conscience compels action for the public interest, this rationale can serve as a self-protective cover. Whistle-blowers may be trying to seize more power within the company or to cover up personal inadequacies that repre-sent a legitimate reason for discipline or dismissal.

Management has often denounced whistle-blowing as a despicable act of disloyalty, but loyalty to the corporation is no more an absolute obligation than is loyalty to any organization. Cases of whistle-blowing usually involve bal-ancing an obligation of loyalty with an obligation to the public interest. Such cases also raise interesting questions about which types of management prac-tices could have been employed to prevent these kinds of conflicts. In this chapter, the cases "The DC-10's Defective Doors" and "The Reluctant Security Guard" feature the issue of whistle-blowing. They stimulate reflection on whether, by whom, and *when* the whistle should be blown.

Also included in this chapter are cases that explore the employee's right to privacy. Questions of rights of privacy and confidentiality (or, correlatively, obligations to respect privacy and confidentiality) have arisen in many areas of business, including the screening of employees for genetic diseases or use of illicit drugs. *Privacy* may be defined as a state or condition of limited access to a person. A person has privacy if others do not have access, or do not use their access, to him or her. A loss of privacy occurs when others gain any form of access to a person—for example, by intervening in zones of secrecy, anonymi-ty, and solitude. Privacy extends to a person's intimate relationships with friends, lovers, spouses, and physicians or other health care professionals.

Although employee privacy is a treasured value, corporations may be jus-tified in enacting tough rules that intrude on privacy. For example, managers of day care centers are obligated to determine whether a potential employee has ever been convicted of child molestation, and an airline company has a right to know if its pilots are taking narcotics. But even if an employer can rightfully invade an employee's privacy to obtain such information, the ques-tion of appropriate means needs resolution. For example, the degree of inva-sion (and the appropriateness of that invasion) is different if an employer asks the employee if he or she takes drugs, requires that the employee submit to urinalysis, or actually hires a private investigative firm to poke into intimate aspects of the employee's personal life. There are similar related questions about the kinds of disclosures that may be made to the corporation by persons who possess sensitive information about employees. These questions domi-nate much of the case "The Open Door at IBM" in this chapter.

As for restricting conduct off the job, employees tend to believe that pri-vate life is absolutely private. But this response is unrealistic. Many private situations might embarrass or otherwise negatively affect the company. For example, what the president of the bank does at a private club in his or her off hours may affect investor confidence in the institution. The problem of how businesses should respond to employee conduct that embarrasses or harms the business's interests is an unavoidable one.

In addition, to affirm a right of privacy does not nullify criticism of various exercises of the right. Persons may exercise their right with poor judgment. A company may also be justified in some cases in overriding rules of privacy to protect other institutional or moral objectives, such as ensuring corporate security and protecting third parties against harmful outcomes. Usually it is possible for society to handle these conflicts by establishing *zones of privacy* that cannot be invaded, while distinguishing other zones in which conduct can be prohibited and punished. But, as the IBM case indicates, the line between these zones is often unclear.

DU PONT'S POLICY OF EXCLUDING WOMEN FROM THE WORKPLACE

In January 1981 *The New York Times* examined a startling development in the nation's workplaces. Fertile women workers were, in increasing numbers, electing to undergo voluntary sterilization rather than give up high-paying jobs involving exposure to chemicals that are potentially harmful to a developing fetus. This disclosure precipitated discussion of a new civil rights issue with "questions . . . raised about whether a company should be allowed to discriminate against a woman to protect her unborn child, or whether the practice of keeping a woman out of certain well-paying jobs because she was fertile was simply another form of sex discrimination in the workplace."[1]

Ten years later, on March 20, 1991, the United States Supreme Court decided in the case of *Auto Workers v. Johnson Controls, Inc.*[2] that employers cannot legally adopt fetal protection policies that exclude women of childbearing age from a hazardous workplace because such policies involve illegal sex discrimination. However, the Supreme Court decision was, in some respects, narrow. It left American corporations in a state of uncertainty about what type of policy would effectively protect fetuses from reproductive hazards.

HISTORICAL AND BIOLOGICAL BACKGROUND

The causes of congenital (birth) defects in humans are not well understood. Although specific drugs and environmental chemicals cause approximately 5 percent of these defects, the causes of at least 65 percent are unknown. Of the 28,000 toxic substances listed by the National Institute of Occupational Safety and Health (NIOSH), over 50 are animal mutagens (that is, they cause chromosomal damage to either the ova or the sperm cells), and roughly 500 are animal teratogens (that is, they can cause deformations in a developing fetus).

Some tragic events in the 1960s alerted the public to the devastating effects that a teratogenic substance can have on a developing fetus, although the drug may be perfectly harmless to the mother. Doctors had prescribed the drug thalidomide for pregnant women as a tranquilizer, but they discovered that the drug caused fetal defects such as missing or deformed arms, legs, hands, and feet, in addition to many soft tissue malformations. Fetal defects

This case was prepared by Martha W. Elliott and Tom L. Beauchamp and revised by Linda Kern, Anna Pinedo, and Kier Olsen. Not to be duplicated without permission of the holder of the copyright, © 1992, 1996 Tom L. Beauchamp.

included both physical and functional alterations, such as the possibility of growth retardation, deformities, behavioral problems, genetic alterations, or a higher than normal tendency to develop cancer.[3]

U.S. federal agencies (particularly the Food and Drug Administration and the Environmental Protection Agency) require animal testing of drugs to ensure that any new product to which pregnant women may be exposed is harmless to the fetus. Animal testing is a costly and lengthy process that involves the testing of more than one species for a three to six month period. The results are often uncertain.

Industries such as chemical manufacturing and zinc smelting with high concentrations of lead have dealt with this potential threat to the fetus in several ways. The standard strategy until the March 1991 Supreme Court decision was to make jobs that involve the risk of exposure off limits to women "of child-bearing potential." That is, companies excluded fertile women in their late teens to their forties from those particular positions. Department of Labor statistics show that the employment rate for women between the ages of 18 and 54 is approximately 60 percent. Because women in this age range are assumed to be fertile until proven otherwise, corporate policies affected a large portion of the female workforce in certain industries.[4]

These protective exclusion policies angered and offended participants in the women's movement and many civil libertarians, who viewed them as a form of sex discrimination. Women's groups also noted a dearth of well-supported evidence about exposure to certain alleged toxic hazards and a general lack of consensus in government and industry about appropriate levels of unsafe exposure. One charge of discrimination involves the male's contribution to birth defects. Mutagenic substances affect the sperm as well as the egg. Exposure to these toxins can result in sterility for the man and can produce mutated sperm and ultimately a malformed fetus. Therefore, any policy designed to protect the fetus should include considerations of both the sperm and the egg that form it, eventuating in a more expansive protective policy than gender-based exclusion of women from the workplace.

Exposure of workers to toxic substances is currently complicated by the fact that a workplace chemical usually does not occur in isolation, but rather in combination with other chemicals. Fetal exposure to teratogenic drugs is even more complex. The human embryo is most susceptible to toxic agents during the gestation period of day 18 to day 60, which is often before the pregnancy is detected. It is also easier to calculate the permissible levels of exposure for adults than for fetuses. Pregnancy tests are not accurate during these early stages when the fetus is most susceptible to the damaging toxins.

THE DU PONT POLICY: PAST AND PRESENT

E. I. Du Pont de Nemours and Company, the world's largest chemical manufacturer, has long been concerned with chemical toxicity and exposure. Du Pont uses only a small number of hazardous substances—such as lead, aniline, and orthotoluidine—that require special controls. Over the years, the company has promulgated several policies dealing with reproductive hazards, particularly one that (until 1991) addressed the problem of fetal damage from chemical exposure.

If Du Pont discovers that a chemical is a developmental toxin (toxic to the fetus), the company first uses engineering and administrative procedures to eliminate the risk of exposure or to reduce it to an acceptable level. Engineering procedures might, for example, require special ventilation equipment; administrative procedures might involve regulation of exposure time or the required use of protective clothing. However, if no "acceptable exposure level" has been determined or if engineering and administrative procedures cannot reduce exposure to an acceptable level, the Du Pont policy until 1991 read: "females of child bearing capacity shall be excluded from work areas."[5]

Before the Supreme Court decision, Du Pont rejected the suggestion that a woman who was apprised of the health risk could then sign a legally valid waiver if she chose to accept the risk. Du Pont held that the exclusionary policy was to protect the fetus, not the woman. Bruce W. Karrh, an experienced vice-president for Safety, Health, and Environmental Affairs at Du Pont, argued that "the issue with exposure to embryotoxic chemicals is one of protecting the susceptible embryo or fetus from chemical substances which can cross the placenta and cause damage to the developing embryo or fetus at concentrations which would have no adverse effects on the female or male adult."[6] Accordingly, Du Pont developed a specific procedure for managing the issue, upon determination that a substance presents a risk to the fetus:

1. Employees who may be affected shall be informed of the possible consequences of exposure to such substances and appropriate handling procedures shall be established and communicated.
2. Engineering controls shall be used to the extent practical to reduce and maintain exposure to embryotoxins to acceptable levels. Such controls shall be augmented by administrative controls as appropriate.
3. Whenever engineering and administrative controls are not practical to keep exposure at or below acceptable levels, personal protective equipment, where appropriate, and training for its proper use shall be provided to and required to be used by employees who may be affected by such compounds.
4. Females of childbearing capacity shall be excluded from work areas:
   a. where there is potential for exposure to an embryotoxin for which an acceptable level cannot be set, *or*
   b. whenever engineering and administrative controls augmented as appropriate by personal protective equipment are determined to be inadequate to insure acceptable levels of exposure.[7]

Under this policy Du Pont stated that "the waiver of subsequent claims by the female worker would be of no legal significance because the deformed fetus, if born, may have its own rights as a person which could not be waived by the mother."[8] Although some state supreme courts upheld this position, women's groups continued to view protective exclusion as sex discrimination, especially given the growing evidence that industrial chemicals that can affect a future fetus may also adversely affect the male reproductive system.[9]

Du Pont considered the excluded party's sex to be irrelevant, on grounds that the policy's goal is to protect the susceptible fetus. Du Pont noted that "the complexity of the issue lies in the separate, but not separated, nature of the affected groups—fetuses and females." Du Pont excluded women only because they are capable of becoming pregnant and bringing the fetus into the workplace.[10] Du Pont regarded the difficulty of determining pregnancy during the early stages, when the fetus is most vulnerable to damage, as a sound reason for the exclusion policy. The company also reported that implementation of the previously mentioned four-step procedure costs more than a policy that would allow women to make their own choices.

However, women's advocates continued to view companies such as Du Pont as simply remiss in developing technological solutions for the control of embryotoxins. A common union complaint is that industry makes the worker safe for the workplace to the point of exclusion, rather than making the workplace safe for the worker and fetus. Management, however, contends that acceptable levels of exposure cannot be achieved using available risk data.

THE DECISION IN JOHNSON CONTROLS

Many prematurely believed that these controversies would end when the U.S. Supreme Court determined in 1991 that fetal protection policies constituted illegal sex discrimination. The Court's opinion attacked not only the particular policy of a battery manufacturer (Johnson Controls, Inc.) but all fetal protection policies. The majority held that neither an employer's legitimate "ethical concerns" about health risks for fetuses nor concern about legal liability for injury caused in the workplace constituted a sufficient ground for a gender-based policy that excluded only women.

The majority further held that fetal exclusion policies are discriminatory because they do not apply to male employees in the same way they do to females, despite the previously mentioned debilitating effects of hazardous chemicals on the male reproductive system. These policies permit only fertile men, and not fertile women, to choose whether they wish to assume reproductive risks. The Court reasoned that decisions about the welfare of future children must be reserved for parents, not employers. The obligation of an employer is to fully inform the potential parents of risk, not to make the decision for them. Once a company has provided such information, the Court held it immune from liability charges for harm to the fetus or to children born with defects.[11]

Although every justice on the U.S. Supreme Court found Johnson Controls' policy to be unacceptable, three filed a concurring opinion in which they criticized their colleagues for failing to note subtle problems in these controversies about fetal protection policies. Writing for these justices, Justice Byron R. White asserted that a fetal protection policy could be justified if it were truly necessary to avoid substantial liability for injuries caused to a third party (the fetus or future child). White noted that every state in the United States allows children to recover for prenatal injuries caused by another party. White argued that the law generally, and antidiscrimination law in particular, does not adequately specify that an employer would be protected from suits by those born with defects caused in the workplace, because the child's right to sue cannot in law be waived by the parents. White rejected the claim that female exclusionary policies could not be valid for pregnant women in a highly toxic environment. White and those who concurred with him wished to leave it open to future court decisions to establish whether fetal protection policies could be refashioned so as to exclude pregnant women. They also indicated a need in law and public policy to remove employers from the dilemma of having to comply with antidiscrimination law only to face potentially enormous damage suits for their adherence to the law.[12]

CORPORATE RESPONSE

In response to the *Johnson Controls* decision, legal experts and business leaders acknowledged that corporations needed to modify their present policies. However, no one seemed certain of how to develop a policy that would ensure a safe workplace. Bruce Karrh at Du Pont said simply, "We are naturally going to comply with the law. . . . We'll have to find some means to comply and still provide a safe workplace." Many corporations are still working to make progress in that direction by implementing extensive applicant and employee education programs. Pat Conry, health services coordinator at Johnson Controls, explained that the company has continued to ensure that applicants are fully informed of the risks of lead exposure through films and posted notices. The primary goal of these educational efforts and the requirement that applicants sign a form indicating that they understand the extent of the risks is to facilitate "good decisions." Some applicants actually decide to withdraw their application upon learning of the risks of lead exposure.

Conry also emphasized the need to redo studies conducted by Dr. Herbert Needleman of the University of Pittsburgh, whose conclusions were instrumental in motivating the Centers for Disease Control to lower the threshold level at which blood lead concentrations would be considered dangerous. Conry maintained that the media presentation of the controversy surrounding Needleman's studies[13] has prompted physicians to consider any level of lead present in the blood to be "poison."[14]

Until threshold blood-lead requirements can be set at a level that all corporations find acceptable, companies are working within existing guidelines by taking steps to reduce toxin exposure and clean up the workplace. For example, Johnson Controls has improved ventilation in plants and covered assembly lines with steel to reduce worker contact with lead. Employees must submit to regular blood-lead level evaluations and maintain good personal hygiene. General Motors has supplemented its educational program by responding generously and compassionately to female employees who become pregnant. For example, the company reportedly allowed two pregnant workers with elevated blood-lead levels to take voluntary, paid sick leave throughout their pregnancies.[15]

Although costly, these efforts to comply with the Johnson Controls decision may spare corporations the expense and worry associated with lawsuits by impaired children of employees. Conry claimed that tort liability is not yet a concern at Johnson Controls because even employees whose blood-lead levels are high have given birth to healthy children. However, as Justice White warned in the Johnson Controls decision, a cavalier dismissal of the possibility of tort liability may not be warranted. A particularly salient concern is the shift from a negligence standard to a strict liability standard, which assigns even more severe penalties to defendants if manufacturing processes are deemed "abnormally dangerous."[16] Stephen Bokat of the U.S. Chamber of Commerce described this concern from a legal perspective: "Frankly, the majority [on the Court is] fooling themselves if they think the American public would stand for injured children having no remedy against deep-pocket companies."[17]

To date, many companies and unions still believe that no adequate response has been found to protect workers and their offspring from the potential dangers of mutagenic and teratogenic substances. The lack of accurate scientific data concerning the developmental toxicity of substances and an uncertain legal situation further aggravate the problem. Cooperation among the Occupational Safety and Health Administration, private industry, and workers seems essential for the formulation of a policy acceptable to the Supreme Court as well as the larger American society.

NOTES

1. Philip Shabecoff, "Industry and Women Clash over Hazards in the Workplace," *The New York Times,* January 3, 1981.
2. Slip opinion. Argued October 10, 1990—decided March 20, 1991.
3. Bruce W. Karrh, "Reproductive Hazards: Evaluation and Control of Embryotoxic Agents" (Du Pont: 1983), p. 4.
4. Albert Rosenfield, "Fertility May be Hazardous to Your Job," *Saturday Review* 6, no. 9, p. 12.
5. Bruce W. Karrh, "A Company's Duty to Report Health Hazards," *Bulletin of the New York Academy of Medicine* 54 (September 1978), esp. pp. 783, 785; and private correspondence to Tom L. Beauchamp of April 5, 1988.
6. Karrh, "Reproductive Hazards," p. 7.
7. Bruce W. Karrh, "Women in the Workplace," an address on May 2, 1978, as quoted in Earl A. Molander, "Regulating Reproductive Risks in the Workplace," in his *Responsive Capitalism: Case Studies in Corporate Social Conduct* (New York: McGraw-Hill, 1980), p. 16.
8. Molander, "Regulating Reproductive Risks," p. 16.
9. M. Donald Whorton et al., "Testicular Function among Carbaryl-Exposed Employees," *Journal of Toxicology and Environmental Health* 5 (1979), pp. 929–41; H. Northrop, "Predictive Value of Animal Toxicology," a paper presented at the Symposium on Reproductive Health Policies in the Workplace, Pittsburgh, PA, May 10, 1982; Vilma R. Hunt, "The Reproductive System Sensitivity through the Life Cycle," a paper presented at the American Conference of Governmental Industrial Hygienists, Symposium: Protection of the Sensitive Individual, Tucson, AZ, November 9, 1981.

10. Karrh, "Reproductive Hazards," p. 1.
11. *Automobile Workers v. Johnson Controls*, at pp. ii, 7, 17, 19.
12. *Automobile Workers v. Johnson Controls*, Justice White concurring, pp. 1–3, 9.
13. For further information, see Gary Putka, "Research on Lead Poisoning Is Questioned," *The Wall Street Journal*, March 6, 1992, p. B1; Phillip Bennett, "Lead-Hazard Research Questioned," *The Boston Globe*, March 25, 1992, p. 27; Gary Putka, "Pittsburgh Professor Sues School, NIH, to Block Inquiry into Lead-Poison Study," *The Wall Street Journal*, April 2, 1992, p. B6; Philip Hilts, "Hearing Is Held on Lead-Poison Data," *The New York Times*, April 15, 1992, p. D28; Gary Putka, "Professor's Data On Lead Levels Cleared by Panel," *The Wall Street Journal*, May 27, 1992, p. B5; David Stipp, "Top Lead Researcher Came in for Criticism in Probe of Methods," *The Wall Street Journal*, September 16, 1993, p. A16; David Stipp, "Probe Finds Errors, but No Misconduct, in Work by Lead-Poisoning Researcher," *The Wall Street Journal*, March 9, 1994, p. B6; Philip Hilts, "Errors Found but No Misconduct in Study on Lead," *The New York Times*, March 11, 1994, p. A22.
14. Telephone conversation between Kier Olsen and Pat Conry, Johnson Controls, Milwaukee, WI, February 29, 1996.
15. Meg Fletcher, "Fetal Protection Ruling Spurs Employee Education Efforts," *Business Insurance* 27 (December 27, 1993), pp. 2+.
16. Ellen Frankel Paul, "Fetal Protection and Freedom of Contract," *Public Affairs Quarterly* 6 (July 1992), pp. 305–26.
17. As quoted in Barbara Vobejda and Frank Swoboda, "Court's Removal of Workplace Barrier Shifts Difficult Question to the Woman," and Ruth Marcus, "Justices Find Bias in 'Fetal Protection,'" both in *The Washington Post*, March 21, 1991, pp. A1, A14–A15.

PEER REVIEW
AT SHAMROCK-DIAMOND
CORPORATION

The Shamrock-Diamond Corporation was founded by an entrepreneur in 1895 as a manufacturer of cutting, drilling, and grinding instruments. By 1912 the company had begun to build overseas plants. Then, as the oil industry grew, Shamrock-Diamond expanded further. In 1965 sales exceeded $300 million for the first time. In this same year the corporation's status progressed from privately held to publicly held. Today it consists of 72 distinct firms employing 18,600 workers at 96 plant sites in 15 countries. The company specializes in cutting tools, drilling equipment, grinding machines, sealants, and safety products.

Mr. Mario Pellegrino has been chief executive officer of this corporation for 12 years. The company has been profitable and has increased its dividends and workforce every year that it has been under his direction. For the past week, Pellegrino has been preparing a presentation and proposal for a meeting of his board of directors. After he calls the meeting to order, he gives his explanation about an additional agenda item. The agenda for the meeting had been mailed but this item was not listed. Pellegrino considered the matter to be too touchy, and instead he selected this occasion to approach the board with his strong views. He does not expect these views to be fully shared by his board members.

Pellegrino begins his presentation to the board as follows:

You know that we have always been keen on a high standard of ethics in this corporation. Over the years we have developed separate codes of ethics to govern problems of "questionable payments" abroad, acceptable advertising of our products, and nondiscrimination in employment. These proposals put us out front in the late 1960s, and we are still ahead of other American corporations.

Two years ago, as some of you know, I took part of my vacation and attended a two-week seminar on "Ethics and the Business Corporation" at Dartmouth College. To my surprise, the focus of the discussion among the participants in this seminar was on employee discontent and the responsibilities of management to ameliorate this discontent. I discovered that only a tiny minority of American corporations have institution-

This case was prepared by Tom L. Beauchamp. Not to be duplicated without permission of the holder of the copyright, © 1992, 1996 Tom L. Beauchamp.

alized ethics programs directed at employee-management relationships. These programs include ethics committees and management development programs that have ethics units in their curriculum. Many corporations, of course, have so-called "open-door grievance" policies, but these are intimidating to employees and rarely eventuate in truly objective grievance hearings.

One idea that has met with increasing acceptance but also increasing resistance is the use of Peer Review Panels to resolve employees' complaints and grievances. This idea was constantly discussed at Dartmouth, and I was deeply impressed with the idea while I was there.

Pellegrino pauses to measure the reaction from his board, which is composed of successful businesspersons, none of whom had previously reflected much on the ethics of management-employee relationships. He then proceeds to explain that upon returning from the Dartmouth seminar, he immediately set up a meeting with his Council of Managers at a large plant site in Worcester, Massachusetts, for the purpose of implementing a small-scale two-year test period for peer review at the plant.

Under his insistent guidance, the managers agreed to the experiment. During the planning stages, they reached the conclusion that one of the potential advantages of having a more explicit personnel policy was that formal rules would protect good managers and good employees alike. Before they began to implement their ideas, the managers established more explicit standards for firing, merit evaluation, retirement, and participative management by workers. The first decision they reached was that they would no longer permit a manager to fire an employee without a stated reason or without informing the employee of his or her right to an independent hearing.

Working closely with some of the most influential managers, Pellegrino quickly implemented his—and now their—ideas for peer review of grievance cases. They appointed four peer employees and three managers to hear each case and ruled that the conclusions of this group were absolutely binding, with no further appeal possible for a losing party. They also devised an intentionally informal arrangement for hearing the complaint and reviewing evidence. No representation by lawyers was permitted for any party, and the hearings were conducted in a room with only eight chairs arranged in a circle. The manager, the grievant, and individual witnesses were each called into the room separately. Coffee was served during the interview, and the discussion proceeded on the model of a conversation among friends.

Their first case involved a five-year employee who had received only modest raises for three straight years, whereas comparable male colleagues had received raises that were almost twice as large. The employee had prepared a massive pile of exhibits to show that the manager had a history of downgrading women and upgrading men. Upon review, it was established to the satisfaction of all seven members of the committee that the manager did have a history of favoring men, at least for promotions and raises. Although the manager at first insisted on his objectivity and fairness, he came to see that his record did not support his claim. The employee was given her full raise, retroactive for three years, and her performance ratings were upgraded.

Everyone was buoyed by the success of this first case. Even the manager who had been shown to be biased praised the fairness of the process. But as time wore on, the managers became less satisfied with the experimental procedure. Over the full two-year period, management decisions were upheld in 59 percent of the cases, but managers came to view this statistic as more a failure than a success. Most management victories were won in cases in which employees under their supervision were desperate and had no real opportunity to win. Moreover, virtually every manager had been overruled in a case in which he or she was certain that an unfair decision had been reached. The managers had lost 86 percent of the cases in which they had fired an employee. These employees were typically reinstated under the same manager's supervision, leading to hostility and tension. The reinstated employees disliked working under someone whose authority they had undermined by filing and winning a grievance.

Managers came to believe that a system of four peers and three managers was unbalanced and unfair. They felt embarrassed by many of the decisions and believed that their authority was undermined by a procedure that could overturn any of their decisions at any time. Most concluded that they had been asked by the company to be supervisors, but that the authority that permitted them to supervise was then denied. They were now leery of firing any employee, no matter how poor the person's performance. Almost anything was preferable, they thought, as compared with another grievance hearing. The plant manager who had most closely monitored the hearings admitted that after the end of the two-year experiment, the morale of the managers was at an all-time low.

Pellegrino is fully aware of this history as he stands before his board. He has repeatedly interviewed the managers at the plant, 85 percent of whom would like to see the peer review process either dismantled or its composition changed so that managers are in the majority. But Pellegrino disagrees. He wants to make the process more objective by adding one outside member to the committee, a person from neither labor nor management. Although his managers are highly skeptical of the adequacy of this idea of including a third party, Pellegrino is firm in his convictions. He now concludes his presentation to the board with the following statement of what are for him heartfelt views:

> Business firms have typically been organized hierarchically, with production line employees at the bottom and the CEO at the top and the interests of the stockholders given supremacy. However, there are now many reasons to challenge these arrangements. Employees want to make an essential contribution rather than serve as means to the end of profit. They want decent salaries and job security, and they also want appreciation from supervisors, a sense of accomplishment, and fair opportunities to display their talents. Many employees are also interested in participat-

ing in the future of the company, defining the public responsibilities of the corporation, and evaluating the role and quality of management.

Although it will be expensive, I want to give our employees all these opportunities. If we can implement this plan for grievance hearings and peer review in all our plants, I am confident we will be a much happier family. I also believe that the corporation as a whole will be better off. We will be more attractive to potential employees, our plants will be built on trust, unions will find no reason to organize our labor forces, and costly lawsuits by employees will not arise.

I want to assure you that if we do successfully implement this program, I will be back asking for more in the way of programs to protect the employment rights of our employees. These policies will cover maximum-hour workweeks, rights against discharge and discipline, privacy rights, severance pay, and standards for pensions. I simply want you to know now what the implications are of your approval of this plan.

At this point Pellegrino turns to his board and asks the members to approve his plan without modification and without further experimental testing at other plants. He notes, however, that there may be room for compromise, despite his strong preference that the package be implemented as a whole.

THE OPEN DOOR AT IBM

Robert Bratt has been employed by International Business Machines Corporation (IBM) in Massachusetts since March 1970. Bratt sought to resolve several personal grievances through a company policy known as the open door procedure. This policy is described as follows in the IBM *Manager's Manual*:

A. Employee Appeal
  1. Any employee who has a problem which has not been resolved to that employee's satisfaction by his or her immediate manager may bring the complaint or concern to the attention of higher management.
  2. While the employee will normally choose to address an appeal first at the local level, the Open Door procedure makes available to an employee either direct or progressive access to any level of management in the Corporation. . . .
  4. If the employee is still not satisfied the problem may be reviewed with the IBM Chief Executive Officer by mail or personally if that is appropriate to the resolution.
  5. Management should be sensitive to assure that no action is taken which may appear to be retaliation for an employee's appeal under the Open Door Policy. . . .

B. The Investigation Process
  4c. The investigation cannot be anonymous; however, the discussion will be restricted to those necessary to resolve the issues. Those consulted will be advised to keep the matter confidential.

Bratt used the open door procedure approximately four times between 1971 and 1978 to complain about company practices. In 1971 Bratt was promised a promotion and a salary raise if he transferred from Waltham to Cambridge. He agreed to the transfer, but he did not receive the promotion or the raise. After participating in the open door procedure, Bratt was granted the promotion. In 1975 he used the policy again, this time without success, to

This case was prepared by Anna Pinedo and Tom L. Beauchamp, and modified in form by Brian Tauscher and Jeff Greene. Not to be duplicated without permission of the holder of the copyright, © 1992, 1996 Tom L. Beauchamp.

inquire about a promotion he thought he was due. He was then transferred back to the Waltham office without a promotion or raise.

While working in the Waltham office, Bratt made several suggestions about ways of improving control of a cash-fund account. His suggestions were implemented with good results, although they had been initially rejected. The cash-fund office was given credit as a unit for the innovations, thus minimizing Bratt's individual contribution. In July 1977 Bratt was given a lower work rating than he thought he deserved, and his immediate manager refused to discuss the rating with him. At the same time Bratt's wife was undergoing tests for cancer. Bratt was denied time off by his immediate manager. After appealing to higher authorities, he received the requested time off.

In 1978 Bratt discovered that copies of some suggestions he had made for preventing embezzlement in the Waltham office were not in his files. One of these suggestions had been adopted throughout the company, and this time he had received *no* credit for the innovation. Inquiries to the Suggestions Department revealed that Bratt's suggestions were not listed in any existing records. Bratt once again invoked the open door process in May or June 1978, arguing that his manager was discriminating against him.

The investigation of this matter was conducted by a higher level manager, David Blackburn. After failing to receive a response from Blackburn, Bratt brought his problems with the open door procedure to the chairman of the board of IBM in September 1978. The chairman appointed Wesley Liebtag, director of personnel programs at IBM corporate headquarters in Armonk, New York, to investigate Blackburn's handling of the open door complaint and to resolve Bratt's grievances. Bratt also asked Liebtag to look into the unfavorable 1977 work rating.

In investigating the open door grievances, Liebtag judged it essential to disclose certain information concerning Bratt's complaints to other IBM personnel. He was also obligated to report the results of the investigation and his recommendation to D. E. McKinney, vice-president of personnel, and to T. A. Vadnais, administrative assistant to the chairman of the board, from whom he received the assignment. Liebtag completed his inquiry on October 3, 1978, at which time he discussed his findings with Bratt and recorded them in a letter, dated that same day. Liebtag assured Bratt that his suggestions had been properly reviewed and evaluated and that the 1977 work appraisal would be destroyed. Liebtag explained in his letter that he was going to receive for review a new "performance plan" for Bratt in 30 days.

After the meeting with Liebtag, Bratt complained about the findings to his supervisor, Rita Lynch, and said he thought Liebtag, Blackburn, and others were involved in a cover-up. Several days later, on October 13, Bratt complained to Lynch of "bad nerves," headaches, and an inability to sleep. He told her that he had seen a doctor, and he agreed to Lynch's suggestion to see an IBM-employed physician. On October 16 Bratt requested a transfer within IBM. He gave as his reasons an unfair management situation, an unfair work situation, and poor health.

On October 18 Bratt saw a general practitioner, Dr. Martha Nugent, who was not part of the IBM in-house medical staff but was an independent physician retained under contract by IBM. Dr. Nugent reported to Lynch, who had set up the appointment, that Bratt seemed paranoid, and she suggested that he see a psychiatrist. Nugent, who had not been apprised of IBM's policy limiting management access to employee medical records, proceeded to discuss Bratt's presumed medical condition with his managers and with members of IBM's medical staff.

Lynch informed her supervisor, Johanna Crawford, of Dr. Nugent's report, and Crawford communicated this information to Liebtag, who was still considering Bratt's open door complaints and was charged with finding him another work assignment. Crawford told Liebtag that Bratt had seen Dr. Nugent and that the doctor felt Bratt was paranoid and suggested that he see a psychiatrist. Dr. Nugent recommended that Bratt receive no changes in assignment, including transfer, until his medical evaluations were complete.

Liebtag made notes on what he was told about Bratt's condition in a memorandum labeled to *File*, dated October 18, 1978, and marked *IBM CONFIDENTIAL*. The following day Liebtag received a second call from Bratt's branch manager, Crawford, explaining that Bratt was distraught and in tears upon receiving a "close out" letter denying his most recent open door complaint. This call was recorded in a memorandum dated October 19, 1978, also labeled *IBM CONFIDENTIAL*. Liebtag wrote in this memorandum that "it appears that the psychiatrist's first reaction, that there is a mental problem that goes beyond IBM, is accurate." Copies of these memoranda were sent to Mr. McKinney and Mr. Vadnais.

Bratt took a three-month leave of absence beginning December 14, 1978. Upon his return Bratt was given a temporary position at the Cambridge Center office. Bratt's psychiatrist reported that Bratt was enjoying his job. He was considered for a permanent assignment at this office, but the office manager did not want someone with a history of using the open door policy. Bratt initiated another grievance procedure when this fact came to his attention in September 1979. He complained to Liebtag about not having a permanent position, and he said that he thought the poor work rating from 1977 was still in his file. The rating was, in fact, still in his file, but it was promptly destroyed.

Bratt's dissatisfaction with his working conditions continued. He felt that he had been discriminated against or penalized for his use of the open door policy. Bratt felt that his rights to privacy and confidentiality had been violated by IBM personnel. Shortly thereafter Bratt brought a lawsuit against IBM and charged Liebtag and Dr. Nugent with improper disclosure of both his use of the open door grievance procedure and his medical condition.

The case, *Robert Bratt et al. v. International Business Machines Corporation et al.*, began a long litigation history in the Superior Court of Middlesex County, Massachusetts, in February 1980. The initial complaint charged IBM with intentional infliction of emotional distress and included a claim by Robert Bratt's wife, Carol Lee Bratt, for the loss of her husband's consortium ("the legal right of one spouse to the company, affection, and service of the other").

Bratt later amended his complaints: He added libel and breach of privacy claims, including a count based on Dr. Nugent's alleged publication of his confidential medical information without his authorization. The third amended complaint, as presented to the U.S. District Court, District of Massachusetts, included the charge that Dr. Nugent violated Bratt's right to privacy by disseminating confidential medical information through oral and written communications with IBM employees.

In November 1982 the U.S. District Court entered a judgment in favor of the IBM defendants on all counts of Bratt's third amended complaint and denied Bratt's motion to file a fourth amended complaint. The district court's decision was based on two grounds. First, the court concluded that Massachusetts courts would not support a breach of privacy claim when an employee alleged that his employer disclosed private information among other employees in the course of their employment. Second, the court concluded that Massachusetts courts would recognize a "qualified privilege for legitimate business communication."[1]

Bratt appealed the district court's decision to the U.S. Court of Appeals for the First Circuit.[2] The court of appeals ruled that there was no clear precedent in Massachusetts concerning the issues of breach of privacy and libel. The court sent a series of certified questions to the Massachusetts Supreme Judicial Court, which then ruled on a standard for an employee's right to privacy in the workplace. The court ruled on July 16, 1984, that "the disclosure of private facts about an employee among other employees in the same corporation can constitute sufficient publication under the Massachusetts right of privacy statute" so as to breach the employee's right to privacy.[3] The court concluded that "no conditional privilege for legitimate business communications exists under the Massachusetts right of privacy statute."[4]

Violations of the privacy statute, according to this ruling, must be determined by balancing "the employer's legitimate business interest in obtaining and publishing the information against the substantiality of the intrusion on the employee's privacy resulting from the disclosure."[5] Finally, concerning the disclosure of medical information, the court found that "when medical information is necessary reasonably to serve a substantial and valid interest of the employer, it is not an invasion of the employee's statutory right of privacy for the physician to disclose such information to the employer."[6]

After the Supreme Judicial Court responded to the legal questions that had been posed, the defendants once again moved for summary judgment on the privacy claims in the U.S. District Court.[7] IBM counsel explained that the company and the parties involved had a legitimate business interest in the disclosures that were made concerning Bratt's use of the open door policy and his medical condition. They maintained that Liebtag was charged with investigating Bratt's use of the open door procedure and was involved in finding a suitable work assignment for Bratt. IBM contended that Liebtag followed the standard practice in investigating and following up on open door complaints. IBM submitted that the two memoranda that Bratt relied on most heavily[8] were not disseminated beyond managerial employees with a legitimate interest in Bratt's work assignments.

Robert Bratt then narrowed his lawsuit to a few basic complaints. He contended that Liebtag violated his privacy by informing an estimated 16 other managerial employees not directly involved in the open door process of his assertion of open door rights. He also charged that copies of Liebtag's memos (dated October 18 and 19, 1978) were included in the *Waltham file* kept at the Waltham office, and that these were made available to Waltham employees, including the manager of the Cambridge Center. In addition Bratt claimed that Liebtag violated his right to privacy by distributing the memos dated October 18 and 19, 1978, which stated that Bratt was considered paranoid by Dr. Nugent and that he had "a mental problem beyond IBM." IBM is charged with having intruded upon Bratt's privacy by allowing Dr. Nugent and the IBM medical staff to discuss his medical condition with IBM management without his consent.

The argument made by IBM in response is the following: Liebtag was responsible for conducting an investigation of Bratt's open door complaints and for finding him an appropriate work assignment. Liebtag followed the standard procedure for open door grievances and then made limited disclosures about Bratt's use of the open door procedure. He reported his findings to his superiors, McKinney and Vadnais, from whom he had received the assignment. Liebtag made note of Bratt's medical condition because Bratt's health was pertinent to his job placement. In addition, Bratt used the open door procedure knowing that some disclosure was necessary for an investigation of his complaints. Bratt, the defendants claimed, also volunteered information concerning his health. For example, he told his manager that he had seen his doctor because he was having headaches and was unable to sleep.

The IBM defendants asserted that Bratt was aware, in accepting IBM's offer of medical assistance, that Dr. Nugent was "being retained by IBM, at its expense, to conduct an examination of Bratt for the purpose of advising IBM concerning his medical condition."[9] Bratt could not have expected the confidentiality of a doctor-patient relationship to have existed. Defendants' counsel cited a precedent from *Hoesl v. United States*[10] that when a physician is employed by an employer to evaluate the fitness of employees, the physician's "duties run primarily" to the employer. Dr. Nugent's assessment of Bratt's medical condition, they argued, was necessary for evaluating his request for transfer (in which Bratt had cited health reasons) and in assigning him to a new position.

District Court Judge Robert E. Keeton ruled in favor of the IBM defendants on the breach of privacy issues. Keeton stated, "It is clear that defendants had a legitimate interest in disclosing the information at issue. I conclude that a fact finder, weighing all of the factors discussed above in applying the balancing test set out by the Supreme Judicial Court in *Bratt*, could not, with support in the evidence, find that the defendants unreasonably interfered with Bratt's right of privacy."[11]

Robert Bratt appealed the district court ruling of June 1985 to the U.S. Court of Appeals, First Circuit. The court considered whether the district court erred in saying that no rational fact finder could conclude that IBM had violated Bratt's right to privacy in communicating his use of the open door grievance procedure and his medical problems to IBM personnel. In considering the alleged violation of privacy that occurred when Liebtag disclosed Bratt's use of the open door procedure, the court observed that the open door process at IBM necessarily involves disclosure of a complaint for a thorough investigation. Disclosure was limited to approximately 16 persons, most of whom were directly involved in or had a legitimate business interest in the process. The court concluded, "There can be no question that these individuals had a legitimate business need for this information and that Bratt's voluntary use of the open door process essentially waived any claim of breach of privacy *vis-à-vis* these persons."[12]

Concerning the allegation that Liebtag violated Bratt's privacy by disclosing memoranda making mention of Bratt's medical condition, the court again applied a balancing standard. The nature of this intrusion was at once more substantial and more personal. However, the employees to whom the disclosure was made had a legitimate business interest in the information. The court of appeals affirmed the district court's judgment for the defendants.

Bratt has argued that Dr. Nugent owed him a duty of confidentiality, regardless of her contract with IBM. He testified that he believed that everything he said to Dr. Nugent would be held in confidence. Dr. Nugent did not inform Bratt that she would report the results of his examination to IBM personnel, nor did she ask Bratt to sign a disclosure form. The defendants asserted that Dr. Nugent was employed by IBM to assess its employees' health and provide an evaluation for the company.

The court of appeals referred to the Massachusetts Supreme Judicial Court's statement in *Bratt* that "[w]hen an employer retains a physician to examine employees, generally no physician-patient relationship exists between the employee and the doctor."[13] However, the Massachusetts court later ruled in another case, *Alberts v. Devine*, that "in this Commonwealth all physicians owe their patients a duty, for violation of which the law provides a remedy, not to disclose without the patient's consent medical information about the patient, except to meet a serious danger to the patient or to others."[14] Consequently, the Massachusetts court did not conclusively address the conditions under which a physician-patient relationship is established. Nor have the other issues in the Bratt case been resolved in the courts.

NOTES

1. *Robert Bratt et al. v. International Business Machines Corporation et al.*, No. 80-547-K, slip op. at 13–14 (November 10, 1982).
2. *Bratt*, 467 N.E.2d 126, 129 (1984).
3. *Ibid.* at 134.

4. *Ibid.* at 135.
5. *Ibid.* at 135–36.
6. *Ibid.* at 137.
7. Once the Supreme Judicial Court had defined a standard for deciding an employee's right to privacy claims against an employer, the issue returned to the U.S. Court of Appeals for a ruling. The court of appeals affirmed the district court's dismissal of the libel claims against the defendants; however, the district court's grant of summary judgment as to the privacy claims was reversed. The case was remanded for additional findings and rulings by the district court on the privacy claims.
8. Dated October 18, 1978, and October 19, 1978.
9. Appellee's Brief at 10, *Bratt v. IBM*, 785 F.2d 352 (1st Cir.) (No. 85-1545) (1986).
10. 451 F. Supp. 1170, 1176.
11. *Bratt v. IBM*, No. 80-547-K, slip op. at 13 (June 26, 1985).
12. *Bratt*, 785 F.2d at 359.
13. 467 N.E.2d at 136 n. 21.
14. 479 N.E.2d 113 at 119 (Mass. 1985).

THE DC-10'S DEFECTIVE DOORS

The Douglas Company had dominated the commercial aviation industry until the late 1950s, when the Boeing Company captured a significant portion of the jet market with its 707. The 707 was similar to Douglas's already-in-service DC-8. The Douglas Company, keenly aware of the new and stiff competition, decided to manufacture a wide-bodied jet that would be attractive to international markets. Management considered this new airbus to be crucial to its long-term economic well-being (although no wide-bodies were produced for another ten years).[1]

Douglas was taken over by McDonnell Aircraft in 1967, by which time pressure to produce a wide-bodied jet had intensified. The Boeing Company had already introduced its 747, and neither Douglas nor the Federal Aviation Administration (FAA) wished Boeing to have exclusive control over this aspect of the air travel market. The McDonnell Douglas firm therefore searched for a structural design subcontractor capable of sharing the short-term financial burdens of a wide-bodied jet construction program that would realize long-term profits. General Dynamics' Convair Division, with its excellent reputation for structural design, was such a subcontractor. Under the agreement between the two companies, McDonnell Douglas had the primary authority to furnish design criteria and to amend design decisions. Convair's role was to create a design that would satisfy the stipulated criteria.[2]

In August 1968 McDonnell Douglas awarded Convair a contract to build the DC-10 fuselage and doors. The lower cargo doors became the subject of immediate discussion. These doors were to be outward-hinging, tension-latch doors, with latches driven by hydraulic cylinders—a design already adequately tested in the DC-8 and DC-9 models. In addition, each cargo door was designed to be linked to hydraulically actuated flight controls and was to have a manual locking system designed so that the handle or latch lever could not be stowed away unless the door was properly closed and latched. McDonnell Douglas, however, decided to separate the cargo door actuation system from the hydraulically actuated primary flight controls. This maneuver involved using electric rather than hydraulic actuators to close the cargo doors. Fewer moving parts in the electric actuators presumably made for easier maintenance, and each door would weigh 28 pounds less.

This case was prepared by Barbara Humes and Tom L. Beauchamp and revised by Cathleen Kaveny, John Cuddihy, and Jeff Greene. Not to be duplicated without permission of the holder of the copyright, © 1986, 1991, 1996 Tom L. Beauchamp.

However, the Convair engineers had considered the hydraulic actuators critical to safety. They were not satisfied with these changes, and they remained dissatisfied after the introduction of further modifications. As Convair engineers saw the situation, the two actuator systems would respond very differently to the buildup of forces caused by increasing pressure. If hydraulic latches were improperly secured, they would smoothly slide open when only a small amount of pressure had built up in the cabin. Although the doors would be ripped off their hinges, this would likely occur at a low enough altitude so that the shock from decompression would be small enough to land the plane safely. By contrast, if an electric latch failed to catch, it would not gently slide open due to increasing pressure. Rather, it would be abruptly and violently forced open, probably at a higher altitude where rapid decompression would dangerously impair the plane's structure. Convair's Director of Product Engineering F. D. "Dan" Applegate was adamant that a hydraulic system was needed. However, McDonnell Douglas did not yield to Convair's reservations about the DC-10 cargo door design.

Once McDonnell Douglas had decided to use an electrical system, the plane required a new and foolproof checking and locking backup system. In the summer of 1969 McDonnell Douglas asked Convair to draft a Failure Mode and Effects Analysis, or FMEA, for the cargo door system. An FMEA assesses the likelihood and consequences of a specific system failure. In August 1969 Convair engineers found nine possible failure sequences that could result in destruction of the craft and loss of human lives. One major problem involved the warning and locking-pin systems. The door could close and latch, but without being safely locked. Furthermore, the warning indicator lights were prone to failure, in which case a door malfunction could go undetected. The FMEA also concluded that the door design was potentially dangerous and lacked a reliable failsafe locking system. It could in theory open in flight and present a considerable danger to passengers.[3]

The FAA requires that it be given an FMEA covering all systems critical to safety, but McDonnell Douglas made no mention to the FAA of this particular hazard prior to certification of the DC-10 model. McDonnell Douglas maintains that its officials did not file a report because this cargo door design was not implemented until all defects noted in the FMEA were removed. Officials contend that the FMEA that they submitted was the final FMEA and did not discuss already repaired defects.[4] As lead manufacturer, McDonnell Douglas took full responsibility for certification of the aircraft and, in seeking the certification, maintained that all defects had been removed. By contrast, Convair was not formally responsible because its contract with McDonnell Douglas forbade Convair from reporting directly to the FAA.

During a model test run in May 1970, the DC-10 blew its forward lower cargo door, and the plane's cabin floor collapsed. Because the plane's vital electric and hydraulic subsystems are located under the cabin floor (unlike in the 747, in which they are above the ceiling), the collapse was doubly incapacitating.[5] A McDonnell Douglas spokesperson placed the blame for this particular malfunction on the "human failure" of a mechanic who had incorrectly sealed the door. Although the manufacturers did not consider this mishap to be indicative of serious design problems, they did respond by modifying the design of the cargo doors somewhat, purportedly to provide better checks on the locking pins. As modified, the cargo door design was properly certified and authorities at McDonnell Douglas claimed it was safe. Five DC-10s were then flight tested for over 1,500 hours prior to craft certification.

Certification processes are carried out in the name of the FAA, but they actually are often conducted by the manufacturers. As a regulatory agency, the FAA is charged with overseeing commercial products and regulating them in the public interest. However, the FAA is often not in an independent position. The FAA appoints designated engineering representatives (DERs) to make inspections at company plants. These are company employees chosen for their experience and integrity who have the dual and sometimes conflicting obligations of loyalty to the company that pays them as design engineers and also of faithful performance of inspections to see that the company has complied with federal airworthiness regulations. The manufacturers are in this respect policing themselves, and it is generally acknowledged that conflicts of interest arise in this dual-obligation system.[6]

Beginning in November 1970, a number of internal memos were written at both McDonnell Douglas and Convair that cited old and new cargo door design problems. New structural proposals were made, but none were implemented, in part because McDonnell Douglas and Convair were having disagreements over cost-accounting and accountability for the remaining design flaws. The FAA finally certified the DC-10 on July 29, 1971, and by late 1971 the plane had received praise for its effectiveness and safety at virtually all levels. Under rigorous conditions it boasted excellent performance ratings. The company vigorously promoted the new aircraft.

But on June 12, 1972, an aft bulk cargo door of a DC-10 in flight from Los Angeles to New York separated from the body of the aircraft at about 11,750 feet over Windsor, Ontario. Rapid cabin decompression occurred as a result, causing structural damage to the cabin floor immediately above the cargo compartment. Though the pilot was able to land the plane safely, nine passengers and two flight attendants were injured. An investigation by the National Transportation Safety Board (NTSB) concluded that the probable cause of the malfunction lay in the cargo doors' latching mechanisms and recommended changes in the locking system. The NTSB's specific recommendations were the following:

1. Require a modification to the DC-10 cargo door locking system to make it physically impossible to position the external locking handle and vent door to their normal locked positions unless the locking pins are fully engaged.
2. Require the installation of relief vents between the cabin and aft cargo compartment to minimize the pressure loading on the cabin flooring in the event of sudden depressurization of the compartment.[7]

The FAA administrator, John Shaffer, could have issued an airworthiness directive that required immediate repairs. However, he elected not to issue the directive, choosing instead to make an informal agreement with McDonnell Douglas that allowed the company to complete the necessary modifications and recommend new procedures to affected airlines. All actions by the company were to be voluntary.

Fifteen days subsequent to the blowout over Windsor (June 27, 1972), Dan Applegate wrote a stern memo to his superior at Convair that expressed his doubts about the entire project and offered some reflections on "future accident liability." The following excerpts from the memo reveal Applegate's anguish and concerns:[8]

The potential for long-term Convair liability on the DC-10 has caused me increasing concern for several reasons.

1. The fundamental safety of the cargo door latching system has been progressively degraded since the program began in 1968.
2. The airplane demonstrated an inherent susceptibility to catastrophic failure when exposed to explosive decompression of the cargo compartment in 1970 ground tests.
3. Douglas has taken an increasingly "hard-line" with regards to the relative division of design responsibility between Douglas and Convair during change cost negotiations.
4. The growing "consumerism" environment indicates increasing Convair exposure to accident liability claims in the years ahead. . . .

In July 1970 DC-10 Number Two was being pressure-tested in the "hangar" by Douglas, on the second shift, without electrical power in the airplane. This meant that the electrically powered cargo door actuators and latch position warning switches were inoperative. The "green" second shift test crew manually cranked the latching system closed but failed to fully engage the latches on the forward door. They also failed to note that the external latch "lock" position indicator showed that the latches were not fully engaged. Subsequently, when the increasing cabin pressure reached about 3 psi (pounds per square inch) the forward door blew open. The resulting explosive decompression failed the cabin floor downward rendering tail controls, plumbing, wiring, etc. which passed through the floor, inoperative. This inherent failure mode is catastrophic, since it results in the loss of control of the horizontal and vertical tail and the aft center engine. We informally studied and discussed with Douglas alternative corrective actions including blow out panels in the cabin floor which would accommodate the "explosive" loss of cargo compartment pressure without loss of tail surface and aft center engine control. It seemed to us then prudent that such a change was indicated since "Murphy's Law" being what it is, cargo doors will come open sometime during the twenty years of use ahead for the DC-10.

Douglas concurrently studied alternative corrective actions, in house, and made a unilateral decision to incorporate vent doors in the cargo doors. This "bandaid fix" not only failed to correct the inherent DC-10 catastrophic failure mode of cabin floor collapse, but the detail design of the vent door change further degraded the safety of the original door latch system by replacing the direct, short-coupled and stiff latch "lock" indicator system with a complex and relatively flexible linkage. (This change was accomplished entirely by Douglas with the exception of the assistance of one Convair engineer who was sent to Long Beach at their request to help their vent door system design team.)

This progressive degradation of the fundamental safety of the cargo door latch system since 1968 has exposed us to increasing liability claims. On June 12, 1972 in Detroit, the cargo door latch electrical actuator system in DC-10 number 5 failed to fully engage the latches of the left rear cargo door and the complex and relatively flexible latch "lock" system failed to make it impossible to close the vent door. When the door blew open before the DC-10 reached 12,000 feet altitude the cabin floor collapsed disabling most of the control to the tail surfaces and aft center engine. It is only chance that the airplane was not lost. Douglas has again studied alternative corrective actions and appears to be applying more "band-aids." So far they have directed to us to install small one-inch diameter, transparent inspection windows through which you can view latch "lock-pin" position, they are revising the rigging instructions to increase "lock-pin" engagement and they plan to reinforce and stiffen the flexible linkage.

It might well be asked why not make the cargo door latch system really "fool-proof" and leave the cabin floor alone. Assuming it is possible to make the latch "fool-proof" this doesn't solve the fundamental deficiency in the airplane. A cargo compartment can experience explosive decompression from a number of causes such as: sabotage, mid-air collision, explosion of combustibles in the compartment and perhaps others, any one of which may result in damage which would not be fatal to the DC-10 were it not for the tendency of the cabin floor to collapse. The responsibility for primary damage from these kinds of causes would clearly not be our responsibility, however, we might very well be held responsible for the secondary damage, that is the floor collapse which could cause the loss of the aircraft. It might be asked why we did not originally detail design the cabin floor to withstand the loads of cargo compartment explosive decompression or design blow out panels in the cabin floors to fail in a safe and predictable way.

I can only say that our contract with Douglas provided that Douglas would furnish all design criteria and loads (which in fact they did) and that we would design to satisfy these design criteria and loads (which in fact we did). There is nothing in our experience history which would have led us to expect that the DC-10 cabin floor would be inherently susceptible to catastrophic failure when exposed to explosive decompression of the cargo compartment, and I must presume that there is nothing in Douglas's experience history which would have led them to expect that the airplane would have this inherent characteristic or they would have provided for this in their loads and criteria which they furnished to us.

My only criticism of Douglas in this regard is that once this inherent weakness was demonstrated by the July 1970 test failure, they did not take immediate steps to correct it. It seems to me inevitable that, in the twenty years ahead of us, DC-10 cargo doors will come open and I would expect this to usually result in the loss of the airplane. [Emphasis added.] This fundamental failure mode has been discussed in the past and is being discussed again in the bowels of both the Douglas and Convair organizations. It appears however that Douglas is waiting and hoping for government direction or regulations in the hope of passing costs on to us or their customers.

If you can judge from Douglas' position during ongoing contract change negotiations they may feel that any liability incurred in the meantime for loss of life, property and equipment may be legally passed on to us.

It is recommended that overtures be made at the highest management level to persuade Douglas to immediately make a decision to incorporate changes in the DC-10 which will correct the fundamental cabin floor catastrophic failure mode. Correction will take a good bit of time, hopefully there is time before the National Transportation Safety Board (NTSB) or the FAA ground the airplane which would have disastrous effects upon sales and production both near and long term. This corrective action becomes more expensive than the cost of damages resulting from the loss of one plane load of people.

F. D. Applegate
Director of Product Engineering

If this memo had reached outside authorities, Applegate might have been able to prevent the events that (to some extent) he correctly foresaw. However, this memo never reached McDonnell Douglas or the FAA. Applegate received a reply to his memo from his immediate supervisor, J. B. Hurt. Both Applegate and Hurt realized that such major safety questions would not be addressed further at McDonnell Douglas. In his reply to Applegate, Hurt pointed out that if further questions about the plane's design arose, Convair, not McDonnell Douglas, would likely have to bear the costs of necessary modifications. Higher management at Convair subsequently agreed with Hurt that nothing further could realistically be done. Without taking other routes to express his grave misgivings about the DC-10, Applegate filed away his memo, rather than taking his concerns to higher corporate authorities at McDonnell Douglas or to federal agents.

In July 1972, Ship 29 of the DC-10 line was inspected by three different inspectors at McDonnell Douglas's Long Beach plant. All three certified that the ship had been successfully altered to meet the new FAA specifications. In fact, *none* of the recommended cargo door modifications had been implemented. Two years later, Turkish Airlines purchased Ship 29. This ship crashed near Paris in 1974, killing all 335 passengers and 11 crew members, the worst single-plane disaster in aviation history. Experts agreed that the immediate cause of the crash was a blowout of the rear cargo door approximately 12 minutes after liftoff. Cargo bay decompression collapsed the cabin floor, thereby severing control cables. Sanford Douglas, president of McDonnell Douglas, alleged that the Turkish airline involved in the crash had attempted to "rework" the door rigging or latching mechanism, was working with an inadequately trained ground crew, and failed to follow specified procedures for proper latching. The Turkish airline denied the charges. Recovery of a flight recorder indicated that there was no explosion, fire, or evident sabotage, and that the cargo door blew because it was not securely sealed.

In 1980 the McDonnell Douglas Corporation issued a special report addressing the public's growing fears about the DC-10's design. The corporation's report aimed to prove "that the DC-10 meets the toughest standards of aerospace technology."[9] The report did not mention the cargo door defects. Although the company eventually corrected the cargo door *locking* systems, the DC-10 still suffered from *hydraulic* failures. On May 25, 1979, an American Airlines DC-10 crashed shortly after takeoff from Chicago's O'Hare Airport, killing 275 passengers and crew members in the worst air disaster in U.S. history. Subsequent examination revealed that the plane's left engine had ripped loose, carrying away vital hydraulic lines and control cables. The resulting massive system failures rendered the flight crew unable to land the plane safely.[10] More recently, in July 1989, United Airlines Flight 232 crashed near Sioux City, Iowa, killing 112 of its 296 passengers and crew members. On emergency approach to the Sioux City airport, the pilot informed air traffic controllers that he was confronted with a "complete hydraulic failure."[11] NTSB investigators concluded that an engine explosion had severed the plane's hydraulic control cables, rendering the plane unflyable.

The DC-10's hydraulic failures may be due to improper maintenance, or perhaps the model's basic design, which includes placement of the hydraulic lines on the wings' leading edges. By contrast, Boeing designers located the lines on the 747's wings' trailing edges, widely considered to be a less exposed position. In 1990, the FAA proposed modifications to the hydraulic system that would install shut-off valves in case of emergency and hopefully make the plane easier to land. DC-10 pilots still were not satisfied. "We aren't sure that the airplane will be capable of being flown to landing," said Harold Marthinson, director of the Air Line Pilots Association accident investigation department.[12] However, regardless of the model's history, aviation experts and airline executives give the DC-10 "generally high marks."[13] Air force crews flying the KC-10, the DC-10's military counterpart, call the model reliable and safe. The military uses KC-10s extensively for resupply missions, including the 1990

Operation Desert Shield in Saudi Arabia. McDonnell Douglas is currently building the MD-11, an updated version of the DC-10.

NOTES

1. This paragraph profited from three unpublished sources: Fay Horton Sawyier, "The Case of the DC-10 and Discussion" (Chicago: Center for the Study of Ethics in the Professions, Illinois Institute of Technology, December 8, 1976), mimeographed, pp. 2–3; correspondence with John T. Sant of the McDonnell Douglas Corporation's legal department in St. Louis; and correspondence with Professor Homer Sewell of George Washington University (see his article in footnote 5).
2. See Paul Eddy, Elaine Potter, and Bruce Page, *Destination Disaster: From the Tri-Motor to the DC-10* (New York: Quadrangle Books, New York Times Book Co., 1976); John Newhouse, "A Reporter at Large: The Airlines Industry," *The New Yorker*, June 21, 1982, pp. 46–93.
3. Eddy et al., *Destination Disaster*; see also Martin Curd and Larry May, *Professional Responsibility for Harmful Actions* (Dubuque, IA: Kendall/Hunt Publishing Co., 1984), pp. 11–21, and Peter French, "What Is Hamlet to McDonnell-Douglas or McDonnell-Douglas to Hamlet: DC-10," *Business and Professional Ethics Journal* 1 (Winter 1982), pp. 1, 5–6.
4. John T. Sant, personal correspondence.
5. See Homer Sewell, "Commentary," *Business and Professional Ethics Journal* 1 (Winter 1982), pp. 17–19.
6. Eddy et al., *Destination Disaster*, pp. 180–81.
7. National Transportation Safety Board, Aircraft Accident Report no. NTSB-AAR-73-2 (February 28, 1973), p. 38.
8. Eddy et al., *Destination Disaster*, pp. 183–85.
9. McDonnell Douglas Corporation, *The DC-10: A Special Report* (Long Beach, CA: McDonnell Douglas Corporation, 1980).
10. Newhouse, "A Reporter," p. 89; *The New York Times*, June 7, 1979, p. B13, and *The New York Times*, June 19, 1979, p. D19; see also "New Testing Methods Could Boost Air Safety," *Science* 205 (July 6, 1979), pp. 29–31.
11. Michael York, "DC-10 Became a Casualty of Its Reputation," *The Washington Post*, July 20, 1990.
12. Laurie McGinley, "DC-10 Hydraulic Plan Doesn't Satisfy Pilots," *The Wall Street Journal*, June 22, 1990, p. B1.
13. *Ibid.*

THE RELUCTANT SECURITY GUARD

David Tuff, 24, is a security guard who has been working for the past 17 months for the Blue Mountain Company in Minneapolis, Minnesota. Blue Mountain manages and operates retail shopping malls in several midwestern states. The company has a security services division that trains and supplies mall security guards, including those for the Village Square Mall where Tuff has been employed.

Minnesota state and local laws require that security officers be licensed and approved by the county police department. Security officers are required to obey the police unit's rules. Tuff completed the required training, passed the security guard compulsory examination, and was issued a license. Tuff has consistently carried out his guard duties conscientiously. Previously a four-year military policeman in the U.S. Marine Corps, his commanding officer had praised both his service and his integrity.

Part of his job training at Blue Mountain required that Tuff learn the procedures found in the *Security Officer's Manual*, which uses military regulations as a model. Two sections of this manual are worded as follows:

Section V, subsection D.
Should a serious accident or crime, including all felonies, occur on the premises of the licensee, it shall be the responsibility of the licensee to notify the appropriate police department immediately. Failure to do so is a violation of the provisions of this manual.

Furthermore, the manual permits the following action if the provisions are violated:

Section XI—disciplinary and deportment
    A. General
        1. The Private Security Coordinator may reprimand a licensee as hereinafter provided. In cases of suspension or revocation, the licensee shall immediately surrender his identification card and badge to the County Police Department. . . .

B. Cause for Disciplinary Action

13. Any violation of any regulation or rule found in this manual is cause for disciplinary action.

The reverse side of a security officer's license bears these statements:

Obey The Rules And Regulations Promulgated By The Superintendent Of Police.

We will obey all lawful orders and rules and regulations pertaining to security officers promulgated by the superintendent of police of the county or any officer placed by him over me.

Given this language, Tuff believed that his license could be revoked or suspended for *any* failure to report illegal behavior such as drunk driving and selling narcotics. He had sworn to uphold these regulations at the end of his training and had later signed a statement acknowledging that he knew a police officer could ask for his badge if a conflict should arise.

Fourteen months after Tuff joined the company, Blue Mountain issued new rules of procedure outlining certain assigned duties of its security guards. These rules required security officers "to order and escort intoxicated persons, including persons driving under the influence of alcohol, off its parking lots and onto the public roads." The rules did not instruct security officers to either arrest the drivers or to contact or alert the police.

Tuff immediately, and publicly, opposed the company's new policy. Over the ensuing months, he expressed his dissatisfaction to every company officer he could locate. He complained to his immediate superiors, sometimes several times a day, that he was being asked to set a drunk out on the road who might later kill an innocent person. Tuff described to these supervisors imagined scenarios in which a drunk clearly violated the law, and he then asked them what he would be expected to do in these circumstances under the new rules.

His immediate supervisor, Director of Security Manuel Hernandez, told him that if any such situation arose he should contact the supervisor in charge, who would make the decision. Hernandez noted that most drunks do not weave down the road and hit someone. Tuff was not satisfied and used abusive language in denouncing the rules. Hernandez became angry and told Tuff that his complaints irritated his supervisors and that they could tolerate only so much of his behavior. Hernandez also cautioned him that he should worry less about his license and more about his paycheck. Neither man put any complaint in writing. Tuff never received a written warning or reprimand from any company official. Tuff maintained that he considered the policy to be illegal, violative of the rules he had sworn to uphold, and dangerous to the maintenance of his license. Neither his supervisor nor the company manager agreed with his interpretation. They encouraged him to continue his job as usual, but under the new rules.

Tuff then contacted a volunteer organization working to prevent drunk driving. At first he simply sought the organization's interpretation of the law, but later, he voiced a specific complaint about the Blue Mountain policy. His supervisors were approached by some representatives of the volunteer organization, who expressed strong opposition to Blue Mountain's policy for security guards and treatment of drunk drivers.

In the following weeks, Tuff discussed the company policy with several other concerned security guards. He met with security officers Fred Grant and Robert Ladd at a restaurant after work. They discussed the company procedure and its conflict with their licensing requirements and sworn commitments. They considered going to the local newspaper with their grievances against the company policy.

Tuff then contacted a local television news station and a local newspaper. He talked to four reporters about several drunk driving incidents at Blue Mountain parking lots. The reporters pursued Tuff's complaint by talking to company officials about the policy. The reporters proved to their editors' satisfaction that Tuff's complaints to the media were not given in reckless disregard of the truth and were, in fact, entirely truthful.

Hernandez called Tuff into his office to discuss these disclosures to the newspaper. Hernandez asked Tuff to sign a document acknowledging that he had spoken with news reporters concerning Blue Mountain company policies, but he refused to sign. Hernandez reminded him of a company policy prohibiting an employee from talking to the media about company policies. This policy is mentioned on a list of company rules distributed to all employees that states that violation of the rules could result in dismissal or in disciplinary procedures. Tuff knew the company rule but did not consider his revelations a violation, because he had not spoken with the press *on company time*.

Hernandez considered Tuff's interpretation of the rule's scope ridiculous. He consulted with the company's Council of Managers that afternoon. Every manager agreed that Tuff's interpretation of the rule showed a blatant disregard for company policy and that Tuff's excuse was an ad hoc rationalization. They also agreed that Tuff had shown himself to be a complainer and a man of poor judgment, qualities that rendered him unsuitable to be a Blue Mountain security guard. The discussion of this problem at the meeting took little more than five minutes. Council members instructed Hernandez to give Tuff a few days' leave to reflect on the situation. Hernandez duly reported this conclusion to Tuff, who then departed for his home. The number of days of leave he should take was not specified, but both men agreed in an amicable though tense setting that they would be in touch.

Three days later an article about the company's policies appeared in the local newspaper, along with a picture of Tuff in the mall, about to report for work. This story prompted an editorial that was critical of the company on a local television station. The story relied entirely on data provided by Tuff, some of which had been copied from his nightly shift reports.

The newspaper had also interviewed Sergeant Shriver of the county police department. He corroborated Tuff's interpretation that any failure by a security guard to report those driving while intoxicated or those under the influence of drugs constituted a violation of the security manual and the specific terms of the officer's license. He also confirmed Tuff's statement that police officers routinely inspect security officers' activities and that the police have instructions to look for failures to comply with license requirements.

After the television editorial, Blue Mountain began to receive phone calls at a rate of approximately 15 per hour, with over 90 percent of the callers expressing opposition to the company's policies. Several callers indicated that they would no longer patronize the malls mentioned in the newspaper story.

The Council of Managers immediately reconvened to consider this escalation of the problem. Its members agreed that Tuff had to be fired for his violation of the company rule against disclosures to the news media. The managers considered Tuff's revelations an unforgivable act of disloyalty. They discussed whether the proper and precise reason for Tuff's dismissal was his disclosure of confidential information or his approaching the media. Their decision on this point required a sharpening of a vaguely worded corporate rule; a careful process of interpretation revealed that approaching the media is grounds for dismissal even if no disclosure of confidential information is made.

Five working days later, Tuff was called into the company manager's office and dismissed. The manager informed him that the reason for his dismissal was his discussions with the press, a violation of company policy.

Tuff then issued a public statement. He explained that his complaints against Blue Mountain Company's procedures had stemmed from his concern to protect the public and other security officers. Tuff had discussed the policy with the company's other security guards, who had all expressed some degree of concern over the policy because it forced them to violate their licensing requirements and subjected them to possible license suspension or revocation. Based on these encounters, Tuff believed that he was acting on their behalf as well as on his own.

Tuff also disclosed a legal argument he wanted to pursue: He contended that his admissions to the media and his complaints about company policy were protected activities. The company interfered with, restrained, and coerced its employees in the exercise of their rights, as protected by the National Labor Relations Act of 1935, by suspending and eventually dismissing Tuff for his disclosures to the press, which violated company policy.

Tuff brought his case to the National Labor Relations Board (NLRB), whose members determined that Blue Mountain was within its legal rights to fire him. The board found that whistle-blowers are legally protected only if they engage in "concerted activity" together with their fellow workers. Because Tuff had acted alone for the most part, he was not protected. However, a NLRB spokesperson said the board made no moral judgment on either the employer's or the employee's conduct. The parties' moral behavior, he said, was not at stake in the NLRB decision.

VENTURE CAPITAL FOR RUBBERNEX

On a Saturday morning in April 1987, five good friends met in the basement of John Kleinig's house near Palo Alto, California. They saw each other frequently because they carpooled to work at the Globe Coating Company, one of the world's largest manufacturers of fine paints and varnishes. Globe had consistently surpassed other manufacturers in the development of several new products and had the industry's finest research staff. The five commuters and friends were all members of this exceptionally capable research staff, although only two were research scientists. The other three handled administration and computer records.

Kleinig was Globe's research division manager, a position he had obtained five years ago after 15 years of working with the company. He also was the clear leader of this group. Each of the other four had more than 10 years of experience with the company. They all believed Kleinig was the person most responsible for making their research division the best in the world. These five men knew virtually everything about research, administration, secret formulas, the competition, suppliers, and the general industry. Along with 13 other key people in the division, these five men had helped develop several products vital for Globe's leading position.

During their commutes, the five had ample opportunity to criticize their peers and to discuss the cumbersome and slow operation of Globe. Over a period of several months they gradually became convinced that they could conduct more advanced research on new coatings in upcoming years than their employer.

Therefore, they met on this Saturday morning to put the final touches on a business plan for which they hoped to find funding. Kleinig and another group member, Jimmy Liang, had already drafted and discussed a tentative plan.

Their idea for a new business venture centered on the strategy of constructing a plant to manufacture "thin film" coatings. These coatings are new products pioneered and marketed by Globe, which devoted 10 years of research to the development of three forms of the coating. The film coating is so thin that it is invisible to the eye and allows various forms of electrical and adhesive contact as though no coating existed. Yet it provides all the protection of traditional clear coatings. The technology has a marvelous potential for application, from oak floors to computer parts, and yet it slashed production costs as compared with standard polyurethane coatings by 32 percent. It is the most innovative new product in the coating industry.

Between July and the end of August 1987, a friend of Kleinig's, Jay Ewing, critiqued the evolving business plan numerous times and helped Kleinig develop contacts with several venture capitalists. He also arranged for a meeting with the Los Angeles specialty law firm of Lion and Lion to provide legal counsel.

In early September Kleinig met with various venture capitalists, and a September 9, 1987, meeting proved to be the decisive one. Kleinig hit it off beautifully with a representative of a large East Coast venture capitalist, HH Ventures of Philadelphia. This representative was already convinced that thin coating promised major technological innovations in the paint and varnish industry and that the five men represented the epitome of coating knowledge. Their discussion of personnel and business plans lasted approximately two and a half hours, and both admired each other's integrity and capability by the end of the meeting. Between September 10 and 18, Kleinig and HH representatives placed 15 evening phone calls to cement the basis for an agreement between HH and what was to be Rubbernex Industries.

On September 19, 1987, Kleinig resigned from Globe. Nearing an agreement with HH Ventures, he felt that he could no longer in good conscience remain a loyal Globe employee. The other four group members did not resign at this point, since they were not holding direct discussions with HH. At his "exit interview" with his supervisor and a Globe lawyer, Kleinig encountered a hostile and intimidating environment. Globe told him in straightforward terms that if he were to put his skills to work with another company by utilizing Globe trade secrets, he would face a massive lawsuit. His supervisor told him that Globe was seriously concerned that its trade secrets and confidential business information would be misappropriated. Kleinig was asked to sign a letter that enumerated 168 broadly worded trade secrets that he could not transmit or use. He refused to sign it but assured Globe that there would be no misappropriation. His supervisors nonetheless continued to focus heavily on moral and legal questions about trade secrets.

By the conclusion of the exit interview, those present had negotiated the following tentative arrangement: In advance of taking a new job or developing any product, Kleinig would consult with his ex-supervisor at Globe to ensure that there would be no trade secret violations. He also would submit a plan to show that any market he wished to explore would not conflict with already established Globe markets. The interview participants discussed neither the nature of trade secrets nor trade secrets specific to thin film technology.

In a September 21, 1987 meeting, Kleinig, three HH representatives, and lawyers representing both signed a tentative agreement to fund Rubbernex. The contract gave Rubbernex funding for one month to allow for further development of the business plan. HH had one month to evaluate its position with the choice of dropping its interest at the month's end or trying to reach a final agreement for major funding. The agreement included an offer of further financing after one month conditional on what is called *due diligence* in the venture capital industry (and elsewhere). In this context, due diligence means, in part, that HH has obligations of due care when money is given to assist in a business startup. It is a standard of proper care that requires an investigator to competently and thoroughly investigate a proposal's business viability as well as to protect against violations of the rights of all affected parties.

The September 21 meeting involved lengthy discussions about Kleinig's exit interview, about Globe's concerns for its trade secrets, and about HH's need for assurances that no trade secrets problem existed. Kleinig reassured them that he could "build thin film coatings using many different alternative chemicals and processes" and that Globe should have no basis for concern by the time Rubbernex developed the new processes. The next day, Jimmy Liang and the group's chief scientist, Jack Kemp, resigned from Globe. One week later the final two group members resigned. Globe officials told all four during their exit interviews that the company was considering a suit against Kleinig to protect its trade secrets and warned all that if they joined him, they faced the same suit. Globe officials told all four that company officials could prove Kleinig had conspired with other individuals to steal Globe's secrets as early as nine months before leaving the company. These officials would not, however, specify the trade secrets when requested by Kemp to do so.

Whether this package called a *tentative agreement* between venture capitalist HH and the five entrepreneurs would be rewritten and result in a new manufacturing company rested in the hands of Henry Hardy, the man whose massive personal fortune constitutes the venture capital that fuels HH. He had at first decided not to fund Rubbernex, based on his lawyer's explicit concern that Globe's threat of a lawsuit was not an idle one. But Mr. Hardy had left open the possibility that Globe could be mollified or that the trade secrets problem could be otherwise dispatched in an honest and forthright manner.

Mr. Hardy had personally taken charge of HH's due diligence review, which he usually leaves to subordinate officers. He first hired the best firm in New York to do reference checks on the entrepreneurs. These consultants were asked to examine both professional credentials and former or existing employment contracts. Mr. Hardy next commissioned a thorough review of the legal questions surrounding trade secrets by a specialist law firm. He also hired 12 outside consultants at American universities to review the feasibility of the entrepreneurs' scientific claims and asked in each case for an evaluation of whether the venture could be successfully launched without using Globe's trade secrets. He then requested a thorough review of the company's financial and legal position by his in-house lawyer and three of his program directors.

Furthermore, Mr. Hardy examined the enterprise's business viability by having two of his trusted consultants check the Rubbernex proposal. He commissioned a review by a Wall Street security analyst of the coating industry and held discussions with two other venture capitalists who had in the past been involved with trade secrets issues. He also asked for an appraisal by Kleinig of whether he would need further direct hires from Globe to fulfill his plan's staffing requirements.

Mr. Hardy then attempted to contact Globe executives to ask them to review the Rubbernex business plan for possible trade secrets problems. Following the course sketched out during Kleinig's exit interview, Mr. Hardy's proposal to Globe invited company engineers and chemists to spend time in any future Rubbernex manufacturing facility for observational purposes to ensure that there were no trade secrets violations. He was prepared to divulge any formulas used for thin film coatings and allow a neutral inspector to examine Rubbernex's formulas by comparison to Globe's to see if there were any violations. In their reply, Globe lawyers issued a warning that the technology of thin film coatings was proprietary to Globe and that if any venture capital was forthcoming from HH, Mr. Hardy would personally be named in a lawsuit.

This response angered Mr. Hardy. He felt that, whereas he had offered numerous concessions to Globe to ensure that there were no moral or legal violations, Globe had taken a hostile position of non-negotiation solely to prevent potential competition. At about this time, Mr. Hardy's internal and external legal advisers submitted reports that stating that with enough chemical and engineering ingenuity and sufficient venture capital to buy expensive new West German machinery, the potential existed to introduce modifications to claim a new product rather than a mere clone of the Globe product. However, his advisers judged it necessary to qualify their reports with roughly the following statement: "I cannot ensure that there will be no violation of trade secrets unless I am able to examine the trade secrets, and law and ethics prohibits me from doing so."

HH Venture's due diligence standards had consistently equaled or surpassed those of any business competitor, and Mr. Hardy could not imagine a more thorough review than he had done. But this was his first foray into the territory of a trade secrets problem, and he was perplexed by the fact that there is no way to examine whether a trade secrets violation is likely to occur. He remained uncertain of both how much ingenuity the entrepreneurs have (although in the past they have not lacked for a wealth of new ideas) and what the trade secrets are that cannot be utilized. He now realized that his consultants could not recognize the exploitation of a Globe trade secret by the entrepreneurs. Each consultant said the potential existed for the entrepreneurs to make thin film coatings through, as one recent court opinion put it, "skillful variations of general processes known to the particular trade,"[1] but no one could say for sure whether the potential would be actualized.

Mr. Hardy's legal consultants had supplied him with the standard legal definition and analysis of trade secrets, which his consultant report-sheet summarized as follows:

> A trade secret consists of any formula, device, pattern, or compilation of information used in business that gives one an opportunity to obtain advantage over competitors who do not know or use it. It is not a secret of any sort, but a process or device for continuous use in the operation of the business. An exact definition of trade secrets is not possible, but there are factors that can be considered in determining whether something is

a trade secret: general knowledge, employee knowledge, the adequacy of protective guarding, the value of the information, the amount of money expended in development of the secret, and ease of acquisition or duplication. An employee in possession of confidential information that could damage the economic interests of an employer if disclosed is under an obligation of confidentiality that remains in force when the employee leaves the firm and takes employment elsewhere. However, under common law it is not a breach of any obligation owed to an employer to plan for a new competitive venture while still employed, even though the employee has an opportunity to observe (what will later be) a competitor's secrets, and even though the employee may leave with a wealth of experience in and knowledge about the competitor's processes, products, research, and financial matters.

Mr. Hardy saw that this legal definition makes a sharp distinction between a company that *owns* a formula, device, or process that has been *disclosed* in confidence to one or more employees, and a company whose formula has been developed by those employees while employed at the company. In some of the more innovative industries, employees are typically instrumental in creating or advancing a formula, device, or process through their own ingenuity and skills. The greater the extent of an employee's role in creating or otherwise improving the confidential information or property, the greater the employee's apparent claim to a right to use it elsewhere, and the less an employer's right to claim sole possession. Mr. Hardy believes that the entrepreneurs who came to him for funding were, and still are, in this latter circumstance.

It therefore seemed unfair to the entrepreneurs to keep them from starting Rubbernex simply because their former employer was intimidating them. As Mr. Hardy sees it, these employees have several types of obligations to Globe: contractual obligations based on their employment contracts; a responsibility to avoid conflicts of interest such as remaining employed by the firm that will become a competitor of the firm being planned; and a duty to ensure that the new venture will use independently developed competitive technologies, thus avoiding violations of trade secrets, patents, and proprietary designs.

Although there is some disagreement and ambiguity, Mr. Hardy's reference checks and technical consultants said that these conditions have been at least minimally satisfied in this case. They all emphasized that the law of trade secrets is amorphous, conceptually muddy, and formed from a number of different areas of law in a patchwork manner. The law attempts to foster innovation and progress without leaving firms the victims of faithless employees or placing employees in a situation of servitude. An employer has a right to his or her intellectual property, but the employee also has a right to seek gainful employment that requires the application of his or her knowledge and abilities. If employees could be prevented by intimidation from moving from one firm to another, technological growth and diffusion could be stifled.

Mr. Hardy agreed with this argument and conclusion. He favored funding the entrepreneurs although he sensed that two lengthy lawsuits were now a virtual certainty, one against the former Globe employees for misappropriation of trade secrets and the second against HH Ventures for a failure of due care. Mr. Hardy denied the latter charge because it implied that he performed an inadequate due diligence review prior to an investment. He considered this charge to be groundless.

NOTES

1. *Aetna Building Co. v. West*, 39 Cal. 2d 198, at 206.

Chapter Two

THE CONSUMER, CUSTOMER, CLIENT, AND COMPETITOR

INTRODUCTION

The title of this chapter reminds us that business incorporates a multitude of social relationships, many involving both the obligations of some parties and the rights of others. Just as we studied the relationship between business and its employees in the first chapter, we now explore the relationships between a business and its consumers, customers, clients, and competitors. We encounter cases about the obligations of a business to advertise its products truthfully, to sell products at reasonable and clearly identified prices, to market only quality products, to provide relevant information to its consumers, to avoid profiting from inside information that gives an unfair advantage, to avoid conflict of interest, and to avoid sharp practices (shrewd practices bordering on dishonesty) that give an unfair advantage in a competitive situation. The case "Seizure of the S.W. Parcel" in this chapter focuses almost entirely on the issue of sharp practices and morally unfair competition in a legally ambiguous situation.

The circumstances under which markets are created and goods sold are notoriously complex, yet few deny that advertising is marketing's primary instrument. Advertising is unrivaled by the use of sales representatives or other alternative techniques. Critics have consistently denounced misleading or information-deficient advertising, but the moral concepts underlying these denunciations have seldom been carefully examined. What is a deceptive or misleading advertisement? Is it, for example, deceptive or misleading to advertise presweetened children's cereals as "nutritious" or as "building strong bodies"? Are such advertisements forms of lying? Are they manipulative, especially when children are the primary targets or people are led to make purchases they do not need and would not have made had they not seen the advertising? If so, does the manipulation derive from some form of deception? For example, if an advertisement that touts a particular mouthwash as germ-killing manipulates listeners into purchasing the mouthwash, does it follow that these consumers have been deceived?

In light of certain free market theories, the question arises whether unjustifiable advertising or competition ever occurs. If market supply shifts in competitive struggles to meet consumer, customer, or client demands, is not the purchaser king, and is not advertising simply a medium to provide information about products consumers demand? Or is this depiction a convenient fiction that is utilized to justify beliefs about the market? Other marketing practices present similar problems. Even the ostensibly simple issue of how to display counter goods in a grocery store can hint at the moral problems of deception and manipulation.

The case "KCRC's Program of Incentives for Advertisers" points to a number of subtle problems about means that might be used to market radio air time so as to secure the friendship, loyalty, and commitment of client advertisers. "Commissions on Sales at Brock Mason Brokerage" explores a different set of problems that arise in marketing investment opportunities. Here we encounter a complex set of relationships that may contain problems of conflict of interest, deception, and manipulation. The case "Lilly's Consultation with Hostile Corporations" presents difficulties that arise when interests conflict and examines problems of limited disclosure in negotiations about services to be performed. In this particular case, the limited disclosure involves undisclosed information about past associations with a client's hostile associate.

Whether marketing practices can be justified by the "rules of the game" in business is another major question. Some have argued that marketing is analogous to ordinary arms-length transactions in which we all engage, for example, when purchasing a house or bargaining about the price of a rug. In these situations bluffing, overstatement, and enticement are expected and invite similar countermoves. Although abuse and contempt are not tolerated, deception is, as long as all players know the rules of the game and occupy roughly equal bargaining positions. This model suggests, on the one hand, that deceptive practices and sharp practices can be justifiable. On the other hand, limits must be set to restrict deception, manipulation, and cunning maneuvers that take advantage of a competitor's misfortune. For example, potentially harmful products cannot be marketed as if benign, a problem explored in "Removing Rely Tampons from the Market."

According to the rules-of-the-game model, there are established procedures for marketing a product or making a business move; consumers, customers, clients, and competitors are well acquainted with these rules of the game and are often in an equal bargaining position. Although advertisements that use subliminal influence or that are inherently offensive to large segments of the population are not permitted, it has been argued that sexual suggestion in ads pitched to adults, strong pitches to young children in toy advertisements, and sharp practices carried out under open rules of law are simply facets of the established game. This defense of prevailing business practice has its advocates, but remains controversial.

The Federal Trade Commission (FTC) and other regulatory institutions hold that the rules of acceptable marketing encompass more than the mere creation of a market, because marketing involves the dissemination of information that helps persons make an informed choice. If consumers are misled in the attempt to make an intelligent choice or are enticed into a choice by deception, the advertising cannot be justified, regardless of the game's rules. The FTC has therefore placed strict regulations on industries that produce potentially harmful products, cigarettes being one of the best- known examples (see Chapter 4, "Banning Cigarette Advertising").

The case "Putting the Squeeze on Citrus Hill Orange Juice" in this chapter shows how the government and consumer protection groups focus on consumer *response* to advertising and on its social effects, rather than on the *intention* of the creators of that advertising. By contrast, those who defend controversial advertising focus more on the intentions of advertising agencies and manufacturers in marketing a product, namely, the intent to sell a good product. These different emphases complicate the issues, because a product marketed with good intentions can nonetheless be advertised in a misleading way or otherwise have negative consequences.

However, not everyone has the same threshold of deception. What deceives one person can be ignored by another. As federal agencies have pointed out, the so-called "reasonable person" and "ignorant person" are both approached by advertising and marketing techniques. The rules-of-the-game defense of advertising and marketing practices has the same problem: How skillfully a person understands and deals with the rules of a game is relative to an individual's capacities of resistance and acceptance. Children's abilities to grasp the nature of advertising and to distance themselves from its appeal is a celebrated issue featured in the Kellogg cereals case in Chapter 4.

A related and widely discussed issue is the extent to which a consumer's, customer's, or client's desires and needs originate with the person, and the extent to which those desires and needs are created by marketing. Debates on this subject are difficult to assess, because our desires and needs commonly derive from social causes and conventions. Moreover, even if a desire or need for a product does not originate from a person's completely autonomous choice, it does not follow that it is an unfortunate desire or that it has not been freely accepted by the person. The desire of a person who sells an old car and buys a new Chrysler because of the advertised rebate may have been stimulated or even created by marketing, but this source is not necessarily manipulative or regrettable. These debates are especially heated when a product is considered harmful, as some have alleged about presweetened children's cereals, tampons, cigarettes, risky forms of investment, and various automobiles.

A different, but important, perspective on these issues is that of quality control. If products like orange juice, cereals, and cupcakes had to be certified as nutritious, fat free, low in sugar, and free of harmful artificial coloring before being allowed on the market, we would care much less about the messages of advertisements or sales representatives. This assertion amounts to a call for higher qualitative standards in industry and regulatory branches of government as a means to resolve consumer protection issues. (Consumerism and consumer advocates have focused more on quality control than on marketing practices.) Higher standards would also protect quality manufacturers from inferior-quality competitors. There are, however, liberty issues at stake—for example, the freedom of consumers to purchase "junk food" or of manufacturers to place products of differing quality on the market.

PUTTING THE SQUEEZE ON CITRUS HILL ORANGE JUICE

In April 1991 the U.S. Food and Drug Administration (FDA) charged Procter & Gamble in federal court with fraud and violation of the 1963 Food and Drug Act, alleging that the company had included false and misleading statements on its Citrus Hill orange juice cartons. The FDA particularly criticized Procter & Gamble's use of the word *fresh* on its Citrus Hill label as misleading to consumers, because the company processed and produced Citrus Hill from concentrate. The FDA also objected to advertisements claiming that the juice was "pure," "squeezed," and free of additives. The following are the primary aspects of the Citrus Hill label that the FDA found misleading or false:[1]

1. Citrus Hill Fresh Choice
2. Fresh Choice . . . Means Fresh Taste
3. We pick our oranges at the peak of ripeness, then we hurry to squeeze them before they lose freshness
4. Pure squeezed 100% orange juice[2]
5. Guaranteed: No additives 100% pure
6. We don't add anything

The FDA was interested in this case because of the agency's overall goal of promoting sound nutrition and public health. Following federal law, the FDA commissioner determined that the agency must use its expertise in science and food safety to ensure honest labeling of food products so that consumers are not the victims of fraud and have the opportunity to select foods that promote good health.[3] By statute the FDA is mandated to eliminate false and misleading advertisements.

David Kessler, who headed the FDA during the Citrus Hill controversy, criticized the FDA for its history of slow and ineffective prosecution of misleading advertising and enforcement of agency regulations. Kessler made enforcement a top priority as commissioner. The Citrus Hill case was his initial step in making the FDA a more effective oversight agency, especially since it was brought against a large and prestigious company.[4]

The FDA believed that the phrases advertised on the Citrus Hill carton label were misleading and perhaps false. For instance, FDA officials main-

This case was prepared by Tom L. Beauchamp and Nicole Herb and revised by Jeff Greene. Not to be duplicated without permission of the holder of the copyright, © 1992, 1996 Tom L. Beauchamp.

tained that using the word *fresh* on a label for a processed food product constituted false advertising. When used in orange juice advertising, the FDA contended that *fresh* leads consumers to assume erroneously that the product is
freshly squeezed. The FDA also attacked the phrase *no additives* as false, on
grounds that Procter & Gamble added water to the orange concentrate.[5]

Procter & Gamble interpreted the advertisements differently, although
both parties agreed that Citrus Hill orange juice was processed and made from
concentrate. The company believed that the slogans used and the phrase
"made from concentrate" effectively conveyed to the consumer that the
orange juice was processed.[6] Procter & Gamble also argued that the brand
name "Citrus Hill Fresh Choice" is no more misleading than its former, FDA-
approved, label "Citrus Hill Select." Company executives also pointed to a
Procter & Gamble study, which involved four groups of 300 subjects each, of
the public's perception of its labels. The following percentages of those studied made an inference from the label listed that the product was *fresh squeezed*:

Citrus Hill Select	21%
Citrus Hill Fresh Choice	22%
Minute Maid	34%
Tropicana	41%

This survey indicated that changing the name from "Select" to "Fresh Choice"
had no significant effect on consumer perception of whether the product was
fresh squeezed; the labels "Citrus Hill Select" and "Citrus Hill Fresh Choice"[7]
were seen as almost identical. However, competitors' brands without the word
fresh were more likely to be perceived as fresh squeezed, presumably because
of advertising. Procter & Gamble also maintained that *fresh* never modified the
label's common food name and therefore was never used in a context implying the orange juice was fresh.[8] Procter & Gamble claimed that *fresh* was not
misleading when used in expressions such as "Citrus Hill Fresh Choice,"
"Fresh Choice . . . Means Fresh Taste," and "we pick our oranges at the peak of
ripeness, then we hurry to squeeze them before they lose freshness."

The two sides also disagreed about whether Procter & Gamble's advertisements violated the law. According to FDA spokesperson Jeff Nesbit, the
FDA ruled in 1963 that *fresh* could not be used to describe commercially
processed orange juice, including concentrate. In Nesbit's interpretation, the
FDA has had a clear policy since 1969 that *fresh* cannot be applied to heated or
chemically processed foods, including food made from concentrate.[9]

However, Procter & Gamble sharply challenged this interpretation, arguing that regulations forbidding the use of the word *fresh* on processed food
product labels apply only when *fresh* modifies a common or usual food name
and is written entirely in small letters.[10] According to this interpretation, Citrus Hill's label could not read "fresh orange juice," but phrases such as "Citrus
Hill Fresh Choice" and "Fresh Taste" would be perfectly acceptable. Procter &
Gamble also argued that FDA regulations that prohibit the use of the word

fresh with respect to processed foods have never been applied to brand or trade names, "particularly where those words are not used in connection with the common or usual name of the food and are clearly distinguished by size and style of type and appear in a different part of the label."[11] Company lawyers cited a legal opinion that established that using *fresh* on trademark names of pasteurized orange juice products may be permissible in some cases.[12]

Procter & Gamble also noted some inconsistencies in the food labeling rules and guidelines of various government agencies that contradicted the FDA's policy on the use of the word *fresh*. Procter & Gamble pointed out that the U.S. Department of Agriculture's (USDA) Food Safety and Inspection Service follows guidelines on the use of the word *fresh* on labels of processed meat products that support Procter & Gamble's practice of precise labeling. The USDA standard is as follows:

> "Fresh" may be used on processed products containing ingredients that could not be labeled "fresh" since the term has acquired acceptance when used to identify products sold in the refrigerated state. . . . We also recognize that, in many instances, the word "fresh" could be incorporated into the firm name or brand name and used on cured, preserved, and frozen or previously frozen poultry products where it would be highly unlikely that the consumer would be led to believe that he or she was purchasing a fresh product.[13]

Accordingly, Procter & Gamble's use of the word *fresh* in its brand name is arguably an accepted practice. Procter & Gamble also produced a list of 79 beverage industries that use the word *fresh* as part of the label's brand or trademark name.[14]

After the FDA notified Procter & Gamble that its Citrus Hill orange juice advertising label was unacceptable, Procter & Gamble did revise the label, to a limited degree, before the FDA prosecuted the company. The company removed the term *squeezed* from the phrase "pure squeezed 100% orange juice," enlarged the words "from concentrate," and made them more visible by providing a new background color that contrasted with, and therefore emphasized, the phrase "from concentrate."[15]

However, the FDA remained dissatisfied with other aspects of the label, particularly the continued use of the word *fresh* in the revised Procter & Gamble label phrases "Fresh Choice" and "Means Fresh Taste." Procter & Gamble claimed replacement of "New!" and "Fresh Sealed Carton" with "Fresh Choice" and "Means Fresh Taste" accurately described the company's processing changes, which allowed for the faster preparation of oranges after harvest and the creation of a fresher tasting product. The company contended that consumers who purchase Citrus Hill Orange Juice really are choosing a fresher juice.[16] The company also claimed that the label alterations announced to the FDA on October 31, 1990, had been FDA-recommended.[17] However, this recommendation, if it occurred, is inconsistent with longstanding FDA policy; and earlier, on October 19, 1990, the FDA had informed Procter & Gamble that it considered all uses of the word *fresh* on its Citrus Hill packaging to be misleading and unacceptable.[18]

On April 24, 1991, the FDA charged Procter & Gamble in a Minneapolis federal court with making false and misleading freshness claims on its Citrus Hill label.[19] After a federal judge's authorization, Minneapolis authorities seized all of the Citrus Hill orange juice products in a local supermarket warehouse.[20]

Procter & Gamble did not cooperate with the FDA because its executives believed that the FDA was applying its policies inconsistently and unfairly. Although Kessler pledged to enforce FDA policies fairly and consistently,[21] Procter & Gamble feared that a changed label would shrink its already small orange juice market share, while other competitors would continue to advertise without FDA criticism and interference. The company noted that some of the criticism that the FDA received about its Citrus Hill label came from a competitor's law firm. Procter & Gamble accordingly notified the FDA that its research indicated both Tropicana's and Minute Maid's use of the phrase "Florida squeezed" on their pasteurized orange juice products caused 41 percent and 34 percent of consumers respectively to incorrectly assume that these products were in fact *freshly squeezed*. Having removed the word *squeezed* from its label, Procter & Gamble wanted the FDA to enforce its regulations consistently and evenly on all of the industry competitors.

Procter & Gamble also asked the FDA to require that all Citrus Hill competitors print their product statements, such as "made from concentrate," in the same color and on the same colored background as Procter & Gamble to enforce advertising consistency.[22] The FDA thanked Procter & Gamble for the information on its competitors' labeling practices but reiterated that it merely wished to ensure Procter & Gamble's conformity with the law, and it reminded the company that its complaints about competitors' advertising did not excuse its reluctance to comply with FDA regulations.[23]

This dispute raises the question of whether it is fair for a regulatory agency to direct action against one company, while delaying investigation or prosecution of competitor companies accused of similar legal violations. Did the FDA have the right to prosecute Procter & Gamble, and delay acting on Procter & Gamble's claims that 79 different beverage labels and approximately 500 different food products use *fresh* in advertisements?[24] Even a brief delay in FDA action with respect to misleading advertising among other orange juice companies could result in economic losses for Procter & Gamble by reducing its share of the orange juice market.

A related question is whether Procter & Gamble followed advertising regulations according to the law's *letter*, but without obeying the law's *spirit*. In advertising Citrus Hill, did Procter & Gamble provide correct advertising information in good faith, as required by law, or did the company manipulate consumers to increase profits, while only technically adhering to the law? If the FDA designed regulations to ensure that advertisements that include the word *fresh* do not mislead consumers to believe that processed foods are fresh, does this create an obligation for companies to comply not only with the letter of the law but with its spirit and intent as well?

Procter & Gamble flatly refused to remove the word *fresh* from the Citrus Hill label throughout ten months of negotiations with the FDA. The two sides did not resolve the labeling dispute until the FDA filed suit against Procter & Gamble.[25] As mentioned earlier, the company defended its new trademark name "Citrus Hill Fresh Choice" by citing the results from its brand name survey. Based on the these results, Procter & Gamble contended that the 22 percent of people misled by Citrus Hill's name constituted an acceptable percentage, on grounds that some people will always believe that frozen orange juice is fresh. However, Procter & Gamble produced no evidence to support its belief in consumer gullibility. The company did not attempt to further reduce the 22 percent survey result through additional label modifications. Procter & Gamble also added the sentence "We pick our oranges at the peak of ripeness, then we hurry to squeeze them before they lose freshness" to its Citrus Hill label, without considering its impact on consumer perceptions.[26]

Some FDA officials have questioned whether this controversy over the use of the words *fresh, squeezed,* and *pure* with respect to orange juice warrants such a large share of the FDA's limited time and resources. Critics note that orange juice, unlike other falsely or deceptively advertised products, does not cause any immediate or visible harm to consumers. These critics argue that the FDA should focus its regulatory actions on products inimical to the public health. A typical example is that of Bioplasty Inc., a St. Paul, Minnesota-based company that failed to obtain FDA approval to market manufactured breast implants. After investigation the FDA charged that Bioplasty Inc. marketed its breast implants illegally and also made false and deceptive medical claims on the product label. The agency charged that the information on the label led consumers to assume that the product had passed safety tests and that information on the risks associated with breast implantation was accurate. The FDA eventually seized these illegal and fraudulently advertised breast implant products.

However, not all false advertising cases clearly violate agency regulations. Moreover, misleading advertisements that are technically free of false statements can often prove to be as harmful to the public as those containing false statements. Misleading advertisements may cause people to purchase a product without proper information. For example, some people develop heart problems and high cholesterol or triglyceride counts from regularly consuming products advertised as "low cholesterol" or "no cholesterol." Though these products have no or low cholesterol, their labels often do not document their high fat or high sugar content, which can contribute to a cholesterol or triglyceride problem.

In comparison to these cases, the Citrus Hill case may appear less important, because Procter & Gamble's false and deceptive advertising claims do not conceal a health threat to consumers. Many government officials believe that the FDA should concentrate on regulating advertising that endangers the public health by not adequately explaining the health risks associated with the product. However, if the FDA prosecuted the Citrus Hill case to enforce rules of unambiguous advertising, consistent and fair policy implementation may be the agency's only viable alternative.

In 1992, Procter & Gamble decided to end the company's 11-year foray into the orange juice business. Citrus Hill was never able to gain a significant market share in the $10 billion industry, which is dominated by the Seagram Company's Tropicana and the Coca-Cola Company's Minute Maid. Attempts to improve the appeal of Citrus Hill with the addition of calcium, use of the word *fresh* on the label, and a new easy-pour spout proved unsuccessful. The FDA's attacks and the ensuing bad publicity led Procter & Gamble to decide that it had had enough. The Cincinnati-based company took a $200 million loss, or 30 cents a share in the division. Repercussions of the move also included a 20 percent drop in earnings for the first quarter of 1992 and either layoffs, reassignments, or potential transfer to a new owner for about half of the 2,300 juice division employees.[27] Future production plans include a focus on the more promising blended juice industry that includes Hawaiian Punch and Sunny Delight.

NOTES

1. Letter dated January 25, 1991, from L. Robert Lake, director of Office of Compliance, Center for Food Safety and Applied Nutrition, to lawyer George Burditt of the Burditt, Bowles & Radzius, chartered law firm representing Procter & Gamble, p. 2.
2. The term *squeezed* was later removed during negotiations with the FDA. *Ibid.*, pp. 1–3.
3. Remarks by David A. Kessler, M.D., commissioner of Food and Drugs, pp. 3–4. This text was used as the basis for Commissioner Kessler's oral remarks on April 24, 1991, from the Office of Public Affairs of the FDA.
4. *Ibid.*, pp. 2–3, 6–7.
5. Lake, letter dated January 25, 1991, pp. 2–3.
6. Letter dated February 6, 1991, from George Burditt of the Burditt, Bowles & Radzius, chartered law firm representing Procter & Gamble, to Janice Oliver, director of Division of Regulatory Guidance, Office of Compliance, Center for Food Safety and Applied Nutrition, p. 2.
7. Memorandum of a meeting held between the FDA and Procter & Gamble dated June 14, 1990, and written by Martin Stutsman of the Case and Advisory Branch, Division of Regulatory Guidance, Center for Food and Safety and Applied Nutrition, p. 2.
8. Letters dated June 22, 1990, and February 6, 1991, from George Burditt of the Burditt, Bowles & Radzius, chartered law firm representing Procter & Gamble, to Janice Oliver, director of Division of Regulatory Guidance, Office of Compliance, Center for Food Safety and Applied Nutrition, pp. 3–4 and 2, respectively.
9. "FDA Puts Squeeze on P&G Over Citrus Hill Labeling," *The Wall Street Journal*, April 25, 1991, pp. B1, B4.
10. Burditt, letters dated June 22, 1990, and February 6, 1991, pp. 1–5 and 1–2, respectively.
11. Burditt, letter dated February 6, 1991, pp. 1–2.
12. Burditt, letter dated June 22, 1990, pp. 2–3.
13. *Ibid.*, pp. 4–5.
14. Burditt, letter dated February 6, 1991, pp. 1–2.
15. Letter dated October 31, 1990, from George Burditt of the Burditt, Bowles & Radzius, chartered law firm representing Procter & Gamble, to L. Robert Lake, director of Office of Compliance, Center for Food Safety and Applied Nutrition, pp. 1–2.
16. Memorandum of June 14, 1990, meeting, p. 2.
17. Burditt, letter dated February 6, 1991, p. 3.

18. Memorandum of meeting held between the FDA and Procter & Gamble dated October 19, 1990, and written by Martin Stutsman of the Case and Advisory Branch, Division of Regulatory Guidance, Center for Food Safety and Applied Nutrition, p. 2.
19. Kessler, p. 7; "FDA Puts Squeeze on P&G," p. B1.
20. "FDA Puts Squeeze on P&G," p. B1.
21. Kessler, p. 7.
22. Burditt, letter dated October 31, 1990, pp. 1–2.
23. Lake, letter dated January 25, 1991, p. 1.
24. Burditt, letter dated February 6, 1991, pp. 1–2.
25. "FDA Puts Squeeze on P&G," p. B1.
26. Memorandum of June 14, 1990, meeting, pp. 2–3.
27. Valerie Rietman, "Procter & Gamble to Scrap Citrus Hill, Plans to Take Charge of $200 Million," *The Wall Street Journal,* September 18, 1992, p. A3.

KCRC'S PROGRAM OF INCENTIVES FOR ADVERTISERS

San Francisco radio station KCRC is owned by ACME Investments, a much larger company with many subsidiary interests. KCRC broadcasts a classic rock format popular with the city's 25–to-49 age group, which accounts for about 50 percent of the metropolitan population. In operation since 1986, KCRC currently leads in the Arbitron Radio national ratings for the classic rock category. Approximately 25 radio stations in the same division directly compete with KCRC.

Radio stations generate income by selling advertising air time. The radio industry competes directly with newspaper or television syndicates for advertising clients, and rival local radio stations compete for the available advertising dollars. Bay area radio stations earned approximately $200 million in advertising revenues in 1995. Advertisers must allocate their funds among the competing radio, television, print, and billboard markets; radio garners only about 9 percent of all media advertising dollars. (A single large newspaper often receives $400 million in advertising revenues in a single year.)

To maintain station profitability in the competitive advertising market, KCRC station manager and part owner, Scott Reed, together with ACME's top management, created an "incentive" program for advertisers. ACME designed the plan to ameliorate the annual first quarter revenues slump (known in the industry as "soft time"), during which there is extensive air-time availability. Under the plan, clients who spent $36,000 in "new" money in first quarter advertising would receive a free, all-expenses-paid (and tax-free) cruise for two to Cozumel, Mexico, with travel to, and tickets for, the Super Bowl (on the return trip). "New" money meant that *existing* clients had to increase current advertising by $36,000, and *new* clients had to spend $36,000 to be eligible. The first quarter ran from December 17, 1991, to April 15, 1991 (which included the pre-Christmas advertising period as an incentive to provide additional benefit for advertisers). Each client received air time during the quarter for the $36,000. The trip cost KCRC $8,500 per client (each "client" being a couple).

As the incentive plan evolved, Scott became concerned for two primary reasons. First, he believed that some clients were purchasing unneeded and perhaps unwanted air time to obtain the vacation. The businesses that partici-

This case was prepared by Tom L. Beauchamp, with research assistance from John Hannula and revisions by John Cuddihy, Katy Cancro, and Jeff Greene. It is entirely based on fact, but names have been changed to protect the sources of the information. Not to be duplicated without permission of the holder of the copyright, © 1992, 1996 Tom L. Beauchamp.

pated in the incentive program were usually small and family owned, with the owner doubling as the business's financial manager. Scott wondered if the cruise offer led the owners to make unsound business judgments, based on personal or family reasons, rather than business reasons. Upon "earning" the incentive cruise, one diamond merchant stated flatly that the station's offer was instrumental in his decision to purchase the additional air time.

Second, Scott thought the plan might function to lower KCRC's overall profit margin. More cost-effective options and better business incentives, such as decreased advertising rates, could have been used instead to attract the same business. ACME had employed Scott to increase station profits, but he worried that maybe the Super Bowl cruise was not the best possible strategy with which to achieve the station's financial goals. The incentive program, from his perspective, ran the risk of undercutting potential profits with its considerable expenditure on clients, even though revenue would actually increase. Although Scott's regional vice-president at ACME and his staff adamantly disagreed with him, there seemed to be no way to demonstrate who was more likely to be correct.

One client, Ray Manta, raised a special concern. He was employed by a new publishing company owned by the largest bookstore chain in the United States. When approached about the cruise trip, he reported to Scott that, "I can't accept anything as a gift, because my employer has strict rules against both gifts and kickbacks." However, three hours later, Ray was back on the phone with Scott. He wanted to know if the station considered the incentive plan a *gift*. Scott informed him that the station viewed the offer as a *bonus*, not as a gift. Ray still felt that under the rules of his parent company, he could not accept such a bonus. He did believe, however, that if he paid for the actual cost of the trip out of his personal funds, he would not be violating company rules. Ray had discussed the trip with his wife, who was enthusiastic about the prospect.

After further reflection, Ray called Scott and said, "I know the actual cost to you can't be $8,500, so can you tell me the real cost?" Scott's actual costs were in fact $8,500, but he knew that Ray was tempted by the carrot. He said he would check the "real costs" and get back to him. Scott called a travel agent and confirmed that some much less elegant cruise and Super Bowl trips were being marketed at $3,400.

Scott then went to Ray's office. With a wink, Ray asked, "What are the real costs?" With a wink back, Scott queried, "What do you think they are?" Ray said, "Oh, I imagine $3,200 is about right." Scott, with mock surprise, said that Ray had almost exactly hit the nail on the head. Ray pulled out his personal checkbook and wrote a check to the station for $3,400. He said he was confident his employer would accept the arrangement without reservations.

The incentive plan also raised other questions. Since the station could not arrange group fares with a travel agent or cruise line, KCRC paid the full cost of the trips. The station also required $13,500 as an advertising minimum to cover its air time costs for the time sold in the package. Added to this was the $8,500 cost of the trip to KCRC. In short, KCRC needed $22,000 from each new advertiser to break even from the incentive program. Theoretically, the $36,000 in advertising revenues from each incentive program participant would give the station a net profit of $14,000 per client. In reality, however, KCRC salespeople offered advertisers reduced rates on quarterly contracts in order to maintain a strong clientele (Table 2.1). Consequently, the program participants rarely paid the actual $36,000 necessary for program eligibility. Table 2.1 shows the total dollars received from each client who elected to participate in the incentive program and how many of these dollars are actual "new dollars" (new money that was not already accounted for in a quarterly package with the client).

TABLE 2.1 Incentive Program Eligibility

Business Name	Total $	New $
1. Smith & Smith Jewelers	36,000	17,000
2. Burger Express	56,300	17,000
3. Emerald Car Rental*	36,000	36,000
4. Healy Diamond Import	36,000	15,000
5. Gaston Auto Sales*	27,000	27,000
6. Captial Racquet Club	36,000	17,000
7. Kohn Tapes & cds	21,000	8,000
8. Alfonso's Restaurants	27,000	27,000
9. Morgan Sporting Goods	27,000	17,000
10. Prospect Grocery*	27,000	27,000
11. Poulton Breweries*	32,000	32,000
Total	$361,300	$240,000

* denotes new client

Scott calculated that the incentive program technically ran a $2,000 overall deficit, because the *new* money did not quite cover the air time and trip expenses [($93,500 + $148,500 = $242,000) - $240,000 = $2,000]. Since Ray Manta was returning $3,400, the figures could be legitimately changed to show a profit on paper of $1,400. However, acknowledged expenses for the trip did not reflect the program's secondary costs, including client dinners, gifts, and car rentals while on the trip.

Although Scott considered the program unprofitable, he did not want to stress his assessment to the ACME management. They emphasized the new dollars and deemphasized the internal cost issues. They were pleased with the resulting client relations and viewed these relationships as intangible benefits not subject to financial calculation. ACME management favored more incentives to advertisers, not fewer and they made their view clear to Scott. "One cannot measure the value of solid client relationships," said the CEO of ACME.

Scott agreed with this statement, because he had carefully watched the development of client relationships during the trip (in which he was permitted to participate). Spouses got to know other spouses, and couple friendships flourished. The environment was intimate, the evening meals fun, the scenery spectacular, and the Super Bowl exciting. How could personal relationships not develop? However, Scott knew that KCRC's cruise guests may also be one-time advertisers, attracted only by the Cozumel trip. He worried that some advertisers would come to resent the $36,000 requirement and look elsewhere, or else expect an incentive more frequently. But these were not consequences he could predict with any accuracy, and he shrugged them off as intuitions rather than hard evidence.

Quite apart from his reservations from a business standpoint, Scott loved the trips. They were not only free for him, but his salary was paid while on the trip without the time counting against his annual vacation leave. But from a business perspective, he did not know what he was getting in return for what he was giving, and he saw no way to prove profitability. He also had a more general sense, which he had not been able to articulate well, that he did not like being involved with his clients in the way this program required.

REMOVING RELY TAMPONS FROM THE MARKET

Procter & Gamble voluntarily withdrew its Rely tampons from the market on September 22, 1980. To date, the company has not reintroduced a tampon to the feminine hygiene market. The media at that time reported the unusual withdrawal under headlines about TSS, or toxic shock syndrome. TSS was unknown to the medical profession until 1978. Not until May 1980 did the Centers for Disease Control (CDC), a division of the U.S. Public Health Service charged with monitoring the incidence of disease in the United States, alert physicians to the problem. The center reported a disease characterized by a sudden onset of high fever (usually over 104 degrees), vomiting and diarrhea, a rapid drop in blood pressure (usually below 90 systolic in adults), and a sunburn-like rash that later peels in scales with a four to five day acute phase.

These conditions have persisted, but the mortality ratio has plummeted since the first TSS cases, from 10 percent of afflicted people to less than 1 percent in the early 1990s. The disease has primarily affected women under age 30, especially those who have just had their menstrual periods. However, studies have also found TSS cases in nonmenstruating women, males, and young girls and boys. Ironically, cases in which males are vaginally infected with TSS "are 3.3 times as likely to be fatal as female vaginal cases."[1]

Rely tampons became widely identified with toxic shock syndrome when the CDC released a TSS report on September 19, 1980. The report indicated that 71 percent of the women in the study (a total of 52) had been Rely users,[2] but research also indicated that TSS cases occurred with tampons produced by all five of the major U.S. tampon manufacturers. At the time, Procter & Gamble had developed the Rely tampon as its entry in the financially secure arena of feminine hygiene products. Introduced to the marketplace in 1974, Rely had captured about 25 percent of the tampon market by September 1980.[3] Rely's design, consisting partly of the use of superabsorbent cellulose and polyurethane, made innovations in the superabsorbent category. Procter & Gamble test marketed Rely in Ft. Wayne, Indiana, in 1974, and in Rochester, New York, in 1975.[4]

Consumers resisted the new product due to its use of polyurethane as an absorbent material. Women who were interviewed reported fears of cancer and other health risks. The Center for Health Services at the University of

This case was prepared by Louisa W. Peat O'Neil and Tom L. Beauchamp and revised by Joanne L. Jurmu, John Cuddihy, and Kier Olsen. Not to be duplicated without the permission of the holder of the copyright, © 1991, 1996 Tom L. Beauchamp.

Tennessee concluded that polyurethane was not carcinogenic and, thus, that these fears were unfounded. Aware of consumer concerns, however, Procter & Gamble reformulated Rely. The revised tampon encased polyester foam and superabsorbent cellulose sponges in a polyester sack.[5] The U.S. Food and Drug Administration (FDA) had over the years recorded unconfirmed claims of certain injuries related to such tampons, including Rely, before release of the TSS studies. Although complaints by consumers and physicians usually involved difficulty with tampon removal and vaginal ulcerations and lacerations, two pages of the FDA's Device Experience Network computer printout listed citations about other Rely-related problems.[6]

The FDA's regulatory role was unclear when the TSS problem first arose because no research had at that time demonstrated that tampons caused TSS. On the other hand, Congress mandated the FDA to test all medical drugs and devices prior to public marketing. Prior to 1974–1976, the FDA regulated tampons under its drug section, although they were not technically classified as drugs. In a reorganization process begun in 1974, the FDA reclassified tampons and other feminine hygiene products as medical devices. Because tampons were considered to have a "history of safe use," they were placed in Class II, which bases safety on past performance rather than on specific premarket testing,[7] as required for Class III medical devices. Small changes in Class II devices are permitted without FDA review or testing. Critics have therefore argued that, because of the Class II classification, tampon manufacturers have been permitted to alter tampons by introducing minor changes over time without regulatory challenge.[8] Tampax, however, has denied that such changes have been made.[9]

When presented with the 1980 CDC study findings, Procter & Gamble executives faced a crisis. They could continue to market Rely tampons despite the publicity linking the product to TSS; they could wait until the FDA attempted to restrict product sale; or they could voluntarily withdraw the product from the market. At first, when scientific research indicated that tampon composition did not encourage bacterial growth, Edward G. Harness, chairman of the board and chief executive of Procter & Gamble, said he was "determined to fight for the brand, to keep an important brand from being hurt by insufficient data in the hands of a bureaucracy."[10]

At the time the FDA did not have sufficient data to order a legal recall. Nonetheless, Procter & Gamble had ceased all Rely tampon production by September 18, 1980, as a result of negative publicity and the CDC report that statistically linked Rely to TSS. The latter was a report that Procter & Gamble's physicians, microbiologists, and epidemiologists could not refute. "That was the turning point," Mr. Harness said. The company subsequently pledged its research expertise to the Centers for Disease Control to investigate TSS and agreed to finance and direct a large educational program about the disease. In addition, the company agreed to issue a warning to tampon users to discontinue and avoid Rely use. Referring to the Rely case, Mr. Harness later made the following public announcement:

Company management must consistently demonstrate a superior talent for keeping profit and growth objectives as first priorities. However, it also must have enough breadth to recognize that enlightened self-interest requires the company to fill any reasonable expectation placed upon it by the community and the various concerned publics. Keeping priorities straight and maintaining the sense of civic responsibility will achieve important secondary objectives of the firm. Profitability and growth go hand in hand with fair treatment of employees, of direct customers, of consumers, and of the community.[11]

Although some executives inside Procter & Gamble strongly resisted the methodology and scope of the CDC studies, the company believed it could not risk its reputation on a product subjected to massive adverse publicity. A prominent question in the deliberations of corporate executives had been whether a profit-making company could continue to market a product associated with the sudden death, illness, and disfigurement of young women (even if a causal relationship was not confirmed). Harness said the withdrawal was intended to remove Rely from the controversy "despite evidence that the withdrawal of Rely will not eliminate the occurrence of TSS even if Rely's use is completely discontinued."[12]

FDA officials met with Procter & Gamble executives, representatives of other tampon manufacturers, and consumer groups to determine how best to publicize the relationship of TSS and all tampons, lest the public think that Rely's withdrawal ended the problem. On October 20, 1980, the FDA proposed a voluntary warning label for packages and shelves that directed its message to the population at risk, including new tampon users. Most tampon manufacturers volunteered to place the warning label on the outer packages.

Tampax did not volunteer, and it has been reported that this company increased its advertising budget while printing only part of the FDA's advice, omitting the FDA recommendation that women could reduce or eliminate TSS risk by avoiding tampon use. In its package inserts, Tampax did mention TSS but asserted that TSS is a "very rare illness" and that "tampons do not cause TSS," because "it is caused by a type of bacteria present in some women." Tampax's strategy was financially successful. In the month following Rely's withdrawal, Tampax's market share grew from 43 percent to 56 percent.[13] Tampax Executive Vice-President Thomas J. Moore explained the company's perspective:

Research has not demonstrated *any* causal connection between tampons and TSS. . . . Tampax omitted from its warning a statement that TSS could be almost entirely avoided by not using tampons because that statement could not be proved true. It is now known that TSS affects non-menstruating women and girls and also men.

The implication that Tampax increased its sales by the use of misleading advertising cannot be supported. Its advertising was complete and correct. In the eleven weeks following the withdrawal of Rely, the total U.S. tampon market shrank by nearly 20 percent. It should not be surprising that Tampax's share of the market increased following the withdrawal of a competitor that had accounted for 20–25 percent of the market.[14]

All warning labels on these products were voluntary, that is, not required by federal regulations. The FDA had provided only a *proposed* rule to require warnings.

Procter & Gamble initiated an unprecedented four-week advertising campaign announcing the association between TSS and Rely, including TV and radio commercials and half-page newspaper ads in 1,200 papers. The firm also took a $75 million after-tax write-off on Rely in fiscal 1981 to account for both its unrecovered investment in Rely and costs associated with the growing number of legal cases arising out of damages or death allegedly caused by Rely.[15] These lawsuits against Procter & Gamble were filed shortly after the first public announcement of the link between tampons and TSS. Within a year, approximately 200 cases named Rely as the cause of death or disfigurement from toxic shock syndrome.[16] By 1990, the company had faced more than 1,000 such lawsuits.[17] Some plaintiffs also named the Department of Health and Human Services and the Food and Drug Administration in their suits, claiming that federal negligence permitted Rely to remain on the market. Procter & Gamble's decision to remove Rely from sale may not have enhanced its position in these product liability suits, but the withdrawal did improve the company's tarnished public image.

Procter & Gamble executives continued to believe that the evidence linking Rely to TSS was unconvincing. They subsequently undertook further independent research. In the first year alone, Procter & Gamble had begun to research TSS extensively at a cost of around $2 million.[18] This financial commitment enabled researchers to better explore TSS's origins and effects. Research has continued now for more than a decade. Unfortunately, medical uncertainties linger still today over TSS and its causes. First, scientists have not yet articulated a pathological mechanism that explains the causal relationship between tampons and TSS. Though researchers recognize the link between tampons and TSS, "the mechanisms by which tampons increase the risk of TSS are unknown."[19] Second, *staph aureus* (the implicated TSS organism) is well known for changes in patterns of presentation and severity. It may be that the TSS epidemic was secondary to the emergence of a strain or strains of *staph aureus*. The simultaneous emergence of other unusual staphylococcal disease supports this hypothesis. Procter & Gamble's early research failed to produce evidence sufficient to support Rely's remarketing. Consequently, the company ceased Rely production. The Rely tampon stock was destroyed beginning in June 1981, used as fuel in a company plant.

Following the release of information linking toxic shock syndrome and all high-absorbency tampons, consumer tampon-buying patterns changed. Before the Rely-TSS crisis, studies indicated that 42 percent of menstruating women used high-absorbency tampons. In 1983 the percentage of high-absorbency tampon users had declined to 18 percent. A 1990 study reported that by 1986, the percentage had plummeted to 1 percent.[20] To adjust to changing preferences, companies abandoned production of high-absorbency tampons. Kimberly-Clark Corporation began replacing its superabsorbent Kotex brands with regular tampons late in 1980. As a company representative explained to *The Wall Street Journal,* "consumers no longer show a preference for the superabsorbent" product.[21] Tampax's president noted that, "There isn't any question that many women have an objection to them."[22] The CDC noted that since withdrawal of Rely and decreased use of high-absorbency tampons, TSS cases have declined. However, the drop in TSS cases could also be attributed to changes in reporting patterns and the general decline in tampon use following the TSS publicity. Media coverage may also have caused increased reporting by physicians and consumers during the time between the May–June 1980 CDC announcements and withdrawal of Rely. TSS cases were reported throughout 1981–1982, and by late December 1981, the CDC had 1,400 cases on file, almost all involving menstruating women who used tampons.[23]

For several months after TSS came to public attention, the FDA considered a ban on tampon products. After extensive investigation the agency concluded that the benefits of tampon use outweighed the risks, but that more consumer information on the risks of TSS had to be made available. The FDA has never maintained that tampon use is a sufficient cause of TSS. However, the agency does believe there is a statistically significant association between tampon use and increased risk of TSS, and that, therefore, some type of causal connection exists.

In June 1982 the FDA promulgated a mandatory use-labeling program. The rule instituted both a mandated warning label for the package's exterior and guidelines for information to be enclosed in each package. The mandated warning was "ATTENTION: Tampons are associated with Toxic Shock Syndrome (TSS). TSS is a rare but serious disease that may cause death. Read and save the enclosed information." The manufacturer had flexibility with the content and setup of the insert provided certain information was disclosed, including warning symptoms, what to do if these symptoms occur, and how to avoid the risks of TSS (viz., by not using tampons). Today there is far more uniformity in manufacturer-provided information than there was before the initiation of mandatory labeling.[24]

The FDA also instituted other regulations. In April 1985, "on the basis of an in vitro laboratory study and a March judicial decision" (*O'Gilvie v. International Playtex*),[25] the FDA removed polychrylate from tampon composition. Studies indicated that the use of polychrylate in production of high-absorbency tampons may have contributed to TSS infection. Twenty months after polychrylate removal, TSS cases dropped almost 400 percent, from 457 to 116 reported cases.[26]

On March 1, 1990, the FDA issued a regulation requiring standardization of tampon absorbency levels. In an accompanying press release, the FDA stated, "It has been shown that tampon use can increase the risk of TSS, and that the higher the absorbency of the tampon, the higher the risk."[27] The new regulation requires that tampon manufacturers standardize their tampon absorbency ratios according to the following scale:

Absorbency Term	Ranges of fluid absorbed in grams
Junior Absorbency	under 6
Regular Absorbency	6 to 9
Super Absorbency	9 to 12
Super Plus Absorbency	12 to 15

The FDA also requires manufacturers to include "an explanation of the absorbency ranges and how women can use this information to compare tampon absorbencies to select those with the lowest absorbency to meet those needs."[28] FDA officials and consumer groups hope that the standardization will further reduce cases of TSS infection. A 1989 study noted that "for each 1 gram increase in absorbency, the risk of TSS increases by 37 percent."[29] The regulations also strengthen the 1982 mandatory use-labeling requirement. Prior to March 1990 manufacturers could place the TSS-tampon link information on package inserts. Tampon producers are now required by regulations to place the information on the outer package.

Debate continues in the medical and scientific communities on the possible causal or catalytic role of tampons in toxic shock syndrome. Both diaphragms and sea sponges have been implicated in TSS cases, although in numbers too small to be studied. The causal relation between Rely and TSS is not understood beyond the fact that the company's product was a high-absorbency tampon.[30] Marketing and purchasing patterns could conceivably account for the increased statistical association of Rely with TSS. Removal of Rely from the marketplace clearly did not eradicate TSS, though there has been a massive decrease in tampon use and in reported cases of TSS since September 1980.[31] However, both the CDC and the FDA continue to maintain that Rely posed a risk significantly above other tampon brands.

Research is still underway today, and Procter & Gamble continues to fund TSS research groups. Over the past decade, the company has spent over $5 million in assistance to 24 university-based TSS research groups. The FDA, the CDC, and the National Institutes of Health continue to administer a joint project of active surveillance, trying to catch cases of TSS not usually reported in order to obtain a better idea of the actual number of cases. In 1987 the project averaged 13 cases per month, as opposed to 9 cases per month when no active surveillance was used.

To date, CDC officials estimate close to 3,300 TSS cases have been reported since the establishment of active surveillance, but the "current incidence of diagnosed TSS in the United States is unknown."[32] Reported cases of TSS substantially declined with the removal of Rely in 1980 and the removal of polychrylate in 1985. Market preference away from high-absorbency tampons further reduced TSS infections. However, TSS maintains a core infection rate among tampon and nontampon users. The CDC recorded no deaths from TSS in 1988–1989, and the TSS contraction ratio has continued to drop, but doctors and researchers have not discovered how to eradicate TSS infection. The disease continues to afflict new persons every year. In fact, although the CDC reported only one "definite" death from TSS each year since 1991, that number unexpectedly jumped to five deaths in 1994 (four of which were associated with menstruation).[33]

Current litigation indicates that TSS continues to warrant investigation. On May 25, 1994, two Kansas women filed a lawsuit against Playtex and Tambrands, alleging that they contracted the syndrome by using these manufacturers' tampons. They charged that the companies have ignored recent research by Philip M. Tierno and Bruce A. Hanna of New York University indicating that all-cotton tampons sold by certain foreign manufacturers are constructed so that they do not induce toxin production.[34] Tierno has been uncompromising in his defense of the natural-fiber tampon. In contrast to all-cotton tampons that do not amplify the toxin in vitro, Tierno explains that the synthetic fibers polyacrylate rayon, polyester, carboxymethylcellulose, and the viscose rayon used today heighten a woman's risk of developing TSS by creating a physical-chemical environment conducive to toxin creation. For this reason, he firmly believes that cotton-fiber tampons are the least risky for women.[35]

This type of evidence prompted the Kansas women to question the motives and responses of tampon companies that continued to market a synthetic-fiber product even in the light of such information. They claimed that the refusal on the part of Playtex and Tambrands to produce the more costly cotton-fiber tampon reflected concern for profit rather than commitment to the safety of the women using their products. The women sought restitution, better warning labels stressing the risks of tampon use, and the creation of a fund to provide monies for aggressive research about causes and treatments of the disease.[36] At the time of this writing, the decision as to whether the case will attain class action status (on behalf of all TSS sufferers) is pending.

A Tambrands legal spokesman explicitly denied that tampons composed of rayon fibers pose a higher risk of TSS than the cotton-fiber tampons that Dr. Tierno advocates. Bruce Garren criticized Tierno's study as less than credible in light of its failure to include a "blinded" scientist, which he characterized as questionable scientific methodology. He appealed to several recently released studies that support Tambrands' position. For example, a study conducted by Dr. Jeffrey Parsonnet of Dartmouth-Hitchcock Medical Center replicated Tierno's study yet included what Garren called more modern measuring techniques and the more impartial blinded scientist methodology.[37] Replication of the Tierno/Hanna study led Dr. Patrick Shlievert of the University of Minnesota to conclude in a 1995 publication, "In contrast to their [Tierno and Hanna's] findings, the cotton regular tampon used in the present study led to the greatest average amount of toxin production. . . . Cotton tampons offer no protective advantage over cotton/rayon tampons with regard to prevention of TSS."[38]

According to Garren, studies performed at Rockefeller University, the University of Hawaii, Harvard University, and the Centers for Disease Control also contradicted Tierno's conclusions. However, Tierno has suggested that one of the scientists who has done work in support of Tambrands' position has received funds from tampon manufacturers. Tierno decried this particular scientist's "absurd observations" and "bad science."[39] Thus, assignment of the term *impartial* in this case may not be the straightforward task that one might expect.

Garren stated that, because there has been no conclusive demonstration of a difference of toxin risk for women using rayon- and cotton-fiber tampons, Tierno's study will not be considered a basis for corporate or public policy. He indicated that women should simply continue to choose the lowest possible absorbency, watch for TSS symptoms (particularly in younger users), and avoid continuous tampon use. He expressed concern that Tierno's findings could be "outright dangerous" if women assume that they can avoid TSS risk simply by using all-cotton tampons.[40]

Tambrands launched the first all-cotton tampon (Tampax Naturals) in January 1996. Still maintaining that the rayon-fiber product is completely safe and insisting that the new tampon has nothing to do with new information about toxic shock, Tambrands officials commented that they hoped the imagery of cleanliness and naturalness would be marketable. However, one lawyer suspected that there was more to the introduction of the all-cotton product than Tambrands officials acknowledged: "The company has developed the so-called all new, natural product and is tacitly admitting that the product that's out there wasn't quite safe."[41]

Hopefully, further scientific data will demonstrate whether, in light of the continuing risk of TSS, cotton or synthetic fibers are safer materials with which to construct tampons. Regardless of how this empirical dispute is resolved, however, the case stimulates interesting and important questions about corporate responsibility. Do tampon manufacturers have an obligation (legal or moral) to construct the product that has been determined to be safer, even at great financial cost? How definitive should data be before a company has a responsibility to shift manufacturing gears? If complete information about risks and options is prominently displayed on packaging and other companies offer the "safer" product, must the manufacturer follow suit?

Interesting comparisons may be made to other potentially dangerous products such as high-tar cigarettes and fat-laden foods, with which consumers are still permitted to take risks despite the availability of less risky alternatives and extremely strong evidence of their potential for harm. Considering that the ostensibly safer tampon was not made available, should we align our sympathies with the Kansas women suffering from a potentially fatal disease that, in their minds, could and should have been prevented?

Another issue is the possible presence of the carcinogenic and toxic substance dioxin in tampons. In June 1992, a congressional panel accused the Food and Drug Administration (FDA) of failing to adequately investigate the dangers of this substance, which is sometimes present in the wood pulp that comprises part of the tampon. An FDA scientist reportedly determined in 1989 that the risk of dioxin in tampons "can be quite high" and thus that "the most effective risk strategy would be to assure that tampons . . . contain no dioxin."[42] The congressional investigators maintained that the FDA deleted a key warning sentence that identified the dioxin risk in tampon use.

FDA officials denied claims that they failed to investigate the matter thoroughly. They contended that the risk of developing cancer from using a dioxin-laced tampon (if such traces are indeed present) would be less than 1 in 100 billion.[43] Melvin Stratmeyer, chief of the FDA health sciences branch, explained that the FDA performed risk assessment studies to measure the effluence of paper pulp. The resultant risk level was so low, he said, that measuring dioxin levels in the finished product (tampons) was unnecessary and unjustified.[44]

Whereas the FDA contended that the level that would be present in tampons would be 1/100,000th the amount found in foods such as the fat of fish, subcommittee chairperson Representative Ted Weiss (D-NY) argued that "Dioxin is unsafe at any dose."[45] Stratmeyer considers the case resolved since "there is no reason to open it up again."[46] However, there is more work to be done in exploring fully the implications of dioxin exposure. A 1994 Environmental Protection Agency preliminary study indicated that even mere traces of dioxin may suppress the human immune system and slow fetal development. The draft copy of the report included this worrisome comment: "A picture emerges of [dioxin] and related compounds as potent toxicants producing a wide range of effects at very low levels when compared to other environmental contaminants."[47] Many would argue that even a remote possibility that such a carcinogen may be associated with tampons is a cause for continuing concern and scientific exploration.

NOTES

1. Claire V. Broome, "Epidemiology of Toxic Shock Syndrome in the United States: Overview," *Reviews of Infectious Diseases* 11, Supplement 1 (January–February 1989), p. S19.
2. U.S. Public Health Service, "Follow Up on Toxic Shock Syndrome," *Morbidity and Mortality Weekly Report* 29, no. 37 (September 19, 1980), pp. 443–44.
3. Carol J. Loomis, "P&G Up against a Wall," *Fortune* 103, no. 4 (February 23, 1981), p. 53. Some sources gave Rely only a 20 percent market share.
4. From a series on Rely by the *Chicago Tribune*, called to the case writers' attention by Tampax.
5. Nancy Friedman, "The Truth about Tampons," *New West* 5, no. 21 (October 21, 1980), pp. 35–36.
6. *Ibid.*, pp. 38, 40.
7. More precisely, Class II devices are those devices that for safety and efficacy can be guaranteed by performance standards. As an "old" device, tampons are assigned to Class II, as devices were classified after the Medical Device Amendments of 1976.
8. Charlotte Oram and Judith Beck, "Tampons: Looking beyond Toxic Shock," *Science of the People* 13, no. 5 (September/October 1981), p. 16.
9. Private correspondence from the executive vice-president of Tampax, Thomas J. Moore, June 1, 1982.
10. Dean Rotbard and John A. Prestbo, "Killing a Product," *The Wall Street Journal*, November 3, 1980, p. 21.

11. Edward G. Harness, "Views on Corporate Responsibility," *Corporate Ethics Digest* 1 (September–October 1980). This citation and other points in this paragraph are indebted to Elizabeth Gatewood and Archie B. Carroll, "Anatomy of a Corporate Social Response: The Procter & Gamble Rely Case," *Business Horizons* (September 1981).

12. Richard Severo, "Sharp Decrease in U.S. Reported in Toxic Shock Syndrome Cases," *The New York Times*, January 30, 1981, p. D15.

13. Pamela Sherrid, "Tampons after the Shock Wave," *Fortune* 104 (August 10, 1981), p. 116.

14. Private correspondence from the executive vice president of Tampax, Thomas J. Moore, June 1, 1982.

15. Loomis, "P&G Up against Wall," p. 53.

16. Dean Rotbart, "Rely Counterattack: P&G Is Going All-Out to Track Toxic Shock and Exonerate Itself," *The Wall Street Journal*, June 26, 1981, p. 1.

17. Stacy Adler, "Appellate Court Deals P&G Coverage Setback," *Business Insurance* 25 (February 18, 1991), pp. 2+.

18. "Jury Still Out on Toxic Shock," *Globe and Mail* (Toronto, Canada), July 6, 1981, p. 13.

19. Broome, "Epidemiology of Toxic Shock Syndrome," p. S14.

20. Centers for Disease Control, *Morbidity and Mortality Weekly Report* 39, no. 25 (June 29, 1990), p. 422.

21. Dean Rotbart, "State of Alarm: Tampon Industry Is in Throes of Change after Toxic Shock," *The Wall Street Journal*, February 26, 1981, p. 1.

22. *Ibid.*

23. "Toxic Shock Linked to Diaphragms," *The Washington Post*, December 24, 1981, p. A2.

24. *Federal Register* 21, Part 801 (1982), 26, 982-26, 990.

25. Broome, "Epidemiology of Toxic Shock Syndrome," p. S19.

26. *Ibid.*, p. S19.

27. U.S. Food and Drug Administration Press Release, "Using New Tampon Absorbency Labeling to Help Prevent Toxic Shock Syndrome," May 11, 1990.

28. *Ibid.*

29. Broome, "Epidemiology of Toxic Shock Syndrome," p. S19.

30. Jerry Bishop, "New Study Links Toxic-Shock Syndrome to the Use of High-Absorbency Tampons," *The Wall Street Journal*, February 19, 1981, p. D16.

31. Charles E. Irwin and Susan G. Millstein, "Emerging Patterns of Tampon Use in the Adolescent Female: The Impact of Toxic Shock Syndrome," *American Journal of Public Health* 72 (May 1982), pp. 464–67.

32. Broome, "Epidemiology of Toxic Shock Syndrome," p. S16.

33. If, then, there were 5 deaths out of 24 "definite" cases, the mortality rate of TSS would be over 20 percent in 1994. Calculating this rate for "definite" and "probable" cases and deaths results in a 11 percent mortality rate.

34. Philip M. Tierno, Jr., and Bruce A. Hanna, "Propensity of Tampons and Barrier Contraceptives to Amplify *Staphylococcus aureus* Toxic Shock Syndrome Toxin-1," *Infectious Diseases in Obstetrics and Gynecology* 2 (1994), pp. 14045. For more information, see the following: Philip M. Tierno, Jr., and Bruce A. Hanna, "Ecology of Toxic Shock Syndrome: Amplification of Toxic Shock Syndrome Toxin 1 by Materials of Medical Interest," *Reviews of Infectious Diseases* 2 (1989), pp. S182S185; Philip M. Tierno, Jr., and Bruce A. Hanna, "Toxic Shock Syndrome: An Epilogue," *Clinical Microbiology Updates* 6 (no. 1), pp. 16.

35. Telephone conversation between Kier Olsen and Dr. Philip Tierno, New York University, New York, February 7, 1996.

36. "Two Kansas Women Sue Tampon Makers Playtex, Tambrands," *The Wall Street Journal*, May 31, 1994, p. B2.

37. Jeffrey Parsonnet, Paul A. Modern, and Kristine D. Giacobbe, "Effect of Tampon Composition on Production of Toxic Shock Syndrome Toxin-1 by *Staphylococcus aureus* in Vitro," *Journal of Infectious Diseases* 173 (1996), pp. 98–103.

38. Patrick M. Schlievert, "Comparison of Cotton and Cotton/Rayon Tampons for Effect on Production of Toxic Shock Syndrome Toxin," *Journal of Infectious Diseases* 172 (1995), pp. 1112–4.

39. Philip M. Tierno, Jr, "Comparison of Cotton and Rayon/Cotton Tampons for Efficacy of Toxic Shock Syndrome Toxin-1 Production," *Journal of Infectious Diseases* 1996 (as yet unpublished letter to the editor).

40. Telephone conversation between Kier Olsen and Bruce Garren, Tambrands, White Plains, New York, February 6, 1996.

41. Yumiko Ono, "Tambrands to Offer All-Cotton Tampon Amid Controversy," *The Wall Street Journal*, October 12, 1995, p. A11.
42. Walt Bogdanich, "House Panel Charges FDA with Neglect in Citing Danger of Dioxin in Tampons," *The Wall Street Journal*, June 11, 1992, p. B8.
43. Christopher Boyd, "Cancer Risk? FDA Defends Stance on Tampon-Dioxin Link," *Chicago Tribune*, July 19, 1992, p. 1.
44. Telephone conversation between Kier Olsen and Melvin Stratmeyer, Food and Drug Administration, Rockville, MD, February 7, 1996. Please see the following for additional information: United States Environmental Protection Agency, Office of Toxic Substances, "Integrated Risk Assessment for Dioxins and Furans from Chlorine Bleaching in Pulp and Paper Mills," July 1990.
45. Boyd, "Cancer Risk?" p. 2.
46. Telephone conversation between Kier Olsen and Melvin Stratmeyer, February 7, 1996.
47. Gary Lee, "Dioxin: Hazard at Low Levels," *The Washington Post*, May 12, 1994, p. A3. For additional information, see Amanda Husted, "Dioxin Traces May Suppress Immune System, Study Says," *Atlanta Constitution*, May 12, 1994, p. E7.

LILLY'S CONSULTATION WITH HOSTILE CORPORATIONS

Lilly Advisors is a consulting firm based in the Maryland suburbs of Washington, DC. The firm consults about contract administration and construction management with architectural firms and construction companies and their respective clients. The firm employs attorneys, engineers, architects, and accountants. They work in teams assembled for individual, discrete projects. The company secures properly written contracts for clients, protects against failures to execute contracts, and prepares contract releases.

Merv Rodgers is the president of Lilly. He is a lawyer specializing in conflict resolution, breach of contract, and contract amendment. He previously worked for the American Arbitration Association and two smaller consulting firms. He is a member of several professional organizations in both law and engineering. He has twice been retained by the governor of Maryland as an expert consultant to assist in the construction of state-owned buildings in Maryland. His dossier contains a strong letter of praise and recommendation from the governor for his contribution to the state.

Several years ago Lilly entered into a consulting agreement with the Green Acres School System in Northern Virginia to address some problems that had arisen during the construction of two new high schools. Merv personally directed the team of consultants. A small construction company was awarded the contract for the two schools. However, the entire project was under the direct supervision of Stewart & Sons, a large, experienced, and prestigious architectural firm heavily involved in construction management. Due to unseasonable rains, add-ons to the contract, subcontractor delays, and disagreements between the architects and the school board, the project was running behind the major dates in the contract. More important, the school board had encountered a series of difficult disagreements with both the architects and the construction company. At one point it was unclear whether any party involved in the contract wished to start construction on the second high school.

The school board hired Merv and his team to advise its members about how to proceed under these circumstances. After several weeks of investigation, the Lilly team submitted a confidential written report called the *First High School Report* to the Green Acres School Board on February 15, 1990. This report analyzed the contract and critically evaluated the work performed to

This case was prepared by Tom L. Beauchamp and revised by Jeff Greene. Not to be duplicated without permission of the holder of the copyright, © 1992, 1996 Tom L. Beauchamp.

date. Lilly was already familiar with Stewart & Sons because it had worked as an adviser for Stewart & Sons on three previous projects, all of which had been successfully completed. The consulting work associated with these projects, none of which involved Green Acres, had been smooth, efficient, and free of any obstacles. Each project involved consulting on an out-of-state construction contract. Lilly had thereby come to know how Stewart & Sons operates and the methods it endorses. It knew, for example, that Stewart & Sons thinks of itself as a construction manager no less than a group of advisory architects.

In the *First High School Report* the Lilly team for Green Acres, which Merv headed, criticized Stewart & Sons's on-site management. Lilly argued that Stewart & Sons had (1) taken too much control over scheduling, (2) abused its position by improperly supervising the construction developments, (3) let several construction company failures go unreported, and (4) assumed scheduling duties not granted in the contract. Lilly argued that Stewart & Sons's failures to control the scheduling properly had largely caused the construction delays. In addition, Lilly concluded that the architectural firm was likely making its largest profit ever on a project over which it had administrative control.

After Lilly filed the report with the school board, its existence and contents remained confidential, although Stewart & Sons knew that Lilly had been retained by Green Acres as a consultant. Based on this report, the Green Acres School Board demanded that the construction firm and Stewart & Sons renegotiate. After two months of negotiation, all parties successfully agreed on an amendment to the contract, called "amended agreement." They settled all outstanding issues and ended the first phase (the first school) of the two-phase project. They also agreed to move next to the second phase (the second school) under the altered format presented in the amended agreement.

However, the haggling over the amended agreement sparked tension, and each party felt abused by the other. The school board believed that, based on Lilly's evaluation, Stewart & Sons had assumed a very uncompromising and aggressive negotiating stance. Each party felt it had compromised too much, but all signed the legally binding amended agreement on June 30, 1990. Construction resumed under the new terms.

During the next eight months, however, additional problems arose over the construction of the second high school. The school board and the architects again found themselves in a series of disagreements about the architects' performance. The two parties were quarreling over several problems about specifications, quality of materials, and management responsibility. At this point, Stewart & Sons—unaware of the contents of the written *First High School Report*—contacted Lilly to see if Lilly would be interested in becoming a consultant for Stewart & Sons in the new round of disputes with Green Acres. Neither company considered this contact surprising, because Stewart & Sons had worked successfully with Lilly on the three previous projects. They agreed over the phone to meet informally to further discuss the possibility.

On September 24, 1991, Lilly made a formal sales presentation to Stewart & Sons. At this meeting Merv represented Lilly. He reported to representatives of Stewart & Sons that Lilly had performed prior consulting work for

Green Acres on several of its projects, including the first high school. Merv explained that Lilly had "evaluated the construction management documents and contracts" for the school board. He said they had made some suggestions to school officials about the various issues of which owners and contractors need to be aware, especially when disputes exist among the parties. However, Merv disclosed neither the existence of the *First High School Report* nor the critical character and magnitude of the consulting.

On November 7, 1991, the architects' lawyer, Sam Shapiro, contacted Merv about the precise kind of representation made in the past to the Green Acres School Board and whether there might be any problem of conflict of interest. They talked for a few minutes by phone, and Merv assured Sam that "there was nothing in any work for the school board that would stand in the way of Lilly's now advising Stewart & Sons." Merv noted that Lilly has a mechanical, well-designed system that is applied to each potential consulting job that explores whether conflicts of interest exist. He said that he personally had reviewed the work for Green Acres and found no problem of conflict of interest. Merv reported that he had to be especially diligent in screening for conflicts because Lilly had worked for *both* clients on several previous contracts. Merv concluded by saying, "If there had been any sort of conflict that would now put Stewart & Sons at risk, I would not even consider accepting the job." Foremost in Merv's mind in making this statement was that the work done for Green Acres was done for a *former* client on a *former* project—the first high school. In his view, this consulting project was concluded.

Neither of these two lawyers asked the other for anything in writing; nor did either take notes about the telephone conversation. Sam assumed that Merv meant that no negative judgments had been reached in the report to Green Acres about the architects' performance. Stewart & Sons had always believed that any problems about the construction contract had been between the construction firm and the school board. They had no reason to suppose that Lilly might have negatively evaluated Stewart & Sons's performance. Based on this assurance, on November 8, 1991, Sam Shapiro and other representatives of Stewart & Sons authorized a contract for Lilly's services. Merv himself signed the agreement.

During the next four weeks the disputes over the construction worsened between Stewart & Sons and Green Acres, and the Green Acres School Board sued both the construction firm and the architects. Lawyers for Stewart & Sons soon discovered the *First High School Report*, which Lilly was required by law (at the demand of the Green Acres School Board) to deposit with the court. As soon as representatives of Stewart & Sons read this report, they were astonished and bitterly angry over what they saw as misrepresentation and conflict of interest by Lilly officials, principally Merv.

As Stewart & Sons saw it, a conflict of interest existed for Lilly *and* an inadequate disclosure had been made of prior consulting work for Green Acres; these failures now placed the firm in legal jeopardy because its own chosen consultant is on record as challenging the firm's competence (in the *Report*). Stewart & Sons had known all along that Lilly had the *potential* for some sort of conflict because there *might* have been something in the relationship with Green Acres that would have presented a conflict. But Lilly had assured Stewart & Sons that there was no reason to be concerned about that past relationship. Lilly did not disclose the contents of the report, the report's negative evaluation, or the possible implications of the report. Lilly disclosed only the presumably innocent consulting relationship with Green Acres.

Merv evaluated the situation very differently. He knew that he had a potential conflict of interest in coming to an agreement with Stewart & Sons. But he had worked very hard within his firm to overcome the potential conflict by assigning an entirely different consulting team for Stewart & Sons than the team that had been assigned to consult with Green Acres. He had carefully instructed every employee associated with the first project not to disclose anything about that project to those assigned to work with Stewart & Sons on the second project. He also isolated himself from any knowledge of the facts during the Stewart & Sons consultation, because he had been on the first consulting team. He did not permit second-team members to have access to the *First High School Report* or any documents involved in the first consultation. He did not allow any knowledge or discussion of the vital services that Lilly had performed for Green Acres to reach the second consultation team. He restricted access to documents that criticized Stewart & Sons's performance, which were in a corporate file.

But as Stewart & Sons saw it, in the absence of an adequate disclosure about the nature and existence of the *First High School Report*, the conflict of interest was actual, not merely potential, and was not eliminated by Merv's various maneuvers. Stewart & Sons also believed that Merv failed to discharge an obligation to contact Green Acres and obtain a waiver to enter the new consultation agreement. Given the confidential nature of the relationship between Lilly and Green Acres, the architects deemed unethical Lilly's failure to warn officials at Green Acres that information from confidential documents might surface at some point.

But the fundamental problem, as Stewart & Sons saw it, was that Lilly should have declined to enter the arrangement because of the conflict of interest. Lilly should have foreseen the moral problems involved, as well as the legal dangers. The architects think it is virtually certain that in a circumstance of adequate disclosure, neither Stewart & Sons nor Green Acres would have consented to Lilly's business arrangement with Stewart & Sons. Stewart & Sons believed it was owed a disclosure of the existence of opinions by Lilly officials that impugned the integrity and honesty of Stewart & Sons, thereby exposing them to legal jeopardy. The confidential nature of the report to Green Acres provided no excuse for the failure to disclose that *some* statements in the report might prove to be detrimental to Stewart & Sons's interests.

Merv was puzzled by this controversy over his actions. He had designed what he saw as a flawless strategy of eliminating all possible revelation of the original consulting arrangement. He did so precisely to prevent all problems of conflict of interest. The accusation that he should have disclosed both the existence and the nature of the report to Stewart & Sons irritated him. Because the report was confidential, he believed that he had an ethical obligation *not* to disclose its content. He therefore could not have disclosed either the services that Lilly had performed for Green Acres or the fact that Lilly criticized Stewart & Sons's performance. He had chosen his words very carefully in all conversations with Stewart & Sons so that they knew that Green Acres had consulted with Lilly about the high schools contract but did not know anything confidential. Now he was being personally attacked for both misrepresenting Lilly's involvement and having an unresolvable conflict of interest. "Doesn't Stewart & Sons appreciate," he said to himself, "that any such consultation is by its very nature confidential? What did they expect me to say about a confidential relationship other than that it existed? Is not that disclosure as much of a disclosure as is ethically permissible?"

The more he thought about the situation, the more Merv believed that these charges against him were simply fabricated to extricate Stewart & Sons from a difficult situation. The conflict of interest charge seemed to him enormously exaggerated. He had told Stewart & Sons everything it could have expected to know, given that the relationship was a confidential one. The architects initiated the contact with Lilly knowing that there had been a consulting relationship and that the contracts had been evaluated. With that knowledge, it was up to Stewart & Sons to decide whether to write a contract with Lilly, and it had decided to do so. He thought he had disclosed all that a client could reasonably ask, and that the client had in fact been in a good position to make a reasonable judgment about whether to come to an agreement with Lilly. Why would anyone suppose that he should have been the person to decide not to proceed, rather than the client's being responsible for the decision?

Moreover, when the company signed the contract with Stewart & Sons, Merv knew little about the nature of the later disputes. He was not in a good position to refuse the job. But, the most important element of Merv's thinking was the conviction that no conflict truly existed, because the job that Lilly performed for Green Acres was not the same as the Stewart & Sons project. Therefore, there was no reason to think that the earlier job conflicted with the later job. At other companies he had often known consultants to work for two different parties who were both contractually involved in the same construction project. This practice was, so far as he could see, acceptable and prevalent in the world of construction consultants. The decisive industry standard for conflict of interest was not "both parties are on the same project" but, rather, "one party is placed at risk by virtue of consulting with both parties." As long as there is no significant risk of harm, Merv had never worried about working for more than one of the different parties to the same contract.

As he slumped into his office chair, Merv noticed the latest letter from Stewart & Sons. This letter informed him that Stewart & Sons would not pay a penny of the $102,500 owed on the consulting contract. Stewart & Sons had good lawyers, and Merv knew that if he became involved in a lawsuit, he could spend more than $100,000 in legal fees, with no guarantee as to outcome. "But," he thought, "I should spend the hundred grand." Merv's considerable anger had settled into determination.

COMMISSIONS ON SALES AT
BROCK MASON BROKERAGE

James Tithe is the manager of a large branch office of a major midwestern brokerage firm, Brock Mason Farre Titmouse. He now manages 40 brokers in his office. Mr. Tithe formerly worked for E. F. Hutton as a broker and assistant manager, but when that firm merged with Shearson-Lehman/American Express (later Smith Barney), he disliked his new manager and left for Brock Mason. He knew the new firm to be aggressive and interested primarily in limited partnerships and fully margined common stock. He liked the new challenge. At Hutton his clients had been predominantly interested in unit investment trusts and municipal bonds, which he found boring and routine forms of investment aimed at people at or near retirement age. He also knew that commissions were higher on the array of products he was hired to sell at Brock Mason.

Although he became bored at Hutton, James had been comfortable with the complete discretion the firm gave him to recommend a range of investments to his clients. He had been free to consult at length with his clients and then to sell what seemed most appropriate in light of their objectives. Hutton skillfully taught its brokers to be salespersons, to avoid lengthy phone calls, and to flatter clients who prided themselves on making their own decisions. At the same time, the firm also did not discourage the broker from recommending a wide variety of products including U.S. government bills, notes, and bonds, which averaged only a $75 commission on a $10,000 investment.

This same array of conventional investment possibilities with small commissions is still available to him and to his brokers at Brock Mason, but the firm has an explicit strategy of trying to sell limited partnerships first and fully margined common stock second. The reason for this strategy is that commissions on a $10,000 investment in a limited partnership run from $600 to $1,000, and commissions on a $10,000 investment in fully margined common stock average $450.

James has been bothered for some time by two facts. The first is that the largest commissions in the brokerage industry are paid on the riskier and more complicated forms of investment. In theory, the reason is that these investments are more difficult to sell to clients. Oil and gas drilling and real

This case was prepared by Tom L. Beauchamp. Not to be duplicated without permission of the holder of the copyright, © 1992, 1996 Tom L. Beauchamp.

estate partnerships, for example, typically return between 4 and 8 percent to sellers, although lately most have been arranged to return the full 8 percent. Some partnerships return more than 8 percent, because they rebate management fees to any securities firm that acts as a participant in the partnership.

The second fact is that James has been instructed to train his brokers to make recommendations to clients based on the level of commission returned to the broker and the firm. He is therefore training his brokers to sell the riskier and more complicated forms of investment, even if that particular investment is not necessarily in the best interest of the client. Although Brock Mason, like all brokerage firms, advertises a full range of products and free financial planning by experts, all salespersons dislike financial planning per se because it takes a large amount of time and carries zero commission.

James has long appreciated that there is an inherent conflict of interest in the brokerage world. Although the broker is presumed to have a fiduciary responsibility to make recommendations based on the financial best interest of the client, the broker is also a salesperson who makes a living by selling securities and who is obligated to attempt to maximize profits for the brokerage house. The broker's rule, though seldom advantageous to the client, is: The more trades made, the better. Commissions are thus an ever-present temptation for a broker attempting to objectively present alternatives or make a recommendation.

Brock Mason does have a house mutual fund that is a less risky form of investment—the Brock Mason Equity-Income Fund—but the return to brokers and to the firm is again substantial. The National Association of Securities Dealers (NASD) allows a firm to charge up to 8.5 percent commission or load on a mutual fund; Brock Mason charges the full 8.5 percent. As an extra incentive, an additional percentage of the commission on an initial investment is returned to a broker if he or she can convince the client to automatically reinvest the dividends rather than have them sent by mail. Brock Mason also offers a fully paid vacation in Hawaii for the five brokers who annually sell the largest number of shares.

The firm has devised the following piggyback strategy: Brokers, as we have seen, are trained to sell limited partnerships first and fully margined stock accounts second. In the latter accounts an investor is allowed to purchase stock valued at up to twice the amount of money deposited in the account. The "extra" money is a loan from the brokerage firm. Twice the normal stock entails twice the normal commission on the amount of money in the account. In addition, salespersons are given a small percentage of the interest earned on the loan made to the client.

Brock Mason, like most brokerage firms, suffered financially as a result of a stock market slump that caused business to fall off sharply in the early 1990s. Business declined 24 percent, and Brock Mason encountered difficulty in paying for the sophisticated electronic equipment that sits on each broker's desk. James's superiors pressured him to persuade his brokers to aggressively market limited partnerships as a solid form of investment during the period of instability in stocks.

In 1991, the average annual commission brought into a firm by a broker in the U.S. brokerage industry was $259,600. Each broker usually takes home between 25 and 50 percent of this amount, depending on the person's contract and seniority. James's take-home earnings last year amounted to $198,000, 35 percent more than he had ever earned at Hutton. A friend of his began his own financial planning firm last year and retains 100 percent of his commissions, netting him $275,000 in his first year. His friend rejected the idea that he charge a flat fee or a percentage of profits in lieu of commissions for his recommendations and services. In his judgment, flat fees would have cost him more than 30 percent of his earnings.

Securities firms are required by law to disclose all commissions to clients. However, James and his brokers are aware that limited partnerships and mutual funds are usually easier to sell than straight stock and bond purchases, because the statistics on fees are buried beneath an enormous pile of information in a prospectus that most clients do not read prior to a purchase. Most clients do not obtain the prospectus until after the purchase, and there is no report of a dollar figure for the commission. Brokers are not required to disclose commissions orally to clients and rarely do; moreover, it is well known that clients virtually never ask what the commission is. James has been instructed to tell his brokers to avoid all mention of commissions unless the subject is explicitly raised by the client.

The Securities and Exchange Commission (SEC) does not set ceilings on commissions and does not require a broker to obtain a written consent from a client prior to a purchase. The SEC does occasionally determine that a markup is so high at a brokerage house that the commission amounts to fraud. It is here that James has drawn his personal "moral line," as he calls it. He has tentatively decided that he will market any product that has passed SEC and NASD requirements. Only if the SEC considers a markup to be fraudulent will he discourage his brokers from marketing it.

But James also wonders about the prudence and completeness of these personal guidelines. He has been around long enough to see some unfortunate circumstances—they are *unfortunate* but not *unfair*, in his judgment—in which unwary clients bought unsuitable products from brokers and had to live with the consequences. Recently, one of his brokers steered a 55-year-old unemployed widow with a total account of $380,000 (inherited upon the death of her husband) into the following diversification: 25 percent in limited partnerships, 25 percent in dividend-paying but margined stocks, 25 percent in corporate bonds yielding 9.8 percent, and 25 percent in the mutual fund. But the woman did not understand at the time of purchase how low the dividends on the stocks and the mutual fund would be. She now has far less annual income than she needs. Because she cannot sell the limited partnerships, she must now sell the stock at a loss and purchase a high dividend-paying instrument.

James and the woman's broker have been somewhat shaken by this client's vigorous protest and display of anger. James decided as a result to take the case to the weekly staff meeting held on Wednesday mornings, which all brokers attend. There was a lively discussion of the best form of diversification and return for the widow. But James's attempt to introduce and discuss the problem of conflict of interest during this session fell completely flat. His brokers were not interested and could not see the problem. They argued that the brokerage industry is a free market arrangement between a broker and a client, who knows that fees are charged. Disclosure rules, they maintained, are well established, even if particular percentages or fees are sometimes hidden in the fine print. They viewed themselves as honest salespersons making a living through a forthright and fair system.

James walked away from this meeting thinking that neither the widow nor the broker had been prudent in making decisions that met her specific needs, but again he viewed the outcome as unfortunate rather than unfair. He had to agree with his brokers. No client, after all, is forced either to deal with the firm or to make any purchase.

SEIZURE OF THE S.W. PARCEL

The European Petroleum Consortium (EPC) is a major European oil company with several affiliates and subsidiaries in the United States. In November 1983 EPC leased three contiguous parcels of land near Chico, California— exactly 300 acres, subdivided into three distinct units of 100 acres—from a wealthy farmer, Mr. Buck Wheat, who owned the property. The parties signed three oil and gas leases, one for each of the three contiguous parcels, which were labeled N.W., S.W., and N.E. because of their geographical location.

Within a year a significant gas-producing well had been drilled on the S.W. property, and Mr. Wheat was earning royalties from the gas production. In the four years following the sale, Mr. Wheat earned in excess of $500,000 in royalties from this well. He was already a multimillionaire by virtue of other wells that oil and gas companies had long operated on his property.

Under the terms of the lease, EPC had the option to extend the lease under the original terms of royalty payments for as long as oil or gas was being produced on any parcel of the land that had been leased. If production ever ceased for a period of one year, the agreement would be invalid. If there were no producing wells on a parcel and EPC wished not to extend the lease on that parcel, EPC was required to file a quitclaim deed (a deed of conveyance that is a form of release of rights) to this effect.

In November 1988, five years after the initial agreement, the lease was scheduled to expire. EPC notified Mr. Wheat by a phone call 90 days prior to the expiration date of the lease of its intention to extend the lease on one parcel of land, the S.W. parcel, but not on the other two. Mr. Wheat responded that he naturally was pleased that royalty payments would continue. Under the terms of the lease, EPC had 30 days beyond the date of expiration to record the quitclaim deed with the county and to record the continuation of the lease arrangement. Twenty-two days beyond the expiration date, EPC did file both the quitclaim and the extension, and 29 days beyond the expiration date an EPC official had a copy delivered to Mr. Wheat by a messenger service. EPC was not required by the terms of the lease to deliver this copy, because Mr. Wheat had already been notified by phone of its intentions.

Thirty-one days beyond the expiration date, Mr. Wheat signed an oil and gas lease on all 100 acres of the producing S.W. parcel with Oklasas Oil Com-

This case was prepared by Tom L. Beauchamp. It is based entirely on factual circumstances, but all names have been changed. Not to be duplicated without permission of the holder of the copyright, © 1992, 1996 Tom L. Beauchamp.

pany, a small independent headquartered in Anadarko, Oklahoma. That is, Mr. Wheat leased to Oklasas the very same S.W. parcel on which EPC believed it had an exclusive lease. Obviously two leases to competitors on the same property cannot be valid.

Mr. Wheat's new lease of the S.W. parcel and his rapid change in relations with EPC were the result of an inadvertent clerical error and the enterprising activities of Mr. B. Sly, president of the Oklasas Oil Company. He devised a method of acquiring land that is highly unconventional but that has thus far paid off handsomely. He hired a low-salaried clerk to go into several California counties known to have a large number of producing gas wells. The clerk checks all the leases that have been filed, looking for technical violations of the law or for lease loopholes. Whenever a technical violation or potential problem is found on the lease of a producing property, Mr. Sly contacts the owner of the property and makes a lease offer that exceeds the terms found in the original lease. Mr. Sly can afford to give the property owner a much larger percentage of the royalties than is conventional, because he has no drilling costs and encounters no real speculative risk in an industry filled with drilling risk.

Only about 15 percent of the landowners are willing to meet and discuss the possibility of a lease with Mr. Sly because most believe they have a prior commitment to the company with which they have signed an agreement. About 10 percent renegotiate with the company with which they originally signed the lease; they often use Mr. Sly's offer as a way of obtaining better terms in the new lease, although they do not negotiate terms as favorable as Mr. Sly's. Instead of providing the landowner with the standard one-sixth royalty share, Mr. Sly offers one third, doubling the owners' royalties overnight.

Mr. Sly has been able to sign agreements with approximately one third of the 15 percent who are willing to meet with him. Thus, he eventually comes to terms with about 5 percent of his contacts. His clerk finds one promising legal problem or technical violation that suggests an invalid lease for every nine days of full-time research. Mr. Sly is already bringing in over $3 million annually for Oklasas from the wells he has acquired on these properties, and his operating costs are extremely low because he only obtains properties with producing wells.

Very fortunately from Mr. Sly's perspective, his clerk was working in the county offices on the day EPC filed its quitclaim deeds and extension. The clerk's trained eye detected a serious error almost immediately: EPC had inadvertently quitclaimed the S.W. parcel and extended the lease on the nonproducing N.W. parcel. This error resulted from a slip of the pen; the clerk at EPC had written "N.W." on the form rather than "S.W." Although EPC had a system that was set up to avoid such "erroneous legal descriptions," the error passed through six checkpoints in six offices at EPC without detection.

Within two hours of the clerk's discovery of the misfiling in the county office, the relevant papers had been copied and sent by overnight mail to Mr. Sly. Two days later he was in California to pay a visit to Mr. Wheat. After a two-hour meeting they were joined by their lawyers for a lunch and afternoon meeting, and by 5:00 an agreement had been signed. Neither party had contacted EPC to ascertain whether a mistake had been made, but it was only too obvious to them that a mistake had indeed been made.

Mr. Wheat asked not only for a one-third royalty share but also that Mr. Sly lease, for a sum of $7,500 per year, the N.E. property that had been quitclaimed and drill on that property. (EPC had said several times that it was not interested in drilling on this property after it had discovered gas on the S.W. property.) Mr. Wheat also asked for a full indemnification in the event of a lawsuit by EPC. That is, he asked to be fully secured against loss or damage in the event of a lawsuit over the leases, including any loss from the shutdown of operations at the well. Mr. Sly agreed that he would pay all legal costs and reimburse for any loss that Mr. Wheat might incur.

This was not a difficult decision for Mr. Sly. In oil and gas leases, the written record is everything, so far as the law is concerned. One simply cannot tell the legal status of the property unless there is a written legal record. Unrecorded statements of intention and verbal promises count for nothing. Mr. Sly's lawyer was certain that no suit by EPC would stand a chance of success.

The next day lawyers notified EPC of the new arrangement and told it to abandon the property immediately. Within 24 hours EPC replied that it considered the negotiations over this property to have been in bad faith. EPC said it considered any entry upon the land and any drilling to constitute a trespass and also to be in bad faith. EPC added, however, that it was willing to negotiate and settle out of court, because it was responsible for the clerical error. Oklasas replied immediately that it was not interested in negotiation.

Chapter Three

THE ENVIRONMENT

INTRODUCTION

Over the last decade the subject of corporate environmental responsibility has been as widely discussed as any other topic in business ethics. The public has become increasingly concerned about the environmental impact of chemical dumping, airborne emissions, nuclear power, oil pipelines and shipping, endangered species, and the like. A widespread consensus now exists that environmental problems such as global warming, ozone layer deterioration, the decline of water and air quality, and the extinction of endangered species—whether or not hastened by business—are critical and immediate problems that demand the mobilization of efforts in public policy and international cooperation. However, no comparable consensus has emerged regarding the proper lines of responsibility or the seriousness of the threat to the environment and to human and animal health.

People often say that contemporary environmental problems are novel and lack historical precedent. In fact, environmental problems have a long history. In eighteenth-century English courts of common law and equity, many individuals filed cases against various businesses to recover the costs of pollution. As early as 1273, certain English jurisdictions prohibited coal burning on grounds that it harmed property and public health. In this chapter, the salience of this concern is evident in the case of "Acid Rain and the Uses of Coal." This case serves to remind us that many environmental problems are global and so cannot be resolved without viable forms of international cooperation. The case also raises many questions of fairness. Tough regulations present severe economic difficulties for firms in underdeveloped countries, but lax regulations create a situation of unfair competition for companies that must conform to stricter standards than a competitor.

The early history of environmental problems serves only as a weak precedent for many contemporary issues. Court cases involving industrial discharge, the use of asbestos, hazardous waste disposal, and the like were largely unprecedented until recently. Millions of dollars are now at stake in the courts in the effort to secure compensation for such harms. Society now confronts sometimes tragic trade-offs, including choices between the health of workers and corporate economic health. The "Reserve Mining's Silver Bay Facility" and "Hooker Chemical and Love Canal" cases in this chapter provide instances of such trade-offs. Recent discoveries of serious degradation of the major river systems in Eastern Europe serve as a reminder of the fact that we have only started to resolve these pressing environmental problems.

These environmental debates spawn classic conflicts between public and private interests. For example, in recent years disposal of industrial hazardous wastes that include mercury, benzene, dioxin, ethyl ether, grout, epoxies, concrete additives, and the like has been faulted for the contamination of public ground water, landfills, and even waste recovery plants. In one of the most famous cases in U.S. legal history, *U.S.A. v. Allied Chemical,* Judge Robert R. Merhige stringently penalized the Allied Chemical Corporation in 1976 for the pollution of a river. This case has a bias and therefore is not included in this chapter. Nonetheless, the case symbolizes the struggle between environmentalists and business interests, and it warrants brief mention.

In this case Allied and five of its employees were indicted on 153 charges of conspiracy to defraud the Environmental Protection Agency and the Army Corps of Engineers in their efforts to enforce water pollution control laws. Allied denied all charges, saying the indictments reflected an extreme reaction by public officials. However, Allied nonetheless pleaded *nolo contendere* (no contest) to the charges. Judge Merhige fined Allied $13.2 million but later reduced the fine to $5 million because Allied contributed $8 million to a fund established to repair the damage resulting from its pollution. This fine was the largest ever imposed in an environmental case, and the case also involved the greatest number of indictments in a single such case.

In his ruling, Judge Merhige argued that corporations will "think several times before anything such as this happens again." But he also proposed what many in the business community believe to be an unacceptable thesis: "I don't think that commercial products or the making of profits are as important as the God-given resources of our country." He then advanced the striking claim that we are all collectively responsible for the results of pollution because we tolerate too much of it. Business community representatives have severely criticized this judicial ruling.

The quality of air, water, soil, food, and health all occupy center stage of discussions about the environment, the public interest, and corporate interests. Since 1960 the U.S. Congress has enacted several major pieces of legislation addressing these problems. But legislative documents are generally vague, broadly worded pronouncements that direct federal agencies to act "in the public interest" or "to protect the public health." The federal government charters agencies to regulate business by deciding which chemicals require regulation and determining the discharge and dose level standards. Many value judgments must be made as to reasonable levels of discharge and dangers to human health.

Environmental problems cannot always be construed as a conflict between the interests of the public and business. Sometimes environmental problems involve the interests of one business in conflict with another. Thus, a fishing industry may be crippled by the airborne or waterborne discharges of chemical industries, oil tankers, or factories. Naturalists' interests in species or wilderness preservation may also conflict with business ambitions. These conflicts call for the balancing of considerations that fairly account for the disputing parties' different interests. They also require difficult judgments about the extent to which business or government can be trusted to pursue reasonable courses of action.

A less thoroughly explored range of environmental issues concerns whether businesses and other responsible parties have obligations to natural objects, especially to certain forms of animal life that are part of the living environment. Some contend that various forms of nonhuman life deserve the same general moral protections afforded humans. For example, animal protection leagues denounce businesses that poison, slaughter, and trap animals without utilizing humane methods and without formal penalty as barbaric. Animals are often more convenient and profitable for businesses than alternative sources that might be used for research, labor, and food.

Research involving the use of animals and various techniques of raising animals for food have gone largely unchallenged in the past. However, critics now argue that animal life deserves new protections against various methods of research, production, and slaughter. They ask, "What justifies the food and research industries in treating animals in ways they would never treat humans?" This question asks for some morally relevant property of human beings that will justify restricting the protections afforded by principles of the sanctity of life to *human* life.

Furthermore, many argue that animals deserve protection not because it is in the interest of humans to protect them, but because animals inherently deserve and have a right to protection. This debate focuses on whose interests count, and how much weight they should be given. But the debate also concerns the value of nonhuman life, if it has any form of value. Two cases in this chapter directly address these questions. The case of "Pâté at Iroquois Brands" raises the issue of the force-feeding of geese and ducks for commercial sale, and "The Cosmetics Industry and the Draize Test" focuses on the testing of cosmetics by dropping irritants into the eyes of rabbits. The pâté industry has to date proved unresponsive to its critics, whereas the cosmetics industry has shown concern about the issue for years. Companies such as Avon, Revlon, and Procter & Gamble, for example, have reduced the volume of irritants to one-tenth the amount they previously used and have funded research of viable alternatives to the use of animals. However, many in the industry continue to use the irritant tests and to defend the research based on its protection of human consumers.

In addition to considerations of whose interests are to count, it is important to ascertain where the burden of proof rests in environmental destruction. Many major controversies involve considerable uncertainty about the extent to which a chemical discharge, storage procedure, and the like present a threat to human or nonhuman life. Does the burden of proof rest on industry or on governmental regulatory agencies to establish that a product or practice is safe or harmful? If government or industry can make this determination, who should bear the responsibility for eliminating the problems, especially when these problems are unprecedented? How do we weigh possible future harm to the environment against the economic harms of more tightly regulating business? These issues are featured in the cases of "Reserve Mining's Silver Bay Facility," "Hooker Chemical and Love Canal," and "Acid Rain and the Uses of Coal."

Almost everyone now believes that there will be further erosion of the liberty of corporations to utilize the environment. But, on the brighter side, many corporations have developed constructive programs both to repair the environment and to prevent further pollution. A massive plastics recycling program spearheaded by Du Pont is a typical example. Undertaken in 1991 at a projected cost of $10 million, the goal is to recycle 1.5 billion to 2 billion pounds of plastics that ordinarily would not be recycled and that, when recycled, will change the way the entire industry does business. Such voluntary programs represent the cutting edge of corporate environmental ethics.

RESERVE MINING'S
SILVER BAY FACILITY

Four steel firms formed the Reserve Mining Company in 1939 for the purpose of mining and crushing taconite (low-grade iron ore). The company's name included the word *Reserve* because in 1939 the iron ore was considered to be a long-term investment still in need of new technology to be processed efficiently. In an expensive and innovative move, Reserve Mining decided in 1944 to locate its prospective plant on Lake Superior and so began to acquire the land in 1945. Establishing the plant on this great body of water was considered essential because taconite processing requires large amounts of water. The taconite must be crushed into fine granules and collected into pellets before the residue is flushed back into the water.

After nine hearings, the state of Minnesota issued the necessary environmental permits in 1947. In 1948 the U.S. Army Corps of Engineers granted Reserve a permit to construct harbor facilities that called for the deposit of tailings (the residue waste product) in Lake Superior. The taconite was to be mined near Babbitt, Minnesota, and then shipped by rail approximately 45 miles to the plant on Lake Superior's northwest shore. Both the Minnesota tax laws and mining technology had improved dramatically by then to the point that efficient mining and crushing were possible. Work began on the Lake Superior facility in 1951, and full operations commenced at the plant in 1955.

The tiny town of Silver Bay was built especially for these mining operations. Soon thereafter Reserve employed 80 percent of the 3,000 adult inhabitants of Silver Bay, and the state's total taconite workforce grew to 9,000. The operation proved so successful that between 1956 and 1960 Reserve sought and received permission for substantially increased production and correspondingly increased discharges of waste products into Lake Superior. Reserve achieved a final modest rise in production in 1965. This increase brought Reserve's annual production capacity to 10.7 million tons of pellets. To achieve this level of production, Reserve dumped 67,000 tons of waste material into Lake Superior each day. The state had approved these discharges under the assumption that this waste would sink and remain forever at the lake bottom.[1]

Professor S. Shane of the George Washington University School of Business has described the basic technology at the facility as follows:

This case was prepared by Tom L. Beauchamp and revised by John Cuddihy and Joanne L. Jurmu. Not to be duplicated without permission of the holder of the copyright, © 1992, 1996 Tom L. Beauchamp.

Taconite is a hard, gray rock in which are found particles of magnetite, a black oxide of iron which is magnetic and has the approximate oxygen content designated as Fe_3O_4. The deposits of taconite near Babbitt, Minnesota are sufficiently near the surface to permit their being taken from open pits. The taconite is crushed to a nominal 4 inch size and hauled along the Reserve railroad line to Silver Bay at a rate of about 90,000 tons per day.

At Silver Bay the crushing operation is continued in order to free the particles of iron oxide for recovery and molding into pellets. A series of crushers, rod mills, ball mills, and magnetic separators are operated in processing the water slurry of ore. Two million tons of water are taken from Lake Superior each day (and returned) in the processing. The low-iron tailings are discharged back into the lake in the direction of a trough about 500 feet deep a few miles offshore. The discharge stream comprises the tailings, and the finest fraction, about 1 1/2 percent solids, forms a dense current which flows toward the bottom of the lake. The magnetically recovered particles are the concentrate which is compressed to a cake with 10 percent moisture. It is then mixed with bentonite, which is a cohesive agent, and rolled into green pellets about 3/8 inch in diameter. The pellets are hardened by heating to 2350°F and are then ready for loading into ore boats at Silver Bay for the trip to the blast furnaces in Cleveland, Youngstown, Ashland, etc.[2]

ENVIRONMENTAL LITIGATION BEGINS

Serious environmental questions about Reserve's discharges first arose in 1963, when U.S. Senator Gaylord Nelson of Wisconsin investigated the possibility of water pollution violations. Various forms of new environmental legislation were passed in the next few years, and by 1968 Senator Nelson, a Taconite Study Group, and Secretary of the Interior Stewart Udall began to express concern about Lake Superior. A Save Lake Superior Association was founded in 1969. In 1971–1972 the Environmental Protection Agency, the U.S. Justice Department, and the Minnesota Pollution Control Board all charged Reserve with violations of the Federal Pollution Control Act. They argued that the plant was discharging mineral fibers into the air, that the water could be hazardous to health, and that drinking water supplies were endangered. Similar fibers were known to cause asbestosis, mesothelioma, and various cancers. Past concerns had primarily pertained to water pollution, including effects on fish life and the water supply, but as the courts began to tackle these issues, the focus quickly shifted to threats to human health.

In 1973 a U.S. District Court in Minnesota entered an order closing Reserve's Silver Bay facility on grounds that it was discharging dust-like asbestiform (asbestos-like) particles into both the air and the water at substantial threat to human health. Asbestos workers had been shown to be vulnerable to cancer when they inhaled the product. Some 200,000 persons drank the water from Lake Superior, and many more might potentially be affected by airborne fibers. Reserve appealed this decision to the Eighth Circuit Court of Appeals, where Judge Myron H. Bright summarized the situation as follows in an extremely influential opinion delivered on June 4, 1974 (139 days had been spent in the courtroom, and the testimony of over 100 witnesses and 1,620 exhibits had been considered):

> Although there is no dispute that significant amounts of waste tailings are discharged into the water and dust is discharged into the air by Reserve, the parties vigorously contest the precise nature of the discharge, its biological effects, and particularly with respect to the waters of Lake Superior, its ultimate destination. . . .
>
> The suggestion that particles of the cummingtonite-grunerite in Reserve's discharges are the equivalent of amosite asbestos raised an immediate health issue, since the inhalation of amosite asbestos at occupational levels of exposure is a demonstrated health hazard resulting in asbestosis and various forms of cancer. However, the proof of a health hazard requires more than the mere fact of discharge; the discharge of an agent hazardous in one circumstance must be linked to some present or future likelihood of disease under the prevailing circumstances. An extraordinary amount of testimony was received on these issues. . . .
>
> The theory by which plaintiffs argue that the discharges present a substantial danger is founded largely upon epidemiological studies of asbestos workers occupationally exposed to and inhaling high levels of asbestos dust. A study by Dr. Selikoff of workers at a New Jersey asbestos manufacturing plant demonstrated that occupational exposure to amosite asbestos poses a hazard of increased incidence of asbestosis and various forms of cancer. Similar studies in other occupational contexts leave no doubt that asbestos, at sufficiently high dosages, is injurious to health. However, in order to draw the conclusion that environmental exposure to Reserve's discharges presents a health threat in the instant case, it must be shown either that the circumstances of exposure are at least comparable to those in occupational settings, or, alternatively, that the occupational studies establish certain principles of asbestos-disease pathology which may be applied to predicting the occurrence of such disease in altered circumstances.
>
> Initially, it must be observed that environmental exposure from Reserve's discharges into air and water is simply not comparable to that typical of occupational settings. The occupational studies involve direct exposure to and inhalation of asbestos dust in high concentrations and in confined spaces. This pattern of exposure cannot be equated with the discharge into the outside air of relatively low levels of asbestos fibers. . . .
> In order to make a prediction, based on the occupational studies, as to the likelihood of disease at lower levels of exposure, at least two key findings must be made. First, an attempt must be made to determine, with some precision, what the lower level of exposure is. Second, that lower

level of exposure must be applied to the known pathology of asbestos-induced disease, i.e., it must be determined whether the level of exposure is safe or unsafe.

Unfortunately, the testimony of Dr. Arnold Brown indicates that neither of these key determinations can be made. Dr. Brown testified that, with respect to both air and water, the level of fibers is not readily susceptible of measurement. This results from the relatively imprecise state of counting techniques and the wide margins of error which necessarily result, and is reflected in the widely divergent sample counts received by the court. . . . In commenting on the statement, "This suggests that there are levels of asbestos exposure that will not be associated with any detectable risk," Dr. Brown stated: "As a generalization, yes, I agree to that. But I must reiterate my view that I do not know what that level is. . . ."

A fair review of this impartial testimony by the court's own witnesses—to which we necessarily must give great weight at this interim stage of review—clearly suggests that the discharges by Reserve can be characterized only as presenting an unquantifiable risk, i.e., a health risk which either may be negligible or may be significant, but with any significance as yet based on unknowns. . . .[3]

The court's reluctance to pronounce or even attempt to quantify an actual health hazard was a victory for Reserve, although the court went on to suggest that better air control and the "termination of Reserve's discharges into Lake Superior" should take place as quickly as possible. Judge Bright, speaking for the court, then granted Reserve a 70-day stay of Judge Lord's order on the condition that Reserve submit an adequate pollution-control plan. During this 70-day period Reserve jostled still further with Judge Lord, who, in August 1974, declared a new Reserve disposal plan environmentally inadequate. Reserve then asked the Eighth Circuit Court of Appeals for an extended stay, which was granted, but the judges who heard the application for a stay warned Reserve officials that they must continue work underway on development of alternate disposal sites.

DISPOSAL PLANS PROPOSED

Reserve quickly announced plans for an on-land disposal facility to be called Mile Post 7. Reserve applied to the state of Minnesota to construct this new facility. However, the state was displeased with these plans and entered negotiations with Reserve. On April 8, 1975, the Eighth Circuit Court of Appeals handed down its much anticipated final decision on the merits of Judge Lord's order and on Reserve's responsibilities. The key parts of this decision, which to many were surprising, read as follows:

We adhere to our preliminary assessment that the evidence is insufficient to support the kind of demonstrable danger to the public health that would justify the immediate closing of Reserve's operations. We now address the basic question of whether the discharges pose any risk to public health. . . .

Plaintiffs' hypothesis that Reserve's air emissions represent a significant threat to the public health touches numerous scientific disciplines, and an overall evaluation demands broad scientific understanding. We think it significant that Dr. Brown, an impartial witness, whose court-appointed task was to address the health issue in its entirety, joined with plaintiff's witnesses in viewing as reasonable the hypothesis that Reserve's discharges present a threat to public health. Although, as we noted in our stay opinion, Dr. Brown found the evidence insufficient to make a scientific probability statement as to whether adverse health consequences would in fact ensue, he expressed a public health concern over the continued long-term emission of fiber into the air. . . .

The . . . discussion of the evidence demonstrates that the medical and scientific conclusions here in dispute clearly lie "on the frontiers of scientific knowledge." . . . As we have demonstrated, Reserve's air and water discharges pose a danger to the public health and justify judicial action of a preventive nature.

In fashioning relief in a case such as this involving a possibility of future harm, a court should strike a proper balance between the benefits conferred and the hazards created by Reserve's facility.

Reserve must be given a reasonable opportunity and a reasonable time to construct facilities to accomplish an abatement of its pollution of air and water and the health risk created thereby. In this way, hardship to employees and great economic loss incident to an immediate plant closing may be avoided. . . .

We cannot ignore, however, the potential for harm in Reserve's discharges. This potential imparts a degree of urgency to this case that would otherwise be absent from an environmental suit in which ecological pollution alone were proved. Thus, any authorization of Reserve to continue operations during conversion of its facilities to abate the pollution must be circumscribed by realistic time limitations. . . .[4]

In all essentials, Judge Bright and his colleagues on the court of appeals had reversed their earlier views, now holding that Reserve's water and air discharges did create a major public health threat and that the courts need not shy away from decisions in the face of scientific uncertainties. (The judges shrouded their apparent reversal in some legal technicalities.)[5]

For several years following this decision, various courts argued that, as the court of appeals put it, "the probability of harm is more likely than not." Neither side succeeded in providing definitive scientific evidence, and the controversy's focus shifted to the problem of finding a satisfactory on-land disposal site. A major battle erupted over Mile Post 7. Reserve was encouraged when the Eighth Circuit removed Judge Lord from the case because of his bias against Reserve. Lord's replacement, however, quickly fined Reserve almost

$1 million for past violations, and the search for a proper on-land site continued both inside and outside of the courtroom. The state preferred an alternative to Mile Post 7, known as Mile Post 20. Reserve complained bitterly about the potential on-site construction costs and began to negotiate over possible financing. (Reserve and the state submitted separate cost estimates that varied by $50 million to $60 million.)

ON-LAND DISPOSAL FACILITY BUILT

Reserve and the state continued to dispute every health issue previously mentioned among others and each won several major victories in the courts. Reserve repeatedly threatened to permanently close its Silver Bay facility in the face of costs imposed by courts and the state. Finally, the two sides struck a bargain. On July 7, 1978, Reserve agreed both to build the new facility at Mile Post 7 and to satisfy the stringent conditions on which the state insisted for approval of the permits. The total investment in the new facility was set at $380 million. The renovated facility contained one of the world's largest and most expensive pollution control programs. In addition, the company agreed to stop all discharges into Lake Superior by April 15, 1980. It faithfully carried out this promise, and the new facility began operations in August 1980.

Several scientific studies of health hazards had been completed by July 1978 and other studies followed. These studies, several of which were sponsored by Reserve, did not show any significant increase in disease related to asbestos in the region or in plant workers. Studies have not even shown a build up of asbestiform bodies in the lung tissue (of sufficient size to be detected) or in the bloodstream of persons drinking the water from Lake Superior. Reserve's workforce did not show a significant outbreak of asbestosis or any similar disease. Reserve claimed that none of its employees developed a single dust-related disease.[6]

Nevertheless, Reserve's claim depended in part on a lack of clear-cut evidence. Just as government officials could never show any increased incidence of disease as a result of the Silver Bay facility, so Reserve could not prove that there would not be latent and serious long-term effects in 20 years, as is commonly the case with asbestos-caused diseases.

RESERVE CEASES OPERATIONS

With the decline of the steel industry in the early 1980s, Reserve's economic usefulness also declined. High-grade Brazilian ore became available to steel makers for a price well under that of taconite.[7] The decline in the auto industry also contributed to the steel industry's problems. Auto sales plunged, and technological advances allowed auto makers to reduce by hundreds of pounds the amount of steel in their cars.

After 1982 Reserve also experienced a number of temporary shutdowns and employee layoffs. While operating at 40 percent of capacity, Reserve was forced to lay off 1,200 of its 2,600 employees between 1982 and 1986.[8] Shutdowns were long, with Reserve losing six and a half months in 1982 and nine months in 1983.[9]

After using the on-land settling pond for four years, Reserve requested permission to build a filtration plant to allow the company to resume the dumping of waste water into Lake Superior. According to Reserve, the operation needed the filtration plant because its settling ponds were filling up sooner than expected. This was due to the fact that Reserve's facilities were operating well under capacity. Water was collecting quicker because less of it was being recirculated through the plant.[10]

Reserve claimed that the filtration plant was the only viable alternative to a complete shutdown. Management claimed that the filtration process would remove more than 99 percent of the pollutants and make the water "safe to drink."[11] Plant discharge would be between 2,500 and 3,500 gallons per minute. The estimated cost of plant construction was approximately $2 million. Reserve hoped to have it operational within six months. The Minnesota Pollution Control Board received the request and after three board meetings mired with controversy, approved the permit, under the assumption that the proposed filtration plant represented the best available technology.[12]

This permit allowed Reserve to dump water into Lake Superior as long as the fiber content was at or below one million fibers per liter. On those days when the fiber content exceeded that limit the water was to be dumped on land and recycled until it met standards. The filtration plant was built and became operational late in 1984. Reserve monitored the fiber content by sending samples to the Minnesota Health Department Laboratory for analysis.

Reserve was dealt a severe blow on July 17, 1986, when LTV Steel, which owned 50 percent of Reserve, declared Chapter 11 bankruptcy. Problems included smaller than expected steel shipments in the second quarter and lower pricing levels. LTV abandoned all responsibilities for Reserve. Reserve's facilities temporarily closed while Armco surveyed the situation. Armco considered operating Reserve on its own or finding another partner for the operations, but neither option was deemed financially feasible. On August 7, Armco placed Reserve into Chapter 11 bankruptcy. The move was linked to industry conditions; no connection was made between the installment of the on-land disposal site and the bankruptcy.

In August 1986 unemployment for the state of Minnesota was between 5 and 6 percent, while Lake County (including Silver Bay) experienced rates of approximately 40 percent. Some families of laid-off workers had remained in the area, but many others elected to leave in search of other employment. All of the 2,200 laid-off or retired Reserve employees lacked health care and pension benefits until mid-1987. At that time company officials established a trust by using three sources: (1) a portion of tax overpayments owed to Reserve by the state of Minnesota; (2) funds from the sale of pellets stockpiled before the shutdown; and (3) 10 percent of revenues from the sale of Reserve assets. Reserve had sold off all equipment that was not necessary to process 4 million tons of taconite per year. They originally had a capacity of 9 million tons per year.[13]

Although the plant did not operate again until 1990, Reserve continued to recycle water into Lake Superior that collected in the on-land facility. After the shutdown the water quality improved significantly and was well below the 1 million fibers per liter limit.

RESERVE FACILITY REOPENS

On June 12, 1989, the Colorado-based Cyprus Minerals Company acquired Reserve's assets with a successful $52 million bid in New York's Federal Bankruptcy Court. The purchase followed a year of negotiations between Cyprus and state representatives, and Reserve's court-appointed trustee. Cyprus, the second-largest copper producer in the United States, purchased Reserve to "enter the iron ore industry, and to provide stability for the company."[14] Immediately after the acquisition, Cyprus renamed Reserve the *Cyprus Northshore Mining Corporation*, and implemented a $29.9 million "program to refurbish the former Reserve mining and processing operations for production of high quality [taconite] pellets."[15]

In conjunction with the renovation plans, Cyprus Northshore called for regional employment applications from former Reserve employees. Cyprus quickly received over 3,000 applications for the initial 150-200 available positions. As of 1992, Cyprus Northshore employed 420 people, 94 percent of whom are former Reserve employees. Although sharply down from Reserve's employee levels, Cyprus is enlarging its employee roster as taconite production increases. According to industry sources, "The company promises slow, stable growth to avoid the roller-coaster production and employment levels common to the domestic steel industry."[16]

Cyprus Northshore blasted and mined its first crude taconite load on December 27, 1989. In 1990 Cyprus mined over 6 million tons of crude taconite, producing 2.2 million tons of pellets. Once pellet production reaches 10.5 million tons over a five- to six-year period, Cyprus will assume responsibility for the upkeep and oversight of Mile Post 7, the facility's on-land tailings disposal basin. Until then, the state of Minnesota regulates the basin and its environmental safety. Cyprus's acquisition of Reserve, combined with Lake Superior's improved water quality, has for now silenced questions over lingering danger to the environment. However, once Cyprus Northshore expands its taconite production, concerns about the environment are likely to surround Silver Bay again.

NOTES

1. The early history in this case relies on E. W. Davis, *Pioneering with Taconite* (St. Paul: Minnesota Historical Society, 1964). Points of history in the 1970s sometimes depend on Robert V. Bartlett, *The Reserve Mining Controversy* (Bloomington: Indiana University Press, 1980); and on a telephone conversation with Professor Bartlett in April 1982.

2. Presson S. Shane, "Silver Bay: Reserve Mining Company" (1973). Reprinted by permission of Professor Shane.

3. 498 F.2d 1073 (1974).

4. 514 F. 2d Series, 492 (1975).

5. A useful analysis of this second decision is found in William A. Thomas, "Judicial Treatment of Scientific Uncertainty in the *Reserve Mining* Case," *Proceedings of the Fourth Symposium on Statistics and the Environment* (Washington, DC: American Statistical Association, 1977), pp. 1–13.

6. Bartlett, *Reserve Mining Controversy*, p. 209.

7. Bill Richards, "Minnesota Iron Range Is Hurt and Despairing as More Plants Close," *The Wall Street Journal*, November 26, 1984, p. 1.

8. "Reserve Mining Schedules Another Operations Suspension," *Skillings' Mining Review* (March 26, 1983), p. 5.

9. *Ibid.*; also "Reserve Will Cut Taconite Output in Half," *Minneapolis Star and Tribune*, September 19, 1984.

10. Bill Sternberg, "Reserve Mining Waste Plan Draws Fire from Activist Mize," *Marquette Mining Journal* (May 26, 1984).

11. *Ibid.*

12. The following information on the filtration plant is the result of a telephone conversation with Robert Criswell of the Minnesota Pollution Control Agency on April 1, 1987.

13. Telephone interview, Gene Skraba, staff representative, United Steelworkers of America, Hibbing, Minnesota, April 6, 1987.

14. "Cyprus Minerals Co. Enters Iron Ore Industry with Start of Pellet Production at Cyprus Northshore Mining Corp.," *Skillings' Mining Review* (January 13, 1990), pp. 2–8.

15. *Ibid.*

16. John Myers, "Babbitt Mine Reopens with a Bang," *Duluth News-Tribune*, December 30, 1990, p. 5.

HOOKER CHEMICAL
AND LOVE CANAL

THE HISTORY OF LOVE CANAL

Love Canal is named for William T. Love, a businessman and visionary who in the late nineteenth century attempted to create a model industrial city near Niagara Falls. Love proposed that a canal be built to facilitate the generation and transmission of hydroelectric power from the falls to the city's industries. The combination of an economic recession that made financing difficult and the development of cheaper methods of transmitting electricity destroyed Love's vision, and the partially dug canal in what is now the southeast corner in the city of Niagara Falls remains the project's sole tangible legacy.

However, the area still attracted industrial development because it provided easy access to transportation, cheap electricity, and abundant water for industrial processes. Several chemical companies joined other corporations in taking advantage of the region's natural resources. The Hooker Electrochemical Company, now absorbed into the Occidental Chemical Corporation, built its first plant in the area in 1905. An Occidental Petroleum Corporation subsidiary since 1968, Hooker manufactures plastics, pesticides, chlorine, caustic soda, fertilizers, and a variety of other chemical products. With over 3,000 employees, Hooker remains one of the region's largest employers and a Niagara Falls area economic force.[1]

In the early 1940s Love Canal's abandoned section—for many years a summer swimming hole—became a dump for barrels of waste materials produced by the various area chemical companies. Hooker received state permission in 1942 to use the site for chemical dumping. Although no accurate records were kept, it is estimated that between the early dumping period and 1953, when this tract of land was sold, these corporations deposited approximately 21,000 tons of different kinds of chemical wastes, some extremely toxic, in the old canal. The companies stored the chemicals in drums, and considered the site ideal for chemical dumping. Located in an undeveloped, largely unpopulated area, the canal featured highly impermeable clay walls that retained liquid chemical materials with virtually no penetration. Research indicated that the canal's walls permitted water penetration at the rate of a third of an inch over a 25-year period.

In 1953 Hooker closed the dump and covered it with an impermeable clay top. The Niagara Falls School Board then acquired the land that encom-

This case was prepared by Martha W. Elliott and Tom L. Beauchamp, and revised by Joanne L. Jurmu, Anna Pinedo, John Cuddihy, and Blaire Osgood. Not to be duplicated without the permission of the holder of the copyright, © 1989, 1992, 1996 Tom L. Beauchamp.

passed and surrounded the dump for $1.00.[2] Hooker advised against the acquisition and warned the school board of the toxic wastes. However, the board persisted and started condemnation proceedings to acquire land in the area. The city subsequently built an elementary school and a tract of houses adjacent to the site. The constructors removed thousands of cubic yards of topsoil. The construction apparently damaged the integrity of the clay covering. Water from rain and heavy snows then seeped through the covering and entered the chemical-filled, clay-lined basin. The basin eventually overflowed into the houses, and the unfortunate residents had to endure the noxious smell and unwholesome sight of chemicals seeping into their basements and surfacing to the ground.

In 1978 evidence of toxic chemicals was found in the living area of several homes, which prompted the state health commissioner to order an investigation that brought a number of health hazards to light. Several adults showed incipient liver damage; young women in certain areas experienced three times the normal incidence of miscarriage; and the area had three and one-half times the normal incidence of birth defects. The investigation also uncovered epilepsy, suicide, rectal bleeding, hyperactivity, and a variety of other ills—all at above normal rates of occurrence.

Upon review of these findings, the health commissioner recommended that the elementary school be temporarily closed and that pregnant women and children under the age of two be temporarily evacuated. Shortly thereafter the governor of New York announced that the state would purchase the 235 houses nearest the canal and would assist in the relocation of dispossessed families. President Carter declared Love Canal a disaster area, qualifying the affected families for federal assistance.[3] However, families in the adjacent ring of houses did not receive federal assistance, although they believed that the canal chemicals endangered their health as well. Early studies tended to confirm this view, but in mid-July 1982 the Environmental Protection Agency (EPA) released a study that concluded there was "no evidence that Love Canal has contributed to environmental contamination" in the outer ring of 400 homes. This report focused solely on health hazards and did not address documented symptoms of stress. For example, the divorce rate among remaining families soared as wives and children fled the area, while husbands tried to hold on to their houses and jobs.[4]

Since the investigation first began, more than 100 different chemicals, some of them mutagens, teratogens, and carcinogens, have been identified. A number of investigations are continuing to resolve unanswered questions, including the long-range effects of chemical exposure. Cancer, for instance, often does not develop for 20 to 25 years after exposure to the cancer-producing agent. Chromosomal damage may appear only in subsequent generations.

For years many unanswered questions persisted about how to clean up the pollution and who should be held responsible for it. In many cases, these issues remained unresolved until 20 years after residents of Love Canal first found out about the condition of their yards and homes.

CRITICISMS OF HOOKER

The Hooker Chemical company figures prominently in the minds of many who raised and sought to resolve these questions. In 1977 the city of Niagara Falls employed an engineering consulting firm to study Love Canal and make cleanup recommendations. Hooker supplied technical assistance, information, and personnel. The cost of a second study was shared equally by Hooker, the city, and the school board that had originally purchased the land from Hooker. Hooker also offered to pay one third of the estimated $850,000 cost of cleanup.[5]

In 1980 Hooker faced over $2 billion in lawsuits stemming from its activities at Love Canal and other locations. Thirteen hundred private suits had been filed by mid-1982. The additional complaints and suits stemmed from past and current activities in other states as well as from other New York sites. In addition, in 1976 Virginia employees of Life Sciences who had been exposed to Kepone, a highly toxic chemical known to cause trembling and sterility in humans, filed suits totaling more than $100 million. The suits named Hooker as a supplier of some of the raw materials used in the Virginia manufacturing process. (The parties ultimately settled the suit out of court.) In 1977 Hooker was ordered to pay $176,000 for discharging HCCPD, a chemical used in the manufacture of Kepone and Mirex, which had caused cancer in laboratory animals, into Michigan's White Lake. In 1979 that state's officials sued Hooker for a $200 million cleanup due to air, water, and land pollution around its White Lake plant.[6]

While Hooker was defending its actions in Virginia and Michigan, the state of California investigated the company and ultimately brought suit on charges that Hooker's Occidental Chemical plant at Lathrop, California, had for years violated state law by dumping toxic pesticides, thereby polluting nearby ground water. Hooker officials denied the charges, but a series of memos written by Robert Edson, Occidental's environmental engineer at Lathrop, suggested that the company knew of the hazard as early as 1975 but chose to ignore it until pressured by the state investigation. In April 1975 Edson wrote, "Our laboratory records indicate that we are slowly contaminating all wells in our area, and two of our own wells are contaminated to the point of being toxic to animals and humans." A year later he wrote, "To date, we have been discharging waste water . . . containing about five tons of pesticide per year to the ground. . . . I believe we have fooled around long enough and already overpressed our luck." Another year later, Edson reiterated his charges and added that "if anyone should complain, we could be the party named in an action by the Water Quality Control Board. . . . Do we correct the situation before we have a problem or do we hold off until action is taken against us?"[7]

Other complaints about Hooker stemmed from the same area of Love Canal. In 1976 the New York Department of Environmental Conservation banned consumption of seven species of fish taken from Lake Ontario, claiming that they were contaminated with chemicals, including Mirex. The department alleged that Hooker's Niagara Falls plant had discharged the Mirex. A Hooker-sponsored study of Lake Ontario fish disputed this allegation of Mirex contamination. Although this study has not been accepted by the state, the ban has, for the most part, been lifted.

Hooker's Hyde Park chemical waste dump, located in the Niagara Falls area, has also been a source of continuing concern and dispute to residents and government officials. In 1972 the manager of a plant adjacent to the dump complained to Hooker about "an extremely dangerous condition affecting our plant and employees . . . our midnight shift workers has [*sic*] complained of coughing and sore throats from the obnoxious and corrosive permeating fumes from the disposal site."[8] The dangerous condition was not adequately rectified, and in 1979 Hooker's Hyde Park landfill became the subject of a nearly $26 million lawsuit filed by the town of Niagara Falls. New York State also filed a suit for more than $200 million for alleged damages at the Hyde Park site.

In 1980 the EPA filed four additional suits against Hooker for $124.5 million in remedial work. The EPA explained that the actions against Hooker involved: (1) litigation under "imminent hazard" provisions of existing EPA laws, and (2) the creation of programs, financed by government and industry, to clean up hazardous waste sites. EPA administrator Barbara Blum described the imminent hazard litigation as follows: "This program seeks to halt dangerous disposal practices and to force privately funded cleanup. This approach gets results, of course, only where a responsible party can be identified and has adequate financial resources to carry some or all of the cleanup costs."[9]

Blum also detailed the specific statutes under which the EPA was acting and discussed the EPA's collaboration with the Justice Department in enforcing the statutes:

> Sections of the Resource Conservation and Recovery Act, Safe Drinking Water Act, Toxic Substances Control Act, Clean Water Act, and Clean Air Act all authorize EPA to ask the court for injunctive relief in situations which pose threats to public health or the environment. Section 309 of the Clean Water Act levies a penalty of up to $10,000 a day for unpermitted discharges to navigable waters (a leaking dump can be considered a discharge). . . .
>
> People are frightened by Love Canal and by the emergence of threatening hazardous waste sites in their local communities. They are demanding action—and they are getting it.[10]

The EPA has estimated that only 10 percent of all hazardous wastes are disposed of in strict compliance with federal regulations. According to Thomas H. Maugh II, "nearly 50 percent is disposed of by lagooning in unlined surface impoundments, 30 percent in nonsecure landfills, and about 10 percent by dumping into sewers, spreading on roads, injection into deep wells, and incineration under uncontrolled conditions."[11] Maugh argues that "legal dump sites gone awry" are a lesser problem than the growing problem of illegally dumped wastes in unsecured dump sites, often in the middle of cities.[12] In October 1981 the EPA announced that "there are at least twenty-nine toxic waste disposal sites around the country as dangerous or more so than Love Canal."[13]

HOOKER'S DEFENSE AGAINST THE CHARGES

Hooker Chemical believes that its role and position have been misunderstood. Although the company neither denies using the canal as a chemical dump nor denies that the dump has created a serious problem, company officials contend that (1) the company's efforts to prevent first the public and then the canal area private development are generally unrecognized; (2) the company has been an industry leader in safety; (3) Hooker is being unfairly singled out for waste disposal practices that were then almost universal throughout the chemical industry; and (4) a certain level of risk is an inevitable hazard in an industrial society.

Hooker has marshaled data to support these contentions. In the first place, Hooker believes that its efforts to warn the school board and city against interfering with the waste disposal area have gone unappreciated. When the Niagara Falls School Board expressed an interest in selling a portion of the Love Canal tract to a developer, Hooker representatives argued against the plan in a public meeting and later reiterated to the board the possible hazards of developing the site. When the school board persisted in its plans and began to obtain adjacent parcels of land through condemnation proceedings, Hooker, in the school board's deed, again referred to the property's past use and stipulated that all future risks and liabilities be passed to the school board. One part of the deed stipulated that

> Prior to the delivery of this instrument of conveyance, the grantee herein has been advised by the grantor that the premises above described have been filled, in whole or in part, to the present grade level thereof with waste products resulting from the manufacturing of chemicals by the grantor at its plant in the City of Niagara Falls, New York, and the grantee assumes all risk and liability incident to the use thereof. It is, therefore, understood and agreed that, as a part of the consideration for this conveyance and as a condition thereof, no claim, suit, action or demand of any nature whatsoever shall ever be made by the grantee, its successors or assigns, against the grantor, it successors or assigns, for injury to a person or persons, including the death resulting therefrom, or loss of or damage to property caused by, in connection with or by reason of the presence of said industrial wastes.[14]

When the school board later sold part of the land to a private developer who planned to build houses, Hooker officials protested the sale both verbally and in writing. Executives contend that the company has been unjustly blamed for others' imprudence. Hooker also claims that it has no legal responsibility for the Love Canal problem and that it has more than met its social and moral obligations in time and money spent on the cleanup effort. Through its Love Canal experiences, Hooker environmental health and safety specialists have developed knowledge and skills that have enabled the company to take a leadership role in problems of underground pollution.

Hooker officials also argue that their past practices satisfied and even exceeded the then-operative industry standards for waste disposal. During the 1942 to 1953 period, when Hooker filled Love Canal with barrels of chemical wastes, neither the industries involved nor the health and regulatory professions recognized the long-term environmental and personal hazards of these industrial "leftovers." Storing the chemical wastes in a clay canal at the time represented an improvement over common methods of disposal in unlined and unsecured landfills.

The company's defense of its behavior in the Love Canal situation parallels in some respects the reaction of certain Love Canal residents. They directed the major thrust of their antagonism not toward Hooker Chemical, but toward the New York State Health Department, which had failed both to provide open access to the results of state-conducted health studies and to admit in a timely and responsible fashion that a health problem existed. The health department attempted to discourage and in fact actively thwarted independent researchers whose reports indicated more widespread risks to the community's health than the department was willing to admit or was prepared to pay to rectify. Given these premises, these residents have concluded that the health department, not Hooker Chemical, failed to meet its obligations to the community.[15]

Hooker supports the common industry position that society will have to learn to accept a certain level of risk in order to enjoy the products of industrial society. Environmental hazards are one form of industrial "trade-off." Industrialists cite persons such as Margery W. Shaw, an independent scientist who reviewed a chromosomal study of Love Canal residents. She pointed out that the need to determine a level of acceptable risk is indicative of a more general societal problem:

> In our democratic society, perhaps we will decide that 500,000 deaths per year is an acceptable price for toxic chemicals in our environment, just as we have decided that 50,000 traffic deaths per year is an acceptable price for automobile travel. On the other hand, we may say that 5,000 deaths per year is an unacceptable price for toxic chemicals.[16]

THE CONTINUING CONTROVERSY
OVER HOOKER AND THE CANAL CLEANUP

Over the years, Hooker has been among the most heavily criticized corporations for its environmental policies. Ralph Nader attacked Hooker as a "callous corporation" that has left toxic "cesspools." An ABC news documentary that focused on the increased incidence of disease at Love Canal harshly criticized the company. Nonetheless, Hooker has won a number of defenders. A

Fortune magazine editorial defended the corporation for having explicitly conformed to government waste disposal standards, for resisting the canal area construction, and for being the victim of exaggerated and irresponsible reports about the regional incidence of disease.[17] A *Discover* magazine editorial laid the blame for the Love Canal on the school board (but argued that Hooker did act irresponsibly in waste dumpage at a number of other sites).[18] The 1982 EPA study blunted some federal efforts and some lawsuits.

In 1983 the U.S. Centers for Disease Control (CDC) conducted a study of Love Canal residents. The CDC examined 44 residents and compared them to a control group chosen from Niagara Falls residents living at least one mile from the evacuated area. The CDC concluded that residents of Love Canal do not show increased incidence of cancer or reproductive abnormalities when compared to residents of other Niagara Falls neighborhoods. CDC critics claim the study was too small to be conclusive. Health officials and state legislators called for more conclusive information.[19]

Amidst the controversy, Niagara Falls city officials had a list of more than 100 families from the Love Canal neighborhood that were waiting for housing.[20] Many people eagerly awaited the final word on Love Canal's conditions. Although the 1982 EPA study contended that adjacent neighborhoods met safety requirements, New York state health officials reported that they found dioxin (one of the world's most toxic chemicals) at levels eight times higher than the lethal dose.[21] The U.S. Office of Technology Assessment undertook an evaluation of all available evidence, but its report shed no additional light on the conditions at Love Canal. It stated that "with available information it is possible either that unsafe levels of toxic contamination exist or that they do not exist."[22]

Voles (field mice common to the Love Canal area) were the subject of another 1983 study. The mice were ideal for the study because they are sedentary, rarely moving appreciable distances. The number of voles found living in the canal area was less than in the control area, which was one mile from the canal. Mice living near the canal evidenced liver damage. Life expectancies varied significantly. Whereas a vole in the control area would be expected to live 100 days past the 30-day mark, any vole in the canal area that reached an age of 30 days could only be expected to live an additional 54 days. The life expectancy thus was cut in half for those mice living near the canal.[23]

Another study of live birth weights of children born to Love Canal women has also provided cause for concern. Children born to women who lived near chemical swales had significantly lower birth weights in the years 1940–1978 than the state average. A swale is a natural low area along water drainage pathways where chemicals might collect. Several drainage pathways pass through the Love Canal region. Researchers found that 12.1 percent of the children born to women who had lived near one of the swales showed lower than average birth weights as compared to a 6.9 percent average for the state of New York (excluding New York City).[24]

Citizens and health officials mobilized in an attempt to force the cleanup of Love Canal and keep area inhabitants informed of new findings and projects. Local citizens grew weary of the problems and demanded a more rapid cleanup. A complex cleanup project began in the spring of 1987 with the dredging of three local creeks. The site, which had remained covered with plastic sheeting and earth, was uncovered. Officials began to dredge dioxin-contaminated mud and tainted sediment from the creeks. The creeks were dewatered, and waste was removed. The EPA and the State Department of Environmental Conservation stored the wastes in a temporary landfill and storage facility near the site.

Citizens opposed the storage, fearing that it would delay possible rehabilitation of the area. They charged the EPA with negligence and undue delay. In October 1987 the EPA announced plans to complete the cleanup. The EPA planned to incinerate the stored wastes at an expected cost of $26 million to $31 million. The incineration process, though costly, is considered a permanent solution. Buried wastes or other disposal methods, such as deep well injection, are considered hazardous.[25] A Technical Review Committee (TRC) oversees testing of Love Canal air and soil samples and will compare its findings to those from other neighborhoods. The TRC also develops criteria for making final Love Canal resettlement decisions. Under the TRC plan, parts of Love Canal will be converted to a reforested park.[26]

In February 1988 a new court decision altered the circumstance of legal liability for Love Canal. Federal Judge John Curtin of the U.S. District Court for the Western District of New York ruled that Occidental Petroleum Corporation's chemicals unit is responsible for the costs of cleaning up Love Canal—costs estimated at $250 million. This decision was made under the 1980 Superfund Act, the federal program to clean up the nation's most polluted environments.[27] Curtin found Occidental "at least partially responsible" for the initially inadequate storage and for leakage that has occurred over the years. Occidental argued in the case that the city of Niagara Falls was solely responsible for release of the toxic wastes because city officials ignored warnings about the site and then disrupted its hydrology. But Judge Curtin rejected this "third-party defense" because Hooker Chemical had brought the wastes to the site.[28] New York State Attorney General Robert Abrams said that the judge's opinion constituted "a tremendous victory for the state and federal governments and a resounding defeat for Occidental's strenuous and expensive public-relations campaign to shift the entire blame for Love Canal to the city of Niagara Falls, the board of education, the state of New York, and even the people who were forced to abandon their homes."[29]

In 1992 Occidental again tried to claim that the federal government was partially at fault for the Love Canal disaster. The company attempted to prove that the Army had dumped toxic wastes at Love Canal and then destroyed the relevant records. Although the Justice Department has denied such claims, Occidental insists that the Army dumped approximately 4,000 tons of chemicals at Love Canal.

The 1988 case that found Occidental the sole party responsible for the clean-up of Love Canal did not come to closure until June 21, 1994, after the settlement of various countersuits. On March 17, 1994, the federal court decided not to hold Occidental responsible for punitive damages. *The New York Times,* quoting Judge Curtin, who was still presiding over the case, said "that while Occidental was negligent 'on a number of occasions,' the state failed to prove that the company acted with 'reckless or wanton disregard of safety or rights,'" the standard he said was necessary to assess punitive damages.[30] This decision does not affect the previous 1988 ruling. In June 1994, after the long awaited out-of-court decision, Occidental agreed to pay New York State $98 million for damages and expenditures and to take full responsibility for cleanup work. The state estimates that the cleanup charges will be approximately $22 million, but Occidental put the value at only $8 million. Whatever the precise figure, G. Oliver Koppel, the state attorney general, said, "the settlement was by far the largest in state history."[31] Occidental views the June decision as a vindication of its actions at Love Canal, because the company was cleared of wrongdoing. The chairman of the Chemical Manufacturers Association argued further that the decision sets a precedent that chemical companies cannot be held responsible for waste disposal practices that were appropriate at the time: "You cannot judge people or a company based on today's standards or knowledge for actions taken 40 to 60 years ago," he said.[32]

The effects of the Love Canal decision extend beyond the realms of New York State and the Occidental Chemical Company. Love Canal has become an example of how slow and costly cleanup of Superfund sites has become. Because of the attention raised by Love Canal, in 1994 the Clinton administration proposed an overhaul of the 14-year-old superfund program. The purpose of this overhaul was to redefine the criterion of a "clean" site so that government programs would not recognize or permit different standards of cleanliness. Love Canal suggests to many that a flexible standard is problematic because, over the course of many years, property can change hands and be used for a variety of purposes, each falling under a different standard of "clean." For this reason, the Clinton administration has insisted on implementing a definition of cleanliness that can apply to all waste sites.[33]

CONCLUSION

In May 1990, Environmental Protection Agency Chief William K. Reilly announced that the government had opened the Love Canal neighborhoods for resettlement. After a 12-year, $250 million cleanup, the EPA concluded that four of the area's seven districts were habitable. The other three could be converted to park land and industrial areas.[34] Sixty of the area's 2,500 original residents remained through the years of turmoil. On August 15, 1990, the planning director of the Love Canal Area Revitalization Agency, James Carr, placed 236 houses on sale, at 20 percent below market value. Armed with a list of over 200 eager potential Love Canal home buyers, Carr predicted that the area would quickly regain residents.

He was right. In 1992 the Federal Housing Administration started offering mortgages when banks declined involvement. This allowed 100 eager buyers to afford new homes. Success in sales allowed the houses' discount to be reduced to approximately 15 percent below market value. Kenneth Denman, the sole sales agent for the Love Canal Area Revitalization Agency, said that "no sooner were the words 'Love Canal' back in the news than the sales office for [the agency was] jamming up like a Tokyo subway."[35] Given the enormous government cleanup and protection programs, Love Canal's environmental dangers appear to have been eradicated; as Carr has argued, "A child runs far, far greater health risks if his parents smoke or drink than he does living in Love Canal."[36] Nevertheless, many observers remain skeptical.

Love Canal, now changed in name to Black Creek Village, has a state-of-the-art containment system, with two three-foot-thick caps over the dump site. The authorities razed the roughly 240 houses nearest the site and enclosed the entire area within a chain-link fence. Home buyers ready to reinhabit Love Canal have put their faith in the cleanup process, despite environmentalists' continuing fears, which spring from inconclusive studies and uncertain conditions. One environmentalist, National Resources Defense Council attorney Rebecca Todd, commented, "Love Canal is a ticking time bomb."[37] Lois Gibbs, who in 1970 led the evacuation of residents from Love Canal and in 1994 was the director of the Citizens' Clearinghouse for Hazardous Waste in Washington, has never waned in her opposition to the resale of homes in the area. Gibbs argues that the attempt to move people back into Love Canal is "a matter of the state trying to cover up Love Canal and pretend that it didn't exist, pretend like it was not a threat."[38]

The state and federal governments continue to assure new and potential residents that the area is habitable. Reports of tests run on neighborhood soil, air, and houses indicated that "this section of Niagara Falls was no more polluted or toxic than other parts of the city."[39] However, critics are quick to point out that no tests were conducted on former residents since 1983. Skeptics wonder why, if health concerns were the major reason to evacuate in the first place, no one has followed up on their health 15 years later.[40]

Despite the court cases, lawsuits, and cleanup responsibilities, uncertainty remains regarding safety and health risks, as well as the correct causal explanation of disease. As one former Love Canal resident puts it, "We'll still have the same question: Is it [a disease] because I live in Love Canal? Or is it not? because those questions have never been addressed."[41]

NOTES

1. John F. Steiner, "Love Can Be Dangerous to Your Health," in George A. Steiner and John F. Steiner, *Casebook for Business, Government and Society*, 2d ed. (New York: Random House, 1980), pp. 108–9.
2. Sam Borenkind, "Environmental Laws: How Far-Reaching?," *NPN—National Petroleum News* (March 1991), p. 60.
3. Thomas H. Maugh II, "Toxic Waste Disposal a Gnawing Problem," *Science* 204 (May 1979), p. 820.
4. Constance Holden, "Love Canal Residents Under Stress," *Science* 208 (June 13, 1980), pp. 1242–44; and Sandra Sugawara, "Some Love Canal Areas Safe, a New EPA Study Concludes,"

The Washington Post, July 15, 1982, pp. A1, A9. See also Beverly Paigen in note 15 on the earlier data.

5. Steiner, "Love Can Be Dangerous," p. 112.
6. Michael H. Brown, "Love Canal, U.S.A.," *New York Times Magazine* (January 21, 1979), p. 23, *passim;* and Gary Whitney, "Hooker Chemical and Plastics" (HBS Case Services, Harvard Business School, 1979), p. 3.
7. "The Hooker Memos," in Robert J. Baum, ed., *Ethical Problems in Engineering,* 2d ed. (Troy, NY: Center for the Study of the Human Dimensions of Science and Technology, Rensselaer Polytechnic Institute, 1980), Vol. 2, p. 38; and "An Occidental Unit Knowingly Polluted California Water, House Panel Charges," *The Wall Street Journal,* June 20, 1979, p. 14.
8. Whitney, "Hooker Chemical and Plastics."
9. *Ibid.*
10. *Ibid.,* p. 8.
11. Maugh, "Toxic Waste Disposal," pp. 819–21.
12. *Ibid.*
13. Joanne Omong, "EPA Names 115 Toxic Waste Dump Sites for Cleanup," *The Washington Post,* October 24, 1981, p. 4.
14. Steiner, "Love Can Be Dangerous," p. 110.
15. Beverly Paigen, "Controversy at Love Canal," *Hastings Center Report* 12 (June 1982), pp. 29–37.
16. Margery W. Shaw, "Love Canal Chromosome Study," *Science* 209 (August 15, 1980), p. 752.
17. *Fortune* (July 27, 1981), pp. 30–31.
18. *Discover* 2, no. 4 (April 1981), p. 8.
19. "CDC Finds No Excess Illness at Love Canal," *Science* 220 (June 17, 1983), p. 1254.
20. "Love Canal: Still a Battleground," *U.S. News and World Report* 93 (July 26, 1982), p. 6.
21. *Ibid.*
22. "Hazards in Love Canal Monitoring," *Science News* 124 (July 9, 1983), p. 29.
23. John J. Christian, "Love Canal's Unhealthy Voles," *Natural History* 92 (October 1983), pp. 8–14.
24. Nicholas J. Vianna and Adele K. Polan, "Incidence of Low Birth Weights among Love Canal Residents," *Science* 226 (December 7, 1983), pp. 1217–19.
25. "EPA Will Burn Sediment to Clean Love Canal Area," *The Wall Street Journal,* October 27, 1987, p. 72.
26. Carolyn Kuma, "Resampling Could Delay Canal Revitalization Effort," *Niagara Gazette,* November 8, 1986, p. 1.
27. "Milestone in the Love Canal Case," *Los Angeles Times,* July 5, 1994, p. 4B.
28. *U.S.A. v. Hooker Chemicals,* U.S. District Court, Western District of New York, CIV-79-990c (February 23, 1988).
29. Roy J. Harris, Jr., "Occidental Unit Is Ruled Liable in Waste Case," *The Wall Street Journal,* February 24, 1988, p. 2; and Michael Weisskopf, "Company Ruled Liable for Love Canal Costs," *The Washington Post,* February 24, 1988, p. A10.
30. "Ex-owner of Toxic Site Wins Ruling on Damages," *The New York Times,* March 18, 1994, p. 5B.
31. Matthew Wald, "Out-of-Court Settlement Reached Over Love Canal," *The New York Times,* June 22, 1994, p. B5.
32. "Ex-owner of Toxic Site Wins Ruling on Damages," p. 5B.
33. "Milestone in the Love Canal Case," *Los Angeles Times,* July 5, 1994, p. 4B.
34. Anne Underwood, "The Return to Love Canal: Would You Live There?" *Newsweek* (July 30, 1990), p. 25.
35. Evelyn Nieves, "Loving Love Canal Once More," *The New York Times,* July 12, 1994, p. 4B.
36. *Ibid.*
37. *Ibid.*
38. Vince Winkel, "Critics Decry Sale of Homes in Love Canal," *Christian Science Monitor,* November 29, 1994, p. 10.
39. *Ibid.*
40. *Ibid.*
41. *Ibid.*

THE COSMETICS INDUSTRY AND THE DRAIZE TEST

In a survey conducted in the United Kingdom, the vast majority of respondents objected to cosmetic testing on animals.[1] More recently, *Glamour* magazine asked its readers whether we should do cosmetic tests on animals and 84 percent said no.[2] However, in a 1977 BBC television program on animal experimentation, the following question was put to a number of shoppers: Would you use a shampoo if it had not been safety-tested on animals? All answered that they would not. The difference in the responses to the two surveys illustrates the complex nature of the problem.

Some argue that society does not need cosmetics but offer few constructive suggestions as to how a $10 billion industry should be prevented from innovation in Western "free" market economies. Others argue that the products should not be tested on animals since humanity has no right to subject animals to pain and suffering for the sake of frivolous vanity products. However, many consumer organizations consider that cosmetics should be even more closely regulated and subjected to more intensive animal tests.[3]

Faced with the continuing threat of litigation as a result of adverse reactions, the cosmetics industry is unlikely to retreat from animal testing. It is known that tests do not necessarily protect consumers from all risk, but they reduce the extent of risk and also provide some protection for a company in the event of a large claim for damages.

Nevertheless, in a case against Beacon Castile, in which a woman accidentally splashed concentrated shampoo in her eye, the verdict went against the FDA and in favor of the company.[4] The judge's ruling was based primarily on the contention that the concentrated shampoo would be unlikely to enter the eye under normal conditions. However, he also noted that "the rabbit studies, standing alone, do not warrant condemnation of this product." This indicated that this court, at least, was not impressed by the applicability of the rabbit data.

HISTORICAL BACKGROUND ON EYE TESTING

The Draize eye test is a standard testing procedure for eye irritation. It is named after the principal author of a paper that outlined the main element of the test, together with a numerical scoring system to provide an idea of the

This case was prepared by Andrew N. Rowan. The present postscript was prepared by Kier Olsen in 1996. Not to be duplicated without permission of the author and publisher.

irritancy of the tested substance.[5] Such irritancy testing primarily involves cosmetics, toiletries, agricultural chemicals, occupational and environmental hazards, and certain therapeutics, especially ophthalmological formulations. The development of the test followed the passage of the Federal Food, Drug, and Cosmetic Act of 1938 that required, *inter alia*, that cosmetics be free of poisonous or deleterious substances to the user.

In 1933, a woman suffered ulceration of both corneas as a result of having her eyelashes dyed with a coal-tar product called "Lash-lure." She was left blind and disfigured and the American Medical Association (AMA) documented 17 similar cases, some resulting in death. "Lash-lure" remained on the market for five more years—the federal government did not have the authority to seize the product under the 1906 Food and Drug Act because the "Lash-lure" manufacturer made no medical claims.[6] However, the 1938 act did not prevent accidents resulting in eye damage. In a 1952 hearing in Congress, a case was presented of an antidandruff shampoo containing a new polyoxyethylene compound that caused semipermanent injuries.[7] A study of 35,490 people, covering a three-month period, turned up 589 adverse reactions that were confirmed by dermatologists as most likely to have been caused by cosmetics. Of the 589 reactions, 3 percent were classified as severe, 11 percent as moderate, and 86 percent as mild.[8] It is thus clear that there is a need to determine whether or not a new cosmetic product is likely to cause eye irritancy before it is released on the market. The question, therefore, concerns the method of determining a product's potential hazard, rather than whether or not testing is required.

Eye irritation usually has one or more of the following characteristics—ulceration or opacity of the cornea, iris inflammation, and conjunctival inflammation. The Draize test utilizes this fact and scores the extent of the injury to each part of the eye. The various scores are then combined to give a total, which is used to indicate the irritancy potential of the test substance.

The Draize test has undergone several modifications since 1944 and was adapted for use in enforcing the Hazardous Substances Labeling Act. In the modified version, 0.1 ml is instilled into the conjunctival sac of one eye of each of six rabbits, the other eye serving as a control. The lids are held together for one second and the animal is then released. The eyes are examined at 24, 48, and 72 hours.[9] The scoring system is heavily weighted toward corneal damage (80 out of 110) because corneal damage leads quickly to impairment of vision.

The Interagency Regulatory Liaison Group issued draft guidelines for acute eye irritation tests a few years ago.[10] They selected the albino rabbit as the preferred test animal and recommended the use of a single, large-volume dose (0.1 ml) despite the advantages (obtaining a dose-response effect) of using a range of volumes.[11] They also recommended that, in most cases, anesthetics should not be used. However, if the test substance were likely to cause extreme pain, the use of a local anesthetic (0.5 percent proparacaine or 2 percent butacaine) was recommended for humane reasons.[12] The eyes should not be washed. Observations should be made 1, 24, 72, and 168 hours after treatment. The cutoff point for a nonirritant is set very low (i.e., minimal reaction) in order to provide a large margin of safety in extrapolating the human response.

COMPARATIVE STUDIES

The parts of the eye that are most affected by topically applied substances are the cornea, the bulbar and palpebral conjunctivae, and the iris. The corneas of laboratory mammals are very similar in construction[13] and variations are, for the most part, minor. (The mean thickness of the cornea does vary: In humans it is 0.51 mm; in the rabbit, 0.37 mm; and in the cat, 0.62 mm. The composition of the corneas of man and other species differs in the quantity and kind of enzymes.) [14]

The rabbit has historically been the animal of choice for the Draize eye test, but this seems to have occurred more by accident than by design. The use of the rabbit eye for predicting human ophthalmic response has been challenged from time to time. It has been suggested that the greater thickness of the human cornea and other anatomical differences may contribute to the rabbit's greater susceptibility to alkali burns of the cornea.[15] However, the rabbit is less sensitive than humans to some other substances.[16] Tears are produced in smaller quantities in the rabbit than in humans, but the rabbit's nictitating membrane may supplement the cleansing effect of tears.

Procter & Gamble produced an extensive critique of the Draize test in its comments on the draft IRLG Guidelines for Acute Toxicity Tests.[17] It expressed disappointment at the fact that federal agencies have been singularly unresponsive to widespread criticism of the Draize test and have made little or no effort to encourage innovation. It commented on the differences between human and rabbit eyes[18] and the fact that the rabbit's response to the test material is greatly exaggerated when compared to human responses.[19] Procter & Gamble suggests that, when the rabbit result is equivocal, organizations should have the option of using monkeys.

The monkey has been proposed as a more suitable model because it is phylogenetically closer to humans,[20] but there are still species differences.[21] In addition, use of monkeys for eye irritancy testing is inappropriate, in part because of their diminishing availability. Also, the expense does not warrant the purported fine-tuning involved in the use of monkeys. The rat has also been suggested as an alternative model but has not been investigated in any depth. Studies at Avon indicate that the rat may be less sensitive than the rabbit.[22] If one must use an animal for eye irritancy testing, then the rabbit would appear to be as appropriate as any other species.

TECHNICAL

It has already been stressed that the Draize eye irritancy test cannot be *routinely* used to grade substances according to their potential irritancy for human beings but only as a "pass-fail" test. In 1971 Weil and Scala reported the results of a survey of intra- and inter-laboratory variability of the Draize eye and skin test.[23] Twenty-four laboratories cooperated on the eye irritancy testing, including the Food and Drug Directorate (Canada), Hazleton Laboratories (USA),

Huntingdom Research Centre (UK), Avon Products (USA), Colgate-Palmolive (USA), General Foods (USA), and American Cyanamid (USA). Twelve chemicals were selected for ophthalmic irritancy testing and distributed as unknowns to the various companies for testing according to a standard reference procedure employing the original grading scale.[24] Three of the substances were recorded as nonirritants by all the laboratories but there was considerable variation in the results for the other nine. For example, cream peroxide was recorded as a nonirritant by certain laboratories but as an irritant by others.

As a result of this study, Weil and Scala concluded that "the rabbit eye and skin procedures currently recommended by the federal agencies for use in the delineation of irritancy of materials should not be recommended as standard procedures in any new regulations. Without careful reeducation these tests result in unreliable results."[25] It is pertinent to note that Scala considers that the Draize test can be used to grade irritants, but only by experienced and careful researchers.[26]

RECENT PROPOSALS AND POLITICAL ACTIVITY

Development of the Coalition to Abolish the Draize Test.   During the last decade, the humane movement has increasingly called into question the testing of cosmetics on laboratory animals. With one or two minor exceptions, the campaigns that have been launched against such cosmetic testing have been poorly planned and their effectiveness has been undercut by inadequately researched position papers and a dissipation of energy in different directions. All this changed with the development of a coalition of over 400 humane societies aimed specifically at the use of the Draize eye irritancy test by cosmetic companies. This coalition was the brainchild of a New York English teacher, Henry Spira, and the Draize test was selected as the target for the following reasons. First, the test has been criticized in scientific literature as being inappropriate and, in routine use, the data produced are unreliable for regulatory purposes.[27] Second, the Draize test can cause trauma to rabbit eyes that is readily visible and that produces a strong reaction among the general public as well as scientists. As Henry Spira states, "it is the type of test that people can identify with—people know what it feels like to get a little bit of soap in their eyes."[28] Third, the test has remained essentially unchanged for over 30 years despite the fact that the prospects for humane modifications are good. Also, relatively little research has been undertaken in a search for an *in vitro* alternative and even fewer results have been made available in the scientific literature.

The cosmetics industry was selected as the target because it is vulnerable to the image problem raised by the use of the Draize eye test. The picture of the sultry model advertising a new beauty product does not juxtapose readily with an inflamed and swollen rabbit eye. It has been argued that the selection of the cosmetics industry is unfair since its products are, by and large, the least irritant. However, the coalition took the view that the cosmetics industry is not a discrete group, totally separate from other manufacturing companies. In many instances, a single company will make a range of products including household cleaners, toiletries, cosmetics, and drugs. From the coalition's point of view, it is important that the activities of all the members be narrowly focused in order to create the maximum impact and ultimately persuade policy makers that it is worth their while to change their priorities on the Draize test. The campaign's success may be measured by the following actions taken after it started in March 1980.

Government Responses.   The Consumer Product Safety Commission started, on May 8, 1980, a temporary (six-month) moratorium on all in-house Draize testing until the effects of using local anesthetics to reduce pain could be elucidated. It has now identified tetracaine (a double dose) as an effective local anesthetic. The Office of Pesticides and Toxic Substances of the Environmental Protection Agency established a similar moratorium on October 1, 1980. Furthermore, it proposed to "establish the search for alternative test methods to the Draize as a research priority for the coming year." The FDA committed funds in 1981 to study a new *in vitro* technique.[29] In Congress, Senator D. Durenberger (R-MN) and Congressman A. Jacobs (D-IN) introduced resolutions that it was the sense of Congress that funds should be allocated to the development of a nonanimal alternative to the Draize. The National Toxicology Program has yet to make a serious commitment to look for an alternative.

Public pressure on government agencies regarding the Draize test in particular has abated since 1981. Until a feasible alternative (a battery of nonanimal tests) becomes available, little more will be expected of the regulatory bodies than that they exhibit sensitivity to the issue. Recently, however, there has been some suggestion that the agencies could be more responsive. Scientists at Procter & Gamble have produced evidence indicating that use of a smaller test volume (0.01 ml instead of 0.1 ml) improves the predictive accuracy of the Draize test.[30] Nevertheless, the Environmental Protection Agency has not yet shown any inclination to change its testing requirements.

Industry Actions.   The Cosmetics, Toiletries and Fragrances Association (CTFA) established a special task force to review alternative test systems. It sponsored a closed workshop of scientists to investigate the potential for modifying the Draize test and developing an alternative.

A major breakthrough in the controversy occurred on December 23, 1980, when Revlon announced that it was giving Rockefeller University a grant of $750,000 to fund a three-year research effort aimed at finding an alternative to the Draize test. Revlon executives commented that although it would be naive to deny that the campaign, including an effort focused specifically on Revlon, did not have any effect, the grant was part of an ongoing program to research and develop possible alternatives. According to Donald Davis, editor of *Drug and Cosmetic Industry,* Revlon's plight engendered a great deal of sympathy from other leaders in the industry, but there was a distinct lack of volunteers to help take the heat off. Revlon also called upon other cosmetic companies, including Avon, Bristol-Myers, Gillette, Johnson and Johnson, Max Factor, and Procter & Gamble, to join as full partners in supporting this research effort.

The other cosmetic companies were taken by surprise by Revlon's action, but they moved rapidly. Early in 1981, the CTFA announced the formation of a special research fund or trust to support research into alternatives. Avon committed $750,000, Estee-Lauder $350,000, and Bristol Myers $200,000. Chanel, Mary Kay, and Max Factor also contributed undisclosed amounts. These funds have now been passed on to the Johns Hopkins School of Hygiene and Public Health to establish a Center for Alternatives Research. In the meantime, a number of proposed modifications were suggested that would answer some of the human concerns.

Possible Modifications to the Draize Test. Since there is no satisfactory nonanimal alternative currently available for eye irritancy testing, any modifications that can be incorporated now to make the test more "humane" would be welcomed by humane groups. Such modifications range from not doing the test at all to the use of smaller volumes or local anesthetics. These proposals include the following:

1. *Do not test substances with physical properties known to produce severe irritation* such as alkalis (above pH 12) and acids (below pH 3).[31] (Adopted by the IRLG, 1981)
2. Screen out irritants using *in vitro* or less stressful tests. The *in vitro* eye preparations described above could be used to screen unknown substances and irritant substances either labeled as such or discarded. One could also utilize results from skin irritancy studies and human patch testing to avoid testing substances that produce trauma since the skin is likely to be less sensitive than the delicate tissues of the eye.[32]
3. When the test is conducted in the living animal, smaller volumes should be used. It has been argued that the use of 10 ml, rather than the standard 100 ml, would be a far more realistic test in terms of assessing possible human hazard. The use of smaller volumes would produce less trauma and one could also do some superficial dose-response studies to ensure that a nonirritant has a sufficient margin of safety.
4. Where it is necessary to test substances that cause pain and irritation to the rabbit, then local anesthetics should be used. This is recommended by the IRLG.[33]

RECENT DEVELOPMENTS

Since 1981 over $5 million has been provided by industry to support research in America into alternatives to the Draize test. Additional funds have been provided to scientists in Europe, not to mention the costs of intramural industry programs. A number of meetings have been organized to explore the issue.

In 1986, as a result of an initiative by Henry Spira, Bausch and Lomb contracted with the Johns Hopkins Center for Alternatives to Animal Testing to produce a critical evaluation of the research to date and to identify the most promising tests. The resulting monograph reviewed 35 different test methods that have been developed but stopped short of naming the five or six with the most promise on the grounds of insufficient data.[34] However, the volume does provide ample evidence of the thought and effort that has gone into the search for an alternative to the Draize since 1980.

Industry has also reevaluated its safety testing program. Procter & Gamble took the opportunity to review and revamp its toxicology group and has made a serious commitment to reduce animal use. Avon has opened its own cell culture laboratory to validate *in vitro* assays and has reduced its use of rodents and rabbits from 14,500 in 1981 to 4,715 in 1986. Avon has asserted that it intends to be a leader in the industry in switching to *in vitro* assays. Bristol Myers, Noxell, Colgate, and others have also pursued aggressive programs to promote alternatives, and the Soap and Detergent Association organized a validation study for eight *in vitro* tests. Ironically, the study was not made public because there was so much difficulty in obtaining sound, quantified animal data to compare with the *in vitro* results.

CONCLUSION

The results of the campaign indicate that before 1980, the companies and government agencies affected could have made more effort to seek an alternative to the Draize test or to modify the procedure to make it more humane. However, until the public raised the stakes on the issue, there was little motivation for action. Revlon ended up spending $1.25 million instead of the $17,000 suggested at the beginning by the coalition, and all the companies had to deal with large numbers of consumer complaints. Some companies have now made considerable strides in addressing the concerns raised by the animal rights movement, but others have been less progressive. Nonetheless, it is clear that there is a trend to reduce animal use in testing.

POSTSCRIPT

That this trend has continued and, in fact, intensified has become evident in recent years. Scientists have made significant progress since the mid-1980s in the development of alternatives to the Draize test and the reduction of the use of animals in laboratory research. In 1990, the Cosmetics, Toiletry and Fragrance Association pointed to the dearth of viable, safe alternatives to the test in its opposition to bills in eight states that would ban animal testing. Its official position was that "no safe alternative to the Draize test exists; therefore, use of this test must continue to ensure that safe products continue to be placed on America's store shelves."[35] At that time, only a few U.S. cosmetics manufacturers had made a firm commitment to eliminate animal testing altogether. For example, the president of an American distributor of England's Beauty Without Cruelty Cosmetics considered the Draize test unnecessary in light of the availability of vegetarian products and other ingredients that have already been proven to be harmless.[36]

By 1987 scientists were certainly making progress in the development of in vitro alternatives, such as Ropak Laboratories' Eytex, which uses molecules that mimic those in corneas that act up when an eye is irritated. Another test-tube test launched in 1990 was Skintex, which measures the way chemicals damage skin.[37] Though promising, such tests cannot actualize their potential to become viable substitutes for the Draize test until they can be officially endorsed by federal guidelines. Clearly, research that is able to validate the safety and effectiveness of these and other tests will be essential in facilitating such regulation.

A 1990 study contracted by the CTFA indicated that further research is necessary. Ten alcohol-based products were tested first by traditional Draize methods, then evaluated by in vitro procedures that have been developed by Avon, Beiersdorf, Donetics, Colgate, Dial, Estee Lauder, Gilette, Johnson & Johnson, Noxell, Procter & Gamble, and Revlon. The results indicated that the Draize scores that corresponded to in vitro scores associated with low irritancy could be predicted more precisely than those corresponding to in vitro scores associated with high irritancy.[38] When Eytex was tested initially, it failed to detect irritancy 4% to 5% of the time.[39] Clearly, then, in 1990 the need for further research belied the possibility of timely regulatory endorsement.

By the mid-1990s, the need to develop and approve alternatives to the Draize test became increasingly urgent. Adding to the exertion of pressure by animal-rights activists, the European union voted to ban, beginning in 1998, cosmetic products that have been tested on animals. In the words of Myra O. Barker, chief scientific officer at Mary Kay, "That ban has a huge effect on every global cosmetics company."[40] In addition, under the NIH (National Institutes of Health) Revitalization Act of 1993, the Director of NIH must construct a plan for the development and implementation of alternatives to animal testing.[41] Accordingly, many companies have made major efforts to develop such innovations. For example, Procter & Gamble spent $42 million to research alternatives in a single fiscal year.[42] The projection that these alternative tests will prove cheaper than animal testing will possibly provide long-term payback for these large expenditures.

While alternatives are being tested, many companies have already reduced the number of animals that must be tested by using bovine eyes from a slaughterhouse to screen acids and alkalis; adopting a three-rabbit instead of six-rabbit protocol; and using one-tenth the standard dose of eye irritant (Procter & Gamble's LVET or low-volume eye test).[43] Interesting new ideas that will come to fruition in the near future include Xenometrix's skin-irritation test, the use of plant proteins or bacteria that respond to irritants, the development of artificial skin such as Skin2, and the use of genetic engineering in testing the degree of damage done to certain cells.[44]

Andrew Rowan and his colleague, Franklin M. Loew, have concluded that the use of animals in laboratory research has fallen by 25 percent nationwide since 1980.[45] This finding, as well as the progress that has been made in the development of alternatives, seems promising to Rowan and Loew. However, as Rowan himself cautioned, "it's going to take years to establish the tremendous amount of data necessary for people to feel comfortable with these tests."[46]

NOTES

1. National Opinion Polls, *Report to Annual General Meeting of Royal Society for the Prevention of Cruelty to Animals* (June 28, 1974).
2. *Glamour* (December 1981).
3. R. Nader, on the regulation of the safety of cosmetics, in S. S. Epstein and R. D. Grundy, eds., *The Legislation of Product Safety: Consumer Health and Product Hazards—Cosmetics and Drugs, Pesticides, Food Additives,* Vol. 2 (Boston, MA: MIT Press, 1974), pp. 73–141.
4. U.S. District Court of the Northern District of Ohio, Eastern Division, No. C71–53, January 7, 1974, pp. 164–66.
5. J. H. Draize, G. Woodard, and H. O. Calvery, on methods for the study of irritation and toxicity of substances applied topically to the skin and mucous membranes, in *Journal of Pharmacology and Experimental Therapy* 82 (1944), pp. 377–90.
6. R. D. Lamb, *American Chamber of Horrors* (New York: Farrar & Reinhart, 1936).
7. T. Stabile, *Cosmetics: Trick or Treat* (New York: Houston Books, 1966).
8. M. Morrison, "Cosmetics: Some Statistics on Safety," *FDA Consumer* (March 1976), pp. 15–17.
9. F. N. Marzulli and M. E. Simon, on eye irritation from topically applied drugs and cosmetics: preclinical studies, in *American Journal of Optometry, Archives of the American Academy of Optometry* 48 (1971), pp. 61–78.
10. Interagency Regulatory Liaison Group, Testing Standards and Guidelines Workgroup, *Draft IRLG Guidelines for Selected Acute Toxicity Test* (Washington, DC: IRLG, 1979).
11. J. F. Griffith, G. A. Nixon, R. D. Bruce, P. J. Reer, and E. A. Bannan, on dose-response studies with chemical irritants in the albino rabbit eye as a basis for selecting optimum testing conditions for predicting hazard to the human eye, in *Toxicology and Applied Pharmacology* 55 (1980), pp. 501–13.
12. A. G. Ulsamer, P. L. Wright, and R. E. Osterbert, "A Comparison of the Effects of Model Irritants on Anesthetized and Nonanesthetized Rabbit Eyes," *Toxicology and Applied Pharmacology* 41 (1977), pp. 191–92 (abstract).
13. S. Duke-Elder, *System of Opthamology,* Volume 1: The Eye in Evolution (St. Louis, MO: C. V. Mosby Co., 1958), p. 452.
14. R. Kuhlman, on species variation in the enzyme content of the corneal epithelium, in *Journal of Cell Composition Physiology* 53 (1959), pp. 313–26.
15. C. P. Carpenter and H. F. Smyth, on chemical burns of the rabbit cornea, in *American Journal of Ophthalmology* 29 (1946), pp. 1363–72.
16. Marzulli and Simon, on eye irritation.
17. Procter & Gamble Company, "Comments on Draft IRLG Guidelines for Acute Toxicity Tests" (Washington, DC: IRLG, 1979).
18. J. H. Beckley, "Comparative Eye Testing: Man versus Animal," *Toxicology and Applied Pharmacology* 7 (1965), pp. 93–101, and E. V. Buehler, "Testing to Predict Potential Ocular Hazards of Household Chemicals," *Toxicology Annual,* ed. C. L. Winek (New York: Marcel Dekker, 1974).
19. R. O. Carter and J. F. Griffith, on experimental bases for the realistic assessment of safety of topical agents in *Toxicology and Applied Pharmacology* 7 (1965), pp. 60–73.
20. J. H. Beckley, T. J. Russell, and L. F. Rubin, on the use of rhesus monkey for predicting human responses to eye irritants, in *Toxicology and Applied Pharmacology* 15 (1969), pp. 1–9.
21. W. R. Green, J. B. Sullivan, R. M. Hehir, L. G. Scharpf, and A. W. Dickinson, *A Systematic Comparison of Chemically Induced Eye Injury in the Albino Rabbit and Rhesus Monkey* (New York: Soap and Detergent Association, 1978).
22. G. Foster, 1980, personal communication.

23. C. S. Weil and R. A. Scala, on the study of intra- and inter-laboratory variability in the results of rabbit eye and skin irritation test, in *Toxicology and Applied Pharmacology* 19 (1971), pp. 276–360.
24. Draize et al., on methods for the study of irritation and toxicity.
25. Weil and Scala, on the study of intra- and inter-laboratory variability.
26. R. A. Scala, 1980, personal communication.
27. Weil and Scala, on the study of intra- and inter-laboratory variability.
28. L. Harriton, "Conversation with Henry Spira: Draize Test Activity," *Lab Animal* 10, no. 1 (1981), pp. 16–22.
29. Congressional Record E2953, June 15, 1981.
30. F. E. Freebert, J. F. Griffith, R. D. Bruce, and F. H. S. Bay, "Correlation of Animal Test Methods with Human Experience of Household Products," *Journal of Toxicology—Cut. Ocular. Toxicology 1* (1984), pp. 53–64.
31. Interagency Regulatory Liaison Group, *Recommended Guidelines for Acute Eye Irritation Testing* (Washington, DC: IRLG, 1981).
32. Ibid.
33. Ibid.
34. J. M. Frazier, S. C. Gad, A. M. Goldberg, and J. P. McCulley, *A Critical Evaluation of Alternatives to Acute Ocular Irritation Testing* (New York: Mary Ann Liebert Inc., 1987).
35. Kathi Gannon, "CFTA Fights Proposed 8-State Ban on Animal Testing," *Drug Topics* 134 (January 22, 1990), pp. 56+.
36. Ibid.
37. "Eye Tests Without Tears," *The Economist* 315 (June 23, 1990), p. 89.
38. Anne Wolven Garrett, "In Vitro Alternatives," *Drug & Cosmetic Industry* 147 (August 1990), pp. 12, 67.
39. "Eye Tests Without Tears," p. 89.
40. Bob Ortega, "Scientists Engineer 'Smart' Skin Cells to Replace Animal Tests for Cosmetics," *The Wall Street Journal*, October 23, 1995, p. B1.
41. As of this writing, a draft of this plan has been developed and sent to the Department of Health and Human Services for final approval. Andrew N. Rowan and Franklin M. Loew, with Joan C. Weer, *The Animal Research Controversy: Protest, Process & Public Policy* (Center for Animals & Public Policy, Tufts University School of Veterinary Medicine, 1995).
42. Ortega, "Scientists Engineer 'Smart' Skin Cells to Replace Animal Tests for Cosmetics," p. B1.
43. Rowan and Loew, pp. 110–111.
44. Ortega, "Scientists Engineer 'Smart' Skin Cells to Replace Animal Tests for Cosmetics," p. B7.
45. Scott Allen, "Animal Testing Reportedly Falls," *The Boston Globe*, March 3, 1994, p. 20.
46. Ortega, "Scientists Engineer 'Smart' Skin Cells to Replace Animal Tests for Cosmetics," p. B7.

PÂTÉ AT IROQUOIS BRANDS

On April 6, 1985, proxy materials mailed by Iroquois Brands of Greenwich, Connecticut, to its shareholders contained a controversial proposal about its importation of goose liver pâté from French suppliers. The question put to shareholders was whether they wished the corporation to investigate charges made concerning the cruel practice of force-feeding the geese used to make the pâté in France.

The officers of Iroquois Brands did not voluntarily place this proposal on the proxy agenda for shareholders. Instead, the issue had come to prominence through the persistent efforts of a single shareholder, Peter C. Lovenheim, who believed that the charges of inhumane treatment had substance and relevance for shareholders. Lovenheim, who held 200 shares of stock, was initially attracted to the company because of its health food orientation and its broad range of specialty products. When he received proxy materials detailing a new product, Edouard Artzner Pâté de Foie Gras, an expensive food created for French restaurants and the gourmet food market, he was distressed. A proponent of animal welfare, he objected to what he understood as cruelty to geese.

He brought his concerns to a stockholders' meeting and obtained just over the 5 percent support from other stockholders necessary to introduce the issue to shareholders and management. Lovenheim wished to have mailed to the shareholders proxy materials advocating the formation of a committee to investigate the methods used to fatten the geese. However, Lovenheim met with stern resistance from management. Officers refused to include his proxy materials in the shareholders' report because the management believed that the only relevant criteria for shareholder consideration, economic significance, was not met.

Lovenheim rejected this argument. He maintained that ethical and social issues should not be excluded from proxy materials simply because these issues failed to be of economic interest and significance. He and other like-minded shareholders saw the proper treatment of animals as a perennial problem in Western morality that any sensitive person should consider, and therefore as relevant to the operations of a business. These shareholders wanted other members to be aware of the cruelty that was involved in the production of the "specialty food." In a "supporting statement," Lovenheim provided a description of the commercial production that can be paraphrased as follows:

Commercial production involves the enlargement of an animal's liver by means of mechanical force-feeding. The prevailing practice is to restrain the animal's body in a metal brace and mechanically pump [corn] mash [up to 400 grams each feeding] through a funnel [inserted 10–12 inches] down its throat. An elastic band around the throat prevents regurgitation. Feeding is repeated 24 times a day for 28 days until the liver has been enlarged 6 times.

Some geese die from intestinal malfunctions caused by the force-feeding, but most do not.

Lovenheim maintained that if undue stress, pain, and suffering are inflicted upon the geese, it is questionable whether further distribution of this product should continue unless a more humane production method is developed. Lovenheim was able to enlist the support of several animal welfare groups. For example, the American Society for the Prevention of Cruelty to Animals (ASPCA) said of force-feeding: "This is not just raising animals for food. This is an aberrant and unethical practice."[1] John F. Kullberg, the executive director of the organization, explained the ASPCA's position on the force-feeding of geese:

> We consider the force-feeding of geese an act of cruelty and remain committed to having this practice stopped.
>
> Hundreds of thousands of geese are subjected to force-feeding yearly. The pain and stress they endure is very real. The fact that all of this is justified solely on the basis of producing a luxury food item not only promotes the unethical stand that the end justifies the means, but makes the matter even more objectionable because of such a meaningless end.
>
> We are distressed that the results of this inhumane feeding practice are promoted for sale in the United States. It is further the opinion of our legal counsel that force-feeding violates several state anti-cruelty laws.[2]

The Humane Society of the United States also condemned this process as unnecessarily cruel to animals.

In his proposal, Lovenheim requested that a committee be formed to study the methods by which the French supplier produced pâté and then to report to shareholders its findings, together with an opinion about whether this process caused undue distress, pain, and suffering to animals. Management at Iroquois Brands denied the need for such a committee. It cited figures that discounted the financial importance of the pâté, claiming the company suffered a net loss on the product. Its figures may be summarized as follows:

Iroquois's annual revenue:	$141 million
Iroquois's annual profit:	$6 million
Iroquois's sales from pâté:	$79,000
Iroquois's net loss on pâté:	$3,121

Management acknowledged the importance of moral problems that arise when animals are treated in a cruel manner. However, the company contended that the real issue is whether a reseller of the end product should be responsible for the means of production. The board claimed to "deplore cruelty to animals in any form"[3] and commended the Humane Society for its work to alleviate the problem of cruelty to animals in the United States. However, it did not view itself as responsible for French practices over which it had no control. It maintained that, upon importing the pâté, the federal Food and Drug Administration tested and approved the product, thereby lifting any responsibility that Iroquois may have had.

Iroquois also argued that it was illogical to form a panel to study an issue that the company could not control, especially when the costs of obtaining expert consultation would exceed any reasonably anticipated profit from the product. Furthermore, management contended that even if a committee were formed, it would have little if any impact on Iroquois's actual business and even less impact on the world pâté market or the feeding practices in France.

Lovenheim rejected this entire line of argument. He claimed that, although Iroquois Brands might not itself force-feed the geese, it did import, advertise, and sell the end product. If the French supplier was using the process described, the Iroquois company was indirectly supporting animal mistreatment and must be held responsible. The availability of a market for products obtained in this manner, he maintained, contributes to the continuation of such treatment.

This struggle between company and shareholder was presented to a U.S. District court, where the issues turned on legal technicalities rather than on the substantive ethical question. At issue in the courtroom was whether a 1983 rule of the Securities and Exchange Commission (SEC) would determine the outcome of this dispute. This rule allows a company to omit proxy materials proposed by shareholders if the relevant operation of the firm—in this case imported pâté—accounts for less than 5 percent of the firm's total assets and is not "otherwise significantly related to the issuer's business." Because importing and selling pâté did not account for the required 5 percent, Iroquois management did not feel compelled to issue the proxy materials.

Judge Oliver Gasch, admitting that the case involved a close call, sided with Lovenheim.[4] Judge Gasch held that the history of the rule in question showed no decision by the SEC that allowed a company to base its judgments solely on the economic considerations on which Iroquois relied. Upon learning of Judge Gasch's order that the proxy material must be sent to shareholders, Lovenheim said that he hoped his effort "reasserts the rights of shareholders in all companies to bring moral issues to the attention of management."[5]

The unit that imported the pâté was subsequently sold by Iroquois Brands, and management officially then considered the matter a moot issue.[6]

NOTES

1. American Society for the Prevention of Cruelty to Animals, Supporting Statement to Shareholders' Proposal. Included in Appendix 3 in the legal opinion cited in footnote 4.

2. From a letter written January 13, 1984, by ASPCA Executive Director John F. Kullberg. Included in Appendix 5 in the legal opinion cited in note 4 below.

3. Notice of 1983 Annual Meeting of Shareholders and Proxy Statement, Tuesday, May 10, 1983.

4. *Peter C. Lovenheim v. Iroquois Brands Ltd.* U.S. District Court, Washington, DC, Civil Case No. 85-0734 (May 24, 1985). The data and arguments presented before this court have been consulted in developing the basic facts in this case.

5. Philip Smith, "Shareholders to Be Given Pâté Question," *The Washington Post*, March 28, 1985, p. E3.

6. Personal correspondence from attorney Ralph L. Halpern of Jaeckle, Fleischmann & Mugel (Buffalo, New York), April 13, 1988.

ACID RAIN AND
THE USES OF COAL

Acid rain is the term used to refer to pollution caused by higher than normal acidity in rain, fog, snow, and the like. It is created by burning coal and other fossil fuels. It has been cited in numerous scientific studies as the leading cause of lake acidification and fish kills in the northeastern United States and southeastern Canada. It may also adversely affect forest ecosystems, farmlands, ground water, exposed surfaces of buildings, human health, and many manufactured items. Environmental activists have targeted the coal industry and its power-generating and industrial consumers as primary causes of acid rain.

Scientists do not yet fully understand the chemical process that creates acid rain or its environmental impact. Experts do, however, believe that gaseous sulfur dioxide is released into the air when coal with a high sulfur content is burned (primarily in utility power plants and some industrial plants). The sulfur dioxide and nitrogen oxides from transportation vehicles and oil burner emissions combine with water vapor to produce sulfuric and nitric acids. Carried by prevailing winds perhaps far from the emission source, these acids infiltrate precipitation and lower its pH levels. Pure rain is naturally somewhat acidic, with a pH level of 5.6 (6.0 is neutral). The degree of acidity increases exponentially as the pH level decreases. Rainfall with pH levels of 3 or 4 is common in the eastern United States and Canada and thus is anywhere from 10 to over 100 times more acidic than a normal 5.6. Levels as low as 1.5, roughly the acidity of battery acid, have been reported in Wheeling, West Virginia.[1]

Ecological systems have natural alkaline properties that can neutralize moderately acidic rain, but continued precipitation with low pH levels endangers the environment. Large fish kills often occur in the early spring because, as environmentalist Anne LaBastille has graphically depicted,

> all winter, the pollutant load from storms accumulates in the snowpack as if in a great white sponge. When mild weather gives the sponge a "squeeze," acids concentrated on the surface of the snow are released with the first melt. This acid shock . . . produces drastic changes in water chemistry that destroy fish life.[2]

This case was prepared by Nancy Blanpied and Tom L. Beauchamp, and revised by Sarah Westrick, Cathleen Kaveny, Joanne L. Jurmu, John Cuddihy, and Jeff Greene. Not to be duplicated without permission of the holder of the copyright, © 1992, 1996 Tom L. Beauchamp.

Those highly acidified areas in the northeastern United States and southeastern Canada are naturally low in alkaline buffers, which neutralize the acids. As an acidification byproduct, toxic metals such as aluminum are leached from the earth's surface. The aluminum proves lethal to fish and other life forms, and fish that survive may become poisonous to predators who eat them, including, in some cases, humans.[3] The state of Maine has issued the strongest warning yet regarding the consumption of freshwater fish. Concerned about high mercury levels, Maine officials now urge women of childbearing capacity and children under age 8 not to eat fish caught in the state.[4]

In the Adirondack region of New York, which receives some acid rain, residents have noticed a steady decrease in the number of fish and other forms of wildlife. A forest ranger and lifelong area resident has noted that

> the snowshoe rabbit is down, the fox is way down, deer are down, way down, the bobcat is down, the raccoon is down. Even the porcupine is disappearing. . . . Frogs and crayfish are way down. The loon has disappeared. . . . You don't see fish jump anymore. There are no fish to jump, and even if there were, there'd be no insects to make them jump.[5]

A recent EPA study has confirmed this ranger's observations. The study projects that by the year 2040 nearly half of the 700 ponds and lakes it studied in the Adirondacks will be virtually devoid of life due to human pollution.[6]

Many businesses have been affected by these and other problems associated with acid rain. The paint on between 17,000 and 18,000 automobiles owned by Nissan Motor Corporation in Nashville, Tennessee, has been damaged due to acidic atmospheric conditions, probably in the form of morning dew. Other nearby car companies including General Motors, Toyota, Honda, Chrysler, and Ford have all experienced similar problems created by acid rain.[7]

Another example of the concern about acid rain is found in Scandinavia, where a problem has existed for many years due to its location downwind of the heavily industrialized countries of the United Kingdom, Germany, and Poland. Regional scientists have studied the effects of acid precipitation in response to alarming changes in their rivers and lakes; for example, in Norway two thirds of its lakes have lost all their fish over the last century.[8] Folke Andersson, coordinator of the Swedish acid rain research on soils, forests, and waters, found that "'75 percent of nitrogen needed by forests comes from the work of soil organisms.' Laboratory studies show that increased acidity kills these microorganisms. 'Over the long term we ought to see a decrease in forest productivity due to the decrease in organisms releasing nitrogen to the soil. We can't see this yet.'"[9] Swedish researchers have found that soils retain liquid pollution. Even if all sulfur emissions stopped today, the sulfur would not stop flowing from the soil for decades. It has been estimated that 80 percent of acid rain's sulfur is retained in the soil and slowly bleeds out.[10] This effect is compounded by the fact that normal fertilizer use contributes to soil acidity.[11]

In the United States, many of those who wish to prevent acid rain and its possibly devastating consequences focus their attention on the midwestern coal mines. Coal mining is a major industry in southern Ohio and the West Virginia panhandle, employing roughly 15,000 miners. Ohio coal, which has a particularly high sulfur content, is used throughout the region and is thought by environmentalists to be one of the primary sources of the acid rain falling in the northeastern United States and southeastern Canada. However, existing environmental regulations (see the following discussion) controlling the use of high sulfur coal have already decimated the region's economy. The state of Michigan has slashed orders for Ohio coal, and some area power plants have switched to a low-sulfur coal. Miners fear for their jobs, and unemployment in these regions is increasing.

The National Coal Association reports that because of greater use of low-sulfur coal and scrubbers in power plants, there is little more sulfur dioxide in the air than there was in the late 1940s. The Environmental Protection Agency (EPA) found a 28 percent decrease in sulfate levels from 1973, when the Clean Air Act was passed, to 1983. From 1980 to 1985 sulfur dioxide emissions decreased by 2.7 percent, while coal usage increased by 23 percent. Furthermore, pertinent levels of sulfur dioxide dropped by 36 percent from 1975 to 1984.[12] As of 1986, 98 percent of all U.S. counties had complied with the national standard for sulfur dioxide and nitrogen oxide.[13] However, because of the many unknowns about acid rain, *The Wall Street Journal* cautioned as follows in mid-1980:

> At least five more years of study is required to identify correctly the causes and effects of acidic rainfall. Precipitous regulatory action by EPA could cost utilities and other industries billions of dollars. Until more is genuinely known about acid rain, these expenditures may end up only going down the drain.[14]

Despite such warnings, the EPA proceeded with regulatory efforts (by targeting coal and oil-fired power plants) until the Reagan administration ordered that *The Wall Street Journal's* advice become official policy. However, a 1981 National Research Council report thwarted this strategy. It reported that nitrogen oxide levels have tripled in the last 25 years, and the panel placed the burden of responsibility for environmental deterioration on coal-burning industries. The "circumstantial evidence" of a causal connection between coal burning and environmental damage, it argued, is overwhelming. The panel recommended stringent control measures.[15]

Scrubbers, which remove sulfur dioxide from coal, are generally regarded as the most effective control technology, although decreased reliance on fossil fuel may be the most promising policy. Installing scrubbers is costly, but it has proven effective. A cheaper though less efficient alternative is to wash coal prior to combustion. The increased regulations and the need for costly technology have made it difficult for many small industrial coal users to survive.

It is also difficult to determine with precision who is responsible for the deteriorating situation. Tracking the atmospheric routes of acid rain from sources to destinations is a complex problem that some believe must be solved if emissions are to be controlled effectively. Sulfur dioxide over the Adirondacks may vary only 10 percent through a given period while rainfall acid concentration may change 100 percent.[16] A Department of Energy (DOE) report has cast doubt altogether on the delineation of imported coal-produced pollutants as a major cause of acid rain, and has focused instead on the dangers of local automobile and oil-burner emissions.[17] (This report was filed approximately nine months before the release of the National Research Council panel report mentioned earlier. The studies ran concurrently.)

The issue of acid precipitation across the U.S.-Canadian border has received extensive attention. In March 1985 the United States and Canada appointed special envoys to study the issue and make recommendations for its resolution. One major recommendation in their January 1986 report was a five-year, $5 billion program to develop innovative technology for new and existing discharge sources. (This is not to imply that the United States has not been actively funding acid rain research. Between 1982 and 1989 the National Acid Precipitation Assessment Program appropriated over $500 million for such research.)[18]

Coal industry representatives generally contend that there are too few definite answers to warrant further emission regulations and that, should they be instituted too quickly, needless expenditures would result. The Electric Power Research Institute has developed an extensive international research plan to examine the causes and effects of acid rain. The Tennessee Valley Authority, the U.S. Geological Survey, and the other government agencies previously mentioned are also pursuing further research.[19] Industry spokespersons believe that further research is all that can and should be done until we better understand the acid rain phenomenon. For example, Al Courtney, the designated spokesperson for the nation's investor-owned electric utilities, notes the following as the industry's preferred policy:

> A careful examination of the available facts leads to four conclusions: first, the only adverse effect which has been documented is the acidification of certain local water bodies; second, the causes of the acidification are not clear; third, the contribution of power plant emissions to this problem is not known, and as a result, it is not known whether emission reductions would retard or reverse this acidification; and further, requiring substantial additional emission reductions by the electric utility industry would impose great economic burdens on the financially troubled nation and on the already weak economy without assurance of commensurate benefits to the public. . . . It is clear that many of the critical chemical, meteorological, ecological, and economic questions related to acid rain remain unanswered. . . . Pending the completion of the research program established by the Acid Precipitation Act of 1980, claims regarding irreversible ecological impact should be investigated,

and mitigating measures, such as liming, should be instituted where appropriate. . . . In enacting the Acid Precipitation Act of 1980, Congress recognized this essential prerequisite and in response, instituted a program designated to explore the acid deposition phenomenon in a deliberate, methodical manner. We should permit this rational, problem-solving approach to produce the information which we so badly need.[20]

The acid rain receivers, on the other hand, have asked for international cooperation and quick responses to what they consider to be a worsening environmental situation. Cost estimates vary, but whatever the method of calculation, the cost of effectively controlling sulfur dioxide emissions has long been agreed to be substantial. According to Sheldon Meyers of the EPA, to install one scrubber on an existing 300 megawatt utility boiler would cost between $60 million and $90 million in 1985 dollars.[21] Because the scrubber creates a sludge, scientists need to develop new sludge disposal methods. Also, levels of reduction vary in costs:

> There are annual dollar values usually assigned to the phased reductions: $2 billion would buy a reduction of four million tons annually in the thirty-one states east of the Mississippi; $4 billion would buy a reduction of eight million tons per year; and $8 to $10 billion would buy reductions of 12 million tons per year below the 1980 level.[22]

Even the basic facts about acid rain remain in dispute, and the legislative and regulatory situation is uncertain. In a 1981 report, the comptroller general of the United States on the debate over acid precipitation summarized the situation as follows:[23]

> Summing up the evidence on the acid precipitation debate, even the most conciliatory representatives of the opposite sides arrive at different conclusions.
> Those most concerned with the additional costs and problems expected for further emissions controls argue for the point that there is no firm proof that reductions of emissions would result in lessening acid deposition. Therefore, they conclude, it is inappropriate to take any additional control actions at this time, because the controls would be certain to involve costs but would stand the risk of producing no benefits.
> On the other side, those most concerned with the present and anticipated damage due to acid precipitation start from the point that the oxide precursors of deposited acids, particularly SO_2, come predominantly from man-made emissions. From this they conclude that reducing oxide emissions upwind from threatened areas is most likely to prevent or reduce damage, so they urge that at least moderate steps in the direction should be started promptly. They view as inequitable the present situation, in which they see all costs and risks being borne by the regions

suffering damage, contending that the emitting regions should also take some share of risks and costs.

Milton J. Socolar
Acting Comptroller General
of the United States

A decade later, in November 1990, President George Bush signed amendments to the Clean Air Act into law. Among the amendments' major provisions is a nationwide utility emissions cap on sulfur dioxide emissions of 8.9 million tons a year by the year 2000. After 2000 emissions must be kept at this level. The Bush administration argued that this cap represents a 10-million-ton reduction from the levels of a decade ago. The largest sulfur dioxide cuts for the first five years are scheduled to come from roughly 100 of the dirtiest plants, located mainly in Appalachia and the Midwest. Cleaner plants will be required only to cut emissions after the five-year period, but before 2001.

Title IV of these amendments details acid rain controls. A major part of the projected reduction in sulfur dioxide is to come by substituting low-sulfur coal for the now popular high-sulfur coal. Industry watchers call the acid rain provisions "a boon for low-sulfur coal producers, since a large part of this reduction will be obtained through substituting low-sulfur coals for the higher-sulfur fuels now used" and also a boon for rail carriers, which now must truck the coal further and in larger quantities.[24]

Midwestern coal producers have experienced economic problems as a result of this section of the bill. In Illinois, for example, the production level and employee population have dropped from 60 million tons and 18,000 miners in 1980 to only 42.1 million tons and 7,400 workers in 1993. This trend, along with the call for lower-sulfur coal, has prompted several companies to look for alternative methods of using their coal in new, non-polluting ways. Coal gasification is the most advanced of several technologies under development to help save the industry. Coal gasification has been available for decades, but its application to the production of electricity is new. The process involves extracting a gaseous mixture of hydrogen and carbon monoxide from a coal slurry, which is then burned in a turbine to turn a generator and produce electricity. Based on experience from prototypes, the process produces emissions of .02 pound of sulfur dioxide and .08 pound of nitrogen dioxide per million BTUs of coal, well below the 1.2 pounds and .6 pound allowed by the law. Many midwestern coal producers are hoping that technologies such as this one will catch on and allow their industry to survive.[25]

The amendments also establish a pollution-credits system that provides an incentive for plants to restrict sulfur dioxide emissions beyond federally required levels. The legislation provides credits for cleaner plants to allow them greater production flexibility beyond the mandated cap and calls for annual reductions of nitrogen oxides, which contribute to acid rain, through 1996.

The Clean Air Act and some joint ventures between the United States and Canada have strengthened the antipollution activity in North America.

Some environmentalists have been quick to praise these initiatives. However, the new legislation is inadequate from the perspective of many environmentalists, in part because of the go-slow provisions of the legislation. There also are no specific provisions to regulate the emissions of midwestern utilities' tall stacks, which disperse emissions that are generally believed to be primary causes of the damage to the ecology of the northeastern United States and southeastern Canada.

Environmentalists have long viewed the acid rain problem as a dire emergency. Yet the 1990 amendments are not likely to produce ecological improvements for at least a decade. Environmentalists believe that this pace is too slow and that in the long struggle between environmental protection and increased costs, fear of costs has once again dominated ecological interests. They worry that the demands of the legislation are too minimal. Their opponents take a diametrically opposed view. Senator Steve Symms (R-ID), for example, maintained that current legislation is "so costly that it probably will do more damage to the economy than the good it may do for the air."[26] (Costs of compliance with the new amendments are thought to be $4 billion to $6 billion per year.)

The continuing effects of acid rain and the economic and environmental impact of the new legislation are still being debated today in much the same terms they were debated ten years ago. Moreover, government studies of costs and projected damage often reach sharply conflicting conclusions. For example, at the present writing it is not clear whether the acidity in streams and lakes has been increasing or decreasing since the Clean Air Act of 1973. The American public also seems confused and ambivalent. Although public opinion polls have consistently shown that Americans say they are willing to pay higher rates for cleaner air, the polls also indicate that Americans favor the reduction or denial of proposed rate increases for public utilities.[27]

NOTES

1. Lois R. Ember, "Acid Pollutants: Hitchhikers Ride the Wind," *Chemical and Engineering News* (September 14, 1981), p. 29.
2. Anne LaBastille, "Acid Rain: How Great a Menace?" *National Geographic* 160 (November 1981), p. 672.
3. Robert H. Boyle, "An American Tragedy," *Sports Illustrated* (September 21, 1981), p. 75.
4. Scott Allen, "Freshwater Fish Mercury Levels Hint at Larger Problem," *The Boston Globe*, May 26, 1994, p. 29.
5. Boyle, "An American Tragedy," p. 74.
6. "EPA: Acid Rain Imperils Future of Adirondacks," *The Boston Globe*, November 4, 1995, p. 28.
7. Lindsay Chappel, "Nissan Adds to Acid Rain Damage List," *Automotive News* (October 12, 1992), p. 3.
8. Ned Burks and Chris Fordney, "Battle for the Blue Ridge," *The Washington Post*, October 31, 1993, Washington Magazine, p. 15.
9. Ember, "Acid Pollutants," p. 24.
10. Fred Pierce, "Unravelling a Century of Acid Pollution," *New Scientist* 111 (September 25, 1986), p. 24.
11. "Acid Rain Briefing Reviews Recent Research," *Journal of the Air Pollution Control Association* 33 (August 1983), p. 782.

12. Carl E. Bagge, "A Tale of UFOs and Other Random Anxieties," *Vital Speeches of the Day* 52 (September 1, 1986), p. 702.
13. Richard E. Benedick, "U.S. Policy on Acid Rain," *Department of State Bulletin* 86 (September 1986), p. 56.
14. "Review and Outlook: Acid Rain," *The Wall Street Journal,* June 20, 1980.
15. Committee on the Atmosphere and the Biosphere, *Atmosphere-Biosphere Interactions* (Washington, DC: National Academy Press, 1981).
16. "Review and Outlook," *The Wall Street Journal.*
17. Michael Woods, "Theory Blamed Midwest Utilities: Study Disputes Cause of Acid Rain," *Toledo Blade,* January 28, 1981.
18. Alan Skrainka and Daniel Burkhardt, "Acid Rain: What's an Investor to Do?" *Public Utilities Fortnightly* (August 31, 1989), p. 33.
19. "Acid Rain," *Energy Researcher,* Electric Power Research Institute (June 1981).
20. Edison Electric Institute Information Service, Release of October 21, 1981, pp. 1–2.
21. Sheldon Meyers, "Acid Deposition: A Search for Solutions," in Diane Suitt Gilland and James H. Swisher, eds., *Acid Rain Control: The Cost of Compliance* (Carbondale: South Illinois University Press, 1985), p. 7.
22. *Ibid.,* p. 8.
23. *The Debate over Acid Precipitation: Opposing Views; Status of Research,* Report by the Comptroller General of the United States (Washington, DC: General Accounting Office, September 11, 1981), pp. 7–8.
24. Richard G. Sharp, "The Clean Air Act Amendments: Impacts on Rail Coal Transportation," *Public Utilities Fortnightly* (March 1, 1991), p. 26.
25. Stevenson Swanson, "Powerful Visions for Non-polluting Coal Stoke Illinois Hopes," *Chicago Tribune,* May 29, 1994, p. 1.
26. "Congress, Breaking 10-Year Deadlock, Passes Landmark Clean Air Measure," *The Washington Post,* October 28, 1990, p. A16.
27. Skrainka and Burkhardt, "Acid Rain," pp. 33–34.

Chapter Four

THE SOCIETY

INTRODUCTION

The idea that a corporation should be socially responsible and should uphold principles of justice provides the focus for many of the controversies explored in this volume. Many writers in moral and political philosophy hold that the corporation's obligations to society are only obligations not to harm society—not obligations to benefit society. This rule does not mean that the corporation is obligated *not* to benefit society. Rather, the view usually assumes one of two forms: (1) The corporation is a legal fiction and not an agent, and therefore it is not responsible to others; or (2) the corporation's responsibilities are only to its stockholders, employees, and others to whom it has direct obligations.

One abbreviated version of this thesis is found in the maxim "The business of business is business"—meaning that the responsibilities of a business are exclusively the demands found in the business world of contracts, stockholders, profits, record-keeping, taxes, and the like. This position resists the encroachment of government into business decision making and rejects the proposition that corporations have moral and social responsibilities other than the responsibilities that the corporation voluntarily assumes. Some who support this viewpoint maintain the position that if business established social goals for itself, it would be encroaching on the scope of government, which alone functions to protect the public interest. According to this view, the business community has no parallel role, and it has neither the expertise, the motivation, nor the social charter to engage in such activities.

Nonetheless, our legal system holds corporations responsible in a variety of ways. Corporations are chartered, and this charter permits a corporation to conduct business only within certain contractually imposed limits, under the assumption that the contract serves society's overall interests. In this chapter, the cases "Kellogg Cereals and Children's Television Advertising" and "Banning Cigarette Advertising" raise questions about whether corporations should be held as responsible as governments for the public health of consumers and possibly for fairness in the distribution of health care resources. In attempting to answer these questions, it becomes apparent that corporate decision making often involves complicated interactions and procedures and may well involve moral deliberation about communal welfare and even about the welfare of persons beyond the corporation's home country. Moreover, the corporation's welfare and the society's welfare are intimately connected—so closely tethered that it would be artificial to try to delineate exclusive areas of government and business responsibility.

Problems of corporate responsibility are usually raised if a corporation has a myopic focus on profit making while excluding consideration of the other effects of its actions. No one denies that corporations are entitled to profits, but it seems equally undeniable that some means of obtaining a profit are unacceptable. As the previous chapter on the environment shows, corporate activities can cause various kinds of social harm. In this chapter, "Banning Cigarette Advertising" grapples with the obligation not to cause harm, whereas "The NYSEG Corporate Responsibility Program" presents some of the possible obligations business may assume to contribute to the public welfare. These cases focus on the question of a corporation's social responsibilities and explore ways to characterize and limit those responsibilities.

Perhaps the most important of these issues is whether a business, like a government agency or a charitable organization, has some kind of welfare responsibility to the communities in which it operates. If so, should a business assume a position of charitableness in fostering better health, education, and financial welfare for citizens? If so, how much of the corporation's resources may legitimately be devoted to these activities, and what justifies the activity if the justification is not based on profit? That is, if the activity is not directed to improve the corporation's economic welfare, why should it be undertaken? How can the rights of shareholders be balanced? These issues are present, in subtle ways, in the New York State Electric and Gas case.

These problems lead naturally to reflection on the proper corporate objectives, on what constitutes just and worthy business practices, and on obligations of distributive justice—that is, proper or fair distribution in society of social benefits and burdens. The principles of justice relied on in law and morality determine the terms of cooperation in any given society, often specifying what persons or groups may legitimately expect from social transactions. Such requirements of social justice are present in virtually all of society's major and pervasive institutions, including governments, laws of property ownership, banking institutions, and systems of allocating benefits. For example, governments use progressive taxation scales to redistribute wealth in order to satisfy their citizens' welfare needs.

Nonetheless, the rules embodied in law and created by government are rarely adequate to resolve controversial matters of social justice of the sort raised in this chapter. For example, abstract principles of American law and government policy cannot explain or excuse the "justice" of the present national distribution of wealth, in which roughly 20 percent is owned by 5 percent of the population, while the poorest 20 percent of the population controls 5 percent of the wealth. Two cases in the section on "Social and Economic Justice" illustrate these problems as they apply internationally. The "H. B. Fuller in Honduras: Street Children and Substance Abuse," case points directly to problems that businesses encounter about responsibilities in Honduras under conditions of social imbalance. "Marketing Infant Formula" explores the problems that arise when rules are drafted that prohibit the sale of drugs and food in a home country, yet allow the same products to be exported. Other countries may not consider these products to be harmful, even if they are aware of the product's alleged problems. If a corporation then markets a product banned domestically and accepted abroad, is it morally placed in a burden-of-proof situation? Must it disclose to consumers the product's alleged problems? Is the firm obligated to offer good evidence that it is not intentionally releasing a harmful product and that there is a valid local need for the product? Such cases are often difficult to resolve because different *principles* of justice in different societies may affect the discussion.

Among the widely agreed upon principles of social justice is equal access: Programs, services, and opportunities in society must be available to *all* qualified members of the society. To provide some persons with access while denying the same access to others who are equally or more qualified is discriminatory and unfair. But this principle is indeterminate and spawns problems of social inequality, including unfair practices of hiring, promotion, and firing— the subject of *McAleer v. AT&T*. Here a central issue is whether justice is really done when firms hire solely according to principles of equal opportunity and merit. The McAleer case raises questions about whether there are circumstances under which firms should use affirmative action principles that require preferential treatment for women and minorities. The term *affirmative action* here refers to positive steps taken to hire persons from groups historically and presently subjected to discriminatory treatment. The term broadly refers to everything from open advertisement of positions to employment quotas.

For over two decades U.S. federal laws have required corporations to advertise jobs fairly and to promote the hiring of members of minority groups. As a result, corporations have often used employment goals or targeted employment quotas in order to eliminate the vestiges of discrimination. These objectives appear to many to be unfair because these goals can work against the interest of the business while also discriminating against those not favored by the goals. More talented applicants who are excluded would have been hired or accepted on their merits were it not for the preferential advancement of others. Government policies that require preferential treatment are thus said by some commentators to create a situation of "reverse discrimination," because white males, among others, are discriminatorily excluded from consideration, although they may be the most qualified applicants or employees. Such practices therefore seem to violate, rather than uphold, basic principles of justice and equal opportunity.

This viewpoint has provoked sustained controversy. Many hold that these practices reverse the flow of past and present discrimination without perpetuating discrimination at all. They accept a different account of how justice is served in a society characterized by a long history of discriminatory practices. Since discrimination from the past continues today (or at least its effects continue), the claim is that reversal of the effects of this discrimination is not only justified, but demanded by the requirements of justice. Today, there is a sustained discussion about whether the idea of *equal opportunity* has been replaced with the idea of *equal results,* meaning numerical outcomes or quotas that discriminate against "victims" of affirmative action programs. U.S. citizens are today sharply divided over this issue, as are moral philosophers.

THE NYSEG CORPORATE
RESPONSIBILITY PROGRAM

We are responsible to the communities in which we live and work and to the world community as well. We must be good citizens and support good works and charities. . . . We must encourage civic improvements and better health and education.[1]

Many large corporations currently operate consumer responsibility or social responsibility programs, which aim to return something to the consumer or to the community in which the company does business. New York State Electric and Gas (NYSEG) is one company that has created a program to fulfill what its officers consider to be the company's responsibility to its public.

NYSEG is a New York Stock Exchange—traded public utility with approximately 60,500 shareholders. It supplies gas and electricity to New York State. NYSEG currently earns 89 percent of its revenues from electricity and 11 percent from gas sales. The company is generally ranked as having solid but not excellent financial strength. Earnings per share have declined in recent years because of the regulatory climate and the company's write-offs for its Nine Mile Point #2 nuclear unit. In order to finance the unit, the company at one point had to absorb delay costs of several million dollars per month. The setback reduced shareholders' dividends for the first time in many years. NYSEG's financial base is now less secure than in the past because of the lowered earnings per share and the increased plant costs.

The company's corporate responsibility program has been in effect throughout this period of financial reversal. NYSEG designed the program to aid customers who are unable to pay their utility bills for various reasons. The program does not simply help customers pay their bills to the company. Rather, NYSEG hopes the program will locate those people in the community who are in unfortunate or desperate circumstances and alleviate their predicament. The two objectives often coincide.

NYSEG has created a system of consumer advocates, social workers trained to deal with customers and their problems. Since the program's 1978 inception, NYSEG has maintained a staff of eight consumer representatives. Each handles approximately 100 cases a month, over half of which result in successful financial assistance. The remaining cases are referred to other organizations for further assistance.[2]

This case was prepared by Kelley MacDougall and Tom L. Beauchamp, and revised by John Cuddihy and Jeff Greene. Not to be duplicated without permission of the holder of the copyright, © 1991, 1996 Tom L. Beauchamp. This case is indebted to Cathy Hughto-Delzer, NYSEG Manager, Consumer Affairs.

The process works as follows: When the company's credit department believes that a special investigation should be made into a customer's situation, the employee refers the case to the consumer advocate. Referrals also come from human service agencies and from customers directly. Examples of appropriate referrals include unemployed household heads; paying customers who suffer serious injury, lengthy illness, or death; and low-income senior citizens or those on fixed incomes who cannot deal with rising costs of living. To qualify for assistance, NYSEG requires only that the customers suffer from hardships they are willing to work to resolve.

Consumer advocates are primarily concerned with preventing the shutoff of service to these customers. They employ an assortment of resources to put them back on their feet, including programs offered by the New York State Department of Social Services and the federal Home Energy Assistance Program (HEAP), which awards annual grants of varying amounts to qualified families. In addition, the consumer advocates provide financial counseling and help customers with their medical bills and educational planning. They arrange for assistance from churches and social services, provide food stamps, and help coordinate VA benefits.

NYSEG also created a direct financial assistance program called Project Share, which enables paying customers who are not in financial difficulty to make charitable donations through their bills. They are asked voluntarily to add to their bill each month one, two, or five extra dollars, which are placed in a special fund overseen by the American Red Cross. This special Fuel Fund is intended to help those 60 years and older on fixed incomes who have no other means of paying their bills. Help is also provided to the handicapped and blind who likewise have few sources of funds. Many Project Share recipients do not qualify for government-funded assistance programs but nonetheless face energy problems. Through December 1995, Project Share had raised over $2.8 million and had successfully assisted more than 13,700 people.

The rationale or justification of this corporate responsibility program is rooted in the history of public utilities and rising energy costs in North America. Public utilities originally provided a relatively inexpensive product. NYSEG and the entire industry considered its public responsibility limited to the business function of providing energy at the lowest possible cost and returning dividends to investors. NYSEG did not concern itself with its customers' financial troubles. The customer or the social welfare system handled all problems of unpaid bills.

However, the skyrocketing energy costs in the 1970s changed customer resources and NYSEG's perspective. The energy crisis caused many long-term customers to encounter difficulty in paying their bills, and the likelihood of power shut-offs increased as a result. NYSEG then accepted the responsibility to assist these valued customers by creating the Consumer Advocate system.

NYSEG believes that its contribution is especially important now because recent reductions in federal assistance programs have shifted the burden of addressing these problems to the private sector. Project Share is viewed as "a logical extension of the President's call for increased volunteerism at the local level."[3] NYSEG chose the American Red Cross to cosponsor Project Share because of its experience in providing emergency assistance.

The costs of NYSEG's involvement in the program are regarded by company officers as low. NYSEG has few additional costs beyond the consumer advocates' salaries and benefits, which total approximately $500,000 annually and are treated as operating expenses. To augment Project Share's financial support, NYSEG shareholders give the program an annual, need-based grant. In the past, shareholder grants have ranged from $40,000 to $100,000. NYSEG shareholders also pay for some personnel and printing costs. The company has also strongly supported Project Share by contributing $765,000 over a twelve-year period.

The company views some of the money expended for the corporate responsibility program as recovered because of customers retained and bills paid through the program. NYSEG assumes that these charges would, under normal circumstances, have remained unpaid and would eventually have been written off as a loss. NYSEG's bad-debt level is 20 percent lower than that of the average U.S. utility company. The company believes that its corporate responsibility policy is *both* altruistic *and* good business, despite the program's maintenance costs, which seem to slightly exceed recovered revenue.

In 1995, NYSEG initiated another program to assist low-income customers in paying for their utility service. Confronted with an economic recession that resulted in the loss of thousands of jobs in NYSEG's service territory, a reduction in federal and state energy assistance, and increasing electric prices caused by government-mandated purchases of expensive independent power, NYSEG found that more and more of its customers were unable to afford its services. The company responded with Fresh Start, a comprehensive energy education, weatherization, and financial assistance program for 2,500 low-income electric customers. Fresh Start, as its name implies, prevents disconnection of service and gives customers a fresh start in paying their NYSEG electric bill.

This program helps customers gain control of their electric bill by placing any unpaid balance (arrears) in a hold account, giving them a NYSEG grant to bring their energy bill in line with their ability to pay, creating for each customer a monthly budget, and providing weatherization services for heating and water usage. Customers who make their monthly budget payment to NYSEG on time will not receive late payment charges on the outstanding balance and will not receive a termination notice. Those who make all 12 payments to NYSEG will have 10 percent of their arrears forgiven. In addition, if they also reduce consumption they can earn an additional 5 percent arrears forgiveness. Fresh Start began in October 1995 with the understanding that it would continue at least for several years.

NOTES

1. "The Johnson and Johnson Way" (from the Johnson and Johnson Company credo), 1986, p. 26.
2. Consumer advocates are viewed as liaisons between NYSEG and human services agencies. All of these representatives have extensive training and experience in human services, including four to six years of college with a degree in social work or social science. They must also have a minimum of four years of work experience in human services so that they are adequately qualified to deal with the problems facing customers.
3. NYSEG, Project Share Procedures Manual, 1988, p. 2.

KELLOGG CEREALS
AND CHILDREN'S TELEVISION
ADVERTISING

It is both unfair and deceptive . . . to address televised advertising for any product to young children who are still too young to understand the selling purpose of, or otherwise comprehend or evaluate, the advertising. . . . The classical justification for a free market, and for the advertising that goes with it, assumes at least a rough balance of information, sophistication and power between buyer and seller. . . . In the present situation, it is ludicrous to suggest that any such balance exists between an advertiser who is willing to spend many thousands of dollars for a single 30-second spot, and a child who is incapable of understanding that the spot has a selling intent, and instead trustingly believes that the spot merely provides advice about one of the good things in life.[1]

This quotation from a 1978 Federal Trade Commission (FTC) staff report presents the heart of an FTC case against televised advertising directed at children for presweetened, ready-to-eat cereals. This report accompanied a set of proposed regulatory rules that would ban all televised advertising for any product directed at children who are too young to understand the selling purpose of the advertising and all televised advertising for sugared food products that pose serious dental health risks directed at audiences composed of older children.[2]

This proposal on children's advertising was triggered by a 1977 citizen petition from Action for Children's Television (ACT) and the Center for Science in the Public Interest (CSPI). They proposed a ban on the advertising of sugary, in-between-meal (snack) foods for children. ACT and CSPI got more than they requested when the previously mentioned 1978 staff report called for a ban on all children's advertising. This discussion, however, has a prior history.

HISTORY

Circa 1970. A U.S. Senate consumer subcommittee opened hearings on the nutritional value of ready-to-eat cereals in 1970 that reflected a growing national concern about nutrition. Two separate issues set the context of later

This case was prepared by Linda Kern, Martha W. Elliott, and Tom L. Beauchamp, and revised by Anna Pinedo, Nicole Herb, Katy Cancro, and Kier Olsen. Not to be duplicated without permission of the holder of the copyright, © 1992, 1996 Tom L. Beauchamp.

debate. First, does the food industry have an obligation to market a nutritious product? Second, even if a product is highly nutritious, what limits should be placed on advertising this product to children?

Robert Choate, Jr., president of the Council on Children, Media, and Merchandising, made 1970 headlines with his nutritional ranking of 60 leading cold cereals. He said, "I watch TV commercials on Saturday morning and get really mad. The image projected for these cereals is that they give kids muscles and energy so they can catch every football pass. But read the nutrients on the boxes, and there is little to support these claims."[3] Although his criteria for ranking the nutritional value of cereals rested on *vitamin fortification* and not on *sugar content* (later a central concern), his ranking system had significant impact. Within 18 months of Choate's first Senate testimony, 26 of 40 criticized cereals had been reformulated.

At these 1970 Senate cereal hearings, Dr. Frederick Stare, chairman of the Department of Nutrition, Harvard University School of Public Health, and Dr. W. H. Sebrell, Jr., of the Institute of Human Nutrition at Columbia University, testified that cereal with milk and sugar is a nutritionally adequate food and that evaluating the nutritional content of cereal without milk is unfair.[4] Dr. Jean Mayer, Harvard professor of nutrition, agreed with industry experts that "taken in the whole breakfast context, cereals did make an important contribution." Nevertheless, Mayer continued, "There are wide differences in nutritional value between various types of cereals, and these differences could be easily avoided if modern technology and nutritional knowledge were used to upgrade weaker products."[5]

1973–1977. In 1973, a second congressional investigation, this time by the Senate Select Committee on Nutrition and Human Needs, addressed the twin issues of nutritional value and advertising fairness. Action for Children's Television presented evidence that a child watching a particular Boston station from 7:00 A.M. to 2:00 P.M. on Saturday, October 28, 1972, would have seen 67 commercials for sugary foods, including ready-to-eat cereals. Representatives of the cereal companies, including Kellogg and General Mills, testified.[6]

In March 1973 the FDA introduced new standards for recommended daily allowances. Also in 1973 FTC Chairman Louis Engleman set up a task force in the Division of Special Projects to investigate the issue of children's advertising. During his term of office, the FTC staff was granted the use of a compulsory process that gave them the right to subpoena cereal companies for access to their market research data and advertising strategies. In 1974 the FTC staff proposed a guide for advertising that was much discussed and finally rejected in 1976. However, in 1977–1978, the debate flourished again.

1977–1978. In April 1977 ACT and CSPI presented their petitions to the FTC. These proposals included the call for a full ban on the advertisement of sugary, in-between-meal (snack) foods to children. Arguments were also presented against all foods with a high sugar content, including some cereals, and also against the practice of advertising to children in general. Shortly thereafter, in

November 1977, Kellogg ran a newspaper advertisement countering the implication that presweetened cereals are harmful or non-nutritious. A series of facts for which it claimed empirical support included:

1. Ready-sweetened cereals are highly nutritious foods.
2. Ready-to-eat cereals do not increase tooth decay in children.
3. Ready-to-eat cereal eaters skip breakfast less than non-ready-to-eat cereal eaters.
4. There is no more sugar in a one-ounce serving of a ready-sweetened cereal than in an apple or banana or in a serving of orange juice.
5. The sugars in cereals and the sugars in fruit are chemically very similar.
6. Ready-to-eat cereals provide only 2 percent of the total consumption of cane and beet sugars in the U.S.
7. On the average, when children eat ready-sweetened cereals as a part of breakfast, the nutritional content of that breakfast is greater than when they eat a non-ready-to-eat cereal breakfast.
8. Most ready-to-eat cereals are consumed with milk.
9. On the average when children eat ready-sweetened cereals as part of breakfast, consumption of fat and cholesterol is less than when they eat a non-ready-to-eat cereal breakfast.
10. The per capita sugar consumption in the U.S. has remained practically unchanged for the last fifty years.[7]

Three months later, in February 1978, the FTC staff proposed a ban on children's advertising. Its 350-page document included concerns about the effects of advertising on children, and about the nutritional value of the product advertised. This report described the preparation of commercials directed at children and the selling techniques they employ:

1. Magical promises that a product will build muscles or improve athletic performance.
2. The chase or tug of war sequence in which one character tries to take a product away from another.
3. The use of magic, singing, and dancing.
4. The use of super heroes to entice children.
5. The voice of authority.
6. The voices of children agreeing with the announcer.
7. Depictions of children outperforming adults.
8. Animation.
9. Peer group acceptance appeals.
10. Selling by characters who also appear in programming.

Three years later, in 1981, the FTC issued a second staff report. During the interim period, there were hearings, exchanges of papers, interviewing of witnesses, and—when the process was completed—600,000 pages of records.

1980–1991. Public attention shifted away from regulation of children's television advertising in 1980. The FTC Improvements Act passed in May 1980 effectively prohibited the FTC from promulgating children's advertising rules on any basis other than that of preventing deceptive advertisement. On March 31, 1981, the FTC issued its (presumably) final staff report and recommendations concerning children's advertising. It called for a halt on any further attempt to ban children's advertising, thus radically revising its initial position (there was a new administration in Washington). Nonetheless, the staff did issue a set of conclusions that implicitly warned cereal manufacturers about outstanding issues:

> The record developed during the rulemaking proceeding adequately supports the following conclusions regarding child-oriented television advertising and young children six years and under: (1) they place indiscriminate trust in televised advertising messages; (2) they do not understand the persuasive bias in television advertising; and (3) the techniques, focus and themes used in child-oriented television advertising enhance the appeal of the advertising message and the advertised product. Consequently, young children do not possess the cognitive ability to evaluate adequately child-oriented television advertising. Despite the fact that these conclusions can be drawn from the evidence, the record establishes that the only effective remedy would be a ban on all advertisements oriented toward young children, and such a ban, as a practical matter, cannot be implemented. Because of this remedial impediment, there is no need to determine whether or not advertising oriented toward young children is deceptive.[8] Staff's recommendation for this portion of the case is that the proceeding be terminated.[9]

Many of the original claims of the 1978 report were still accepted. The "practical matter" that prohibited the FTC from banning children's advertising was twofold. First, dental research had not been able to positively identify which foods were cariogenic, or cavity producing. There are too many unknown factors. Second, although children under six cannot understand the intent of a commercial message, children over six often can. To ban the advertising to one group would automatically affect the other older group. For these practical reasons—as well as a new political climate in Washington—the FTC terminated all investigative proceedings.

In 1984 the Federal Communications Commission (FCC) also eliminated its guidelines on children's advertising. The FCC had maintained voluntary guidelines that limited the number of advertisements during children's shows to 9.5 minutes each hour on Saturday and Sunday and 12 minutes an hour on other days. But a three-judge panel of the U.S. Court of Appeals reopened this issue by holding that the FCC had not sufficiently justified its policy change eliminating the established guidelines. The FCC announced in October 1987 that it was conducting new inquiries on the issue of regulating children's advertising to assess the need for new guidelines. It planned to consider new developments such as cartoon action shows based on popular children's products.[10]

This debate continued vigorously until October 1990, when Congress approved the Children's Television Act. This act restricted the time allowed for advertising during children's television programming to 10.5 minutes per hour on weekends and 12.5 minutes per hour on weekdays. (Prior to this act, advertising accounted for up to 14 minutes per hour during children's prime time.) The act also directed the FCC to write specific guidelines on the content and allowable messages of children's television commercials. Additionally, the act required the FCC to examine the increasing role of program-length commercials; that is, cartoon shows or movies featuring popular toys such as Teenage Mutant Ninja Turtles.[11] Through cartoons based on popular figures, a child is, in effect, exposed to a program-length advertisement for all products licensed by the owners of the figures presented in the cartoons. These products commonly include lunch boxes, slippers, breakfast cereals, video games, and the like. One concern is that children's food preferences will be established not by health considerations but by advertising and commercial association.

Finally, until August 1991, the FCC required only a 60-second separation between program-length commercials and advertisements for their related products. But the FCC then strengthened this restriction: Networks must separate the material with "intervening and unrelated broadcasting." The longer separation would prevent children from perceiving the program and the advertisements as parts of the same entertainment.[12]

TWO MAJOR ISSUES

Two issues have been present throughout the history of these debates. The first is whether the product (for our purposes, cereal) has significant nutritional value. The second is whether the practice of advertising to children is justified even if a product ranks high on a nutritional scale.

1. The Adequacy of Nutrition. The ACT and CSPI petitions, along with the FTC staff reports and later congressional inquiries, all attacked children's cereals on the basis of high sugar content. The initial 1978 staff report presented expert testimony from several fields on the nutritional value of ready-to-eat cereals.[13] Sugar contributes calories to the human diet but is not otherwise nutritious.[14] Ivalee McCord, chairman of the Child Development and Family Relations Section of the American Economics Association, at one time construed the matter as follows:

> At a time when a body is growing at a more rapid rate and body structures are developing, the need for quality food is crucial. There is no room in the diet for "empty calories"—those represented by most sugar-coated and snack foods. At this time children need balanced diets providing the nutrients needed for growth.[15]

With a few exceptions, manufacturers do not claim that the sugared snack foods and candies that they promote to children on television have any nutritional value apart from calories. But claims are made that presweetened cereals are "highly nutritious."[16] Manufacturers point out that most, if not all, of their cereals have been fortified by adding vitamins and minerals and that by the 1990s the sugar content had been substantially reduced. Fortification began in the early 1970s, following congressional hearings in which participants pointed out that the nutritional value of the unfortified cereals was essentially nil.[17] The manufacturers contended then, and still do, that some children are reluctant to eat breakfast at all, and that some sugar in these cereals is a necessary attraction in order to get them to swallow the now-added vitamins and minerals.[18]

This debate over nutritional value has not changed substantially in 20 years, despite modifications by manufacturers, virtually all of whom have developed attractive new products that are low in sucrose and related sugars, high in dietary fiber, high in complex carbohydrates, and low in fat. The lingering problem is that many of the most advertised and the most attractive cereals from a child's perspective have not had their sugar content decreased substantially, or have other nutritional deficiencies. Currently, some popular children's cereals have as much as 12 grams of sugar in a 3/4 cup serving—the equivalent of three teaspoons of sugar per serving—yet many are advertised as nutritious.[19] For example, Cap'n Crunch contains 45 percent sugar but is marketed as a part of a well-balanced breakfast. This marketing technique appears questionable in light of child nutritionist Ellyn Satter's comment: "Kids are not eating cereal, they are eating candy in a bowl."[20]

In response to growing concerns about food content and labeling, the American Academy of Pediatrics (AAP) issued a report in July 1991 (just prior to the congressional act) holding that food advertising directed toward children has an adverse effect on their health. The academy cited two studies, one published in 1985 and the other in 1990, that established a direct link between children watching TV and the two most prevalent health problems affecting children, obesity and cholesterol. The AAP stated that food ads promoting high-density caloric intake "may contribute to the energy imbalance that results in obesity."[21]

CSPI reported at the same time that these two prevalent problems have increased among children in the 20-year period 1971–1991: Obesity has increased 54 percent in elementary schoolchildren and 34 percent in adolescents. This new report shifted the traditional issue beyond sugared cereals and cavities to the more comprehensive health issues of obesity, cholesterol, and fiber content. But the sugar-content problem had not been forgotten. CSPI noted that in 1976, there were 5 times as many ads for high-sugar cereals as low-sugar cereals, but that by 1991, there were 17 times as many ads for high-sugar cereals as low-sugar cereals. CSPI also argued that nutritional imbalance at a young age is directly correlated with heart disease and related problems in adulthood. Therefore, failure to promote good nutrition in young children creates high health costs in the future.

In its 1991 report, the AAP called for a ban on all food commercials aimed at children, on grounds that advertising food products to children reflects food companies' concerns for profit rather than for the health of young consumers. However, Oregon Congressman Ron Wyden, a leader in the movement for control of advertising, disagreed with the academy's ban strategy for several reasons. Wyden advocated an educational strategy instead of a complete ban. Children are currently receiving images of quality built around sugar and fat; this should change so that advertisements stress the nutritional content of foods and its importance.[22]

Kellogg set an example of positive informational strategies of the sort Wyden had in mind when it aired a 30-second spot for a "good breakfast." This advertisement made no mention of particular brands. In a survey of the broadcasting of five television channels from 7:55 A.M. to 12 noon on Saturday, February 9, 1991, CSPI found that out of 222 food ads, only the Kellogg ad promoted a good breakfast. It found that no other public service announcement promoted good nutrition—the basis of a rare CSPI commendation for Kellogg.[23] CSPI found that the food ads in these broadcasts typically focused on foods that are high in sugar content, fat, and sodium. After analyzing the 222 food ads, CSPI found that 213 were for sugary cereals, candy, chocolate syrup, cookies, chips, fast foods, fruit-flavored beverages, and salty canned pasta. All are high in sugar, fat, or salt.[24] CSPI observed that many recent government policies on nutrition support its claim that these foods do cause health problems. It noted that the Departments of Agriculture and Health and Human Services, the Surgeon General, and the National Academy of Sciences have all published reports urging the American public to eat diets lower in fat, sugar, and salt, and higher in whole grains to reduce the risk of tooth decay, obesity, diabetes, and diseases such as heart disease.[25] Additionally, CSPI criticized advertised food products on grounds that few grain-containing foods use whole grain.[26]

Cereal companies defend these products by citing low sugar content per ounce per serving. However, critics argue that per ounce measurements are deceptive; children eat cereal by the bowl rather than the ounce and often take in more calories and sugar in a bowl of presweetened cereal than they should consume. Critics argue that these cereals are consumed in lieu of more nutritious products often produced by the same manufacturers—both because they taste better and because they are more heavily advertised. The recent growth of fiber-rich adult cereals illustrates the ability of cereal companies to manufacture high-fiber, low-sugar cereals that taste good, although not as good as the heavily sugared cereals.

Technological gaps no longer seem to play a significant role in these debates. Cereal manufacturers made significant developments in fiber extraction technology in the 1980s, creating cereals that are healthy and low in fat. They also substituted honey and natural fruit sugars for refined sugar. These modifications—largely in the adult cereal market—make it possible to modify the children's market in a similar way. However, shelf space, children's preferences, and competition in the industry have far overshadowed further nutrition changes.

2. The Fairness of Advertising. Advertisers and their critics agree that children's advertising should not be deceptive. However, they disagree over their classification of material as deceptive or misleading to young children. The dispute is complicated by many unanswered questions. For example, there are questions about the effect of television advertising on children; about children's cognitive abilities for processing the advertising information; about the ability of children to discriminate between the content of a program and its accompanying commercials; and about the ability of children to resist persuasive appeals even if they understand them to be commercial in character. Although research in this area is relatively recent and still somewhat sparse, a National Science Foundation (NSF) study, *Research on the Effects of Television Advertising on Children*, came to two major conclusions on these questions. The first conclusion was that television commercials do affect children:

> Children have been shown to acquire specific product information presented in food commercials. There is also preliminary evidence indicating that information about the nutritional content and value of food products can be effectively communicated to children both within commercials and in brief (five-second) slide presentations. Studies have also demonstrated shifts in children's beliefs about advertised foods following their exposure to specific commercial messages.

The second conclusion of the NSF study is that specific advertising practices—such as wording—affect the child's ability to understand and remember the message. Some have argued that these problems of comprehension are at the center of the difficulty:

> There is little evidence that children comprehend typical commercial disclaimers much before the age of 7. . . .
> However, the relationship between comprehension of intent to persuade and resistance to persuasive appeals remains uncertain.[27]

The American Academy of Pediatrics argued in its 1991 report that the "commercialization of television exploits children" because they do not understand that the intent of the ads is to sell and are ignorant of the health risks of the advertised foods. According to the AAP, the ads have a documented deleterious effect on children's health. This is the main reason the AAP called for the elimination of food advertising directed at children and asked parents to play a greater role in determining what their children eat.

Advertisers and their critics also dispute the extent of an advertiser's responsibility to the child viewer. Both parties recognize that children are not "capable of acting as rational self-interested consumers" because they lack a complete understanding of the "concepts of time, money and self" necessary to evaluate the information that the advertisers present to them.[28] However, some advertisers do not recognize an obligation to take children's limitations into account in formulating their marketing approaches.

John Culkin quotes an advertisement that appeared in a *Broadcasting* magazine whose purpose was to solicit advertising for a Boston television station. The ad was entitled "Kid Power Is Coming to Boston." It read as follows:

> If you're selling, Charlie's mom is buying. But you've got to sell Charlie first.
>
> His allowance is only 50 cents a week but his buying power is an American phenomenon. He's not only tight with his Mom, but he has a way with his Dad, his Grandma and Aunt Harriet, too.
>
> When Charlie sees something he likes, he usually gets it.[29]

Culkin questions the morality of an industry that would spend half a billion dollars a year on TV advertising directed at children in order to sell to parents: "Quite apart from the question of the real value of the advertised product, what is the propriety of the sponsor contesting the parent for control of the child? . . . Parents have enough difficulty in helping their children make wise choices without skewing the process by $500 million worth of counter-persuasion."[30]

There is empirical evidence that children influence their parents' purchases. A study done by the Harvard Business School found that "5 to 7 year olds successfully influenced parental purchases of cereals (88% of the time), snack foods (52%), candy (40%), and soft drinks (38%)." A survey of almost 600 mothers found that 75 percent of the women chose products and brands that their children requested.[31] Research has shown that, around age nine, children become highly aware of the status of particular brands and make "definite brand choices."[32] Such evidence has lead one consultant to urge manufacturers to "plant the seeds of brand loyalty at an early age. . . . It is effective to show the product big and advertise the brand, not the product, to children."[33] However strategic such instruction may be, there is still no evidence directly linking food commercials to the actual nutritional status of children.

Research indicates, however, that exposure to child-oriented television advertising is correlated with a lower degree of nutritional knowledge and lesser understanding of nutritional terms.[34] Another study demonstrated that first-grade children who viewed commercials for foods that were high in sugar selected more sugary foods, whether advertised or not.[35] These links between the watching of child-oriented or sugary food commercials and reduced levels of awareness of and orientation to nutritious foods indicate that reduced nutritional status among children may to some extent be correlated with exposure to such advertisement.

Culkin points out that, in fairness to the cereal industry, the broadcasters, and the advertising agencies, it should be acknowledged that parents and schools have a responsibility to prevent the abuse of television by children, as well as the abuse of children by television. Culkin maintains that "even the best of all possible programming does not justify the four hours a day spent by the average American in front of the TV set. In our less than perfect world, the uncomfortable fact is that we have to reform ourselves as well as the networks."[36]

The cereal industry and its advertising agencies contend that claims of unfair and deceptive practices are unwarranted and that the cereal industry is being singled out for criticism on an issue that involves numerous products, especially candy and soft drinks. In particular, opponents of federal regulation argue that:

1. Advertising to children is not unfair or deceptive.
2. Sugar in foods has been directly linked to dental caries, but not to many alleged health problems.
3. The conflict between parents and children is an inevitable part of growing up and would not disappear if Frosted Flakes and Milky Way bars were banned from TV.[37]

Opponents of proposed constraints on advertising also contend that First Amendment rights are at stake. Peter McSpadden, president of a large advertising agency, sees the primary issue as censorship: "The question is, do we have a right to market a product to a particular group—in this case, children—and does another group have the right to say, 'no, you can't'?"[38] Members of Congress have also taken seriously the censorship issue, with its implied threat to liberty. In 1978 the Senate Appropriations Committee threatened to cut off all FTC funding if the commission continued its inquiry into these issues. The majority report of the Senate committee took the position that "if the question of how many cavities for how much freedom is to be considered seriously at all, then it should be done with full Constitutional process and not as a matter of regulatory rulings."[39]

KELLOGG'S RESPONSE TO THE ISSUE OF CHILDREN'S ADVERTISING

Kellogg is the nation's largest manufacturer of ready-to-eat cereals. General Foods and General Mills, the next largest producers, have a combined total sales figure equal to Kellogg's. The Kellogg Company has been active over the years in attempting to refute the charges leveled at its cereals in the areas of nutrition and advertising.

The Nutritional Value of Kellogg Cereals. As early as 1971, the Kellogg Company formally published an ambitious corporate nutrition policy. However, it cautioned in the policy that "consumer acceptability of our products in flavor, texture and appearance is essential if they are to make any nutritional contribution." In early 1973 the Kellogg Company, along with General Mills, testified before the Senate Select Committee on Nutrition and Human Needs. Dr. Gary Costley, Kellogg's director of nutrition, argued that (1) "only a small part of a child's sugar intake comes from sweetened breakfast cereals"; (2) "a normal serving of most canned fruits contained far more sugar" than a serving of cereal; (3) presweetened cereals do not cause a child to become "hooked" on sugar; and (4) "research studies show no correlation between new dental caries and the amount of pre-sweetened cereal consumed."[40]

In October 1981 the Consumer Service Department of Kellogg printed and distributed a pamphlet entitled "Cereal Fortification," which followed its 1980 monograph *Ready-to-Eat Cereals and Nutrition*.[41] The pamphlet provided a detailed analysis or nutrient profile of Corn Flakes and Sugar Frosted Flakes. The pamphlet's purpose was to prove that Kellogg cereals, as presently fortified and when used with milk, easily provide the daily nutrient intake recommended by nutritionists. By 1972 Kellogg and all the major cereal companies had introduced 100 percent natural cereals into their product lines.[42] In 1984, Kellogg touted one such cereal, All-Bran, as being part of a diet linked to lower cancer incidence; the manufacturer strengthened those claims ten years later by marketing All-Bran Extra Fiber as possessing anticancerous qualities.[43]

Kellogg's Advertising Practices. The Kellogg Company has worked tirelessly to refute charges that its advertising makes false nutritional claims. Kellogg issued a pamphlet entitled "Advertising" in late 1979. In this pamphlet the company argued as follows:

> Kellogg's has been recognized an unprecedented seven times by *Family Health Magazine* for excellence in nutritional advertising. . . .
>
> For years we have placed great emphasis on creating honest and tasteful advertising for youngsters with messages that convey the inherent nutritional value of our products. We present these messages in a way that is not only informative and interesting, but also appropriate for a child's level of understanding.
>
> Our advertising serves not only as a product selling tool, it also stresses the importance of starting the day with a nutritious breakfast.

The Consumer Service Department at Kellogg has not directed the same level of effort at charges that its advertising practices are an unfair means of influencing children. The views of Seymour Banks, vice-president of the advertising agency that handles the Kellogg account, have been widely quoted:

> Even if a child is deceived by an ad at age four, what harm is done? He will grow out of it. He is in the process of learning to make his own decisions. . . . Even if, as many psychologists claim, a child perceives children in TV advertising as friends, not actors selling them something, what's the harm? All a parent has to say is, "Shut up or I'll belt you."[44]

Kellogg believes that the products in question are nutritious and that children would be worse off if they were not available and not advertised. William E. LaMothe, president of Kellogg at the time of the proposed FTC ban on advertising, commented:

We try to construct our commercials so that they can be entertaining, and have a message. We're convinced that if we could get every young-ster in the country to eat a ready-to-eat cereal—the nutritional informa-tion we have says they would have a better diet than the mix of things they have now with high cholesterol and high fat, or no breakfast at all. We are almost evangelistic in our thrust to try to convince youngsters to be interested in breakfast.[45]

CONTINUING ISSUES

The current non-regulatory status of the cereal market does not belie the exis-tence of pressing issues that need to be addressed. For example, in the 1990s the cereal industry has shown an inclination to defend its advertisements by pointing to the "fun" nature of food. Food is marketed to adults with an emphasis on its nutritional content, but for children advertisements must depict the product in an enjoyable atmosphere in order to be successful. Advertisers also claim that by using the fun approach the advertisements encourage children to eat, implying that children would not be motivated to eat as well without the advertising.

The motivation to select "fun" cereals may be irresistible, thanks to the introduction of such kid-oriented products as Nabisco's Teddy Grahams Breakfast Bears, Post's Croonchy Stars, Ralston's Donkey Kong, Rainbow Brite, Barbie, and Nerds Cereals, and General Mills' Undercover Bears and Rocky Road.[46] Another subscriber to this approach is General Mills's Frosted Chee-rios, which is marketed as a "fun taste" that will hopefully inspire consumers to associate "opening a bag [with] . . . starting a party."[47] Similarly, Kellogg's use of baseball star Ken Griffey Jr. in the marketing of its Frosted Flakes cereal is intended to attract young audiences. The ultimate use of this "fun" tactic is, as its name implies, General Mills's product Circus Fun. The company reported-ly promised grocery buyers that "95% of all children ages 2 through 11 will see the [Circus Fun] TV spot an average of 107 times during the cereal's first year."[48] This practice of bombarding children with ads for presweetened prod-ucts associated with "fun" toys and activities continues today.

Nonetheless, a University of Texas study showed that healthy foods are on the minds of children. When asked to draw a picture of something related to a grocery store, the majority of 150 kids drew pictures of fruit or vegetables. None drew cereal. In addition, a public service advertisement depicting veg-etables in numerous witty situations sparked children's interest. It seems likely, then, that children respond to clever advertisements for healthy products as long as they are "fun."[49]

Possibly, then, a healthier multigrain cereal such as Kellogg's Big Mixx, with its animated chicken/wolf/moose/pig character,[50] will target children with its fun imagery while still encouraging the selection of a more nutritious breakfast product. General Mills has progressed even further with its Kix mar-keting campaign, whose "no funny stuff" approach sells the nutritional value of the product directly to kids.[51] If this trend were to continue, kids might become more conscious of the important benefits (even the fun) of eating healthier, more natural, and less sweetened cereals. However, too much optimism may be unwarranted, considering that a revolution in kids' sweet-toothed tastes is unlikely. Also, as Action for Children's Television president Peggy Charren declared, "I have little hope that ethical marketing decisions will be made by American corporations in this competitive economy."[52] In light of such pessimistic concern, future options might include reconsidering some type of regulation, encouraging further parental involvement in their children's exposure to such advertisements, and more frequently airing pro-nutrition public service announcements.[53]

NOTES

1. FTC, "Staff Report on Television Advertising to Children" (February 1978), pp. 27, 29.
2. *Ibid.*, pp. 345–46.
3. "A Gadfly Buzzes around the Table," *Business Week* (September 26, 1970), p. 116.
4. Earl A. Molander, "Marketing Ready-to-Eat Breakfast Cereals at the Kellogg Company," in *Responsive Capitalism: Case Studies in Corporate Social Conduct* (New York: McGraw-Hill, 1980), p. 130.
5. *Ibid.*, p. 131.
6. *Ibid.*, p. 135.
7. *Ibid.*, App. 11-1.
8. Consumers Union of the U.S., Inc., and Committee on Children's Television, C-9, pp. 1–46, quoted in *FTC Final Staff Report and Recommendation in the Matter of Children's Advertising*, 43 Fed. Reg. 17,967, TRR No. 215–60 (1981), p. 3.
9. *FTC Final Staff Report*, p. 3.
10. Rep. Edward Markey (D-MA), chairman of the House Commerce Committee's telecommunications subcommittee, also began hearings and pressed for a bill to reimpose advertising guidelines. See Bob Davis, "FCC Is Planning to Launch an Inquiry in to Tougher Rules for Children's TV," *The Wall Street Journal*, October 8, 1987, p. 34; and "FCC Takes Second Look at Children's Advertising," *Broadcasting* (October 26, 1987), p. 54.
11. Although consumer advocacy groups hailed this strategy, President Bush withheld his signature, citing First Amendment reservations: "In an effort to improve children's television, this legislation imposes content-based restrictions on programming. The first amendment, however, does not contemplate that Government will dictate the quality or quantity of what Americans should hear. Rather, it leaves this to be decided by free media responding to the free choices or individual consumers." Barbara Gamarekian, "Ads Aimed at Children Restricted," *The New York Times*, October 18, 1990, Business section, p. 1.
12. "FCC Delays Imposing Ad Limits on Children's TV," *The Washington Post*, August 2, 1991, p. D1.
13. FTC, "Staff Report on Television Advertising to Children."
14. U.S. Department of Agriculture, *Nutritional Value of Foods, Home and Garden Bulletin*, no. 72 (April 1977), p. 24.
15. Letter to ACT, February 23, 1972. To similar effect, see Arlen, *The Science of Nutrition* 253 (2d ed. 1977).
16. This phrase was used by the president of the Kellogg Company in threatening to sue the American Dental Association for defamation of its products. See *The Washington Post*, December 2, 1971.
17. *Hearings on Dry Cereal before Consumers Subcommittee, Senate Commerce Committee*, 91st Congress, 2nd session (1970); Robert Choate, "The Sugar Coated Children's Hour," *Nation* (January 31, 1972), p. 146.
18. Kellogg's data, however, show that fewer children (5 percent) than adults (9 percent) skip breakfast, and that fewer consumers of *non*sugared cereals (5 percent) than of sugared cereals (7 percent) skip breakfast. See Kellogg, *Breakfast and Nutrition* (undated pamphlet).

19. Nanci Hellmich, "Sugary Cereal: Make It a Munchie, Not a Meal," *USA Today*, August 17, 1994, p. D6.
20. *Ibid.*
21. "The Commercialization of Children's Television," a Report of the American Academy of Pediatrics (July 1991).
22. Joanne Lipman, "Pediatric Academy Prescribes Ban on Food Ads Aimed at Children," *The Wall Street Journal*, July 24, 1991, p. B8.
23. CSPI, "Content Analysis of Children's Television Advertisements," May 1991, p. 4.
24. *Ibid.*
25. "Food Commercials on Children's TV," a statement issued in a press conference by Michael F. Jacobson, executive director of CSPI.
26. CSPI, "Content Analysis," p. 3.
27. Donald F. Roberts and Christine M. Bachen, "Mass Communication Effects," *Annual Review of Psychology* 32 (1981), section on Effects on Children and Adolescents, pp. 336, 338.
28. Lynda Sharp Paine, "Children as Consumers: An Ethical Evaluation of Children's Advertising," *Business and Professional Ethics Journal* 3, nos. 3 and 4 (Spring–Summer 1984), pp. 123-25.
29. John Culkin, "Selling to Children: Fair Play in TV Commercials," *Hastings Center Report* 8 (1978), p. 7.
30. *Ibid.*, pp. 8–9.
31. As quoted from Linda McJ. Micheli, "Kellogg Company: Sugar, Children, and T.V. Advertising" (Boston: Harvard Business School, 1979), p. 4.
32. As quoted in Jo Marney, "Kids Have Economic Power: Marketing to Youngsters Pays Long-Term Benefits," *Marketing* 96 (October 28, 1991), p. 6.
33. *Ibid.*, p. 6.
34. Alan R. Wiman and Larry M. Newman, "Television Advertising Exposure and Children's Nutritional Awareness," *Journal of the Academy of Marketing Science* 17 (no. 2), pp. 179-88.
35. Marvin E. Goldberg, Gerald J. Gorn, and Wendy Gibson, "TV Messages for Snack and Breakfast Foods: Do They Influence Children's Preferences?" *Journal of Consumer Research* 5 (September 1978), pp. 73–81.
36. Culkin, "Selling to Children," p. 9.
37. See Micheli, "Kellogg Company," p. 6. Craig Shulstad of General Mills helped us formulate the wording here, which modifies Micheli's wording.
38. *Ibid.*, p. 7.
39. *Ibid.*, p. 6.
40. Molander, "Marketing Ready-to-Eat Breakfast Cereals," p. 136.
41. The pamphlet argued that in 1955, Kellogg's "Special K" was introduced to provide higher levels of essential nutrients, and in 1966 "Product 19" was introduced for the same reason.
42. Molander, "Marketing Ready-to-Eat Breakfast Cereals," p. 132.
43. Kevin Goldman, "Advertising: Anticancer Pitch Returns," *The Wall Street Journal*, January 28, 1994, p. B2.
44. Micheli, "Kellogg Company," p. 7. Banks is not an officer of the Kellogg Company.
45. Molander, "Marketing Ready-to-Eat Breakfast Cereals," p. 138.
46. See Judann Dagnoli, "Making Breakfast Bear-Able: Popular Nabisco Cookie Sparks New Kids' Cereal," *Advertising Age* (October 16, 1989), p. 3; Julie Liesse, "General Mills' New Oatmeal is a Cover-Up," *Advertising Age* (July 16, 1990), p. 3; and Cyndee Miller, "Cereal Maker to Kids: Eat Breakfast with Barbie," *Marketing News* (September 25, 1989), p. 10.
47. Kevin Goldman, "General Mills to Launch Frosted Cheerios," *The Wall Street Journal*, July 25, 1995, p. B9.
48. As quoted in Julie Franz, "General Mills Pours Out 3rd Cereal," *Advertising Age* (March 17, 1986), pp. 2+.
49. Bruce Horovitz, "Sugary Pitches to Kids Capture a Sweet Market," *Los Angeles Times*, June 4, 1991, pp. D1, D4.
50. Julie Liesse, "Kellogg Puts $30M on Kids," *Advertising Age* (April 9, 1990), p. 1.
51. Fara Warner, "General Mills Pitches Kix Directly to Kids," *Adweek's Marketing Week* (October 21, 1991), p. 7.
52. Peggy Charren, "Marketing to Children," *Across the Board* 29 (November 1992), pp. 56-57.
53. Wiman and Newman, "Television Advertising Exposure," pp. 183–184.

BANNING CIGARETTE ADVERTISING

Beginning in the late 1950s, there was growing pressure from the health care community for a governmental study on the health hazards of smoking. The hazards had been discussed for several years, but no definite conclusions had been drawn. In response to pressure from the medical community, President Kennedy asked the surgeon general to study the risks of smoking in 1962. Thirty-four years later, in 1996, the Clinton administration, the Food and Drug Administration (FDA), and various antismoking coalitions are still vigorously attacking cigarette manufacturers for the way they market their products without respect to whom they are actually targeting. This evolving history has moved from a focus on the risk of a product to a focus on the ethics of its advertising.

THE EARLY SURGEON GENERAL'S REPORT

In the early 1960s Surgeon General Luther Terry assumed the task of evaluating over 8,000 previous studies on the effects of smoking. No new research was undertaken. The goal of the committee he assembled was to decide, "Is smoking bad?" The committee consisted of persons selected to provide as much impartiality as possible. Members of the committee included smokers and nonsmokers, none of whom had publicly taken a stand on the issue of smoking and its hazards. This committee concluded and reported that smoking was a substantial cause of certain diseases.

Government officials responded by considering the regulation of cigarette advertising. Critics of the tobacco industry claimed that advertisements that showed healthy, happy, and sexually appealing men and women smoking were encouraging increased consumption, especially by American youth. Congressional examination resulted in the passage of the Federal Cigarette Labeling and Advertising Act (1965). The purposes of the act were to provide for the uniform labeling of all cigarette packages and to inform the public of the health risks associated with smoking.[1] The act required that the warning label "*Caution: Cigarette smoking may be hazardous to your health*" be included on every package in a conspicuous location. The act went into effect on January 1, 1966, and expired on July 1, 1969.

This case was prepared by Joanne L. Jurmu and Tom L. Beauchamp and revised by Anna Pinedo, Katy Cancro, and Blaire Osgood. Not to be duplicated without permission of the holder of the copyright, © 1992, 1996 Tom L. Beauchamp.

The act preempted actions by other authorities to regulate cigarette advertising. No state or federal agency could require additional package labeling or warnings in advertisements for the life of the act. Originally, the Federal Trade Commission (FTC) had pushed to extend the act to require the warning label in advertisements.[2] Thus, the FTC was critical of Congress for not taking this and other, more sweeping courses of action.

For their part, members of the tobacco industry were reserved. They agreed that the findings of the committee were significant, but they urged further medical research into the risks of smoking. Many of the studies that the congressional committee had evaluated were statistical. The industry believed that other forms of evidence based on biomedical research of the risks of smoking should be undertaken before definite conclusions could be drawn. Tobacco producers also adopted a voluntary advertising code. They vowed that smoking would not be associated with manliness, sex appeal, or social charm in any of their ads.[3]

Cigarette consumption in 1968 was approximately 530 billion, or over 4,200 cigarettes annually per person in the United States. This was the first year since the surgeon general's 1966 report was released that cigarette consumption had declined. The federal government hoped to further this decline through the adoption of educational programs. For the fiscal year 1968 the U.S. Public Health Service (PHS) expended $4.4 million on tobacco-related education and research. While many educational programs were designed to address all Americans, PHS specifically targeted youths. Health officials believed that the best way to decrease smoking was to reach people before they started to smoke.[4]

Advertising for cigarettes involves large expenditures. In 1967 the industry spent $312 million on ads. Of this figure, 73 percent or $226.9 million was spent on television advertising.[5] Eleven percent of 1967 advertising revenues were generated by cigarette ads.[6] Combative advertising—that is, ads that try to influence brand choice—was the focus of industry attention. Some economists predicted that an ad ban could actually help existing tobacco firms by allowing them to decrease combative advertising and by preventing other firms from entering the industry.

The FTC conducted a new study based on industry figures and found that the average American was exposed to 67 cigarette commercials per month.[7] The agency concluded that such a high exposure rate was encouraging youth to begin the habit. In 1967 the FTC invoked the Fairness Doctrine with regard to cigarette commercials. The Fairness Doctrine, implemented in the 1950s, requires that broadcasters present both sides of a controversial issue. (See the case on the Fairness Doctrine in Chapter 5.) The FTC declared smoking to be a controversial issue and required that broadcasters make significant time available for anti-smoking messages. Anti-smoking interest groups were unable to afford advertising time in proportion to cigarette advertising, so broadcasters had to give them free air time. By 1970 the broadcast media had given anti-smoking messages roughly one third of cigarette-related advertising time, at a cost of $75 million.[8]

BAN PROPOSED

Two factors led to a proposal to ban cigarette ads from all broadcast media. First, the surgeon general and the U.S. Public Health Service issued a follow-up report to the 1964 study entitled "The Health Consequences of Smoking, A PHS Review." This 1967 report supported or even strengthened the 1964 conclusions. Second, in 1968 the Federal Communications Commission (FCC) announced a proposed rule to ban all broadcast ads.[9] Some groups also called for a stronger warning label that cited specific health risks or for warnings plus information on tar and nicotine content to be included on all packaging. Others favored a full ban on cigarette ads in broadcast media. The debate finally narrowed to those in favor of warnings only and those in favor of a ban on all ads.

Arguments in Support of the Ad Ban

Advocates of the ban acknowledged that adult smokers would not stop smoking even if all ads disappeared, but their hope was to prevent youths from starting. Teenagers presumably saw smoking glamorized in ads and tried to duplicate the conduct that was glorified by the ads. Ban supporters predicted that each successive generation would foster a smaller percentage of smokers and eventually smoking would be eliminated. Any risk to jobs and the tobacco industry as a whole would be minimized because those involved would have a chance to find other work and invest in other endeavors. Ban supporters maintained that tobacco was a dangerous substance, unworthy of promotion through federally regulated broadcast media.

Arguments in Opposition to the Ban

Opposition to the ban rested primarily, from the industry perspective, on questions of First Amendment rights. Tobacco is a legal product in the United States, and the federal government helps to subsidize tobacco farmers. State governments and the federal government depend on revenues generated by cigarette taxes. In 1968 the industry paid $4.1 billion in state and federal taxes.[10] With obvious state and federal backing for the manufacture of cigarettes, tobacco product manufacturers seemed to have the right to advertise their products under the freedom of speech provision of the Constitution. Banning tobacco industry ads was viewed by tobacco industry representatives as arbitrary discrimination against a targeted industry. As one advertising executive put it, "No matter how well-meaning the social scientist, the reduction of choice for 'his own good' is the first step towards totalitarianism."[11]

The primary question thus became not whether the product was a health risk, but how its use should be discouraged. Few people would deny that there are some risks associated with smoking. But opponents of a ban noted that there are many "risky" products: Eggs and milk contain cholesterol, which has been linked to heart disease; candy can lead to tooth decay and obesity; driving high-performance cars can be fatal. Opponents of an ad ban argued that one health-related ban could open the floodgates for other bans. These concerns are still at the center of the debate today.

Controversy over the character and strength of the causal link between the decision to smoke and advertising has also continued. Industry marketers often maintained that ads only induce consumers to change the brands they smoke rather than encouraging the practice of smoking per se.[12] Some studies conducted in the 1950s and 1960s found little consumer sensitivity to cigarette ads. Researchers found that ads were necessary for increasing market share, but they did little to increase aggregate demand.[13] In 1994 Thomas Lauria, a spokesman for the Tobacco Institute, defended the need for advertising by stating that "in a $48 billion domestic industry in which 40 percent of customers are constantly shifting brands, [there] is reason enough for advertising among six companies to shift market share among adult users even though the market is shrinking."[14] Armed with this information, ban adversaries claim that banning ads, or any action short of changing the status of tobacco to that of a controlled substance, would not eliminate or substantially reduce cigarette consumption.

The National Broadcasters Association (NBA) viewed the banning of advertisements for cigarettes as inevitable. The association believed that if Congress did not enact the ban, the FCC would lead broadcasters to adopt a voluntary ad ban in 1969. Their strategy was to begin phasing out ads in 1969, with final elimination set for September 1, 1973. The effects of the ban would be far-reaching because NBA membership included two thirds of all commercial networks and 40 percent of all radio stations. In 1969 broadcaster revenues from cigarette ads were over $230 million. The NBA hoped that a gradual phase-out would ease the burden on both industries.[15]

The tobacco industry fought the ban. It defended the use of ads to increase market share and cited its voluntary efforts to monitor the content of ads. The industry also pointed to other countries' failed efforts to ban cigarette advertising. Great Britain, France, Switzerland, and Italy had all banned ads before 1966. Yet each country was experiencing a positive annual growth rate of cigarette consumption between 2.7 and 8 percent.[16]

A BAN ON BROADCAST ADVERTISING

Congress amended the Cigarette Labeling and Advertising Act in 1970 in the Public Health Smoking Act. The 1970 act provided for the banning of all cigarette ads "on any medium of electronic communication subject to the jurisdiction of the Federal Communication Commission."[17] Congress allowed the industry one concession: The effective date was January 2, 1971, to permit advertising during the heavily watched football games on New Year's Day.

To the dismay of cigarette producers, the anti-smoking ads continued in the absence of cigarette ads. The industry petitioned the FCC to be permitted significant time under the Fairness Doctrine to present industry views on smoking. The FCC denied the request, stating that the dangers of smoking were now well known and the issue was no longer controversial. Thus, the FCC concluded that the Fairness Doctrine was no longer applicable to tobacco advertising and that neither anti-smoking messages nor the airing of tobacco industry views would be subsidized by broadcasters.[18]

James Hamilton studied the comparative effects of cigarette advertising and anti-smoking messages. Based on his results, Hamilton argued that "the health scare was a several-fold more potent determinant of per capita consumption than was promotional cigarette advertising, and since anti-smoking advertising simply promulgated and intensified the health scare, finding that anti-smoking ads were more potent than promotional ads does not seem surprising." In fact, Hamilton cited statistics indicating that an advertising ban would be less effective than continuing or intensifying the anti-smoking campaign. Anti-smoking messages from 1968 through 1970 lowered per capita consumption by 530.7 cigarettes per year, while on average, cigarette advertising increased it by 95.0.[19]

The ban has had the desired effect, but only to a limited degree. In 1985, per capita cigarette consumption decreased while the national population increased. This data reflected a significant decline in smoking. The trend was expected to continue, according to projections made by the Centers for Disease Control, Office of Health and Smoking. If these projections were correct, in 1994 the per capita consumption of cigarettes was an estimated 2,493, compared to the consumption of 3,370 cigarettes per capita in 1985.[20] A 1993 report by the California Department of Health Services and the University of San Diego suggests that this trend has indeed continued. Based on California's statistics alone, "smoking is at an all time low." In 1988, 26.7 percent of California's population smoked. In 1993 that number was down to 20 percent.[21]

However, the medical community, especially the American Medical Association (AMA), has not been satisfied with the results. It was disappointed that the tobacco industry was still advertising heavily, generally by switching media—from electronic to print—and undertaking sponsorship of sporting events, such as the Marlboro race car tours.

CIGARETTE ADS IN PRINT MEDIA

After the 1971 ban, newspaper advertising and sponsorship of sporting events became major means of marketing cigarettes, as is still the case today. Newspapers are probably the major source of information transmitted to the public about the dangers of smoking cigarettes. Newspapers thus have an interest both in earning revenue from cigarette advertising and in informing the public about the dangers of what they advertise. Most newspapers are businesses with two goals—making a profit and satisfying the consumer—which in the case of cigarette advertising can conflict.

The *New Republic* once commissioned reporter David Owen to write an article on cancer and the cigarette lobby. He wrote a piece sufficiently blunt in stating the issues and laying blame that the *New Republic*'s editors killed the story. According to *USA Today*, "In the candid (and no doubt regretted) words of Leon Wieseltier, the editor who assigned it, the threat of 'massive losses of advertising revenue' did it in."[22] The editors of the *New Republic* had been willing to report on the dangers of smoking and on the pressures brought by lobbyists, but they were not willing to print the forcefulness with which Owen stated his case. Owen later published his piece in the *Washington Monthly*, where he depicted the industry as using newspapers and magazines to enhance the appeal of smoking by portraying the young smoker as healthy and sexy—precisely what the industry had agreed not to do.

According to research conducted by Kenneth E. Warner, this example of burying Owen's article is but one of many cases in which American news media have refused to report the dangers of smoking for fear of decreased advertising revenue.[23] The *Washington Post*'s ombudsperson, using statistics taken from the *New York State Journal of Medicine*, found that only six out of 1,700 daily American newspapers attempt wholeheartedly to report on the dangers of smoking.[24] However, the American Newspaper Publishers Association and the Magazine Publishers Association continue to appeal to First Amendment protections of the right to advertise and to present the facts as newspapers see fit in order to justify their view that this matter should be left up to each individual newspaper.

In 1985, the AMA set a goal of having a smokeless society by the year 2000. In an effort to achieve this goal, the association proposed a total ban on all cigarette advertising. The proposed ban includes the following components: (1) no distribution of samples or discount coupons; (2) no sponsorship of sporting events; (3) no advertising by skywriting; and (4) no portrayal of smoking in films.[25]

Most, if not all, advertising associations are opposed to a ban on print cigarette ads. Ad agencies maintain that the government cannot ban an industry's ads merely because it does not like that industry's product. They remind Congress that if cigarettes are legal to sell, they should be legal to advertise. Furthermore, agencies believe that banning cigarette ads will not accomplish the goal of reducing consumption by youth. Several studies have found that young smokers are most often influenced to start smoking by friends and parents, rather than by media ads.[26]

Although the AMA's proposed ban has not been implemented, most major cigarette companies have continued to reduce their share of print advertisements. In 1985 tobacco companies purchased $375 million in advertising space, a 12 percent decline in one year. The FTC reports that the amount spent on media advertising was down to $300 million per year by 1994. However, this figure is only a fraction of the $6 billion budget spent on other advertising techniques such as giveaways, coupons, and event sponsorship.[27] Tobacco marketers decided to focus on the use of discount ads, point-of-sale displays, and sponsorship of sports events to replace print advertisements. After television ads were banned and print advertising seemed targeted for strict regulation, the cigarette industry put more than 90 percent of its marketing dollars into nonprint advertising.[28] These techniques are mostly directed to those who already smoke rather than potential smokers. For example, Philip Morris, marketer of the nation's largest selling Marlboro brand, has developed the Philip Morris magazine. The magazine, a voice for industry concerns, is distributed free of charge to 1.3 million smokers.[29]

Congressional and federal agency assessments of the cigarette ad ban are recurrent events. In 1986 the federal government completely banned the radio and television advertising of smokeless tobacco and snuff, a ban similar to that imposed on cigarette manufacturers in 1971. At the same time, and throughout his years in office, U.S. Surgeon General C. Everett Koop repeatedly expressed support for a full industry ban. In 1994, then Surgeon General Joycelyn Elders continued to support a ban on advertising specifically aimed at young people. Based on a report presented to Congress, Dr. Elders argued that "1 of 3 people ages 12 to 18 had used tobacco . . . and at least 3.1 million adolescents, or 1 in 8, are considered smokers."[30] Hearings have subsequently evaluated several alternatives to a ban. One option includes limiting ads to informational, black-and-white text-only ads containing simply the product brand name and a health warning, called "tombstone" ads. Other options would require the tobacco industry to finance a counteractive anti-smoking campaign, or would eliminate the tax deductibility of tobacco ads and promotional expenditures.[31]

New regulations proposed by the Clinton administration in 1995 continued the congressional and federal agency assessments and took into consideration many of the previously suggested restrictions. If put into effect, the Clinton plan would make even alternative methods of print advertising such as discount ads and sponsorship of sports events difficult. The new regulations are targeted at any publication in which 15 percent or more of its readers or viewers are under the age of 18. These publications are limited to tombstone ads. These rules would affect mass-market publications like *TV Guide*, *Sports Illustrated*, and other backbones of cigarette advertising, such as billboard ads in sports arenas or titles of sporting events, as well as promotional giveaways such as T-shirts and hats.[32] The industry may also be required to finance a $150 million anti-smoking advertising campaign if the proposed FDA regulations are passed.[33]

As could be expected, the prospect of such strict restrictions has provoked strong opposition from the tobacco and advertising industries. Roger L. Beahm, president of Coyne Beahm, a small advertising firm in Colfax, North Carolina that supports the tobacco industry's opposition to the advertising rules, says that "it's mind boggling in terms of the impact of these regulations. You don't need an advertising agency to produce black-and-white print text-only ads, billboards and in-store promotions. This is going to have a wide impact on not only advertisers and their agencies but the communications industry as a whole."[34] Support for the new restrictions is being generated by anti-smoking forces. Matthew Meyers of the anti-tobacco Coalition on Smoking or Health says, "The law is clear. The government can restrict commercial speech in order to further a compelling [societal] interest. . . If ever there was a case where the government stepping in will be looked on with favor by the courts, it is this one."[35] A 1994 Gallup Poll indicated that "two-thirds of Americans—including almost half of all smokers—want the U.S. government to impose greater restrictions on cigarette advertising. For 53 percent that means a total ban. And 15 percent, while they don't support a total ban, said there should be greater restrictions." Overall, this poll indicates that "interest in a total ban appears to have gone up since 1991."[36]

CIGARETTE ADS IN THE 1990s

During the 1990s, former Health and Human Services Secretary Louis W. Sullivan mounted a vigorous criticism of cigarette marketing by accusing the industry of incorrect, dishonest, and harmful advertising techniques. Sullivan was particularly distressed by the sponsorship of sporting events. The tobacco industry is firmly entrenched in the sports world with such sponsorships as the Winston Cup race car circuit. Television exposure is a major motivation for these sports sponsorships. In effect, by sponsoring sporting events and splashing their names across billboards, sailboats, or race cars, tobacco companies are purchasing the advertising exposure on television that money cannot legally buy. The most recent leader in the campaign against televised tobacco ads and the founder of the group *Doctors Ought to Care*, Dr. Alan Blum, stated, "I can find you tobacco brand logos on television every hour of every day."[37]

Sullivan judged the industry to be "trading on the prestige and image of the athletes to barter their deadly products," while suggesting in its ads that "tobacco use is compatible with good health." Sullivan criticized social inaction over the last 30 years as vigorously as he criticized the industry: "It is immoral for civilized societies to condone the promotion and advertising of products which, when used as intended, cause disability and death."[38] Sullivan and other critics have used at least two major arguments to challenge these tobacco sponsorships. First, by using athletic men and women in its ads, the tobacco industry is attempting to create an image that the products are positively related to health and fitness. This association runs counter to all collected data on both exercise and disease. Second, many children watch the sporting events live or on television. Thus, they are exposed to cigarette advertising in a way that seems to defeat the purpose of the cigarette advertising ban.

The tobacco industry has reacted sharply to these criticisms, insisting that it has a right to market its product. The industry claims that Sullivan's comments are insulting in that they suggest that people have no choice about whether they should smoke and need the government to make the decision for them. Industry officials also cite the sports world's dependence on tobacco companies' financial support. The industry, which in 1993 spent approximately $80 million in sponsoring sporting events, received some support from the athletes involved. For example, Pam Shriver, a leading tennis player in the once-popular "Virginia Slims" tour, said that critics do not understand "how our tour evolved and how it's progressing and the opportunities that Philip

Morris gave to women over the last 20 years. . . . If they asked us to endorse the product, that would be different. But personal endorsements versus [corporate] marketing vehicles that are perfectly legal are two very different things."[39]

This technique of using sports-related advertising would also be limited by the proposed FDA regulations set out by the Clinton plan. The new rules would limit the amount of exposure that ads would get by permitting only text advertising within 1,000 feet of school grounds and on billboards and buses. The sponsor of any sporting event would also have to change the name of the event that it was sponsoring. For example, the Winston Cup auto racing event would be known only as the R. J. Reynolds Cup.[40]

Even before these proposals to regulate outdoor ads for tobacco were implemented, some cutbacks had already begun to occur. Cincinnati set out in 1994 to remove any ad for tobacco products that appeared in bus shelters, buses, or outdoors. Baltimore has imposed similar regulations.[41] Philip Morris Co. has already begun to feel the affects of restricted advertising. After being accused by the Justice Department of strategically placing billboards in locations at professional sports stadiums that would frequently be shown on TV,[42] the company has agreed to reposition all ads in sports stadiums.[43] In addition to that agreement, in 1994 Philip Morris ended its 25-year connection with the Women's Tennis Association as the sponsor of the Virginia Slims tour.[44]

Target Marketing

According to the Centers for Disease Control and Prevention in Atlanta, the cigarette industry is currently losing approximately 434,000 customers a year to lung-cancer and smoking-related deaths.[45] The percentage of adults who smoke has dropped from 42.4 percent in 1965 to 25.7 percent in 1991.[46] As a result of this declining market, cigarette manufacturers need customers in alternative population segments. They currently favor advertisements that depict an optimum lifestyle, suggesting one could enjoy that lifestyle when smoking certain cigarettes.

Statistics show that almost 50 percent of smokers begin by the age of 15. Recently, a few tobacco companies have been criticized for crossing the fine line between general advertising and advertising directed at children. In 1993, of the 24.2 percent of the total population (estimated at 258 million) that smoked, 9.6 percent of those users were between the ages of 12 and 17.[47] Dr. Elders pointed out that, because tobacco companies wish to survive in a competitive market, "young people are the chief source of new customers. Each day 3,000 young people must be recruited to start smoking in order for the tobacco industry to continue at the same level of business."[48]

Although companies insist that advertising themes such as the animated "Joe Camel" and his female counterpart "Josephine Camel," introduced in 1994, do nothing more than promote the product to users, former Surgeon General Antonia Novello has spoken out against what she sees as misdirected advertising: "Today 16 percent of our youth smoke, many of whom fall into a lifetime of tobacco addiction and die prematurely from a tobacco-related disease. The use of themes in tobacco advertising that appeal to young people is disgraceful."[49] Just as defendants of the tobacco industry claim that people start smoking because of the three P's, Dr. Elders blames the allure of the five S's: slim, sexy, sociable, sophisticated, and successful.[50]

"Joe Camel," in particular, has been brought under scrutiny because of growing concern about advertising directed at youth. The California Supreme Court in San Francisco decided in 1994 to hear the case brought by a California woman against RJR's "Joe Camel" campaign. The court upheld the lawsuit because "the allegations against R.J. Reynolds were based not on smoking and health, but on a 'more general' duty imposed under state law 'not to engage in unfair competition by advertising illegal conduct,' namely, smoking by minors."[51] Alan Mansfield, the attorney representing the California woman, said that the legal challenge "will attempt to show RJR intentionally targeted minors with its ads, or that, upon learning the campaign affected youths, it failed to amend the now 6-year-old campaign." As evidence, Mansfield cites a study that suggests that teen "smokers accounted for $476 million of Camel sales in 1991, compared with just $6 million garnered before the Camel campaign."[52] This and similar cases are proceeding even though the FTC decided in June 1994 not to take action against "Joe Camel." The FTC said that there is no evidence to support the hypothesis that "Joe Camel" entices children to begin smoking.[53] This decision, together with the Freedom of Speech Act and First Amendment rights, strengthens RJR's defense arguments in its various lawsuits.

Brown and Williamson Tobacco company launched its KOOL PENGUIN campaign in the fall of 1991. Arguably, this animated penguin with a spiked haircut and Bart Simpson attitude encourages young people to take up the cigarette habit. The advertisements present the penguin as a rebellious type, with lines such as "So I'm a penguin, deal with it." This rebellious tone appears to reinforce teenage rebellion and beliefs that smoking promotes friendship and social acceptability. Brown and Williamson denied that this campaign was designed to encourage young people to start smoking: "We're interested in reaching anyone over 21," said the spokesperson. "The reaction we got in focus groups was that this is a funny, appealing and eye catching way to sell our product."[54]

Similarly, R. J. Reynolds marketed Uptown Cigarettes, menthol cigarettes targeted specifically at black Americans, but was widely criticized by anti-smoking organizations as exploiting the known fact that economically secure people are withdrawing from smoking while economically disadvantaged people continue to smoke. Since the ban on television advertising, the tobacco industry has customarily concentrated advertising on low-income sectors of the economy by placing billboards in predominantly black or ethnic neighborhoods. In response to a straightforward acknowledgment from R. J. Reynolds that the company was targeting blacks in its advertising, Johnson Publishing Company, a publisher of magazines with a primarily black readership, refused to accept advertising for Uptown, despite the fact that tobacco advertising from many different brands is a vital source of revenue for the magazines and all of it is targeted in some respect at blacks.

Such opposition to cigarette advertising is not confined to the American market. As of October 1, 1991, all cigarette advertising on television was banned throughout Europe. In addition, each European country began some form of prohibition. For example, the United Kingdom began to require tobacco advertisers to place one of six warning labels on cigarette packages including one that reads "smoking kills." In France, tobacco ads must devote 20 percent of the space to warning labels. In 1993, Hungary reinforced a total cigarette advertising ban that it started in 1978 but claims has been violated for many years. Australia passed legislation in 1992 under which tobacco advertising and sponsorship will be entirely phased out over four years. With this relatively new worldwide pressure against tobacco advertising, tobacco companies are looking for new ways to market their products effectively to both current and future users in order to survive.

A final resolution of these advertising issues will prove difficult due to the variety of conflicting interests. Any policy must balance public health concerns and free speech rights. The U.S. tobacco industry is fighting to hold on to its $48 billion market amidst declining domestic sales and continued public attention to the health hazards of smoking. It is virtually certain to hold on to a substantial market, but government regulation now threatens to destroy profitability for even major manufacturers.

NOTES

1 "Controversy Over Cigarette Advertising," *Congressional Digest* 48 (June–July, 1969), p. 168.
2. *Ibid.*
3. "Smoking: One Year Later," *Time* 87 (January 22, 1965), p. 58.
4. *Ibid.*, pp. 164–65.
5. "Controversy Over Cigarette Advertising," p. 169.
6. "Rising Battle," *Time* 93 (February 14, 1969), p. 85.
7. "Controversy Over Cigarette Advertising," p. 168
8. James L. Hamilton, "The Demand for Cigarettes: Advertising, the Health Scare, and the Cigarette Advertising Ban," *Review of Economics and Statistics* 54 (November 1972), p. 408.
9. "Rising Battle," *Time*, p. 85.
10. *Ibid.*
11. "The Moral Minefield of Cigarette Advertising," *Business and Society Review* 51 (Fall 1984), p. 14.
12. *Ibid.*, p. 13.
13. Hamilton, "Demand for Cigarettes," p. 401.
14. Warren Leary, "Surgeon General Urges Banning Cigarette Ads Aimed at the Young," *The New York Times*, February 25, 1994, p. A12.
15. "Cigarettes: Down in Ash," *Newsweek* 74 (July 21, 1969), p. 82.
16. "Where the Cigarette Men Go after the TV Ban," *Business Week* (November 21, 1970), p. 69.
17. 15 U.S.C., #1335.
18. "A Bright Spark for Cigarette Makers," *Business Week* (December 26, 1970), p. 64.
19. Hamilton, "Demand for Cigarettes," p. 408.
20. "Surveillance for Selected Tobacco-Use Behaviors—United States, 1900–1994," *Morbidity and Mortality Weekly Report* 43 (November 18, 1994), p. 7.
21. Dan Morain, "Legislature Aims Fusillade of Bills at Tobacco Industry," *Los Angeles Times*, March 10, 1993, p. A1.

22. Charles Trueheart, "The Tobacco Industry's Advertising Smoke Screen," *USA Today*, March 15, 1985, p. 3D.
23. Kenneth E. Warner, "Cigarette Advertising and Media Coverage of Smoking and Health," *New England Journal of Medicine* 312 (February 7, 1985), pp. 384-88.
24. Sam Zagoria, "Smoking and the Media's Responsibility," *The Washington Post*, December 18, 1985, p. A26.
25. "Cigarette Ads: Round Two," *Newsweek* 106 (December 23, 1985), p. 55.
26. Eugene E. Levitt and Judith A. Edwards, "A Multivariate Study of Correlative Factors in Youthful Cigarette Smoking," *Developmental Psychology* 2, no. 2 (1970), pp. 5–11; and E. E. Levitt, "Reasons for Smoking and Not Smoking Given by School Children," *Journal of Public Health* (February 1971), pp. 10–14.
27. Paul Farhi, "Clinton Mover May Doom Colorful Cigarette Ads," *The Washington Post*, August 11, 1995, p. D1.
28. Anthony Ramirez, "Advertising: Proposed Regulations," *The New York Times*, August 14, 1995, p. D6.
29. "Goodbye to Marlboro Man," *Forbes* (June 2, 1986), p. 208.
30. Warren Leary, "Surgeon General Urges Banning Cigarette Ads Aimed at the Young," *The New York Times*, February 25, 1994, p. A12.
31. Steven W. Colford, "Something Less Than Ban Seen for Cigarette Ads," *Advertising Age* (August 11, 1986), p. 59.
32. Anthony Ramirez, "Advertising: Proposed Regulations," *The New York Times*, August 14, 1995, p. D6.
33. *Ibid.*
34. *Ibid.*
35. Farhi, "Clinton Mover May Doom Colorful Cigarette Ads."
36. Steven Colford and Ira Teinowitz, "Teen Smoking and Ads Linked," *Advertising Age* 65 (February 21, 1994), pp. 1+.
37. Mitchell Zuckoff, "Kicking the Connection," *The Boston Sunday Globe*, July 2, 1995, p. 65.
38. Alison Muscatine and Spencer Rich, "Sullivan: Cut Tobacco, Sports Links," *The Washington Post*, April 11, 1991, pp. A1, A4.
39. *Ibid.*
40. Ramirez, "Advertising: Proposed Regulations," p. D6.
41. "Cincinnati Will Prohibit Outdoor Ads for Tobacco," *The New York Times*, June 4, 1994, p. A9.
42. For example, in Fenway Park in Boston, a Marlboro billboard had been placed above the right field bleachers and could be seen on TV every time the camera has a shot of a home run or a play in the outfield. See Mitchell Zuckoff, "Is It Safe or Out? US, Philip Morris Dispute Marlboro Sign at Fenway Park," *The Boston Sunday Globe*, July 2, 1995, p. 66.
43. Mitchell Zuckoff, "Kicking the Connection," *The Boston Sunday Globe*, July 2, 1995, p. 65.
44. Suein Hwang, "Philip Morris Agrees to Stop Placing Ads in View of TV," *The Wall Street Journal*, June 7, 1995, p. B5.
45. Eban Shapiro, "FTC Staff Recommends Ban of Joe Camel Campaign," *The Wall Street Journal*, August 11, 1993, p. G9.
46. "Surveillance for Selected Tobacco-Use Behaviors—United States, 1900–1994."
47. U.S. Bureau of the Census, *Statistical Abstract of the United States: 1995* (115th ed.). Washington, DC: U.S. Government Printing Office, 1995.
48. Leary, "Surgeon General Urges Banning Cigarette Ads Aimed at the Young."
49. *Ibid.*; Associated Press, "Surgeon General, AMA Seek End to 'Old Joe' Ads," *The Washington Post*, March 10, 1992, p. A3; Stuart Elliott, "Camel Cartoon Draws Buyers, Too," *The New York Times*, December 12, 1991, pp. D1, D17.
50. Leary, "Surgeon General Urges Banning Cigarette Ads Aimed at the Young."
51. Paul Barrett, "Supreme Court Gives Green Light to Suit Against Tobacco Concern's Cartoon Ads," *The Wall Street Journal*, November 29, 1994, p. A24.
52. Steven W. Colford, "Joe Camel Heads for Showdown in California Court," *Advertising Age* (December 5, 1994), p. 16.
53. Stuart Elliot, "The F.T.C. Explains Its Joe Camel Decision," *The New York Times*, June 8, 1994, p. D2.
54. Paul Farhi, "Kool's Penguin Draws Health Officials' Heat," *The Washington Post*, October 23, 1991, pp. C1, C7.

MARKETING INFANT FORMULA

On May 21, 1981, the Thirty-fourth World Health Assembly of the World Health Organization (WHO) passed a resolution adopting the International Code of Marketing of Breastmilk Substitutes, urging all member states "to give full and unanimous support to the implementation of the recommendations made by the joint WHO/UNICEF Meeting on Infant and Young Child Feeding."[1] WHO designed the code to regulate marketing practices related to prepared infant formula and other products designed as partial or total substitutes for breast milk. The code specifies that it makes recommendations, not requirements, for member nations. Article 5 of this code states:

> There should be no advertising or other form of promotion to the general public of products within the scope of this Code.
>
> Manufacturers and distributors should not provide, directly or indirectly to pregnant women, mothers or members of their families, samples of products within the scope of this Code. . . .
>
> There should be no point-of-sale advertising, giving of samples, or any other promotion device to induce sales directly to the consumer at the retail level, such as special displays, discount coupons, premiums, special sales, loss-leaders and tie-in sales, for products within the scope of this Code. . . .
>
> Manufacturers and distributors should not distribute to pregnant women or mothers of infants and young children any gifts of articles or utensils which may promote the use of breastmilk substitutes or bottle-feeding.
>
> Marketing personnel, in their business capacity, should not seek direct or indirect contact of any kind with pregnant women or with mothers of infants and young children.[2]

WHO wrote these limitations on the marketing of breastmilk substitutes to apply to all WHO-member countries. They evolved from a specific controversy that has raged for years about the marketing of prepared infant formulas in Third World countries.

In 1981 annual sales of infant formula, as marketed by approximately 20 multinational corporations, amounted to roughly $2 billion. Third World sales

This case was prepared by Martha W. Elliott and Tom L. Beauchamp and revised by Anna Pinedo, Jennifer Givens, and Kier Olsen. Not to be duplicated without permission of the holder of the copyright, © 1989, 1992, 1996 Tom L. Beauchamp.

were no less than $690 million.[3] Abbott Laboratories, through its Ross Laboratories nutritional division, is the largest domestic manufacturer of infant formula in the United States. Switzerland-based Nestlé, S.A., with over 50 percent percent of total sales, dominates the Third World market. Chicago-based Abbott/Ross has a far smaller percentage of the remaining Third World market. Several companies, including Mead Johnson (Bristol-Myers) and Wyeth Laboratories (American Home Products) share the remainder of the market.[4]

Since 1970 Abbott/Ross and Nestlé have been involved in a controversy over the ethical responsibilities of marketing infant formula in Third World countries. Critics have questioned the morality of *any* infant formula marketing in the Third World and the morality of specific promotional claims and marketing techniques. The controversy has been played out in various health organizations (for example, UNICEF, the World Health Organization, and the Pan American Health Organization), the popular press, consumer boycotts organized primarily by religious groups, the annual meetings of the corporations involved, the Securities and Exchange Commission (SEC), the courts, and federal and international hearing rooms.

The triggering charges were that, in Third World countries, corporations (1) prepared infant formula that is dangerous if improperly used; (2) used aggressive marketing tactics to encourage women to choose bottle feeding and thereby cause a decline in breast-feeding; and (3) failed to emphasize the importance of breast-feeding. In Third World countries the use of prepared infant formulas often is complicated by ignorance and consequent failure to understand the instructions and by poverty. Poor sanitation, lack of adequate water supplies, and improper facilities for cleaning and storing supplies lead women to improperly cleanse the bottles and to mix the formula with impure water. Due to the high cost of infant formula (it can cost 25 to 40 percent of a Third World family's income), mothers sometimes overdilute the preparation to make it go further. Overdilution coupled with bacterial contamination leads to malnutrition, diarrhea, and increased susceptibility to infectious disease.

Marketing strategies to sell infant formula in Third World countries have included direct mass media advertising by radio, television, newspapers, and billboards. Companies also distribute free samples through health professionals in hospitals and clinics. The provision of free samples can be detrimental to breast-feeding because formula use may irreversibly suppress lactation, leaving the mother with no choice but to continue with the formula. The samples are occasionally distributed by milk nurses, company employees dressed like nurses who visit prospective and new mothers at home and in hospitals. Critics have denounced the use of these milk nurses as a deceptive practice, because these company employees are easily confused with bona fide nurses. Critics view these promotional strategies as a major cause of the decline of breast-feeding in some Third World countries.

Critics who see breast-feeding as a free and available resource consider formula unnecessary. Although prepared infant formulas do provide adequate nourishment if properly used, breast-feeding is almost universally agreed to be the superior way to feed infants (assuming a healthy mother).

However, complex situations can be masked by imprecise use of the phrase "Third World countries." Each of these countries is substantially different from the others, and within each the socioeconomic backgrounds of mothers using the formula vary dramatically. Perhaps three fourths of the women in the Third World are not in the cash economy of their country and could not purchase formula even if they wanted to. For example, the Algerian government permits no advertising whatsoever, but it distributes in excess of 20 million pounds of infant formula per year. Breast-feeding rates remain high in this country.[5]

The history of the infant formula debate is marred by lack of clarity and disagreement about all of the relevant cause-and-effect relationships and about the importance of related cultural practices. Health and nutritional experts disagree as to the exact relationship between bottle feeding and infant mortality and morbidity and as to the continuing decline of breast-feeding. Experts do, however, agree that these relationships are complex and multicausal.

In 1970 Dr. Derrick B. Jelliffe, then head of the Caribbean Food and Nutrition Institute in Jamaica, brought the problem of "bottle illness" to the attention of Abbott/Ross, Nestlé, and other infant formula manufacturers. He charged that "infant morbidity and mortality in general were linked in a significant way to the promotion and use of commercial formulas." Jelliffe recommended that prepared formulas be entirely withdrawn from developing countries.[6] Other medical and nutritional experts joined him in favoring the complete demarketing of infant formula and the regulation of the industry as part of a more comprehensive plan of government control.

In 1971 an *ad hoc* committee of the United Nation's Protein Advisory Group observed that "the extensive introduction and indiscriminate promotion of expensive processed milk-based infant foods in some situations may constitute a grave threat to the nutritional status of the infants for whom they are intended." In 1974 the governing body of the World Health Organization passed a resolution that stressed the problems caused by advertisements promoting the superiority of bottle feeding over breast-feeding. The resolution urged member countries to "review sales promotion activities on baby foods and to introduce appropriate remedial measures, including advertisement codes and legislation where necessary."[7]

However, other medical and nutritional experts disagreed with these views. A group led by Dr. Fernando Monkeberg of the Institute of Nutrition and Food Technology at the University of Chile maintained that more serious health and nutrition problems would exist if prepared infant formulas were *not* available. The group argued that the decline in breast-feeding "was largely independent of prepared infant formula promotion." It insisted "that data on morbidity and mortality had to be examined as part of a much larger picture that included maternal nutrition, sanitation, access to health care, purchasing power, education, lactation failure due to family disruption, [and] urbanization with subsequent life-style changes." The UN's Protein Advisory Group modified its earlier position on the basis of a series of international meetings on infant nutrition. Although still critical of industry promotional practices, the group's report included the recommendation that "infant formulas be developed and introduced to satisfy the special needs of infants who are *not* breast fed."[8]

A study conducted by Jose Villar of the Johns Hopkins School of Hygiene and Public Health and Jose M. Belizan of the Institute of Nutrition of Central America and Panama supported the availability of prepared infant formula when used properly in the poorer countries:

> UNSUPPLEMENTED human milk from a well-nourished, well-motivated mother is all that a baby in optimal nutritional condition may require to sustain growth and good nutrition during the first 4 to 6 months of life. To have a healthy, well-nourished, and well-developed infant, the mother must have laid down adequate nutritional reserves during pregnancy, including subcutaneous fat, and must remain well-fed throughout lactation. Unfortunately, in developing countries poorly nourished women give birth to infants of low birthweight (LBW) in bad environmental and sanitary conditions. The frequency of low birthweight (<2500g) is, on the average, three times greater in underdeveloped (17 percent) than in developed countries (6 percent). In some areas 30–40 percent of birthweights may be below 2500g with 75 percent of the infants intrauterine-growth-retarded (IUGR). IUGR infants are the ones most at risk of perinatal death, illness, and subsequent handicap. . . .
>
> A healthy, well-nourished woman must be prepared for successful lactation in two ways:
>
> (a)   by the physiological changes of pregnancy, especially the accumulation of fat reserves. . . .
>
> (b)   by an increased dietary intake during lactation. . . .
>
> Neither of the two physiological processes required for successful lactation is found in poorly nourished mothers from developing countries and these women are, from their first pregnancy, in a state of general "maternal depletion," characterized by progressive weight loss and/or specific nutritional deficiencies.[9]

Villar and Belizan conclude that in the case of malnourished children born to already malnourished mothers, breast-feeding alone neither corrects "malnutrition nor modifies its basic course. When the infant is already malnourished at birth, as are about 40 percent in developing countries, breast-feeding alone during the first four months of life is unlikely to provide adequate nutrition."[10] Villar and Belizan do not take a general position on the controversy surrounding economic and sanitation factors or about marketing practices in the Third World. Like many other scientific studies on this topic, theirs supports the contention that infant formula is not inherently dangerous, yet its abuse may be unavoidable in the face of consumer misuse.

There is also no conclusive evidence to establish a causal link between infant formula advertising and the decline in breast-feeding. Dr. William

Foege, then director of the Centers for Disease Control in Atlanta, examined this relationship and found that significant declines in breast-feeding could be measured in only three countries—Taiwan, Malaysia, and Singapore—which all had comparatively low infant mortality rates.[11]

THE ABBOTT/ROSS RESPONSE

David Cox, then head of Ross Laboratories, agreed with many of the criticisms leveled at some of the companies that market infant formula. He disagreed, however, with both the notion that infant formula sales are responsible for the decline in breast-feeding and across-the-board condemnations of infant formula producers (by the press, the public, and specific action groups). Cox pointed out that infant mortality is closely related to the general level of a country's economic and technological development, the health status of the population, child spacing, the nutritional and educational status of the mother, and the availability of adequate supplies of pure water. He also noted that "infant mortality is often highest in areas where lactation is universal and extended, for example, in the rural areas of the Third World."[12] Cox agreed, however, that breast-feeding is the desirable means of infant feeding and should not be unnecessarily replaced by substitutes: "Breast milk is a relatively inexpensive, nutritionally ideal first food for infants. As a natural fertility regulator, exclusive breast-feeding tends to increase the spacing between births; additionally, its immunological properties can be passively transmitted to the newborn, offering some protection from environmental insult."[13]

Cox held that, despite accusations to the contrary, Abbott/Ross has consistently demonstrated responsible stewardship:

> In 1972, we published our first Marketing Code of Ethics in Developing Countries; it was later strengthened in 1977.
>
> We were the first member of industry to develop such an ethical regulation and believe it remains the most stringent one in the industry. For the most part, our code development was but a clarification of policies already in place and based on the following three marketing philosophies:
>
> (1) Breast-feeding is superior and the preferred method of feeding;
> (2) Our marketing practices should in no way discourage the adoption of breast-feeding; and
> (3) Promotion of our product is limited to the health professional community.
>
> It is our belief that health professionals are best qualified to evaluate and recommend the appropriate use of our products for babies in their care. It is our policy, that where no health care counseling is available, the use of our product is inappropriate.

New labels stress the importance of breast-feeding as the most desirable feeding for infants. The labels also include written and graphic instructions for use, emphasize that the product should only be used under the supervision of a qualified health professional, and warn against the dangers of improper preparation.[14]

Other Abbott/Ross measures initiated to control infant formula abuses include (1) placing an insert in each carton of formula asking Third World distributors to limit the product to consumers who can afford and properly prepare the product; (2) a similar request to Third World health professionals; (3) the limitation of samples to health professionals; (4) the reduction of sample size from 250 grams to 125 grams to preclude the chances of interference with the establishment of lactation; (5) the elimination of bonuses to employees based on sales; and (6) the banning of nurses' uniforms for nurses and midwives hired as company representatives.

Abbott/Ross has also undertaken an extensive program to promote maternal and child health in the Third World. It has a permanent team that includes a nutritionist, an anthropologist, a medical education specialist, and a pediatric consultant to study infant nutrition, formula, and breast-feeding in the Third World. As a result, the company has undertaken projects such as the preparation of posters, sample radio announcements, and films advocating the merits of breast-feeding for distribution to Third World health ministries, and the development of instructional material for training traditional birth attendants in the Arab world.[15]

THE NESTLÉ RESPONSE

A campaign against the Nestlé Corporation began in 1974. First, a Swiss political organization published a United Kingdom report on infant formula marketing in developing countries under the title "Nestlé Kills Babies." In response, the company filed a libel suit in a Swiss court. Nestlé won the libel suit, but the court called on the company to adjust its marketing practices in Third World countries. The court cited questionable mass advertising and sales promotion techniques.[16] Nestlé was also the target of a worldwide boycott initiated in 1977 by the Infant Formula Action Coalition (INFACT). Other church and local groups joined this effort to form the International Nestlé Boycott Committee (INBC). INFACT called for Nestlé to stop mass media advertising, distribution of free infant formula samples, use of milk nurses, and promotion through the medical profession.

Whereas Abbott/Ross relies on health professionals for the distribution and promotion of its products, Nestlé, primarily a producer and distributor of foods, relies more on mass advertising. Nestlé advertised its infant formula on billboards, posters, through radio and television messages, and in newspapers and booklets. The company provided free samples to hospitals and health professionals. Critics of Nestlé cite the following radio message as an example of its aggressive advertising:

> Bring up your baby with love and Lactogen.
> Important news for mothers/Now Lactogen is even better, because it contains more proteins plus vitamins and iron, all essential for making your baby strong and healthy.
> Lactogen Full Protein now has an even creamier taste and is guaranteed by Nestlé.
> Lactogen and love.[17]

Nestlé has made changes in its advertising and marketing tactics as a result of criticism for using gift schemes and premiums to promote its milk products, for establishing baby clubs,[18] and for using milk nurses (or, as the company prefers to say, mothercraft nurses). The company suspended "all consumer advertising of infant formula products in developing countries in order to reevaluate the role of advertising in educating Third World peoples about the use of infant formula."[19] The company has also changed the outfits worn by the mothercraft nurses from white nurses' uniforms to colored company uniforms.

Nestlé agreed early to endorse the "principle" behind the marketing code recommended by the World Health Assembly. On March 16, 1982, the company agreed to abide strictly by the code in the 120 countries in which its product is marketed.[20] Nestlé created the Infant Formula Audit Commission, chaired by former U.S. Senator Edmund Muskie, to review the company's compliance with the WHO code and to investigate any charges of abuse. However, Nestlé executives have voiced concerns over the prohibition of contact between company representatives and consumers. The company holds that improvements in labeling are not adequate to fulfill often illiterate consumers' need for accurate information and that a "show and tell" approach is necessary:

> What we're talking about is not necessarily the *right* but the *responsibility* of industry to communicate with its consumers. . . . If consumers—mothers in this case—are not given adequate instructions which can help them to use a product correctly, there are certain circumstances under which a manufacturer could be held responsible. So if you say, "Treat it like lettuce and just put it on the shelves" you are neglecting what is seen as a manufacturer's basic responsibility to do everything in his power to ensure that the product he sells is used correctly and appropriately.[21]

CONTINUING CRITICISMS

Certain church, medical, and public health groups continue to criticize Abbott/Ross, Nestlé, and other manufacturers. An ecumenical agency of the National Council of Churches argues that corporate "development" often means *creating* a market for a product (that is, creating a need that previously did not exist). They hold Abbott/Ross and Nestlé responsible for increasing the incidence of infant malnutrition and mortality. They are willing to agree that an infant formula product can be benign in developed countries, but they believe that the same product can endanger health and welfare levels in underdeveloped countries.

This group has occasionally met with representatives of Abbott/Ross. The company believes it has done all it can to satisfy the proposed changes in marketing, but the church group cites two remaining problems. First, the company continues to offer "large quantities of free formula" that flow through health professionals to mothers. Second, the company continues to pay its representatives to sell its products. However, the church group has also cited Abbott's code of marketing ethics as making important strides in proper marketing. The group further holds that the effectiveness of the code will depend more on how progressively the company monitors its implementation, including the reporting of abuses, than on the actual wording.

Numerous medical and public health groups have arranged and joined a boycott of Nestlé products. The following official statement (concerning the WHO Code of Marketing of Breastmilk Substitutes) by the board of directors of the Ambulatory Pediatric Association is representative of these concerns:

Despite claims to the contrary, marketing of infant formula influences maternal feeding practices. In recent testimony before the House Subcommittee on International Economic Policy and Trade, Carl Taylor, Professor and Head of the Department of International Health at the Johns Hopkins School of Hygiene and Public Health, presented some evidence: Massive advertising and availability of formula have been associated with a decline in breast-feeding in oil-rich Arab countries so that only 15 percent of mothers are nursing their babies at 3 months of age. In 1977 in Papua, New Guinea, promotion of infant formula was banned and feeding bottles could only be obtained with prescriptions from health workers. Breast-feeding increased from 65 percent to 88 percent, and by 1980 there was a statistically significant association with decreased incidence of gastroenteritis and malnutrition. With the institution of practices to encourage breast-feeding in an area in rural Costa Rica, neonatal mortality from diarrheal infections decreased from 3.9/1,000 in 1976 to near zero in 1980. . . .

Recent hearings by the House Subcommittee on Domestic Marketing, Consumer Relations, and Nutrition and an administrative petition by Public Advocates, Inc. to "alleviate domestic infant formula misuse" indicate growing public concern about the policies of infant formula manufacturers in the United States. The free distribution of formula within health facilities makes health professionals conduits for free advertising.[22]

Abbott/Ross vigorously denies that these claims have been adequately validated in New Guinea, the Arab countries, or elsewhere. Both Nestlé and

Abbott/Ross continue to insist they are providing a product vitally needed by some Third World infants in a way that is not detrimental to the ideal of breast-feeding. Furthermore, they believe that no solid evidence linking infant formula sales to the decline of breast-feeding has yet been produced.[23] Abbott/Ross argues that it has developed a good marketing code and is attempting to enforce it. Tom McCollough of Ross Laboratories argues, in addition, that this controversy is a cover for a number of other agendas that are less openly discussed. In particular, he mentions the conflicts between private enterprise and centralized ownership and between conservative and liberal philosophies.[24]

Nestlé signed a joint statement with the International Nestlé Boycott Committee on January 24, 1984, ending the six-year boycott against Nestlé. The INBC had gradually narrowed its points of disagreement to four concerns: (1) the use of educational materials, (2) hazard warnings on bottle labels, (3) personal gifts to health professionals, and (4) distribution of supplies. Douglas A. Johnson, the national chairperson of the Infant Formula Action Coalition, explained, "The signing of the joint statement . . . represented the [WHO] Code's transition from an urgent moral mandate to the accepted business practice by the largest and singly most important actor [concerning infant formula] in the world."[25]

Despite the end of the Nestlé boycott, the controversy continued. In a May 1986 WHO meeting, member states endorsed new WHO/UNICEF guidelines. These stringent guidelines specify the conditions under which it is advisable to bottle feed an infant and recommend the use of a wet nurse or a breast-milk bank.[26] In October 1988 a public interest group, Action for Corporate Accountability, criticized Nestlé and American Home Products for documented violations of the provisions in the prevailing codes. They were accused of reneging on the most crucial point in the agreement to end the boycott, the promise to restrict the supply of free samples to hospitals. As a result, critics initiated a new boycott. These corporations acknowledge passing out free supplies, but claim to have limited the supply to a small number of infants who need formula while in the hospital. But critics charged that the only rationale for hospital supply in the first place was to entice women to bottle feed their infants.[27]

RECENT DOMESTIC ISSUES

In the early 1990s, these controversies continue, but they have spread from a Third World focus to domestic issues in the United States. The marketing strategies of the industry's leaders have been the subject of serious investigation and litigation by the Federal Trade Commission and several states. The three major players in the formula market whose practices are at issue are Abbott/Ross, Bristol-Myers Squibb, and American Home Products. Rather than spending money on consumer advertising, these companies have carefully created a loyal group of doctors and hospitals to whom they dispense free samples. Their objective is that new mothers will take the free formula home and become loyal to the brand. This strategy has proved to be extremely successful.

However, in 1988 Nestlé expanded into the U.S. market and added to the already heated competition by selling a formula made by Carnation, its U.S. subsidiary. Also that year, the federal government determined that states must buy all infant formula for federal programs such as the Women, Infants, and Children program (WIC) from a single manufacturer in order to keep costs down.[28] Previously, a mother could obtain any brand of formula that her doctor recommended—most likely a formula from the manufacturer (that is, Abbott/Ross) that owned exclusive rights to distribution in that particular hospital. However, upon inception of this requirement, it became immediately apparent that the lower-priced Carnation might have an edge in competing for WIC contracts.

Abbott/Ross and Bristol-Myers have taken a particularly vigorous line against Carnation, sometimes using aggressive tactics to block its entrance into the market and to hamper its potential for success. These companies pointed to Carnation's connection with Nestlé's Third World marketing and its use of mass media promotions directed at mothers. They also criticized Carnation for its advertised claim that its product does not cause allergic reactions. Carnation agreed to drop this claim after competitor complaints and an FDA investigation.

However, these corporations continued to engage in controversial strategic practices. As company and industry records indicate, Abbott/Ross (whose relationships with hospitals were deep-seated and financially rewarding) renewed a line of attack against consumer advertising that had been developed by that company and Bristol-Myers Squibb in a formula-industry code of behavior. The American Academy of Pediatrics (AAP) followed suit by reiterating its disapproval of such advertising, a move that some allege to have been motivated by a desire to preserve financially rewarding relationships with the industry leaders. Although the AAP's position was ostensibly driven by concern over the reduction in the percentage of breast-feeding mothers, a 1993 investigation revealed that this concern might not be the only concern. As an internal AAP document stated, "If there is a marketing war, there may be a shift in industry's distribution of funds and the AAP may have to cut back on anticipated income from industry."[29] As of 1993, formula makers contributed approximately $1 million each year to the AAP. However, James E. Strain, executive director of the AAP, denies any connection between the Academy's views and industry contributions.[30]

The AAP position statement also raised questions about the marketing practices of the larger companies. The letter urged AAP members to pressure hospitals to cease accepting formula makers' financial incentives in the form of grants for education and research and free baby bottles in exchange for exclusive rights to supply their brand of formula. It also criticized the common practice of giving free samples to mothers when they left the hospital. The latter recommendation may be seen as allowing Carnation and Gerber an inroad to penetrate markets that were formerly closed to them. However, as the infant nutrition director at Nestlé's Carnation unit commented, "To say that the academy's position [against advertising] was damaging to our launch is perhaps the biggest understatement you can make."[31]

By criticizing the practice of direct consumer advertising by Carnation and Gerber (which had also just begun to market an infant formula product), this letter and statements by Abbott/Ross and Bristol in effect closed off the only avenue by which these new competitors could enter the market. Because both companies lacked those lucrative and long-time links with the medical field on which their competitors relied, consumer advertising was their only channel into a highly competitive market. Although the AAP can perhaps not be faulted for releasing such a position letter, antitrust laws forbid anti-advertising agreements among competitors (regardless of alleged benevolent motives). For this reason, the Federal Trade Commission (FTC) charged both Bristol and Abbott/Ross in June 1991 with conspiring to eliminate new competition by releasing their industry code of behavior.

The FTC also accused these two companies, along with American Home Products, of fixing infant formula prices in government nutrition programs in 1990.[32] Two Florida supermarket companies participated in a suit against the manufacturers for price fixing at the retail level.[33] Allegations against Abbott were still more serious. In May 1993, the company faced several state-specific lawsuits[34] as well as consolidated antitrust litigation that resulted in a $140 million settlement. In addition to charges of violating antitrust law by barring competition, the company was accused of ethical violations such as destroying relevant documents after being subpoenaed by Florida officials, unreasonably increasing prices, and contributing large cash sums to the AAP and individual physicians and hospitals. Although officials from the implicated manufacturers repeatedly denied any wrongdoing, total settlement payments by all three companies exceeded $230 million.[35]

This venerable war among formula industry competitors continues. As of early 1995, dozens of hospitals were refusing to distribute free formula samples to new mothers in the form of "discharge packets." In a joint venture, the World Health Organization and UNICEF propose to certify as "Baby Friendly" those maternity wards that discourage formula-company marketing; two hundred U.S. hospitals say they intend to join the voluntary certification program.[36] Many other hospitals would like to follow suit but serve too many indigent mothers to be able to afford to do so.

Cost is becoming a central issue in this competitive market. In October 1994 American Home released a lower-priced version of Abbott's Similac formula.[37] As the WIC program continues to facilitate the lowering of prices and the number of hospitals who ban discharge packs burgeons, some doubt that the larger companies' marketing methods and high-priced products will allow them to continue to hold the majority of the market share. Others worry that if the maternity ward is closed off as a major marketing device and competitors continue to wage price wars, formula makers will begin to advertise widely on television. Although Gerber already does so, the prospect of an industrywide televised battle for consumer loyalty is daunting. Such a move would conceivably threaten to further reduce the U.S. breast-feeding rate, representing an even more dramatic disregard of overwhelming medical evidence that breast milk, not formula, is better for babies.[38]

NOTES

1. Thirty-fourth World Health Assembly, "International Code of Marketing of Breastmilk Substitutes," World Health Assembly 34.22 (May 21, 1981), p. 1. Passed under Article 23 of the WHO Constitution.
2. *Ibid.*, p. 7.
3. David O. Cox, "The Infant Formula Issue: A Story in Escalation and Complication," a paper delivered at the Conference on Business Environment/Public Policy and the Business School of the 1980s, College Park, MD, July 12–17, 1981, p. 5.
4. Earl A. Molander, "Abbott Laboratories Puts Restraints on Marketing Infant Formulas in the Third World," in his *Responsive Capitalism: Case Studies in Corporate Social Conduct* (New York: McGraw-Hill, 1980), p. 265.
5. Based on data supplied in correspondence by Tom McCollough of Ross Laboratories.
6. Molander, "Abbott Laboratories," p. 266.
7. David Vogel, "Infant Formulas," in his *Lobbying the Corporation: Citizen Challenges to Business Authority* (New York: Basic Books, 1978), p. 189.
8. Molander, "Abbott Laboratories," p. 267.
9. Jose Villar and Jose M. Belizan, "Breastfeeding in Developing Countries," *Lancet* (September 19, 1981), pp. 621–22.
10. *Ibid.*, p. 623.
11. Carol Adelman, "Closing the Book on Infant Formula Fears," *The Wall Street Journal*, June 19, 1986, p. 30.
12. Cox, "Infant Formula Issue," p. 2.
13. *Ibid.*
14. *Ibid.* In note 3, Cox is referring to a policy and organizational difference between Abbott/Ross and some competitors. Abbott/Ross manufactures pharmaceuticals and health care products, not food products. Abbott/Ross therefore has marketed its products by calls on professionals, rather than through mass marketing practices.
15. *Ibid.*
16. "Infant Formula: An Activist Campaign," reprinted from *Europe's Consumer Movement: Key Issues and Corporate Responses* (Geneva: Business International, S.A., n.d.), p. 9.
17. Marjorie Chan, "Nestlé under Fire for Hyping Infant Formula," in George A. Steiner and John F. Steiner, eds., *Casebook for Business, Government, and Society*, 2d ed. (New York: Random House, 1980), p. 197.
18. *Ibid.*
19. John A. Sparks, *The Nestlé Controversy—Anatomy of a Boycott* (Grove City, PA: Public Policy Education Fund, n.d.).
20. Philip J. Hilts, "Nestlé to Comply with Tougher Code on Infant Formula," *The Washington Post*, March 17, 1982, p. A8.
21. "Infant Formula: An Activist Campaign," p. 13.
22. "Statement," *Pediatrics* 68, no. 3 (September 1981), pp. 432–33.
23. Cox, "Infant Formula Issue," p. 7.
24. McCollough correspondence.
25. Susan Jenks, "Nestle Boycott Ends, Firm Revises Tactics," *The Washington Times*, January 27, 1984.
26. Adelman, "Closing the Book," p. 30.
27. Carol-Linnea Salmon, "Milking Deadly Dollars from the Third World," *Business & Society Review* 68 (Winter 1989), pp. 43–48.
28. Marcia Berss, "Baby Milk Wars," *Forbes* 150 (October 26, 1992), pp. 153–54.
29. Thomas M. Burton, "Spilt Milk: Methods of Marketing Infant Formula Land Abbott in Hot Water," *The Wall Street Journal*, May 25, 1993, p. A7.
30. *Ibid.*
31. *Ibid.*

32. Berss, "Baby Milk Wars," p. 153.
33. Priscilla Donegan, "Formula Controversy Rocks the Cradle," *Progressive Grocer* 70 (February 1991), p. 107.
34. See, for example, *State of Florida, ex. rel. Butterworth v. Abbott Laboratories*, 1993-1 Trade Cases 70,241. Here, state officials and three supermarket chains accuse Abbott of conspiring with competitors regarding the pricing and marketing of infant formula.
35. Burton, "Methods of Marketing Infant Formula Land Abbott in Hot Water," p. A1.
36. Andrea Gerlin, "Hospitals Wean from Formula Makers' Freebies," *The Wall Street Journal*, December 29, 1994, pp. B1+.
37. Richard Gibson, "American Home to Offer Low-Price Infant Formula," *The Wall Street Journal*, Oct. 26, 1994, p. B7.
38. In fact, one study showed that, whereas only 59.3 percent of breast-fed infants experienced illness, 92.9 percent of formula-fed infants became ill. Unfortunately, the nation fell far short of the U.S. Surgeon General's goal of increasing the breast-feeding rate to 75 percent by 1990. As of early 1995, the rate remained below 60 percent. Gerlin, "Hospitals Wean From Formula Makers' Freebies," p. B1.

H. B. FULLER IN HONDURAS: STREET CHILDREN AND SUBSTANCE ABUSE

Resistol is manufactured by H. B. Fuller S.A., a subsidiary of Kativo Chemical Industries, S.A., which in turn is a wholly owned subsidiary of the H. B. Fuller Company of St. Paul, Minnesota.[1] Kativo sells more than a dozen different adhesives under the Resistol brand name in several countries in Latin America for a variety of industrial and commercial applications. In Honduras the Resistol products have a strong market position.

Three of the Resistol products are solvent-based adhesives designed with certain properties that are not possible to attain with a water-based formula. These properties include rapid set, strong adhesion, and water resistance. These products are similar to airplane glue or rubber cement and are primarily used in shoe manufacturing and repair, leatherwork, and carpentry.

Even though the street children of each Central American country may have a different choice of a drug for substance abuse, and even though Resistol is not the only glue that Honduran street children use as an inhalant, the term *Resistolero* stuck and has become synonymous with all street children, whether they use inhalants or not. In Honduras Resistol is identified as the abused substance.

HONDURAS

The social problems that contribute to widespread inhalant abuse among street children can be attributed to the depth of poverty in Honduras. In 1989, 65 percent of all households and 40 percent of urban households in Honduras were living in poverty, making it one of the poorest countries in Latin America.[2] Between 1950 and 1988 the increase in the Honduran gross domestic product (GDP) was 3.8 percent, only slightly greater than the average yearly increase in population growth. In 1986 the Honduran GDP was about U.S. $740 per capita and has grown only slightly since. Infant and child mortality rates are high, life expectancy for adults is 64 years, and the adult literacy rate is estimated to be about 60 percent.

In the 1970s the Honduran government relied on external financing to invest in the physical and social infrastructure and to implement development programs intended to diversify and improve the economy. Government spending increased 10.4 percent a year from 1973. By 1981 the failure of many of

This case was prepared by Norman Bowie and Stefanie Ann Lenway. Reprinted by permission. Not to be duplicated without the permission of the authors.

these development projects led the government to stop financing state-owned industrial projects. The public sector failures were attributed to wasteful administrative mismanagement and corruption. Left with little increase in productivity to show for these investments, Honduras continues to face massive budgetary deficits and unprecedented levels of external borrowing.

The government deficit was further exacerbated in the early 1980s by increasing levels of unemployment. By 1983 unemployment reached 20–30 percent of the economically active population, with an additional 40 percent of the population underemployed primarily in agriculture. The rising unemployment, falling real wages, and low level of existing social infrastructure in education and health care contributed to the low level of labor productivity found in the Honduran economy in the early 1980s. Unemployment benefits were very limited and only about 7.3 percent of the population was covered by social security.

Rural-to-urban migration has been a major contributor to urban growth in Honduras. The urban population grew at more than twice the rural population rate in the 1970s. Tegucigalpa, the capital of Honduras, has had one of the fastest population increases among Central American capitals, growing by 178,000 between 1970 and 1980, with a projected population of 975,000 by the year 2000. Honduras's second largest city, San Pedro Sula, is projected to have a population of 650,000 by the year 2000.

The slow growth in the industrial and commercial sectors has not been adequate to provide jobs for those moving to the city. The migrants to the urban areas typically move first to *cuarterias* (rows) of connected rooms. The rooms are generally constructed of wood with dirt floors, and they are usually windowless. The average household contains about seven persons, who live together in a single room. For those living in the rooms facing an alley, the narrow passageway between buildings serves both as a sewage and waste disposal area and as a courtyard for as many as 150 persons.

Although more than 70 percent of the families living in these *cuarterias* have one member with a permanent salaried job, few can survive on that income alone. For stable extended families, this income is supplemented by entrepreneurial activities such as selling tortillas. Given migratory labor, high unemployment, and income insecurity, many family relationships are unstable. Often the support of children is left to mothers. Children are frequently forced to leave school and support the family income through shining shoes, selling newspapers, or guarding cars, which can bring in essential income. If the mother has become sick or dies, some children are abandoned to the streets.

KATIVO CHEMICAL INDUSTRIES S.A.

Kativo celebrated its fortieth anniversary in 1989. It is now one of the 500 largest private corporations in Latin America. In 1989 improved sales in most of Central America were partially offset by a reduction in sales in Honduras.

Walter Kissling, the chairman of the board of Kativo and senior vice-president for international operations for H. B. Fuller, has the reputation of giving the country managers of Kativo a high degree of autonomy. Local managers often have to respond quickly because of unexpected currency fluctuations. He comments that "In Latin America, if you know what you are doing, you can make more money managing your balance sheet than by selling products."[3] The emphasis on managing the balance sheet in countries with high rates of inflation has led Kativo management to develop a distinctive competence in finance.

In spite of the competitive challenge of operating under unstable political and economic conditions, in its annual report (1989, p. 8), the management of Kativo stressed the importance of going beyond the bottom line:

> Kativo is an organization with a profound philosophy and ethical conduct, worthy of the most advanced firms. It carries out business with the utmost respect for ethical and legal principles and its orientation is not solely directed to the customer, who has the highest priority, but also to the shareholders, and communities where it operates.

In the early 1980s Kativo, which was primarily a paint company, decided to enter the adhesive market in Latin America. Its strategy was to combine Kativo's marketing experience with H. B. Fuller's products. Kativo found the adhesive market potentially profitable in Latin America because of the lack of strong competition. Kativo's initial concern in entering the adhesives market was building market share. Resistol was the brand name for all adhesive products, including the water-based school glue.

KATIVO AND THE STREET CHILDREN

In 1983 Honduran newspapers carried articles about police arrests of *Resistoleros*—street children who drugged themselves by sniffing glue. In response to these newspaper articles, Kativo's Honduras advertising agency, Calderon Publicidad, informed the newspapers that Resistol was not the only substance abused by Honduran street children and that the image of the manufacturer was being damaged by using a prestigious trademark as a synonym for drug abusers.[4] Moreover, the glue-sniffing problem was not caused by something inherent in the product but was a social problem. For example, on one occasion the agency complained to the editor requesting that he "make the necessary effort to recommend to the editorial staff that they abstain from using the brand name Resistol as a synonym for the drug, and the adjective Resistolero, as a synonym for the drug addict."

The man on the spot was Kativo Vice-President Humberto Larach ("Beto"), a Honduran, who headed Kativo's North Adhesives Division. Nine countries, including all of Central America, Mexico, the Caribbean, and two South American countries (Ecuador and Colombia), reported to him. He had become manager of the adhesives division after demonstrating his entrepreneurial talents managing Kativo's paint business in Honduras.

Beto had proven his courage and his business creativity when he was among 105 hostages taken by guerrillas from the Communist Popular Liberation Front in the Chamber of Commerce building in downtown San Pedro Sula, Honduras. Despite firefights between the guerrillas and government troops, threats of execution, and being used as a human shield, Beto had sold two clients (fellow hostages) who had previously been buying products from Kativo's chief competitor! Beto also has a reputation for emphasizing the importance of "making the bottom line," an important part of the Kativo corporate culture.

By the summer of 1985 more than corporate image was at stake. As a solution to the glue-sniffing problem, social activists working with street children suggested that oil of mustard, allyl isothiocyanate, could be added to the product to prevent its abuse. They argued that a person attempting to sniff a glue with oil of mustard added would find it too powerful to tolerate. Sniffing it has been compared to getting an "overdose of horseradish." An attempt to legislate the addition of oil of mustard received a boost when Honduran Peace Corps volunteer Timothy Bicknell convinced a local group called the "Committee for the Prevention of Drugs at the National Level" of the necessity of adding oil of mustard to Resistol. All members of the committee were prominent members of Honduran society.

Beto, in response to the growing publicity about the *Resistoleros*, requested staff members of H. B. Fuller's U.S. headquarters to look into the viability of oil of mustard as a solution with special attention to side effects and whether it was required or used in the United States. H. B. Fuller's corporate industrial hygiene staff found 1983 toxicology reports that oil of mustard was a cancer-causing agent in tests run with rats. A 1986 toxicology report from the Aldrich Chemical Company described the health hazard data of allyl isothiocyanate as:

Acute Effects
May be fatal if inhaled, swallowed, or absorbed through skin.
Carcinogen.
Causes burns.
Material is extremely destructive to tissue of the mucous membranes and upper respiratory tract, eyes and skin.

Prolonged contact can cause:
Nausea, dizziness and headache.
Severe irritation or burns.
Lung irritation, chest pain and edema which may be fatal.
Repeated exposure may cause asthma.

In addition the product had a maximum shelf-life of six months.
To the best of our knowledge, the chemical, physical and toxicological properties have not been thoroughly investigated.

In 1986 Beto contacted Hugh Young, president of SAFE (Solvent Abuse Foundation for Education) and gathered information on programs SAFE had developed in Mexico. Young, who believed that there is no effective deterrent to substance abuse, took the position that the only viable approach to substance abuse was education, not product modification. He argued that reformulating the product is an exercise in futility because "nothing is available in the solvent area that is not abusable." With these reports in hand, Beto attempted to persuade Resistol's critics, relief agencies, and government officials that adding oil of mustard to Resistol was not the solution to the glue-sniffing problem.

During the summer of 1986 Beto had his first success in changing the mind of someone in the press. Earlier in the year Marie Kawas, an independent writer and journalist, wrote an article sympathetic to the position of Timothy Bicknell and the Committee for the Prevention of Drugs in Honduras. In June Beto met with her and explained how both SAFE and Kativo sought a solution that was not product oriented but was directed at changing human behavior. She was also informed of the research on the dangers of oil of mustard (of which additional information had been obtained). Kawas then wrote a new article:

Education Is the Solution for Drug Addiction
LA CEIBA. (By Marie J. Kawas). A lot of people have been interested in combating drug addition among youths and children, but few have sought solutions, and almost no one looks into the feasibility of the alternatives that are so desperately proposed. . . .

Oil of mustard (allyl isothiocyanate) may well have been an irresponsible solution in the United States of America during the sixties and seventies, and the Hondurans want to adopt this as a panacea without realizing that their information sources are out of date. Through scientific progress, it has been found that the inclusion of oil of mustard in products which contain solvents, in order to prevent their perversion into use as an addictive drug, only causes greater harm to the consumers and workers involved in their manufacture.

At first Beto did not have much success at the governmental level. In September 1986, Dr. Rosalis Zavala, head of the Mental Health Division of the Honduran Ministry of Health, wrote an article attacking the improper use of Resistrol by youth. Beto was unsuccessful in his attempts to contact Dr. Zavala. He had better luck with Mrs. Norma Castro, governor of the State of Cortes, who after a conversation with Beto became convinced that oil of mustard had serious dangers and that glue sniffing was a social problem.

Beto's efforts continued into the new year. Early in 1987 Kativo began to establish community affairs councils, as a planned expansion of the worldwide company's philosophy of community involvement. These employee committees had already been in place in the United States since 1978.

A company document stated the purposes of community affairs councils:

To educate employees about community issues.
To develop understanding of, and be responsive to, the communities near our facilities.
To contribute to Kativo/H. B. Fuller's corporate presence in the neighborhoods and communities we are a part of.

To encourage and support employee involvement in the community.

To spark a true interest in the concerns of the communities in which we live and work.

The document goes on to state that "We want to be more than just bricks, mortar, machines and people. We want to be a company with recognized values, demonstrating involvement and commitment to the betterment of the communities we are a part of." Later that year the Honduran community affairs committees made contributions to several organizations working with street children.

In March 1987 Beto visited Jose Oqueli, vice-minister of Public Health, to explain the philosophy behind H. B. Fuller's community affairs program. He also informed him of some of the health hazards with oil of mustard, and they discussed the cultural, family, and economic roots of the problem of glue sniffing among street children.

In June 1987 PRIDE (Parents Resource Institute for Drug Education) set up an office in San Pedro Sula. The philosophy of this organization is that through adequate *parental* education on the drug problem, it would be possible to deal with the problems of inhalant use. PRIDE is a North American organization that had taken international Nancy Reagan's "just say no" approach to inhalant abuse. Like SAFE, PRIDE took the position that oil of mustard was not the solution to glue sniffing.

PRIDE introduced Beto to Wilfredo Alvarado, the new head of the Mental Health Division in the Ministry of Health. As an adviser to the Congressional Committee on Health, Dr. Alvarado was in charge of preparing draft legislation and evaluating legislation received by Congress. Together with Dr. Alvarado, Kativo staff worked to prepare draft legislation to address the problem of inhalant-addicted children. At the same time, five members of Congress drafted a proposed law that required the use of oil of mustard in locally produced or imported solvent-based adhesives.

In June 1988 Dr. Alvarado asked the congressional committee to reject the legislation proposed by the five members of Congress. Alvarado was given 60 days to present a complete draft of legislation. In August 1988 Dr. Alvarado retired from his position. With his resignation, Kativo lost its primary communication channel with the Congressional Committee on Health. This was critical because Beto was relying on Alvarado to help ensure that the legislation reflected the technical information that he had collected.

The company did not have an active lobbying or government-monitoring function in Tegucigalpa, the capital, which tends to be isolated from the rest of the country. (In fact, the company's philosophy has generally been not to lobby on behalf of its own narrow self-interest.) Beto, located in San Pedro Sula, had no staff support to help him monitor political developments. He did this in addition to his daily responsibilities. His ability to keep track of political developments was made more difficult by the fact that he traveled about 45 percent of the time outside Honduras. It took over two months for Beto to learn of Alvarado's departure from government. When the legislation was passed in March, he was completely absorbed in reviewing strategic plans for the nine country divisions that report to him.

On March 30, 1989, the Honduran Congress voted the legislation drafted by the five members of Congress into law. After the law was passed, Beto spoke to the press about the problems with the legislation. He argued that

> This type of cement is utilized in industry, in crafts, in the home, schools, and other places where it has become indispensable; thus by altering the product, he said, not only will the drug addiction problem not be solved, but rather, the country's development would be slowed.
>
> In order to put an end to the inhalation of Resistol by dozens of people, various products which are daily necessities would have to be eliminated from the marketplace. This is impossible . . . since it would mean a serious setback to industry at several levels . . . .
>
> There are studies that show that the problem is not the glue itself, but rather the individual. The mere removal of this substance would immediately be substituted by some other, to play the same hallucinogenic trip for the person who was sniffing it.

H. B. FULLER: THE CORPORATE RESPONSE

In late April 1986, Elmer Andersen, H. B. Fuller chairman of the board, received the following letter:

4/21/86

Elmer L. Andersen
H. B. Fuller Co.

Dear Mr. Andersen:

I heard part of your talk on public radio recently, and was favorably impressed with your philosophy that business should not be primarily for profit. This was consistent with my previous impression of H. B. Fuller Co. since I am a public heath nurse and have been aware of your benevolence to the nursing profession.

However, on a recent trip to Honduras, I spent some time at a new home for chemically dependent "street boys" who are addicted to glue sniffing. It was estimated that there are 600 of these children still on the streets in San Pedro Sula alone. The glue is sold for repairing *tennis shoes* and I am told it is made by H. B. Fuller in Costa Rica. These children also suffer toxic effects of liver and brain damage from the glue. . . .

Hearing you on the radio, I immediately wondered how this condemnation of H. B. Fuller Company could be consistent with the company as I knew it before and with your business philosophy.

Are you aware of this problem in Honduras, and, if so, how are you dealing with it?

That a stockholder should write the 76-year-old chairman of the board directly was significant. Elmer Andersen is a legendary figure in Minnesota. He was responsible for the financial success of H. B. Fuller from 1941 to 1971. He also served a brief term as governor and was extraordinarily active in civic affairs. In 1990 he was elected Minnesotan of the Year, and thousands of citizens attended his eightieth birthday party, which was held on the steps of the state capitol building in St. Paul.

Three years later the Resistol issue was raised dramatically and visibly for a second time by a stockholder. On June 7, 1989, Vice-President for Corporate Relations Dick Johnson received a call from a stockholder whose daughter was in the Peace Corps in Honduras. Her question was how a company such as H. B. Fuller could claim to have a social conscience and continue to sell Resistol which is "literally burning out the brains" of children in Latin America.

Johnson was galvanized into action. This complaint was of special concern because he was about to meet with a national group of socially responsible investors who were considering including H. B. Fuller's stock in their portfolio. Fortunately Karen Muller, director of community affairs, had been keeping a file on the glue-sniffing problem. Within 24 hours of receiving the call, Dick had written a memo to CEO Tony Andersen.

In that memo Dick had articulated some basic values that had to be considered as H. B. Fuller wrestled with the problem:

1. H. B. Fuller's explicitly stated public concern about substance abuse.
2. H. B. Fuller's "Concern for Youth" focus in its community affairs projects.
3. H. B. Fuller's reputation as a socially responsible company.
4. H. B. Fuller's history of ethical conduct.
5. H. B. Fuller's commitment to the intrinsic value of each individual.

Whatever solution was ultimately adopted would have to be consistent with these values. In addition, Dick suggested a number of options including that H. B. Fuller withdraw from the market or perhaps alter the formula to make Resistol a water-based product so that sniffing would no longer be an issue.

Tony responded by suggesting that Dick create a task force to find a solution and a plan to implement it. Dick decided to accept Beto's invitation to travel to Honduras to view the situation firsthand.

Dick understood that this problem crossed functional and divisional responsibilities. Given H. B. Fuller's high visibility as a socially responsible corporation, the glue-sniffing problem had the potential for being a public relations nightmare. The brand name of one of H. B. Fuller's products had become synonymous with a serious social problem. Additionally, Dick understood that this was an issue larger than product misuse: It had social and community ramifications. The issue is substance abuse by children, whether the substance is an H. B. Fuller product or not. As a part of the solution, a community relations response was required. Therefore, he invited Karen Muller to join him on his trip to Honduras.

Karen recalled a memo she had written about a year earlier directed to Beto. In the memo she had articulated her version of a community relations approach as distinguished from the government relations approach that Beto had been following. In that memo Karen said,

> This community relations process involves developing a community-wide coalition from all those with a vested interest in solving the community issue—those providing services in dealing with the street children and drug users, other businesses, and the government. It does require leadership over the long-term both with a clear set of objectives and a commitment on the part of each group represented to share in the solution, . . .

In support of the community relations approach Karen argued that

1. It takes the focus and pressure off H. B. Fuller as one individual company.
2. It can educate the broader community and focus on the *best* solution, not just the easiest ones.
3. It holds everyone responsible: the government, educators, H. B. Fuller's customers, legitimate consumers of our product, social service workers, and agencies.
4. It provides H. B. Fuller with an expanded good image as a company that cares and will stay with the problem—that we are willing to go the second mile.
5. It can de-politicize the issue.
6. It offers the opportunity to counterbalance the negative impact of the use of our product name Resistol by re-identifying the problem.

Karen and Dick left for a four-day trip to Honduras on September 18. Upon arriving they were joined by Beto; Oscar Sahuri, general manager for Kativo's adhesives business in Honduras; and Jorge Walter Bolanos, vice-president and director of finance, Kativo. Karen had also asked Mark Connelly, a health consultant from an international agency working with street children, to join the group. They began the process of looking at all aspects of the situation. Visits to two different small shoe manufacturing shops and a shoe supply distributor helped to clarify the issues around pricing, sales, distribution, and the packaging of the product.

A visit to a well-run shelter for street children provided them with some insight into the dynamics of substance abuse among this vulnerable population in the streets of Tegucigalpa and San Pedro Sula. At a meeting with the officials at the Ministry of Health, the issue of implementing the oil of mustard law was reviewed, and the Kativo managers offered to assist the committee as it reviewed the details of the law. In both Tegucigalpa and San Pedro Sula, the National Commission for Technical Assistance to Children in Irregular Situations (CONATNSI), a countywide association of private and public agencies working with street children, organized meetings of its members at which the

Kativo managers offered an explanation of the company's philosophy and the hazards involved in the use of oil of mustard.

As they returned from their trip to Honduras, Karen and Dick reflected on what they had learned. They agreed that removing Resistol from the market would not resolve the problem, which was extremely complex. The use of inhalants by street children is a symptom of Honduras's underlying economic problems—problems that have social, cultural, and political aspects as well as simply economic dimensions.

Honduran street children are from a wide variety of circumstances. Some are true orphans while others are abandoned. Some are runaways, while others are working the streets to help support their parents' insufficient income. Children doing street jobs or begging usually earn more than the minimum wage. Despite this, these children are often punished if they bring home too little. This creates a vicious circle because the children would rather be on the street than home—a situation that increases the likelihood that they will fall victim to drug addiction. The problems of the street children are exacerbated by the lack of opportunities for young people and by the fact that the regulations concerning school attendance are not enforced. In addition, the policies sometimes abuse street children.

Karen and Dick realized that Resistol appeared to be the drug of choice for young street children. However, the street children seemed to obtain the drug in a number of different ways. There was not a clear pattern, and hence, the solution could not be found in simply changing some features of the distribution system. Children might obtain the glue from legitimate customers, small shoe repair stalls, by theft, from "illegal" dealers, or from third parties who purchased Resistol from legitimate stores but then sold the product to children. For some persons the sale of Resistol to children could be profitable.

Resistol was available in small packages, which made it more affordable, and the economic circumstances of a country such as Honduras made this packaging economically sensible.

The government had a reputation for being unstable. As a result there was a tendency for people working with the government to hope that new policy initiatives would fade away within a few months. Moreover, in government there is a large amount of turnover of officials, little knowledge of H. B. Fuller and its corporate philosophy, and a great desire for a quick fix. Although it was on the books for six months by the time of their trip, the law requiring oil of mustard in Resistol still had not been implemented. Moreover, the country was only three months away from major national elections. During meetings with government officials, it appeared to Karen and Dick that no further actions would be taken as current officials waited for the outcome of the election.

Kativo company officers, Jorge Walter Bolanos and Humberto Larach, discussed continuing the government relations strategy, hoping that the law might be repealed or modified. They also were concerned with the damage done to H. B. Fuller's image. Karen and Dick thought the focus should be on community relations. From their perspective, efforts directed toward changing the law seemed important but would do nothing to help with the long-term solution to the substance-abuse problems of the street children.

Much of the concern for street children is found in private agencies. The chief coordinating association is CONATNSI, created as a result of a seminar sponsored by UNICEF in 1987. CONATNSI began its work in 1988 under the direction of a general assembly and board of directors elected by the general assembly. Its objectives include (1) improving the quality of services, (2) promoting interchange of experiences, (3) coordinating human and material resources, (4) offering technical support, and (5) promoting research. Karen and the others believe that CONATNSI has a shortage of both financial and human resources. Yet, this association appeared to be well organized and emerged as a potential intermediary for the company.

As a result of their trip, they knew that a community relations strategy would be extremely complex and risky. H. B. Fuller is committed to a community relations approach to this problem, but what would a community relations solution look like in Honduras? The H. B. Fuller mission statement does not provide a complete answer. It does indicate that H. B. Fuller has responsibilities to its Honduran customers and employees regarding oil of mustard. But what additional responsibilities does it have? What impact can one company have in solving a complex social problem? How should the differing emphases in the perspectives of Kativo and its parent, H. B. Fuller, be handled? What does corporate citizenship require in situations such as this?

REFERENCES

Acker, Alison, *The Making of a Banana Republic*. Boston: South End Press, 1988.
H. B. Fuller Company, *A Fuller Life: The Story of H. B. Fuller Company: 1887–1987*. St. Paul: H. B. Fuller Company, 1986.
Rudolph, James D., ed., *Honduras: A Country Study*, 2d ed. Washington DC: U.S. Department of the Army, 1984.
Sheehan, Edward, *Agony in the Garden: A Stranger in Central America*. Boston: Houghton Mifflin, 1989.

NOTES

1. The subsidiaries of the North Adhesives Division of Kativo Chemical Industries, S.A. go by the name "H. B. Fuller (Country of Operation)," that is, H. B. Fuller S.A. Honduras. To prevent confusion with the parent company we will refer to H. B. Fuller S.A. Honduras by the name of its parent, "Kativo." The H. B. Fuller Company was founded in 1887 by Harvey Fuller in St. Paul as a manufacturer of glue, mucilage, inks, blueing, and blacking. The founder was an inventor of a flour-based wet paste that paperhangers found especially effective. Harvey's oldest son Albert joined his father in 1888, and the company grew rapidly, making its first acquisition, the Minnesota Paste Company, in 1892.
2. The following discussion is based in part on *Honduras: A Country Study*, 2d edition, ed. James D. Rudolph (Washington, DC: U.S. Department of the Army, 1984).
3. Eric Schine, "Preparing for Banana Republic U.S." *Corporate Finance* (December 1987).
4. Unless otherwise indicated all references and quotations regarding H. B. Fuller and its subsidiary Kativo Chemical Industries S.A. are from company documents.

McALEER V. AT&T

Daniel McAleer was a $10,500-per-year service representative who handled orders for telephone service in AT&T's Washington, DC, Long Lines Division. In 1974 he asked for a promotion that he did not receive. Instead, a staff assistant named Sharon Hulvey received the promotion. She was qualified for the job, but she was not as qualified as McAleer because she had less seniority and had scored slightly lower on the company's employee evaluation scale. The job was given to Hulvey because of an affirmative action program at AT&T. McAleer claimed that he had been discriminated against on the basis of sex. He then brought a lawsuit against AT&T to ask for the promotion, differential back pay, and $100,000 in damages (on grounds of lost opportunity for further promotion). Joined by his union (Communications Workers of America), he also claimed that AT&T had undermined the ability of the union to secure employment rights to jobs and fair promotions under the relevant collective bargaining agreement.

Some historical background is essential to understand how this situation arose, and why AT&T acted as it did.

HISTORICAL BACKGROUND

The U.S. Equal Employment Opportunity Commission (EEOC) had long been in pursuit of AT&T on grounds of its discriminatory practices. In 1970 the EEOC claimed that the firm engaged in "pervasive, system-wide, and blatantly unlawful discrimination in employment against women, blacks, Spanish-surnamed Americans, and other minorities."[1] The EEOC argued that the employment practices of AT&T violated several laws, including the Civil Rights

This case was prepared by Tom L. Beauchamp and revised by Joanne L. Jurmu. Sources consulted include *McAleer v. American Telephone and Telegraph Company*, 416 F.Supp. 435 (1976); Earl A. Molander, *Responsive Capitalism: Case Studies in Corporate Social Conduct* (New York: McGraw-Hill, 1980), pp. 56–70; Theodore Purcell, "Management Development: A Practical Ethical Method and a Case," unpublished; "A.T.&T. Denies Job Discrimination Charges, Claims Firm Is Equal Employment Leader," *The Wall Street Journal*, December 14, 1970, p. 6; "A.T.&T. Makes Reparation," *Economist* 246 (January 27, 1973), p. 42; Byron Calame, "Liberating Ma Bell: Female Telephone Workers Hit Labor Pact, Says Men Still Get the Best Jobs, More Pay," *The Wall Street Journal*, July 26, 1971, p. 22; "FCC Orders Hearing on Charge that A.T.&T. Discriminates in Hiring," *The Wall Street Journal*, January 22, 1971, p. 10; "Federal Agency Says A.T.&T. Job Bias Keeps Rates from Declining," *The Wall Street Journal* December 2, 1971, p. 21; Richard M. Hodgetts, "A.T.& T. versus the Equal Employment Opportunity Commission," in *The Business Enterprise: Social Challenge, Social Response* (Philadelphia: W.B. Saunders Company, 1977), pp. 176–82. Not to be duplicated without permission of the holder of the copyright, © 1992, 1996 Tom L. Beauchamp.

Acts of 1866 and 1964, the Equal Pay Act of 1963, and the Fair Employment Practices Acts of numerous states and cities. In hearings the EEOC maintained that AT&T suppressed women workers and that for the past 30 years "women as a class have been excluded from every job classification except low paying clerical and telephone-operator jobs."[2] AT&T denied all charges brought against it, claiming that its record demonstrated equality of treatment for minorities and women. It produced supporting statistics about minorities in the workforce, but the EEOC vigorously challenged all of these statistics.

In the spring of 1972 the Department of Labor intervened and assumed jurisdiction in the matter. After a period of negotiation, a final agreement was reached on December 29, 1972. The Department of Labor proposed an out-of-court settlement and AT&T entered a Consent Decree, which was accepted by a Philadelphia court on January 18, 1973. This agreement resulted in AT&T's paying $15 million in back wages to 13,000 women and 2,000 minority-group men and giving $23 million in raises to 36,000 employees who had presumably suffered because of previous policies.

Out of this settlement came an extensive, companywide affirmative action recruitment and promotion program. AT&T set rigorous goals and intermediate targets in 15 job categories to meet first-year objectives. The goals were determined by statistics regarding representative numbers of workers in the relevant labor market. The agreement also stated that if, during this campaign, its progress was to fall short of deadlines, AT&T would then have to depart from normal selection and promotion standards by more vigorously pursuing affirmative action goals.[3]

At the same time, AT&T had a union contract that established ability and merit as the primary qualifications for positions, but also required that seniority be given full consideration. This contract stood in noticeable contrast to the Consent Decree, which called for an affirmative action override that would bypass union-contract promotion criteria if necessary to achieve the affirmative action goals. Therefore, the decree required that under conditions of a target failure, a *less* qualified (but *qualified*) person could take precedence over a more qualified person with greater seniority. This condition applied only to promotions, not to layoffs and rehiring, where seniority continued to prevail.

McALEER AND THE COURTS

The McAleer case came before Judge Gerhard A. Gesell, who held on June 9, 1976, that McAleer was a faultless employee who became an innocent victim through an unfortunate but justifiable use of the affirmative action process. More specifically, Gesell ruled that McAleer was entitled to monetary compensation (as damages) but was not entitled to the promotion because the discrimination the Consent Decree had been designed to eliminate might be perpetuated if Hulvey were not given the promotion. The central thrust of Gesell's ruling is as follows:

> After the filing of the Philadelphia complaint and AT&T's contemporaneous answer, and following an immediate hearing, the Court received

from the parties and approved a Consent Decree and accompanying Memorandum of Agreement which had been entered into by the governmental plaintiffs and AT&T after protracted negotiation. This settlement was characterized by Judge Higginbotham as "the largest and most impressive civil rights settlement in the history of this nation."

. . . "Affirmative action override" requires AT&T to disregard this standard [seniority] and choose from among basically qualified female or minority applicants if necessary to meet the goals and timetables of the Consent Decree and if other affirmative efforts fail to provide sufficient female or minority candidates for promotion who are the best qualified or most senior. . . .

This entire process occurred without the participation of Communication Workers of America (CWA), the certified collective bargaining representative of approximately 600,000 nonmanagement employees at AT&T and the parent union with which plaintiff Local #2350 is affiliated. Although it was consistently given notice in the Philadelphia case of the efforts to reach a settlement, and although it was "begged . . . to negotiate and litigate" in that proceeding, 365 F. Supp. at 1110, CWA persistently and repeatedly refused to become involved. . . .

Judge Higginbotham presently has before him and has taken under advisement the question of modification of the Consent Decree because it conflicts with the collective bargaining agreement. . . .

It is disputed that plaintiff McAleer would have been promoted but for his gender. This is a classic case of sex discrimination within the meaning of the Act, 42 U.S.C. § 2000e-2(a)(2). That much is clear. What is more difficult is the issue of defenses or justifications available to AT&T and the question of appropriate relief under the circumstances revealed by this record. McAleer seeks both promotion and damages. The Court holds that he is entitled only to the latter.

General principles of law also support plaintiff McAleer's right to damages. It is true that AT&T was following the terms of the Consent Decree, and ordinarily one who acts pursuant to a judicial order or other lawful process is protected from liability arising from the act. . . . But such protection does not exist where the judicial order was necessitated by the wrongful conduct of the party sought to be held liable. . . .

Here, the Consent Decree on which the defendant relies *was necessary only because of AT&T's prior sex discrimination.* Under these circumstances the Decree provides *no defense against the claims of a faultless employee such as McAleer.* . . . [Italics added]

Since McAleer had no responsibility for AT&T's past sex discrimination, it is AT&T rather than McAleer who should bear the principal burden of rectifying the company's previous failure to comply with the Civil Rights Act of 1964. An affirmative award of some damages on a "rough justice" basis is therefore required and will constitute an added cost which the stockholders of AT&T must bear.

In the year that Judge Gesell's decision was reached, the same Judge (A. Leon) Higginbotham that Gesell mentioned rejected the new union petition to eliminate the affirmative action override from the Consent Decree—a petition that Gesell had considered pending. Higginbotham went out of his way to disagree with Gesell, saying that he had wrongly decided the case. He found AT&T to have immunity as an employer because of its history with and commitments to a valid affirmative action plan. However, because he was hearing a union case, Higginbotham's ruling did not directly overturn or otherwise affect Gesell's ruling. AT&T's lawyers—Mr. Robert Jeffrey, in particular—felt strongly that Judge Gesell's arguments were misguided and that Judge Higginbotham did the best that he could at the time to set matters right.

AT&T and McAleer settled out of court for $14,000, with $6,500 of it going to legal fees for McAleer's attorney. Both McAleer and Hulvey continued their employment at AT&T. Mr. Jeffrey, AT&T's lawyer, maintained that this case was an aberration and that subsequent legal developments vindicated his point of view. From the moral point of view, Mr. Jeffrey believed that both Judge Gesell's ruling and the law being promulgated at the time in the White House deserved the most serious ethical scrutiny and criticism.[4]

REVERSE DISCRIMINATION IN 1996

Numerous large firms have continued to adopt voluntary affirmative action plans to foster the promotion and hiring of women and minorities. Whenever such plans are adopted, questions inevitably arise about the practice of substituting one type of discrimination for another. In March 1987, the U.S. Supreme Court decided a case involving reverse discrimination that many believe set a strong precedent for future affirmative action plans. In this case, *Johnson v. Transportation Agency*,[5] the majority held the affirmative action plan to be proper because it

1. Was intended to *attain*, not *maintain*, a balanced workforce
2. Did not unnecessarily trammel the rights of male employees or create an absolute bar to their advancement
3. Expressly directed that numerous factors be taken into account, including qualifications of female applicants for particular jobs.

Justice Brennan stated in the Court's opinion that "[o]ur decision was grounded in the recognition that voluntary employer action can play a crucial role in furthering Title VII's purpose of eliminating the effects of discrimination in the workplace and that Title VII should not be read to thwart such efforts."[6] Many firms view this and related Supreme Court decisions[7] as encouraging the continuation of affirmative action plans already in place and the adoption of new plans where they have not previously existed. However, corporate America and American courts continue to be divided over both the morality and legality of affirmative action plans such as the one that generated the McAleer case. Many firms continue to adopt plans almost identical to the one that led to the promotion of Hulvey rather than McAleer, whereas other firms insist that these policies involve immoral forms of discrimination.

In March 1988 AT&T's shareholders were in sharp disagreement over the company's employment history and affirmative action program. One set of shareholders fought for a stronger affirmative action program, whereas another set recommended phasing it out.

AT&T's policy as of 1996 uses annual affirmative action plans to identify underutilized groups at particular locations. Hiring and promotional targets (stated as percentage goals) are relative to the geographic location of the establishment and the normal hiring pool within AT&T from which the establishment hires its employees. Because these targets are location-specific, there are no companywide targets at any level. The affirmative action plans also contain a component that focuses on good faith policies to protect certain groups of workers from discrimination. This portion of the plan applies particularly to veterans and disabled employees.[8]

NOTES

1. U.S. Equal Employment Opportunity Commission, "Petition to Intervene," Federal Communications Commission Hearings on A.T.&T. Revised Tariff Schedule, December 10, 1970, p. 1.
2. "Bias Charges in Hiring: A.T.&T. Fights Back," *U.S. News and World Report* (August 14, 1972), p. 67.
3. The stipulations of the agreement were met by the company before an established 1979 deadline.
4. According to Mr. Jeffrey of the legal staff in AT&T's Washington, DC, office, in a phone conversation on March 10, 1982.
5. *Johnson v. Transportation Agency, Santa Clara County, California*, 480 U.S. 616 (1987).
6. *Ibid.*, pp. 18-21.
7. *Fullilove v. Klutznick*, 448 U.S. 448 (1980); *United Steelworkers v. Weber*, 443 U.S. 193 (1979); *United States v. Paradise*, 480 U.S. 149 (1987).
8. Based on phone conversations with Mr. Frank Bloomfield, Equal Opportunity Affirmative Action Manager for the Network Service Division, December 10, 1991; and Ms. Joanne Marleowicz, Corporate Equal Opportunity Affirmative Action Manager, December 10, 1991, and May 7, 1996.

Chapter Five

THE GOVERNMENT

INTRODUCTION

Many industries have long been self-regulated; that is, they have determined their responsibilities to society, to employees, and to others free from government regulation. Some of these industries have adopted formal codes of ethics that presumably serve to regulate their members' conduct. They have institutionalized moral behavior as a part of professional practice. However, society becomes suspicious when a professional or trade group providing public services is allowed to develop its codes of conduct independent of external warrant or scrutiny. Moreover, enforcement of even good codes and corporate review procedures has proved lax in some cases, impossible in others.

The government has sometimes regulated industry in order to ensure that public policy remains fair. As government power has grown in the Western world, some have complained that government has replaced industry as an overbearing wielder of power. The original purpose of regulation had been to help the free enterprise system remain free, but now critics of government contend that regulation actually inhibits the free enterprise system. The system is shackled by other goals, such as nondiscriminatory hiring, a pollution-free environment, and smut-free broadcasting. Consequently, the effort to regulate industry in the public interest has created two major controversies. First, what is the public interest, and how is the protection of a free market related to the public interest? Second, how can the public interest be protected without unduly harming the private interests at stake in free competition?

The second question is addressed in a poignant way in several of this chapter's cases that involve government mechanisms for regulating industry. The Fairness Doctrine, Laetrile, Hazardous Chemicals, Cisco Wine, and AIDS/AZT cases all demonstrate how, as social and political systems have become more complex, the problem of fair and adequate government regulation has compounded in difficulty and become mired in controversy. Skepticism has emerged from various quarters that business has any capacity to regulate itself, and from other quarters that government has an adequate body of information and expertise to regulate business. "Policies for Hazardous Chemicals in the Workplace," for example, examines some of the severe constraints precipitated by lack of information and expertise.

State and local governments have complained almost as much about federal intervention and ownership as have corporate officials. Both tend to view federal, state, and local requirements as collectively overwhelming. One compromise has been to regulate heavily when the problems seem acute; for example, in the regulation of fetus-deforming drugs and dangerous chemicals that produce mental and physical disorders. Such an attempt at compromise does not belie the fact that the resulting governmental uncertainty and political negotiations create a hodgepodge of sometimes inconsistent government regulations directed at particular problems, rather than comprehensive or systematic programs of regulation and enforcement.

Despite the patchwork character of the current regulatory environment, it is suspect to claim, as some critics have, that the United States has remained passively oblivious to problematic issues raised by regulatory activities. Since the inception of government requirements, the regulatory structure has undergone repeated modification and refinement in light of both internal and external scrutiny, even though certain problems persist. The precise and changing implications of the developing regulations are therefore difficult to distinguish, and it is only fair to remember that regulation is an ongoing process often responsive to constructive criticism and legislative initiative.

In domains of business untouched by government regulation, the initiatives of self-regulation previously discussed have often proved unsatisfactory. Professional codes and mechanisms such as internal peer review are beneficial only if they provide effective and defensible rules for the affected relationships. But some of these formal mechanisms oversimplify moral requirements or boast more completeness and authority than they are entitled to claim. As a consequence, the affected professionals may suppose that everything morally required has been done if the rules of the code have been obediently followed, just as many believe that all obligations have been discharged when *legal* requirements have been met. Professional codes and internal corporate mechanisms such as grievance procedures often prove ambiguous, and some moral dilemmas are compounded rather than eased by these procedures. Codes and internal corporate guidelines have also traditionally been constituted in abstract language that either dispenses only vague and nondirective moral advice or is subject to competing interpretations.

The specter of government regulation raises a number of important ethical issues. For example, can the government legitimately play a paternalistic role? Can business activities legitimately be regulated to protect business from itself? to protect customers against their foolish decisions? to protect clients against their ignorant choices? The government often makes judgments about consumer waste, non-nutritious foods, inefficacious drugs, and the like. Are the legitimate freedoms and rights of citizens and businesses unduly restricted by such judgments?

These questions are raised in this chapter in "Manufacture and Regulation of Laetrile," which involves a decision by the U.S. Food and Drug Administration (FDA) to ban the manufacture and marketing of a product popular with cancer patients but declared ineffective by the FDA. These questions are also raised in more subtle forms in "Cisco, the 'Wine Fooler,'" and "The FCC's Fairness Doctrine."

Another question is whether the government should support businesses that have sustained losses because of government intervention but are innocent of moral and legal violations. Occasionally government-imposed standards threaten a business or an entire industry. Is the government acting unfairly by regulating and not indemnifying small, undercapitalized industries that could fold or sustain serious losses due to regulatory intervention? (See, for example, "Reserve Mining's Silver Bay Facility" in Chapter 3.)

Questions have also been raised about the use of cost/benefit judgments of efficiency as a way to establish public policies. Cost/benefit judgments aim to measure costs and benefits objectively, while identifying uncertainties and possible trade-offs, in order to present policy makers with relevant information on which to base a decision. Many believe that such information can be used to clarify which trade-offs are being made and why one alternative is more efficient than another. Yet this ideal has proved difficult to implement, and in many cases we are faced with moral choices rather than economic ones. Considerations of justice, for example, might lead us to choose a *less efficient* but *more just* outcome. What counts as a cost, a benefit, or a valuable outcome is also often debatable; government regulatory activities often spark debates about these matters, as the Hazardous Chemicals, Laetrile, Cisco Wines, AIDS/AZT, and Fairness Doctrine cases all illustrate.

Finally, a consumer, client, customer, member of a board of directors, or corporate officer occasionally obtains inside information and begins to trade in a company's stock. The Securities and Exchange Commission (SEC) regulates insider trading. The SEC operates on the principle that one cannot trade on nonpublic, financially useful information that has been misappropriated or secured by a breach of fiduciary duty. A person cannot legally use information obtained on the inside to buy or sell securities or to pass the information on to others so that they might benefit. However, moral and conceptual ambiguities surround insider trading, and not every authority considers the practice unfair. Several scholars have argued that permitting insider trades would actually make the securities markets more efficient and would involve no moral violation. The case entitled "An Accountant's Small-Time Inside Trading" provides a common circumstance in which this thesis about the appropriateness, fairness, and scope of government regulation of insider trading might be tested.

THE FCC'S FAIRNESS DOCTRINE

Government intervention in the publication and dissemination of news is inconsistent with the notion of a free press. However, the government has a responsibility to ensure fairness in the dissemination of information on matters of community interest. These two obligations often conflict. Until recently, a U.S. government mechanism for media accountability known as the Fairness Doctrine existed. The doctrine attempted to mediate between broadcasters' First Amendment rights and those of the public by requiring broadcasters to provide balanced coverage of important public issues.

The Fairness Doctrine originated in congressional and Federal Communications Commission (FCC) legislation. The FCC's 1949 "Report on Editorializing by Broadcasters" outlined the doctrine and stressed the importance of the role of broadcasting in fostering an informed public opinion in a democracy. It affirmed the "right of the public in a free society to be informed and to have presented to it for acceptance or rejection the different attitudes and viewpoints concerning these vital and often controversial issues."[1] In 1959 Congress amended the Communications Act of 1934 to impose, in section 315(a), a statutory "obligation upon [broadcasters] to operate in the public interest and to afford reasonable opportunity for the discussion of conflicting views on issues of public importance."[2]

The Fairness Doctrine did not require broadcasters to give equal time to contrasting views. However, if "during the presentation of views on a controversial issue, an attack [was] made upon the honesty, character, integrity, or like personal qualities of an identified person or group,"[3] that person or group had to be given an opportunity to respond on the air. The broadcasting company had to bear all presentation costs.

The policy was traditionally confined to broadcast rather than print media, based on the principle of scarce resource allocation. In this case, the resource is broadcast frequencies and the scarcity is that of broadcasting possibilities; the number of people who want to broadcast exceeds the number of available broadcast licenses. The government allocates this limited resource through a licensing system, designed to protect the public interest through the enforcement of various regulations.

This case was written by Tom L. Beauchamp and revised by John Cuddihy, Joanne L. Jurmu, Anna Pinedo, and Jeff Greene. Not to be duplicated without permission of the holder of the copyright, © 1992, 1996 Tom L. Beauchamp.

In 1969 the U.S. Supreme Court held the Fairness Doctrine to be constitutional and consistent with the First Amendment's intent in *Red Lion Broadcasting Co. v. Federal Communications Commission*. The Court ruled that the scarcity of available frequencies justifies the imposition of a government regulatory system intended to ensure that broadcasters, as fiduciaries, act in the public interest. The Court declared the public's First Amendment rights to hear differing viewpoints "paramount" to broadcasters' rights. Justice Byron White expressed the Court's opinion as follows:

> Where there are substantially more individuals who want to broadcast than there are frequencies to allocate, it is idle to posit an unabridgeable First Amendment right to broadcast comparable to the right of every individual to speak, write or publish. . . . A license permits broadcasting, but the licensee has no constitutional right to be the one who holds the license or to monopolize a radio frequency to the exclusion of his fellow citizens. There is nothing in the First Amendment which prevents the Government from requiring a licensee to share his frequency with others and to conduct himself as a proxy or fiduciary with obligations to present those views and voices which are representative of his community and which would otherwise, by necessity, be barred from the airwaves.[4]

The Court reaffirmed the scarcity of the radio airwaves and the responsibility of broadcasters as public trustees in subsequent cases. Similar reasoning served to justify the Fairness Doctrine's application to cable programming.

However, the Fairness Doctrine was neither strictly enforced nor widely applied. From January 1980 through August 1987, the FCC received over 50,000 complaints of alleged Fairness Doctrine violations.[5] The FCC dismissed the vast majority of the charges. The Fairness Doctrine was primarily invoked to restrict virulent racism and other uses of the airwaves that intimidate and attack certain persons and institutions. The FCC also used the doctrine in 1967 to require that broadcasters give significant time to anti-smoking messages (see "Banning Cigarette Advertising," in Chapter 4). It was almost never used to enforce accountability for claims made in documentaries, no matter how hard-hitting or speculative. Although the National Association of Broadcasters (NAB) has reported several cases in which documentaries were accused of violating the Fairness Doctrine, the FCC upheld only one complaint that was later overturned in federal court.

The doctrine was usually applied to ensure that the licensed station owners' political preferences would not control the presentation of candidates for public office. However, these regulations were also loosened over the years. For example, the FCC held that any station endorsing or criticizing a candidate on the air had to give the opposing or criticized candidate air time in which to respond. In 1983 FCC Chairman Mark Fowler revised the commission's policy on televised political debates. He announced that broadcasters could schedule political debates with the candidates of their choice without being required to provide air time to excluded candidates.[6] Broadcasters could cover debates as bona fide news events without having to make time available to those who did not participate.

THE CURRENT LEGAL SITUATION

The Fairness Doctrine has come under fire from both sides of the political spectrum. Conservatives oppose it as an expendable form of government intervention, while many liberals regard it as a disguised means of intimidating or even silencing the expression of journalistic opinion. In October 1981 the FCC recommended that the Fairness Doctrine be repealed. The commission issued a detailed study of the doctrine in 1985. It concluded that the doctrine was "an unnecessary and detrimental regulatory mechanism . . . [that] disserves the public interest."[7] The FCC did not at that point repeal the doctrine because it believed that Congress had already codified it. However, a September 1986 ruling by the U.S. Court of Appeals held that the Fairness Doctrine was not a statutory requirement. According to the ruling, written by Judge Robert Bork and supported by then Appeals Court Judge Antonin Scalia, Congress had merely ratified the doctrine in amending section 315(a) of the 1934 Communications Act. The decision gave the FCC the power to modify or to abolish the doctrine. The commission then abolished the doctrine's chief measures in August 1987, claiming that they violated First Amendment rights and stifled controversial programming.

The court of appeals ruling spurred controversy in Congress, where some members have consistently voiced support for the doctrine. There have been several legislative proposals to codify the doctrine and to make it an explicit requirement of the Communications Act. Representative John Dingell (D-MI), chairman of the House Committee on Energy and Commerce, introduced an amendment to the Communications Act that would "require expressly that licensees of broadcast stations present discussion of conflicting views on issues of public importance."[8] President Reagan vetoed the measure, and Congress lacked the two-thirds majority needed to override the veto. In November 1987 Senator Ernest Hollings (D-SC), chairman of the Senate Commerce Committee, deftly steered a bill through the committee that would have restored the Fairness Doctrine. Although Hollings argued vigorously for the bill, congressional deficit-reduction negotiations eliminated it. Still more recent bills introduced by Senator Hollings and Representative Dingell have either failed to clear their respective committees or died on chamber floors.

THE CURRENT DEBATE

On August 4, 1987, the FCC voted unanimously to eliminate the Fairness Doctrine. In a letter to Representative Dingell, then FCC Chairman Dennis Patrick emphasized that, although the FCC had abolished the doctrine's major clauses, several of the doctrine's regulations remained in force: the political editorial rule, the personal attack rule, the Zapple Doctrine, and the "application of the Fairness Doctrine to ballot issues."[9]

As the FCC stated, "The rules on political editorials and personal attacks do not forbid the broadcast of either. Instead, they require broadcasters who carry such editorials or attacks to offer the persons adversely affected by them a chance to state their side of the case in person or through a spokesman."[10] The political editorial clause currently mandates that TV and radio stations offer political candidates whose opponents have been endorsed by the involved station "a reasonable opportunity to respond" on air to the endorsement. The FCC requires that the opposing candidate be furnished with a transcript of the editorial within 24 hours of a broadcast. If a station broadcasts a political editorial within three days of the election, the station must provide the transcript and a response-time offer prior to the editorial's airing.

Personal attacks also require response time. However, attacks "occurring during uses by legally qualified candidates"[11] are not covered by the Fairness Doctrine. Attacks made on "foreign groups or foreign public figures"[12] are also immune from the doctrine's "personal attack" claims.

Like the political editorial clause, the Zapple Doctrine pertains to political campaigning. Should a TV or radio station run an advertisement during a formal campaign period in which political supporters endorse a candidate, an opponent's supporters have the right to a reasonable opportunity to respond. The Zapple Doctrine may apply only to legally qualified candidates during formal campaign periods. The restrictions "reflect the intent of Congress to confine special treatment of political discussion to distinct, identifiable periods."[13]

The ballot-issue exception requires broadcasters to permit opposing sides equal air time to discuss and advertise for or against ballot propositions. However, "The [Federal Communications] Commission will not intervene in cases alleging false and misleading statements regarding controversial issues of public importance."[14]

Although these clauses remain in force, an FCC employee declared that these exceptions "are not vigorously enforced"[15] and have not been frequently used in recent years. Overall, the FCC has moved away from even the spirit of the Fairness Doctrine, firm in the belief that the doctrine stifled rather than promoted discussion and debate on public issues.

Doctrine opponents have challenged the Supreme Court's *Red Lion* decision, claiming that it is based on the mistaken premise of airwaves scarcity and need for improved communication of information, which are no longer valid. From this perspective, the Fairness Doctrine is now an unfair restraint on free market trade; technological advances since the *Red Lion* case have eliminated the former scarcity. The 1985 FCC report noted a dramatic increase to more than 10,000 radio and television broadcasting stations, a 400 percent growth since 1949.[16] Commercial broadcasters opposed to the doctrine point out that in many cities listeners and viewers can pick up dozens of radio and television stations and have access to only one significant newspaper. The FCC also observed that the growth of cable television, satellite television, and new telecommunications services offer an almost unlimited number of broadcast options.

The 1985 FCC report noted that the "fairness doctrine in operation thwarts the laudatory purpose it is designed to promote. Instead of furthering the discussion of public issues, the fairness doctrine inhibits broadcasters from presenting controversial issues of public importance."[17] Broadcasters sometimes hesitate to air controversial materials for fear that they will be forced to use expensive air time to present another side of the issue. For some broadcasters, the loss of advertising time alone prevents them from making room in their broadcast schedule for these materials. For example, there may be as many as 15 candidates running in a presidential primary, which makes the provision of equal time burdensome for many stations.

Doctrine supporters claim that the relative scarcity of usable airwaves persists. The "scarcity of frequencies should not be measured by the number of stations allowed to broadcast, but by the number of individuals or groups who wish to use the facilities, or would use them if they were more readily available."[18] They point to the economic value of government licenses as a measure of the relative demand. Independent VHF licenses have sold for as much as $700 million in New York. Also, the number of stations has not increased in isolation, but rather in proportion to the nation's population growth. The broadcast medium continues to be more inaccessible to the private citizen than the print medium because the government must allocate the use of airwaves. Finally, the increase in stations does not necessarily correspond to any increase in availability of diverse views on issues.

The Fairness Doctrine has been the only significant mechanism of controlling the dissemination of information in broadcast media. The House Committee on Energy and Commerce Report on the Fairness Doctrine points out that "numerous case histories demonstrate that the Fairness Doctrine promotes carriage of views that would otherwise not be available to the American public."[19] Former FCC Chairman Charles Ferris testified before the Subcommittee on Telecommunications and Finance that "in 1979, during [his] watch, the Commission explicitly found that the Fairness Doctrine enhanced, not reduced, speech."[20] The congressional committee questioned the authority of the 1985 FCC report because it relied solely on broadcasters' accounts of the doctrine's effects.

Opponents argue that the Fairness Doctrine violates constitutional principles by allowing the government to intervene and to define how freedom of expression is to be used and practiced. The doctrine, they say, provides a dangerous potential for government abuse. They point to the FCC's statement that federal law permits government agencies to file Fairness Doctrine complaints against the media, and they maintain that both the Kennedy and Nixon administrations did so in order to counter opposition.[21] This ruling (in July 1985) prompted the CIA to file a complaint charging that ABC's *World News Tonight* had three times distorted the news in broadcasting allegations that the CIA had tried to arrange the assassination of Ronald Rewald, a Honolulu businessman who was under indictment for several crimes. The CIA complaint called for the reversal of past precedents and greater accountability of the media to the government.

Fairness Doctrine supporters face an uphill battle in the judiciary and Congress. A Media Action Project (a public interest law firm in Washington, DC) employee said that when the Supreme Court declined in 1989 to review the 1986 DC Court of Appeals ruling, a legal review of the case became "extremely difficult."[22] If the firm decides to re-file a Fairness Doctrine case, it will certainly "seek a more sympathetic court."[23]

Attempts to revive the Fairness Doctrine in the late 1980s and early 1990s proved unsuccessful in the face of White House vetoes and a conservative FCC. This trend began to change when President Clinton came into office; it looked as if the doctrine would become law once again. However, Congress and the White House were not prepared for the stiff opposition that it would face from influential segments of public opinion. Led by conservative host Rush Limbaugh, the talk show industry mounted a strong public push against revival of the doctrine. Limbaugh, whose show is heard by an estimated 20 million listeners a week, said that if this bill were made law, he would be "gang muzzled"[24] by the White House and Congress. This drive against the bill received some indirect support from then governor of New York, Mario Cuomo. Cuomo said, "Restricting expression, even in the name of balance, is inconsistent with our party's commitment to First Amendment freedoms."[25]

Opponents responded to these various sources of opposition to the bill by overwhelming Congress with phone calls and letters of disapproval. The doctrine was then shelved in Congress, and supporters looked to the FCC for further direction. The makeup of the Commission had changed as the appointments of Presidents Reagan and Bush were leaving office and President Clinton was filling the openings. In light of Clinton's appointments, speculation flourished that the bill would be revived. However, opposition to the bill remained strong and political campaigning prevented the possibility of revival.

U.S. citizens continue to be wary of government intervention in the private sector. The Fairness Doctrine was, until recently, considered a justified exception. Although it is a measure that potentially infringed on broadcasters' freedoms, the doctrine was traditionally designed to protect the individual's moral and political right to the presentation of differing views on important issues.

NOTES

1. "Report on Editorializing by Broadcasters," 13 FCC 1246 (1949), p. 1249.
2. Communications Act of 1934, 47 U.S.C. 315(a).
3. *Red Lion Broadcasting Co. v. Federal Communications Commission* (1969), in Marc A. Franklin, ed., *Mass Media Law*, 2d ed. (Mineola, NY: Foundation Press, 1982), p. 652.
4. *Ibid.*, pp. 658–59.
5. Bob Davis, "Hollings Again Tries to Revive Fairness Doctrine, Abolished by FCC, but Faces Maelstrom of Static," *The Wall Street Journal*, November 18, 1987, p. 68.
6. "More Debates?" *Time* 122 (November 12, 1983), p. 59.

7. "In re Inquiry into Section 73.1910 of the Commission's Rules and Regulations Concerning the General Fairness Doctrine Obligations of Broadcast Licenses," 102 FCC2 143 (1985).
8. Report together with additional and dissenting views submitted by Rep. John Dingell from the House Committee on Energy and Commerce concerning the Fairness in Broadcasting Act of 1987 (HR 1934), p. 2.
9. Letter from FCC Chairman Dennis Patrick to Representative John Dingell, dated September 22, 1987.
10. "Personal Editorials, Personal Attacks," the Federal Communications Commission's *The Law of Political Broadcasting and Cablecasting: A Political Primer, 1984 Edition* (Washington, DC: FCC, 1984), pp. 85–88.
11. *Ibid.* p. 64.
12. *Ibid.* p. 70.
13. *Ibid.* p. 71.
14. *Ibid.* p. 72.
15. Conversation between John Cuddihy and FCC Associate Director of Legislative Affairs Steven Klitzman, on September 12, 1990.
16. FCC, 1985 Report, as quoted in "Report on the Fairness in Broadcasting Act," pp. 38–39.
17. "In re Inquiry into Section 73.1910," 102 FCC2 143 (1985).
18. T. Emerson, "The System of Freedom of Expression," as quoted in "Report on the Fairness in Broadcasting Act," p. 13.
19. "Report on Fairness in Broadcasting Act," p. 19.
20. Charles Ferris at hearing on Fairness in Broadcasting Act of 1987, before the Subcommittee on Telecommunications and Finance on April 7, 1987, as quoted in "Report on Fairness in Broadcasting Act," p. 19.
21. "The Hush Rush Law," *The Wall Street Journal*, September 1, 1993, p. A14.
22. Conversation between John Cuddihy and Gigi Sohen at Media Access Project on September 19, 1990.
23. *Ibid.*
24. Jim Cooper, "Talkers Brace for Fairness Assault," *Broadcasting & Cable* (September 6, 1993), p. 44.
25. Mario M. Cuomo, "The Unfairness Doctrine," *The New York Times*, September 20, 1993, p. A19.

MANUFACTURE AND REGULATION OF LAETRILE

It has been estimated that consumers waste $500 million a year on medical quackery and another $500 million annually on some "health foods" which have no beneficial effect. Unnecessary deaths, injuries and financial loss can be expected to continue until the law requires adequate testing for safety and efficacy of products and devices before they are made available to consumers. (President John F. Kennedy in a message to Congress)[1]

Let me choose the way I want to die. It is not your prerogative to tell me how. (Glenn Rutherford, cancer patient and Laetrile supporter at FDA hearing)[2]

These quotations express the essence of an acrimonious conflict that raged over the better part of the 1970s in the scientific and popular press, in courtrooms and hearing rooms, in prestigious research institutions, and among drug manufacturers. This debate emerged over the regulation, manufacturing, and marketing of Laetrile, a drug said to be a cure for cancer by its supporters but denounced as worthless by much of the scientific community.

The U.S. Food and Drug Administration (FDA) has a responsibility to determine both the safety and the *efficacy* of a drug before allowing it to be marketed in the United States. The FDA's responsibility for drug licensing dates from the passage of the 1906 Pure Food and Drug Act, which primarily addressed safety abuses among patent medicine purveyors. In 1962 new laws were passed (partly in response to the Thalidomide tragedy involving malformed fetuses) that required the FDA to assess a drug's efficacy as well as its safety before the drug could be approved for marketing.[3]

The FDA examined Laetrile for safety and found no significant problems. However, the FDA could not find evidence of the drug's effectiveness and became convinced that Laetrile was worthless for the treatment of cancer. Consequently, the drug was banned from the U.S. market.

Laetrile supporters reacted with fury to the drug ban. Cancer victims demanded the right to use the drug. Over 20 state legislatures that opposed the FDA's decision legalized it for intrastate marketing and consumption. Others felt that the FDA was denying the American people their constitutional right to freedom of choice. Many argued that, because the drug had not been proven unsafe, people should be allowed to use it pending further tests. But many in the medical and scientific communities opposed this laissez-faire attitude. They argued that patients were drawn toward an inexpensive, painless cure for their disease but failed to realize its ineffectiveness. Critics claimed that Laetrile use had caused numerous deaths and that some of these people could have been helped by legitimate alternative forms of treatment.

The debate's ferocity was new, but Laetrile was not. According to Dr. Charles Moertel of the Mayo Clinic, "Amygdalin had many centuries of use for medical purposes. Usually administered in the form of bitter almonds, it was a common ingredient of herbal prescriptions for a variety of illnesses, and by liberal interpretation of ancient pharmacopeias one might conclude that it was used for the treatment of cancer."[4] German physicians briefly used amygdalin in an attempt to treat cancer in 1892, but they discarded the extract as ineffective and toxic.

Modern proponents of Laetrile therapy attribute the beginning of the Laetrile movement to Ernst Krebs, who began experimenting with the extract of apricot pits in the 1920s, and to his son, Ernst Krebs, Jr., who refined the extract to produce Laetrile in 1949 for use in the treatment of disorders of intestinal fermentation—cancer.[5] Since then, pro-Laetrile researchers have experimented with a variety of methods and techniques for using Laetrile in cancer treatment, and they claim that Laetrile is in fact effective. According to Krebs, Laetrile is effective because cyanide, which is an active ingredient, attacks the cancerous cells while an enzyme called rhodanese protects the normal cells.[6]

Initially Krebs's supporters claimed that Laetrile not only cured or controlled existing cancers but also could prevent cancers from forming. They based their claims of Laetrile's efficacy primarily on patients' case histories (some published in a volume called *Laetrile Case Histories*) and on personal testimonials of "cured" cancer patients. However, many in the medical and scientific communities were not impressed with this form of proof. They considered the reported case histories too sketchy and the follow-up times too short to support the claims. Moreover, few patients took Laetrile without first undergoing more traditional forms of cancer therapy. Under these conditions it is virtually impossible to determine which treatment or treatments should receive credit for improvements. Also, the natural history of cancer is not totally understood, and spontaneous remissions can and do occur.[7]

In 1962 the FDA charged Krebs with violating the Federal Food, Drug, and Cosmetic Act, on grounds that he could not prove his drug's effectiveness. In 1963 Laetrile was banned because it was not found to be an effective treatment of cancer or any other health problem. Since then, Laetrile proponents have revised their claims. They no longer proclaim Laetrile an independent cure for cancer, instead emphasizing its role in the prevention and control of the disease. Laetrile supporters also maintain that the standards of proof for Laetrile research have been higher than for other cancer drugs and that pro-Laetrile results have been obtained but suppressed.[8]

The controversy surrounding Laetrile turned largely on the drug's efficacy and on one's right to *manufacture, market,* and *purchase* the product. During the 1970s, the FDA suffered criticisms that it was a paternalistic agency after it attempted to ban the manufacturing and marketing of the popular artificial sweetener saccharin. The Laetrile problem came to light immediately after the institution of this unpopular FDA policy. By mid-1977 FDA head Donald Kennedy said his agency found increasing evidence of Laetrile's inefficacy. However, criticism of the FDA was also increasing and efforts were mounted either to allow free choice of the drug or to test for inefficacy in a public trial using human subjects. Some state legislatures and judges called the FDA's findings into question.[9] Some states had legalized its manufacture and sale, and some courts had criticized the FDA record and policies. Even prestigious physicians and newspapers such as *The New York Times* endorsed the right of individuals to choose to use a possibly inefficacious drug.

Responding to the demands for a Laetrile efficacy trial with human subjects, the National Cancer Institute sponsored a 1981 clinical trial with 178 terminal cancer patients. The trial results dispelled any lingering hope in the medical and scientific communities that Laetrile might indeed be able to destroy cancer cells. Of the 178 trial subjects, only one demonstrated a partial positive response to Laetrile treatment. His gastric carcinoma showed a 10-week retardation period. However, the cancer progressed, and the patient died 37 weeks after the institution of Laetrile therapy. In their conclusion, the trial doctors commented, "No substantive benefit was observed in the terms of cure, improvement or stabilization of cancer."[10] According to the study, several patients displayed symptoms of cyanide toxicity and blood cyanide levels that approached the lethal range. The report concluded, "Amygdalin (Laetrile) is a toxic drug that is not effective as a cancer treatment."[11] In response, Laetrile manufacturers sued the NCI in three lawsuits, claiming the study had drastically reduced demand for Laetrile, thereby inflicting financial damage on the manufacturers. All three suits were dismissed in the courts.

According to pro-regulation partisans, it is desirable and necessary to protect uneducated risk takers who are vulnerable to unsubstantiated medicinal claims: "The absolute freedom to choose an effective drug is properly surrendered in exchange for the freedom from danger to each person's health and well-being from the sale and use of worthless drugs."[12] From this perspective, regulation is not irreconcilable with freedom of choice. If a regulation promotes situations within which more informed and deliberative choices are made, it does not constrict freedom; and a choice cannot be free if the product is a fraud.[13]

By contrast, freedom-of-choice advocates claim that the simple restriction of Laetrile violates the individual's right to autonomous choice and the manufacturers' right to market a product. Supporters of this view resent the characterization of cancer patients as people who are incapable of making rational or free decisions because of the stress of illness. They believe that most of these individuals are able to make well-founded personal decisions and should be allowed to do so.

The economic implications of banning Laetrile have also introduced a significant controversy. Each side has accused the other of economic exploitation of cancer victims. Laetrile proponents say that traditional cancer treatments represent an enormous and profitable industry and claim that patients and insurers would save money if Laetrile were legally marketed in the United States. They note that the American Cancer Society estimated that as early as 1972 the direct costs of cancer treatment totaled over $3 billion (for hospital care, nursing home care, physicians' and nurses' fees, drugs and other treatments, and research).[14] By comparison, Laetrile supporters claim that legalized Laetrile would cost a fraction of conventional cancer therapies.

Laetrile has been primarily manufactured and marketed in Mexico. In one study it was estimated that in 1977 alone, approximately 7,000 patients were treated in two Mexican clinics at an average cost of $350 per day.[15] The United States represents a large potential market for a legalized, over-the-counter Laetrile. However, due to FDA restrictions, one may neither import amygdalin from foreign countries nor ship it across state lines. Although the FDA does not control *intrastate* commerce, it would not be profitable for any one state to manufacture Laetrile in all its stages—that is, from the farming of apricot trees to the laboratory synthesis of the finished drug. Furthermore, the FDA has issued an import alert ban on amygdalin and all corresponding brand names, including Laetrile and vitamin B-17. The FDA refuses to permit importation of Laetrile on the grounds that "it appears to be a new drug without an effective new drug application (NDA)."[16] The FDA also classifies the Laetrile issue as a case of health fraud. As a senior scientist at the AMA commented, "People took Laetrile, ignored other, more conventional cancer treatment, and died."[17] Although NDAs for Laetrile have been submitted to the FDA, none has been approved. Consequently, the FDA currently proscribes all importation and interstate transportation and marketing of amygdalin under any brand name.

However, one may still obtain amygdalin quickly and easily within the United States. VitaChem International/Genesis West in Redwood City, California, offers 50 tablets of "Laevalin, a naturally occurring amygdalin" for $47.50. Mexican-based Vita Inc. will ship 100 Laetrile tablets to a United States address for $65.00. To circumvent FDA regulations, U.S. Laetrile marketers have changed the brand name, but continue to market amygdalin openly, in violation of the FDA import and interstate commerce ban.

The courts as well as the press have provided an arena for the conflict over the patient's right to choose a treatment and the manufacturer's right to market a product. Although Congress did not intend to impose such restrictions on choice, the 1962 drug amendments in fact restrict the patient's choice. Because these amendments limit the market to industry-tested and FDA-approved products, treatment by and manufacturing of alternatives are inevitably constricted.[18]

A series of lawsuits have challenged the FDA restrictions, and a number of states have passed laws legalizing its use. In early 1977 U.S. District Court Judge Luther Bohanon (U.S. District Court for the Western District of Oklahoma) issued a ruling that permitted Laetrile's importation under a physician's affidavit for terminally ill cancer patients. Although overturned by an appeals court in December 1986, Bohanon's ruling allowed Laetrile treatment for terminal patients. Despite the opportunity to convince the FDA of the drug's efficacy, Laetrile proponents were unable to obtain an NDA approval for amygdalin. The judicial and legislative challenges are not, however, without opponents. Lawyer William Curran, for instance, has deplored the action of certain courts in allowing the use of Laetrile for the terminally ill:

> It is understandable that judges have had trouble dealing objectively with the legal pleas of plaintiffs who are dying a painful death and whose only wish is to indulge in a harmless, although ineffective, gesture of hope. The courts have tried to dispense mercy. Their error has been in abandoning the protection of law for these patients.[19]

As the arguments have developed, the issues of choice and fraudulent representation by business have moved to the forefront. Franz Inglefinger, the distinguished former editor of the *New England Journal of Medicine* and himself a cancer victim, was convinced that Laetrile was useless. In 1977 he wrote, "I would not take Laetrile myself under any circumstances. If any member of my family had cancer, I would counsel them against it. If I were still in practice, I would not recommend it to my patients." On the other hand, he said, "Perhaps there are some situations in which rational medical science should yield and make some concessions. If any patient had what I thought was hopelessly advanced cancer, and if he asked for Laetrile, I should like to be able to give the substance to him to assuage his mental anguish, just as I would give him morphine to relieve his physical suffering."[20] Inglefinger did not view truthful marketing of the drug as involving a fraudulent misrepresentation.

In January 1987 a Laetrile bill was introduced into the U.S. House of Representatives. H.R. 651 provided that the controversial efficacy requirements of the Food, Drug, and Cosmetic Act would not be applied to Laetrile if a patient were under a physician's care (see Exhibit 1). The bill's sponsor, Representative Bill Goodling (R-PA) asserted that "the legislation does not state that Laetrile is a cure for pain or a pain reducer."[21] The bill died in the Health and Environment Subcommittee of the House Energy and Commerce Committee.

The National Institutes of Health and most other health care institutions still discourage the use of Laetrile, preferring conventional methods of cancer treatment. The National Cancer Institute's official policy is to encourage conventional methods with the explanation that testing has always shown "evidence of Laetrile's failure as a cancer treatment."[22] The American Cancer Society holds the position that "Laetrile is not effective in the prevention or treatment of cancer in human beings."[23] Despite the medical evidence and the FDA's past efforts to restrict the drug's marketing, one may still today purchase amygdalin by dialing a toll-free number.

APPENDIX

Exhibit 1: H.R. 651

A Bill

To provide that the effectiveness requirements of the Federal Food, Drug, and Cosmetic Act shall not apply to laetrile in certain cases.

Be it enacted by the Senate and House of Representatives of the United States of America in Congress assembled, That in the administration of section 505 of the Federal Food, Drug, and Cosmetic Act, the effectiveness requirement of such section shall not be applicable to Laetrile when used under the direction of a physician for the treatment of pain.

NOTES

1. Quoted by David A. Smith, "The Laetrile Dilemma," *Pennsylvania Medicine* 80 (August 15, 1977), p. 15.
2. Quoted by James C. Peterson and Gerald A. Markle, "The Laetrile Controversy," in Dorothy Nelkin, ed., *Controversy: Politics of Technical Decisions* (Beverly Hills, CA: Sage Publications, 1979), p. 175.
3. Two arguments were advanced in favor of the efficacy requirement. The economic argument had to do with consumer protection; that is, consumers were wasting their money on drugs that were not benefiting them. The second argument had to do with health and safety; namely, that reliance on ineffective drugs could be dangerous when effective alternatives were available. The FDA held that although Laetrile appeared "harmless," it had not been proven effective and therefore should not be approved for manufacture and sale in the United States.
4. Charles G. Moertel, M.D., "A Clinical Trial of Amygdalin (Laetrile) in the Treatment of Human Cancer," *New England Journal of Medicine* 306 (January 28, 1982), pp. 201-6.
5. *Ibid.*, p. 201.
6. Thomas Donaldson, "Case Study—Laetrile: The FDA and Society," in Thomas Donaldson and Patricia Werhane, eds., *Ethical Issues in Business: A Philosophical Approach* (Englewood Cliffs, NJ: Prentice Hall, 1979), p. 208.
7. John M. Yarbro, "Laetrile 'Case Histories': A Review and Critique," *Missouri Medicine* 76 (April 1979), pp. 195–203.
8. Peterson and Markle, "The Laetrile Controversy," p. 170.
9. See, for example, *Rutherford v. United States*, 438 F. Supp. (1977); and John F. Cannizzaro and Madelon M. Rosenfield, "Laetrile and the FDA: A Case of Reverse Regulation," *Journal of Health Politics, Policy and Law* (Summer 1978), pp. 181–95.
10. Moertel, "A Clinical Trial of Amygdalin (Laetrile)," pp. 201–6.
11. *Ibid.*, p. 201.
12. HEW Release, August 4, 1977, as quoted by Marion Smiley, "Legalizing Laetrile," in Amy Gutman and Dennis Thompson, eds., *Ethics and Politics: Cases and Comments* (Chicago: Nelson-Hall Publishers, 1984), p. 198.

13. See Arthur L. Caplan, "When Liberty Meets Authority: Ethical Aspects of the Laetrile Controversy," in Gerald Markle and James Peterson, eds., *Politics, Science and Cancer* (Boulder, CO: Westview Press, 1980), Chapter 6, pp. 133–50; and Smiley, "Legalizing Laetrile," p. 200.

14. Peterson and Markle, "The Laetrile Controversy," p. 172.

15. Donaldson, "Case Study—Laetrile," p. 211.

16. Food and Drug Administration Import Alert Ban Number 62-01, last revised December 7, 1987.

17. September 13, 1990, conversation with Dr. Jerome Seidenfeld, senior scientist with the Chicago-based American Medical Association (AMA).

18. See Don G. Rushing, "Picking Your Poison: The Drug Efficacy Requirement and the Right of Privacy," *UCLA Law Review* 25 (February 1978), p. 587.

19. William J. Curran, "Laetrile for the Terminally Ill: Supreme Court Stops the Nonsense," *New England Journal of Medicine* 302 (March 13, 1980), p. 621.

20. Franz Inglefinger, "Laetrilomania" (Editorial), *New England Journal of Medicine* 296 (May 19, 1977), p. 1167.

21. Letter to fellow members of Congress regarding approval of Laetrile legislation, dated September 15, 1986.

22. "Statement of the National Cancer Institute on Laetrile Tests with Patients," Vincent T. De Vita, Jr., M.D., director, April 30, 1981.

23. American Cancer Society position paper on Laetrile, as updated January 1986.

POLICIES FOR HAZARDOUS CHEMICALS IN THE WORKPLACE

In 1989–1991 the National Institute of Occupational Safety and Health (NIOSH) conducted a study on employees at Goodyear Tire and Rubber Co.'s Niagara Falls, New York, plant. The study results, released on April 2, 1991, showed that workers exposed to two chemicals, aniline and ortho-toluidine, were 6.5 times more likely to develop bladder cancer than the average citizen. The study also found that the cancer risk increased for workers in accordance with their proximity to the chemicals and the size and duration of their exposure at the site. Persons with an average level of exposure for over 10 years were found to be 27.2 times more likely to suffer bladder cancer than the average citizen.

A *Wall Street Journal* article quoted Elizabeth Ward, the study's chief investigator, as follows:

> The chain of evidence here is fairly strong that an increase in bladder cancer is associated with exposure to ortho-toluidine and aniline. . . . We're saying exposure should be reduced to the lowest feasible concentration.[1]

Some 2,300 facilities in the United States expose over 64,000 workers to these chemicals. Upon the study's publication, NIOSH immediately sent a hazard alert to more than 200 American corporations that use these chemicals, including Eastman Kodak, Du Pont, Uniroyal Chemical, First Chemical, and so on. These companies had been preparing for the study's final results for over a year. NIOSH's interim report, issued in December 1989, had stated that 14 cases of bladder cancer had been found in the Niagara Falls facility among workers exposed to ortho-toluidine and aniline, although only 3.54 cases would be expected in a normal population of the same size. Both industry and government consider this ratio significant in the search for cancer-causing environments.

After the 1989 interim report, many American corporations began to examine the medical and personnel files of employees exposed to the suspected chemicals. They discovered statistical excesses similar to those reported by NIOSH. These companies had also noticed a significant excess of urinary can-

This case was prepared by Tom L. Beauchamp; the benzene portions were revised by Joanne L. Jurmu, Anna Pinedo, John Cuddihy, and Kier Olsen. Not to be duplicated without permission of the holder of the copyright, © 1992, 1996 Tom L. Beauchamp.

cer in a similar group of workers. However, such surveillance does not show that exposure to aniline or ortho-toluidine leads to bladder cancer or makes a causal difference. Nonetheless, the study's results raised suspicions. These scientific questions are more complicated than a first-run statistical correlation can show because of the phenomenon of confounding variables, such as whether a worker smoked, had poor dietary habits, or was exposed to other hazardous worksite chemicals.

As industrial epidemiology departments began to study these chemicals' hazardous character, companies notified workers of the NIOSH results and of company studies to be conducted at various plants. Each company also informed its workers that the studies would not be completed for several years. In the meantime, the companies introduced new warnings and controls. Goodyear, for example, followed NIOSH recommendations on warnings, permissible exposures, training, and necessary protective equipment. However, Goodyear and other affected corporations also noted that (1) these chemicals are irreplaceable and therefore are absolutely essential to their major manufacturing processes, and (2) due to the lack of knowledge of safe levels, experiences with other chemicals must guide and shape current policy. For example, it is instructive to examine the history of benzene, perhaps the most widely examined hazardous chemical in recent years.

BACKGROUND OF BENZENE

A colorless, sweet-smelling gas classified as an aromatic hydrocarbon, benzene has long been recognized as a potentially dangerous substance causing toxic effects and diseases after significant workplace exposure.[2] It is used in the processing and manufacturing of tires, detergents, paints, pesticides, and petroleum products. Over 270,000 employees are exposed to benzene in product-related industries.[3]

In May 1977 the U.S. government's Occupational Safety and Health Administration (OSHA) issued an emergency temporary standard (ETS) ordering that worker exposure to benzene be reduced from the regulated level of 10 parts per million (ppm) to 1 ppm (time weighted average [TWA]). In addition, OSHA also proposed 1 ppm as a permanent standard for benzene exposure in all industries (except gasoline distribution and sales), pending a public hearing.

A 1977 report to the National Institutes of Health (NIH) detailed excessive leukemia deaths related to benzene exposure. This precipitated OSHA's decision to lower the 10-ppm standard. These deaths occurred in two Ohio rubber pliofilm plants; both had benzene exposure levels in excess of 10 ppm. No animal or human test data were then available for lower levels of exposure. However, OSHA determined that benzene is a leukemogen (leukemia-causing agent) and ruled that worker safety demanded reduction of exposure to the lowest technologically feasible level. OSHA based its decision to drop the standard exposure level on two assumptions: (1) Adverse health effects were evident at certain exposure levels, and thus a reduced exposure was necessary to maintain a customary factor of safety; and (2) there is no determined safe level of exposure to carcinogens, which suggests that exposure should be reduced to the lowest level that can be monitored without undue burden.

When OSHA issued the ETS, little medical evidence existed to prove a causal relationship between benzene and cancer at any industrial level. The oil industry therefore questioned the wisdom of OSHA's regulation, which would require large public and private expenditures, because some scientific evidence indicated that there are no-effect exposure levels (i.e., harmless levels).

OSHA and the affected industries both determined that compliance costs would be large, with considerable uncertainty regarding the number of workers likely to be protected from cancer. Estimated per employee compliance costs ranged from $1,390 to $82,000, depending on the size and type of industry. The total compliance cost for all industries was projected to surpass $500 million in the first year alone.[4]

OSHA'S AUTHORITY

The fact that benzene, aniline, ortho-toluidine, and other chemicals have been identified as carcinogens, and that workers can be adversely affected by them, gives OSHA a legitimate interest in the regulation of their industrial manufacture. The Occupational Safety and Health Act gives the secretary of labor regulatory authority.[5] If the secretary promulgates a regulatory standard involving toxic materials such as benzene, Section 6(b)(5) provides:

> The Secretary, in promulgating standards dealing with toxic materials or harmful physical agents under this subsection, shall set the standard which most adequately assures, to the extent feasible, on the basis of the best available evidence, that no employee will suffer material impairment of health or functional capacity even if such employee has regular exposure to the hazard dealt with by such standard for the period of his working life. Development of standards under this subsection shall be based upon research, demonstrations, experiments, and such other information as may be appropriate. In addition to the attainment of the highest degree of health and safety protection for the employee, other considerations shall be the latest available scientific data in the field, the feasibility of the standards, and experience gained under this and other health and safety laws.[6]

Throughout 1978–1979, OSHA primarily studied the level at which benzene would be allowed in the environment, not whether its use and manufacture should be regulated. A 1978 study at Dow Chemical Corporation found that 12 out of 52 workers exposed to low levels of benzene showed an abnormally high level of damaged chromosomes in their blood cells, as compared to 1 out of 44 in the control group, whose members were not exposed to benzene. A series of measurements taken over the study's two-year course found the exposure level to have been below 10 ppm. Although damaged chromosomes do not inherently produce injury, they have been linked to an increased risk of cancer.[7]

SUPREME COURT ACTION

Into this uncertainty stepped the U.S. Supreme Court, which announced a decision relevant to the controversy on July 2, 1980. In a case filed by the AFL-CIO (Industrial Union Department) and others against the American Petroleum Institute (the Trade Association of American Oil Companies), the Supreme Court ruled that the proposed OSHA standard was unjustifiably strict. However, the Court was divided. The plurality agreed with the U.S. Circuit Court of Appeals (5th Circuit, New Orleans), which concluded that OSHA had exceeded its standard-setting authority because it had not shown that the new benzene exposure limit was "reasonably necessary or appropriate to provide safe or healthful employment" as required by the OSH Act, and because the act does not "give OSHA the unbridled discretion to adopt standards designed to create absolutely risk-free workplaces regardless of the costs."[8]

Some central findings of the plurality in this case are as follows:

> As presently formulated, the benzene standard is an expensive way of providing some additional protection for a relatively small number of employees. According to OSHA's figures, the standard will require capital investments in engineering controls of approximately $266 million, first-year operating costs (for monitoring, medical testing, employee training and respirators) of $187 million to $205 million and recurring annual costs of approximately $34 million [43 Fed. Reg., at 5934]. The figures outlined in OSHA's explanation of the costs of compliance to various industries indicate that only 35,000 employees would gain any benefit from the regulation in terms of a reduction in their exposure to benzene. Over two-thirds of these workers (24,450) are employed in the rubber manufacturing industry. Compliance costs in that industry are estimated to be rather low with no capital costs and initial operating expenses estimated at only $34 million ($1,390 per employee); recurring annual costs would also be rather low, totalling less than $1 million. By contrast, the segment of the petroleum refining industry that produces benzene would be required to incur $24 million in capital costs and $600,000 in first-year operating expenses to provide additional protection for 300 workers ($82,000 per employee), while the petrochemical industry would be required to incur $20.9 million in capital costs and $1 million in initial operating expenses for the benefit of 552 employees ($39,675 per employee) [43 Fed. Reg. 5936-5938].

Although OSHA did not quantify the benefits to each category of worker in terms of decreased exposure to benzene, it appears from the economic impact study done at OSHA's direction that those benefits may be relatively small. Thus, although the current exposure limit is 10 ppm, the actual exposures outlined in that study are often considerably lower. For example, for the period 1970-1975 the petrochemical industry reported that, out of a total of 496 employees exposed to benzene, only 53 were exposed to levels between 1 and 5 ppm and only seven (all at the same plant) were exposed to between 5 and 10 ppm. . . .

Any discussion of the 1 ppm exposure limit must, of course, begin with the Agency's rationale for imposing that limit. The written explanation of the standard fills 184 pages of the printed appendix. Much of it is devoted to a discussion of the voluminous evidence of the adverse effects of exposure to benzene at levels of concentration well above 10 ppm. This discussion demonstrates that there is ample justification for regulating occupational exposure to benzene and the prior limit of 10 ppm, with a ceiling of 25 ppm (or a peak of 50 ppm) was reasonable. It does not, however, provide direct support for the Agency's conclusion that the limit should be reduced from 10 ppm to 1 ppm.[9]

The Court held that OSHA must make a threshold determination of significant risk at the standard's present level before moving to a lower level. To the Court, a safe work environment does not necessitate a risk-free work environment. Unsafe means the workplace has a *substantial* or *significant* health risk. Under the decision, OSHA must adequately prove that there will be significant health benefits at the lower level. The Court stated that OSHA had established a risk at levels above 10 ppm, yet the agency failed to prove that any substantial benefit would result from dropping the level. The ruling forced OSHA to obtain and appeal to scientific and quantitative data, rather than continuing to promulgate standards based on less compelling evidence. OSHA had no choice but to reinstate the previous 10 ppm standard.

RESPONSES TO THE BENZENE DECISION

The Supreme Court decision prompted mixed reactions. Industrial unions argued that too great a burden had been placed on scientific data. They feared that only a "body count" would prod industry to take protective action.[10] They were concerned that too many employees might be exposed to industrial chemicals at dangerous levels while OSHA waited for research to be completed and data to be interpreted, just as industry must now await the results of aniline and ortho-toluidine studies.

Company spokespersons typically supported the court's ruling. The petroleum and rubber industries had long criticized OSHA for promulgating standards that they believed were based on sheer speculation. Now they contended that some rational boundaries had been established, within which the law compelled OSHA to operate. They hoped that new OSHA regulations would rely on quantitatively significant risk rather than theoretical risk.[11]

The ruling placed OSHA officials in a quandary. The burden of proof that a certain level of chemical exposure was dangerous was shifted to their shoulders. Yet, they believed that the Court did not provide clear guidance in determining the standard's proper level. The Court required that OSHA weigh costs and benefits, but the ruling did not delineate which method to use or at what level a standard should be abandoned as unreasonable.

There are many expenses—for facilities, personnel, and so forth—involved in financing a research project. Questions also arise about the testing methods to be used, particularly concerning the use of animal data as opposed to human-based research. The process is lengthy (perhaps six years); even at the completion of that process, researchers cannot ensure that a substance that is not carcinogenic in animals will prove to be noncarcinogenic in humans. Moreover, the International Agency for Research on Cancer estimates that 92 percent of known or suspected carcinogens have not been adequately tested to identify them as safe or unsafe for human exposure at any level.[12] Epidemiological studies available in 1980 have gradually been updated or replaced, but the regulatory battle over benzene has continued amid scientific inquiries into its effects. In December 1985, OSHA proposed a new rule for occupational exposure to benzene. Once again OSHA proposed that the standard be lowered to 1 ppm. In proposing this new rule, OSHA adhered to the standards set by the Supreme Court in its 1980 ruling. OSHA conducted quantitative risk studies to assess benzene's potential threat to workers. OSHA then assessed the new standard's potentially significant benefits to exposed workers. Unfortunately, few studies are available that are based on exposure levels at or below 10 ppm, so OSHA extrapolated from studies involving higher levels of exposure. For this extrapolation OSHA used a simple linear model that assumes a direct relationship between leukemia development and benzene dosage. Several experimental studies have demonstrated a linear relationship between benzene and chromosomal damage associated with an increased risk of cancer. In addition, U.S. and foreign governments have widely accepted the linear model for the study of chemical carcinogens. When questioned as to whether it was correct to assume a direct link, researcher Charles Brown replied, "The correct model is unknown, and will remain so until we know the mechanistic relationship between benzene exposure and leukemia; however I do not believe that the data warrant more sophistication than the simple linear model."[13]

Finally, OSHA examined available data to set a technologically and economically feasible exposure limit. Though the 1-ppm standard was proposed back in 1977 under substantial industry opposition, technological developments made the proposed rule more feasible and palatable to industry. The EPA had imposed pollution standards that caused industries to install equipment to reduce airborne benzene levels. Surveillance and maintenance standards were also improved. Consequently, average exposure levels had dropped below 10 ppm, with many already close to 1 ppm.

OSHA conducted public hearings on the new proposed benzene exposure rules in March 1986. The agency announced final rules for benzene exposure in all industries on September 1, 1987. OSHA based the final standard on a complete assessment of the proceedings. The new standard, to be met by February 1988, reduced the permissible exposure limit (PEL) from 10 ppm to the proposed 8-hour TWA of 1 ppm and a short-term exposure limit of 5 ppm. The rules also established industrial hygiene requirements, including provisions that called for monitoring, engineering controls, respiratory protection, medical surveillance, and hazard communication.[14] The OSHA benzene guidelines, as revised in July 1995, compel the employer to post a specifically worded sign and to distribute an extensive material safety data sheet in accordance with the latter requirement.[15]

THE CURRENT SITUATION

Industry, organized labor, and government hope not to repeat the uncertainties of the benzene experience now that ortho-toluidine and aniline appear to be similarly dangerous chemicals. Everyone wants standards to be based on more than surveillance of medical records mixed with speculation about appropriate exposure levels. But how are reasoned boundaries to be set? Is it even possible for OSHA to act in a timely manner to promulgate new standards in light of what one scientist calls "the cumbersome regulatory machinery that has evolved since passage of the OSH Act [and] . . . the sheer inertia that must be overcome to proceed step by step through the process"?[16] What is quantitatively significant risk, what is acceptable risk, and how does a public policy flow from our knowledge of risk?

In September 1989 the U.S. Environmental Protection Agency (EPA) established guidelines to remove 90 percent of all industrial benzene emissions into the air. Ironically, the new regulations—written to take effect in 1992—do not affect automobile benzene emissions, which account for almost 80 percent of all airborne benzene. The new laws regulate only pesticide and industrial emissions. The EPA has mandated that benzene pesticide emissions be reduced to 1-ppm exposures, and industrial amounts to 1 part per 10,000 exposures.

However, environmentalists and union representatives objected to the new regulations, calling them too lenient and subjective. According to David Hawkins, a Natural Resources Defense Fund attorney, "[Why] allow a greater risk for the air you put in your lungs than the food you put in your mouth?"[17] Hawkins added that the EPA needed to reduce the industrial exposure rate even further to better protect workers. Though the regulations are arguably too lenient in design, the EPA has enforced compliance with industrial emissions reductions requirements. In 1992, the EPA imposed a $1 million penalty on Chevron U.S.A. Inc. for failure to limit benzene emissions in accordance with regulations. The agency also fined BP Chemicals Inc. for violating hazardous waste laws at its Lima, Ohio, plant.[18]

EPA Deputy Administrator Henry Habicht contended that the new regulations will fully protect 99 percent of the estimated 90 million workers exposed to industrial benzene emissions. Habicht added that the costs of implementing the new requirements to industry would be significant but feasible,[19] requiring a $1 billion expenditure on new pollution controls and annual $200 million operating costs.

Industry representatives contradicted Habicht's estimates, calling the regulations unnecessary. The American Petroleum Institute maintained that the EPA based its benzene limits on "outdated risk assessments that have never been reviewed by the scientific community."[20] A coke mills representative added that the EPA's requirements will force the closure of an undetermined number of marginal plants, which the EPA blames as primary benzene vapor producers.

Responses to the OSHA guidelines, first established in 1987 and revised most recently in 1995, have also been mixed. A study of employees in a petrochemical plant in the Virgin Islands called for an adjustment to the white blood cell cutoffs that OSHA has identified as evidence of benzene exposure. The authors argue that the regulations, which require employers to refer an employee to a hematologist if his or her white blood cell level reaches a certain threshold level, fail to take into account racial differences. Applying OSHA's hematological standard to African-Caribbean adults, who have lower counts than white populations, may thus be unduly strict, even unnecessary.[21] Possibly in response to such criticism, the revised (1995) OSHA standards include the following statement, "The normal ranges for the red cell and white cell counts are influenced by altitude, race, and sex, and therefore should be determined by the accredited laboratory in the specific area where the tests are performed."[22]

Others have questioned the efficacy of utilizing short-term exposure limits (STELs) to determine concentrations of benzene and other hazardous chemicals. S. M. Rappaport has argued that monitoring STELs is actually counterproductive, because it is costly and requires 10 times the resources per worker by comparison to investigation of 8-hour TWA concentrations. He contends that, "OSHA should resist the temptation to add STELs to its standards without reasonable evidence that transient levels either induce acute effects or disproportionally influence the risk of chronic disease."[23]

As neurobehavioral and other assessment methods have grown in popularity and methodological sophistication, we have increasingly come to appreciate that there are many unanswered questions about the very tests used to achieve the results that OSHA and the EPA rely on in making such recommendations. No one set of chemical tests or medical, neurological, or neuropsychological tests is sufficiently comprehensive or accurate to yield the necessary results. As of the mid-1990s, after more than two decades of development, the major tests still appear to be in their infancy.[24]

NOTES

1. Dana Milbank, "Link Is Found Between Bladder Cancer and Two Chemicals Used in Industry," *The Wall Street Journal*, April 3, 1991, p. A2.
2. Carl F. Cranor, "Epidemiology and Procedural Protections for Workplace Health in the Aftermath of the Benzene Case," *Industrial Relations Law Journal* 5 (1983), p. 394.
3. "Benzene, Formaldehyde: Workplace Exposure Limits Proposed," *Chemical and Engineering News* 63 (December 9, 1985), p. 5.
4. R. Jeffrey Smith, "A Light Rein Falls on OSHA," *Science* 209 (August 1, 1980), p. 568.
5. 20 U.S.C., #652(8).
6. 29 U.S.C. ,#655(b)(5).
7. "Research that Clouds the Benzene Issue," *Business Week* (June 26, 1978), p. 43.
8. *Industrial Union Department, AFL-CIO v. American Petroleum Institute et al.*, 100 S.Ct. 2884 (1980).
9. *Ibid.*
10. "The Court Leaves OSHA Hanging," *Business Week* (July 21, 1980), p. 68.
11. "High Court Overturns OSHA Benzene Rule," *Chemical and Engineering News* 58 (July 7, 1980), p. 4.
12. *Ibid.*
13. 50 Fed. Reg. 50533 (1985).
14. 52 Fed. Reg. 34460 (1987).
15. 29 Fed. Reg. 1910.1028 (1995).
16. S. M. Rappaport, "Threshold Limit Values, Permissible Exposure Limits, and Feasibility: The Bases for Exposure Limits in the United States," *American Journal of Industrial Medicine* 23 (May 1993), pp. 683-94.
17. Bill McAllister, "EPA Sets New Rules to Curb Benzene," *The Washington Post*, September 1, 1989, p. A4.
18. "Chevron U.S.A. to Pay EPA Penalties; Agency Charges BP Chemicals," *The Wall Street Journal*, August 6, 1992, p. A4.
19. McAllister, "EPA Sets New Rules to Curb Benzene," p. A4.
20. *Ibid.*
21. Cora L. E. Christian, Bonnie Werley, Angela Smith et al., "Comparison of Employees' White Blood Cell Counts in a Petrochemical Plant by Worksite and Race," *Journal of the National Medical Association* 86 (August 1994), pp. 620–23.
22. OSHA Regulations, p. 312.
23. S. M. Rappaport, "Biological Monitoring and Standard Setting in the USA: A Critical Appraisal," *Toxicology Letters* 77 (May 1995), pp. 171–82.
24. See B. L. Johnson, ed., *Prevention of Neurotoxic Illness in Working Populations* (New York: John Wiley & Sons, 1987); D. E. Hartman, *Neuropsychological Toxicology* (New York: Pergamon Press, 1988); Harvey Checkoway et al., *Research Methods in Occupational Epidemiology* (New York: Oxford University Press, 1989).

CISCO, THE "WINE FOOLER"

On the night of May 27, 1990, intoxicated Maryland teenager Donnell Petite hurled rocks at motorists passing by on the Capital Beltway, causing permanent brain damage to a teenage passenger. Before the incident, Petite and his friends had purchased and consumed two 24-ounce bottles of Cisco, a wine strengthened with grape brandy and manufactured by the Canandaigua Wine Company in New York State. The incident marked a new development in a preexisting controversy between Cisco's manufacturer, state and local governments, and public interest activists. Cisco's clear glass container and wraparound neck label make its appearance almost identical to standard wine coolers. However, the alcohol content is not equal. The wine industry divides its products into three categories, each roughly defined by average alcohol content. Most wine coolers contain 4 to 5 percent alcohol. In comparison, the industry defines "table wines" as products containing up to a 14 percent alcohol level. Finally, the "dessert wine" category includes all wines with alcohol content above 14 percent, usually an 18 to 20 percent level. Classified by Canandaigua as a "fortified dessert wine," Cisco has a 20 percent alcohol content level, even though its packaging gives Cisco a "cooler style" appearance.

Consumer advocates like the National Council on Alcoholism and Drug Dependence (NCADD) allege that purchasers, particularly underage drinkers, do not realize the wine's potency. Cisco therefore represents a danger to ill-informed drinkers. When compounded by its stylish packaging, Cisco's potency prompted Surgeon General Antonia Novello to declare Cisco "a dangerous fortified wine, and the ultimate 'wine fooler.'"[1]

Before manufacturing Cisco, Canandaigua had established a reputation as a leading wine and wine cooler producer through the marketing of products such as Sun Country Wine Cooler and Richard's Wild Irish Rose, an inexpensive fortified sweet wine. Canandaigua introduced Sun Country in 1986, and it quickly increased company sales by 28 percent and net income by 11.6 percent. However, fiscal year 1987 showed a sales downturn for Canandaigua's coolers, with a total $2.7 million loss in one fiscal quarter. Sun Country's share of the wine cooler market plunged to 11 percent, tied in fourth place with Stroh's White Mountain. Industry sources attributed Sun Country's decline to "poor sales and increased marketing expenses."[2] Over the same period, Wild

This case was prepared by John Cuddihy and revised by Jeff Greene, under the supervision of Tom L. Beauchamp. Not to be duplicated without permission of the holder of the copyright, © 1992, 1996 Tom L. Beauchamp.

Irish Rose's sales soared, resulting in a net corporate profit. Given the wine's success, Canandaigua decided to expand its fortified wine product line. In 1988 Canandaigua purchased Cisco from a California wine producer and introduced it nationally. Canandaigua was rewarded with extraordinary results: Sales soared 50 percent in 1989, and Cisco's total earnings rose 89 percent in 1990.[3]

Consumer complaints about Cisco surfaced shortly after the company marketed the wine on a national level. In Gaithersburg, Maryland, city officials instituted a voluntary ban on cheap, potent wines. Officials hoped that homeless alcoholics, who rely on cheap wines like Thunderbird and Wild Irish Rose to maintain their dependencies, would seek treatment once their wine supplies diminished. Instead, the alcoholics discovered Cisco. According to Gaithersburg homeless advocate Lamont Lawson, "This stuff . . . is what they're turning to when they can't get the other wines."[4] Homeless alcoholics describe Cisco as "liquid crack" and affirm that Cisco became the wine of choice after the ban largely ended the sale of conventional potent wines.

Consumer complaints alerted various public interest organizations, including NCADD and the Center for Science in the Public Interest (CSPI), about the public's concern over Cisco's unadvertised potency. The organizations researched Cisco and its effects, and launched "a grassroots campaign in August 1990 to alert the public to the dangers of Cisco."[5] During this time Canandaigua used the slogan "Cisco takes you by surprise" as a marketing technique. Documented effects of Cisco consumption included "combativeness, hallucinations, disorientation, loss of motor control and consciousness."[6]

Canandaigua sells Cisco in 12-ounce (375 ml) and 24-ounce (750 ml) bottles. The two sizes supply purchasers with approximately four and eight (normal-size) drinks, respectively. Research has shown that consumption of the 12-ounce bottle (equivalent to five shots of 80-proof vodka) within one hour by a person weighing 150 pounds or less will result in a 0.11 blood alcohol content level, which renders people legally unfit to drive in every state except Georgia. Consumption of two 12-ounce Cisco bottles within one hour by a 100-pound person may induce acute alcohol poisoning and death.

Disturbed by the results of the research, NCADD, in cooperation with CSPI, Mothers Against Drunk Driving (MADD), and Representative John Conyers (D-MI), asked Canandaigua to voluntarily withdraw Cisco from sale and to alter its marketing techniques to better inform the public of Cisco's alcohol content. These interest groups feared that the wine's cooler style of packaging could cause people to mistake Cisco for a regular wine cooler with a low-alcohol content. Because it is inexpensively priced, like wine coolers, retail dealers often stock Cisco near or with the wine cooler displays. As U.S. Surgeon General Antonia Novello reported in a January 9, 1991, press conference, "The manufacturer has packaged this drink to appear as a refreshing, cool drink, with a seemingly low alcohol content." Consumer groups and the Surgeon General worried that underage drinkers, pregnant women, and others particularly susceptible to the dangers of alcohol would unwittingly consume Cisco.

Southland Corporation, the owner of 7-Eleven stores, also said it "shares concerns of consumer groups over the marketing and packaging of the product."[7] Because of its concerns, the convenience store decided to remove Cisco from all of the company-owned stores, which account for more than 50 percent of its 6,700 U.S. retail outlets. Southland executives then sent letters to the remaining stores, all of which are run by franchises, strongly urging them to discontinue selling the product. Southland pulled Cisco after CSPI called the company's Northern Virginia regional office to disseminate information on Cisco's unadvertised potency. According to Southland spokeswoman Rosemary Fischer, "We removed Cisco because of the wine's nature; kids were being harmed by it."[8] In similar actions, the state of Maine banned all sales of Cisco, and a midwestern food chain (Food-4-Less) removed the fortified dessert wine from its shelves.

Canandaigua's management has never shared these opinions or had similar concerns. Though the company acknowledged that Cisco's 12-ounce bottle bore "some resemblance"[9] to coolers produced by the Seagram's and Gallo companies, it contended that the superficial likenesses did not warrant a packaging adjustment. Canandaigua highlighted Cisco's distinctive packaging: "Whereas wine coolers are almost universally sold in 4-packs of bottles, Cisco is sold in single bottles."[10] The company also maintained that "Cisco's 'hot,' high-alcohol taste immediately tells the consumer it is not a low-alcohol cooler."[11] However, faced with growing pressure to repackage Cisco and properly identify the drink's potency to distinguish it from a wine cooler, Canandaigua's management announced new marketing and labeling plans in October 1990. It opted to label Cisco bottles with the statement "This is not a wine cooler" in the largest print allowed under federal regulations, and it agreed to remove the controversial point-of-purchase slogan "Cisco takes you by surprise."

However, NCADD and CSPI vowed to continue their grass-roots campaign until Canandaigua further redesigned Cisco's packaging. According to a NCADD statement, "Once [Cisco] has been repackaged to look like a fortified wine [instead of a wine cooler], our work is done."[12] Canandaigua supporters replied that "for years, wine coolers and fortified wines have been produced in a variety of different sizes and shapes."[13]

As consumer advocates feared, teenage intoxication cases involving Cisco continued to increase, despite Canandaigua's improved warning labels. Dr. Joseph Wright, a pediatrician at the Children's National Medical Center in Washington, DC, documented 15 cases in late 1990 of adolescent intoxication cases with 0.1 percent blood alcohol levels. Wright discovered that 10 of these 15 emergency room patients had "cited Cisco as the sole agent of consumption."[14] Wright interviewed eight of these Cisco users, "who all thought Cisco was a wine cooler."[15] Wright cited the average intoxication level of the Cisco users as 200.2 mg/dcl, twice the legal limit for driving in 49 states and the District of Columbia.

These legally drunk patients had consumed an average of only 18 ounces of Cisco (a relatively small quantity) to cause their resulting blood alcohol levels. Dr. Wright observed that the Cisco users' blood alcohol levels rivaled those of patients who drank hard alcohol. Wright maintained that Cisco, a carbonated drink similar to champagne, lends itself to rapid intoxication. Cisco's 20 percent alcohol content also facilitates alcohol absorption by the body. Medical data indicate that beverages with alcohol content between 10 percent and 30 percent usually have a high absorption rate.

Dr. Wright's patients averaged 15.3 years of age, leading him to say, "Kids think it's a more benign product than it actually is. Kids are deceived by the color, taste, and packaging resemblances to wine coolers. Cisco represents an extreme health hazard to underage drinkers."[16] The American Association of Poison Control Centers, Inc. (AAPCC) concurred with Dr. Wright's evaluation of Cisco. Over the winter holidays, AAPCC documented several alcohol poisoning cases. In each instance, the underage drinker ingested only Cisco. Cases ranged from a 14-year-old "drunk and combative"[17] California girl to a 17-year-old New Jersey female "admitted unconscious with a history of Cisco ingestion. Her blood ethanol [alcohol] level was 300 mg/dcl,"[18] triple the legal intoxication level. AAPCC reported other ethanol poisoning cases nationwide, from Minnesota to Rhode Island. In response, advocacy groups accelerated their drive to force Canandaigua to repackage Cisco.

The mushrooming public and business uproar over Cisco also attracted the U.S. government's attention. Congress, the Treasury Department's Bureau of Alcohol, Tobacco and Firearms (BATF), the U.S. Surgeon General, and the Federal Trade Commission all became involved in the Cisco controversy. This involvement gave consumer advocates the opportunity to effect national regulatory action against Cisco. Though some state governments vigorously supported the Cisco recall movement, they wielded little authority outside of their state borders.

In September and October 1990 Representative Conyers and Surgeon General Novello repeatedly criticized Canandaigua's actions in their public appearances. Dr. Novello characterized Cisco as "incredibly potent, [a] potentially lethal beverage."[19] In late 1990 Representative George Miller (D-CA), chairman of the Select Committee on Children, Youth, and Families, wrote a letter to Richard Sands, Canandaigua's president, urging "immediate action to design and market Cisco, to make it unmistakably clear that 'Cisco' is a *high alcohol content wine*, not a wine cooler or soft drink."[20] Miller added, "Cisco should not remain on the market in its present label (even the barely improved 'modified' label) or bottle shape."[21]

Despite the government's discreet requests, Canandaigua did not repackage Cisco by the end of 1990. Accordingly, at a January 9, 1991, press conference, Surgeon General Novello formally asked Canandaigua to repackage Cisco "so that it is not confused with wine coolers."[22] Joined by consumer and health advocacy groups, Novello cited the dangers that Cisco posed to underage drinkers who mistake the wine for a low-alcohol beverage. The surgeon general pledged to have Cisco reclassified as a fortified wine and urged the public to help her "protect a generation of American youth from becoming Cisco Kids."[23]

Canandaigua Chairman Marvin Sands contended in early 1991 that Cisco had been made the scapegoat for the problem of underage drinking. According to Sands, "Cisco doesn't play any more of a role [in alcohol abuse] than any other brand. We've never had a single complaint about it from a consumer, retailer or wholesaler. All we've seen is allegations and accusations."[24] In later correspondence with Representative George Miller, Canandaigua President Richard Sands stated that, "When [Cisco] is consumed responsibly by persons over 21, there is no 'serious health hazard' associated with Cisco."[25]

Nonetheless, NCADD pressed its case: "When something becomes known on the street as 'Liquid Crack,' shouldn't there be some questions raised about a product's promotion that has helped create that imagery?"[26] Federal officials noted that BATF's regulations at that time could not compel a producer to alter its product marketing strategies or distribution procedures. Accordingly, BATF proposed a change in the Code of Federal Regulations to "provide that standard wine containers shall be so made and formed so as not to mislead the purchaser."[27] The revisions also authorized the federal government to prohibit the interstate or foreign shipment of any wine product "unless such wine is bottled or packed in standard wine containers."[28]

These proposed regulations enraged significant sectors of the wine industry, which felt targeted for punitive action by the government and by anti-alcohol activists. One spirits industry correspondent commented that the regulation "sounds like it would open a Pandora's box of subjective judgments about package and label design."[29]

Faced with a potential ban on all Cisco shipments outside New York State—unless it altered Cisco's bottle and label design—Canandaigua's management finally reached an agreement with federal authorities. On February 4, 1991, Canandaigua officials presented proposed modifications to Cisco's packaging to Surgeon General Novello. The plans changed Cisco's bottle color from clear to dark green and replaced the bottle's short neck with a longer, more slender neck. Canandaigua altered the 12-ounce bottle label so that it read "THIS CONTAINER SERVES 4 PEOPLE AND IS BEST SERVED OVER ICE." The company also retained its warning label "This is not a wine cooler" on all Cisco bottles. According to Canandaigua Chairman Marvin Sands, "The new Cisco package looks like no other product on the market today."[30] Company officials made the new bottles available to distributors during the spring of 1991.

The surgeon general, the Federal Trade Commission, and the BATF announced that the changes satisfactorily addressed their objections about the former package, and the government abandoned its plans for regulatory action against Canandaigua.

Despite this apparent resolution of the controversy, the actors still faced obstacles to a final resolution. NCADD announced that its movement to ban Cisco from retail shelves would continue until the new bottles arrived and the existing inventory disappeared. Canandaigua's legal counsel, Robert Sands, criticized the public interest groups for creating "a campaign not based on fact or truth, that uses distorted facts."[31] Marvin Sands also commented, "We never felt a package change would accomplish the purposes advanced by a handful of adversaries."[32] Management considers underage drinking, not Cisco, to be responsible for the rash of alcohol-related injuries and illnesses. According to Canandaigua, "We have [not] seen any evidence that consumers have purchased and consumed Cisco without realizing it was a 20 percent alcohol beverage."[33]

The company insists that consumer groups have targeted Cisco for action, even though other, stronger dessert (strengthened) wines enjoy national marketing without inducing negative publicity. Canandaigua's management argues that popular sherries, ports, and marsala wines rival Cisco's alcohol content levels, while other alcoholic beverages, such as brandy, contain 40 percent alcohol. Consequently, Cisco's producers believe that the advocacy groups unfairly "made what is true of a class of beverages appear to be true of Cisco only."[34] Canandaigua considers the groups' actions discriminatory because they ignore the alcoholic content and effects of other strengthened brands currently on sale.

Canandaigua's claims of discriminatory treatment by interest groups and the government were heightened by a further controversy just as the conflict over Cisco began to subside. During the summer of 1991, the BATF, the surgeon general, and advocacy groups led by the Center for Science in the Public Interest (CSPI) launched a campaign to remove G. Heileman Brewing Company's malt liquor PowerMaster from store shelves. The LaCrosse, Wisconsin-based brewer, which produces the top-selling Colt 45 malt liquor, had recently experienced a series of financial setbacks. In January 1991 the company filed for protection from creditors in a New York bankruptcy court, claiming to be "struggling under a huge debt load."[35] In an attempt to reverse its financial decline, Heileman introduced PowerMaster with a 5.9 percent alcohol content. Most malt liquors (defined by law as beers with alcohol levels above 4 percent) have a 5.5 percent average content, as compared with the typical 3.5 percent alcohol level of standard beers.

PowerMaster came under fire from both anti-alcohol and African-American activists. These groups charged that Heileman had created the name and the accompanying advertising campaign, which featured a black male model, with the intent of targeting young black men, who consume roughly one third of all malt liquors.[36] U.S. Surgeon General Antonia Novello joined the Heileman critics, calling the PowerMaster marketing campaign insensitive.[37] The BATF, which had originally approved the PowerMaster label, withdrew its approval. A bureau spokeswoman said, "In light of the planned marketing campaign to blacks, and the high alcohol content, we took another look at [PowerMaster]."[38] The agency subsequently asked Heileman to remove the PowerMaster label from the product. Citing the economic burden that a legal contest to retain the brand name would entail, the company discontinued the product.

Beer industry executives and members criticized the government's role in the controversy. One newspaper columnist cited race as the critical factor in the campaign to remove PowerMaster, noting that the "It's the power" advertising slogan used in the marketing of Pabst Brewing Co.'s Olde English 800 malt liquor had gone unchallenged.[39] James Sanders, president of the Washington, DC based Beer Institute, contended that the government focused on the PowerMaster label to "take the focus off the effects of other factors"[40] such as unemployment and poverty, the real problems that the black community confronts.

In the aftermath of both controversies, the Canandaigua Wine Company faced considerable negative publicity. However, along the way the company was encouraged by some more flexible, even receptive reactions to its position. In particular, Jack Killorin, spokesperson for the U.S. Bureau of Alcohol, Tobacco and Firearms, said, "We don't think the new packaging is deceptive. We're glad that the company has agreed to make that change."[41]

Canandaigua's management hoped that its latest bottle alterations would defuse public interest in Cisco and allow the company to resume its normal operations with the product.

NOTES

1. Public statement of Antonia C. Novello, M.D., M.P.H., U.S. Surgeon General, press conference, January 9, 1991.
2. "Canandaigua," *Advertising Age* 58, no. 50 (November 23, 1987), p. S17.
3. *Adweek's Marketing Week* (January 14, 1991), p. 6.
4. Beth Kalman, "New Cheap Wine Snags Effort for Homeless," *The Washington Post,* November 8, 1990, p. 1.
5. *FYI—Cisco Campaign Chronology.* Published by the National Council on Alcoholism and Drug Dependence, Inc., n.d., pp. 1–2.
6. "NCADD Demands Removal of Cisco from Market," NCADD press release, September 13, 1990.
7. "7-Eleven Stores to Remove Their Cisco Wine Supplies," *The Wall Street Journal,* January 9, 1991, p. B3.
8. Telephone conversation between Southland spokeswoman Mrs. Rosemary Fischer and John Cuddihy, January 28, 1991.
9. April 24, 1991, telephone conversation between John Cuddihy and Canandaigua Wine Company legal counsel Robert Sands.
10. *Cisco: The Controversy, The Facts, Actions*, p. 12. Privately published by the Canandaigua Wine Company, 1990.
11. *Ibid.*
12. Seymour Leikind, "The Decline of Reason," *Beverage Dynamics* (March 1991), p. 4 [Editorial Note].
13. *Ibid.*
14. Joseph L. Wright, *FORTIFIED WINES: A Wolf in Sheep's Clothing*, press release, November 1990.
15. "Teen Alcohol Poisonings Spur Criticisms of 'Cisco,'" CSPI press release, January 9, 1991.
16. Personal interview with Dr. Joseph Wright, February 6, 1991.
17. American Association of Poison Control Centers, Inc., press release, January 18, 1991.
18. *Ibid.*
19. "Teen Alcohol Poisonings Spur Criticisms of 'Cisco,'" CSPI news release.
20. Letter from Representative George Miller, chairman, Select Committee on Children, Youth, and Families, to Mr. Richard Sands, president, Canandaigua Wine Company, dated January 24, 1991.
21. *Ibid.*
22. Letter from Antonia C. Novello, U.S. Surgeon General, to Mr. Marvin Sands, chairman, Canandaigua Wine Company, dated January 9, 1991.

23. *Ibid.*
24. Laura Bird, "Novello Brands Cisco a 'Wine Fooler,'" *Adweek's Marketing Week* (January 14, 1991), p. 6.
25. Letter from Mr. Richard Sands, president, Canandaigua Wine Company, to Representative George Miller, chairman, Select Committee on Children, Youth, and Families, dated January 29, 1991.
26. "Repackaging of Cisco to Eliminate Confusion with Low-Alcohol Wine Coolers," *NCADD News* (February 8, 1991).
27. Notice 710, "Standard Wine Containers," Bureau of Alcohol, Tobacco and Firearms, *Federal Register* 56, no. 25 (February 6, 1991), p. 4770.
28. *Ibid.*
29. Duncan Cameron, "Cisco Debate Centers on Symptoms, Not Problem," *Ohio Tavern News* (March 5, 1991), pp. 1, 13.
30. *Canandaigua Unveils New Package for Cisco-Brand Fortified Wine*, Canandaigua Wine Company press release, dated February 5, 1991.
31. April 24, 1991, telephone conversation between John Cuddihy and Canandaigua Wine Company legal counsel Robert Sands.
32. *Adweek's Marketing Week* (January 14, 1991), p. 6.
33. *Cisco: The Controversy, The Facts, Actions*, p. 11.
34. *Ibid.*, p. 7.
35. Alix Freedman, "Heileman Will Be Asked to Change Potent Brew's Name," *The Wall Street Journal*, June 20, 1991, p. B1.
36. Courtland Milloy, "Race, Beer Don't Mix," *The Washington Post*, July 9, 1991, p. B3; Ira Teinowitz and Steven W. Colford, "Targeting Woes in PowerMaster Wake," *Advertising Age* (July 8, 1991), p. 35.
37. Milloy, "Race, Beer Don't Mix"; Paul Farhi, "Surgeon General Hits New Malt Liquor's Name, Ads," *The Washington Post*, June 26, 1991, pp. A1, A4.
38. Freedman, "Heileman Will Be Asked to Change Potent Brew's Name," p. B1.
39. Milloy, "Race, Beer Don't Mix," p. B3.
40. *Ibid.*
41. Associated Press, "Cisco Wine to Get New Packaging," *The Washington Post*, February 9, 1991, p. A3.

AIDS AND THE AVAILABILITY OF AZT

The realization that AIDS can potentially harm millions of people worldwide has prompted responses from both government and business. In September 1984 the U.S. National Cancer Institute (NCI) conducted a screening program to discover a drug that would kill, or at least deactivate, the human immunodeficiency virus (HIV) that causes AIDS. Five months later, the Burroughs Wellcome Company, a pharmaceutical company in Research Triangle Park, North Carolina, sent samples of zidovudine (formerly azidothymidine, or AZT) to the NCI for virological, immunological, and pharmacological testing. Burroughs Wellcome had experimented with the drug in the early 1980s as a possible anti-bacterial agent. NCI scientists, led by current NCI Director Dr. Samuel Broder, discovered that AZT slowed the growth of the AIDS virus in the test tube. Following extensive testing and governmental clinical pharmacology studies, Burroughs Wellcome submitted a new drug application (NDA) to the U.S. Food and Drug Administration (FDA) for permission to sell AZT.

On March 19, 1987, the FDA approved the drug for sale, and a year later (on February 9, 1988) Burroughs Wellcome obtained an exclusive license to market AZT under the brand name Retrovir. As is the case with all patents, Burroughs Wellcome received exclusive proprietary rights over AZT for 17 years, until February 9, 2005.

Because AIDS is believed to be inevitably fatal and there is no promising alternative treatment, many have argued that compassion dictates making the drug available to all HIV-infected persons. The practice of prescribing AZT to patients with HIV infection, with or without symptoms, spread quickly during the first few years after its development, due in part to the initial increase in the drug's availability and effectiveness for certain purposes.

Federal regulations require that new drugs be tested extensively before market sale. One standard test is to select two similar groups and give one the new drug and the other a harmless placebo. Burroughs Wellcome, in compliance with federal regulations, created a placebo-controlled trial of AZT to determine its efficacy and its toxicity for HIV-infected patients. However, critics argued that a placebo-controlled trial under such extreme circumstances was morally unacceptable, because the trial itself denied 10,000 patients the only promising drug for treating AIDS. Critics argued that the demands of scientific rigor could not be resolved with justice and compassion for HIV patients. However, trial defenders insisted that it was necessary to determine both AZT's efficacy and whether its negative side effects would outweigh its benefits. Dr. Samuel Broder of NCI denied that "compassion and science are in conflict," on grounds that "we have to be concerned with people who have AIDS both now and in the future." He noted that "serious errors—irredeemable errors . . . can be introduced if we don't undertake appropriately controlled studies. It would be a catastrophe if we dismissed a 'good drug' or if we allowed a 'bad drug' to become the standard of therapy."[1]

Use has shown that AZT neither cures AIDS nor eliminates the virus, and its side effects can often be severe, particularly on bone marrow, which produces red and white blood cells. Some patients experience other adverse effects, including nausea, muscle pain, insomnia, and moderate to severe headaches. AZT's toxicity forces many recipients over time to cease the treatment, while others select reduced doses. In fact, one major problem with AZT is its transitory effectiveness. The drug confers only short-term benefits because the HIV virus mutates rapidly and can no longer be effectively controlled. This process of drug resistance can occur quickly in some AZT recipients.[2]

In response to such shortcomings, the FDA eventually began to give quick approval to other new drugs that could combat AIDS or HIV illnesses. In February 1989 the FDA approved aerosol pentamidine for use under a federal program that allows seriously ill patients access to promising new drugs before formal FDA approval. The program allows legal prescription, but it requires that use be monitored before actual licensing can be approved. In June 1989 the FDA also approved Ganciclovir and Erythropoietin without subjecting the drugs to rigorous clinical trials. In October 1991 the FDA approved dideoxyinosine (DDI) "for use in adult and pediatric AIDS patients who are intolerant to or whose health has significantly deteriorated while on zidovudine (AZT)."[3] The FDA approved the drug for market sale six months after Bristol-Myers's Squibb Co. submitted a new drug application for DDI to be marketed under the trade name Videx. HHS Assistant Secretary for Health James O. Mason, M.D., said that "DDI has benefitted through its development from a number of innovative measures FDA has taken to expedite the availability of potentially promising experimental AIDS therapies."[4] These cases constitute a departure from normal FDA drug testing policy.

Though the FDA has approved drugs such as DDI and Ganciclovir for use in combatting AIDS and AIDS-related complex (ARC), AZT is currently the only drug that has been awarded *full* marketing approval. (In order to receive treatment with DDI, patients must have first exhausted AZT treatment options without success.) As the sole AZT producer, Burroughs Wellcome is free to set the drug price. Pharmaceutical companies typically recover research and development costs by charging whatever the market will bear before competition and new drugs enter the market, even if the cost exceeds some consumers' budgets. This practice, with its potential for abuse of profit, has long been controversial.

Burroughs Wellcome originally listed a $10,000 retail price (the company then wholesaled the drug for $8,300) for a year's supply of the drug, with a projected use by up to 30,000 patients. Estimated (anticipated) annual revenue at this cost was between $130 million and $250 million. By October 1989 the AZT full dosage price had been lowered to approximately $650 per month, or $7,800 per year retail, and by late 1991 the retail price had dropped (partially through the lowering of dosage) to approximately $3,000. (This retail price derives from Burroughs Wellcome's wholesale price of $1.20 for each 100-mg capsule.)

Industry analysts believe that Burroughs Wellcome's cost for bringing AZT onto the market ranged from $80 million to $180 million. Sales quickly exceeded $220 million annually after it entered the market. In 1990 Retrovir sales earned the Wellcome Foundation, the British-based parent company, approximately $287 million.[5] Early in 1990 scientists confirmed that AZT benefited not only patients ill with HIV-related conditions but also some asymptomatic HIV-infected persons. With increased use by patients infected with the AIDS virus but showing no symptoms, sales could reach $1 billion annually. Company figures already show large increases in Retrovir's volume sales, which increased 53 percent in 1990 from 1989 levels.

Burroughs Wellcome, with assistance from experts at the Infectious Disease Society of America, originally set strict criteria to ensure the best utilization of AZT and a continuous supply for patients with the greatest need and the most substantial probability of medical benefit. The criteria excluded children, pregnant women, and nursing mothers, due to the lack of information then available about the drug's effects on children, fetuses, and newborns. However, testing eventually showed AZT to be as effective for AIDS-infected children as for adults in prolonging life and dramatically reversing mental deterioration and dementia, symptoms common to AIDS patients. In May 1990 the FDA announced that AZT would be widely distributed to children for the first time. This action ended what some critics have called an unconscionable delay in administering AZT to children after tests showed that it could prolong their lives and reverse mental deterioration.

Critics have long charged that the company's AZT price was unreasonably high and created a potential hardship for patients who lack any real alternative. In January 1988 police arrested 19 people in a civil disobedience protest at Burroughs Wellcome's Burlingame, California, distribution center. Many physicians and consumer advocates still demand that Burroughs Wellcome justify what appears to them to be an exorbitant price.

Burroughs Wellcome has defended the AZT price as fair and necessary because of the costs it incurred, citing the lengthy and expensive process of manufacturing AZT, as well as intensive and financially burdensome labor and technology. However, the company has consistently refused to provide precise figures on costs to Congress, claiming that these figures are confidential. Burroughs Wellcome does state that it committed $80 million to the drug's research and development, including $10 million in free AZT administered to 4,500 clinical trial patients.

Mr. T. E. Haigler, Jr., president and CEO of Burroughs Wellcome, testified that the company's calculation of AZT's cost included the following:

> [The] costs of developing, producing and marketing the drug, the high costs of research, and the need to generate revenues to cover these continuing costs . . . [including] the possible advent of new therapies, and profit margins customarily generated by significant new medicines. . . . We also examined factors that might be considered to be unique with respect to Retrovir. These included the very real high cost of producing this drug and the very real needs of the patients for whom this drug was developed.[6]

Burroughs Wellcome also claimed that AZT merits its price because it will reduce the costs of treating each AIDS patient by 25 percent, and the costs of treating each ARC patient by 60 percent. The prolongation of life and the reduced incidence of infections achieved by the AZT drug will also result in fewer hospitalizations for AIDS patients.[7]

Some individuals with AIDS, many of whom are young, indigent, and uninsured, cannot pay AZT's market price. Therefore, public programs such as Medicaid have borne much of the treatment cost. The financial burden of obtaining AZT has prompted one physician to say, "Either it'll be on the taxpayer's back, or patients will be robbing pharmacies. These are desperate, dying patients."

By September 1988 a $30 million federal allocation for AIDS patients had been exhausted. Congress did not renew the funds but did twice extend funding to allow states more time to develop their own programs. However, many state and local governments in the United States have not assumed the costs of combating the disease. In some states, health officials have stopped accepting new applications for AZT under existing programs. Many public officials have expressed fears that new funding bills would open a Pandora's box that could lead to enormous federal and state expenditures.

In response to public pressure and the skyrocketing number of reported AIDS cases, U.S. government agencies have implemented streamlined drug approval programs for potential AIDS treatments. Consequently, drugs such as DDI have gained quicker access to the marketplace and needy AIDS patients. However, many people still face severe financial obstacles to AZT treatment. AIDS activists, pharmaceutical companies, and U.S. government representatives therefore contend that Burroughs Wellcome's monopoly on AZT production should be broken to allow generic AZT production. According to some economic and pharmaceutical experts, competitive production of AZT would sharply lower the drug's retail price. Dr. Stephen Schondelmeyer, director of Purdue University's Pharmaceutical Economic Research Center, states, "Many generic drugs enter the market for one-half to two-thirds the price of the innovator drug. I think that the same kind of savings could be achieved with zidovudine (AZT)."[8] Consequently, Burroughs Wellcome has had to confront legal motions that aim to invalidate the U.S. patent that gives the company exclusive production rights on AZT until February, 2005.

On March 18, 1991, Public Citizen, a law firm founded by Ralph Nader, filed suit in Washington, DC, federal court on behalf of the People With AIDS Health Group, hoping to invalidate Burroughs Wellcome's six AIDS-related patents. This group argued that the firm wrongly took credit for developing AZT as an AIDS therapy away from federal scientists and researchers. According to a Public Citizen lawyer, "We cannot allow our government to give away an invention that it paid for and made while at the same time asking people with AIDS and the taxpayers to shoulder the monopoly prices charged by Burroughs Wellcome."[9] Burroughs Wellcome filed a motion to dismiss Public Citizen's lawsuit on May 13, 1991. At this writing, the case remains unresolved.

Some people familiar with the AZT controversy consider the Public Citizen lawsuit "to be part of a larger attempt by scientists at the NCI—where much of the work on the drug was conducted—to be given what they feel is due recognition for their work."[10] The National Institutes of Health (NIH) unsuccessfully negotiated with Burroughs Wellcome through May 1991 to have NCI scientists included on the patent as co-inventors of AZT. NIH Director Bernadine Healy commented during a May 1991 press conference, "The intellectual and scientific contributions made by NCI to the evolution of AZT were essential components of the AZT therapy for AIDS, and deserve recognition."[11]

The patent dispute and collapse of negotiations between NIH and Burroughs Wellcome were related to Burroughs Wellcome's second legal crisis, involving a patent challenge by Barr Laboratories. Barr, a Pomona, NY–based pharmaceuticals firm, filed an abbreviated new drug application (ANDA) with the FDA on March 19, 1991, asking permission to produce a generic equivalent to Retrovir. On April 9, 1991, Barr executives informed Burroughs Wellcome they intended to challenge the company's AZT-related patents. In response, Burroughs Wellcome sued Barr for patent infringement on May 14, 1991, in a Raleigh, North Carolina, federal court.

Barr contends that a generic version of AZT would sell for 40 percent less than the current prices. Edwin A. Cohen, at that time Barr Laboratories' president and CEO, said, "We would like to see zidovudine become available at the lowest possible price." On July 17, 1991, NIH Director Healy announced that the NIH had granted Barr a "nonexclusive patent license to market AZT."[12] According to Healy, "The availability of AZT from additional commercial sources and the resulting competition should cause a marked decrease in the price of AZT."[13] The NIH also gave Barr the right to litigate the government's alleged inventorship and ownership in the AZT patents, and it has agreed to cooperate with Barr in the lawsuit filed by Burroughs Wellcome. According to one pharmaceuticals publication, "The NIH would also allow Barr a credit on future royalty payments if the [legal] dispute resulted in generic zidovudine being marketed."[14]

According to industry observers, "It is rare for the government to step in and take sides in a patent dispute."[15] Although the Barr-NIH agreement is hollow unless Barr succeeds in invalidating Burroughs Wellcome's exclusive patent, the consequences to the British subsidiary are potentially devastating.

According to one pharmaceutical consultant, "Burroughs Wellcome can lose at least half their business in the first year a copy drug reaches the market."[16]

In a November 1994 ruling, Burroughs Wellcome finally prevailed in the legal contest. The U.S. Court of Appeals upheld a July 1993 federal ruling that established Burroughs Wellcome's continued role as exclusive patent holder. This decision effectively denied both Barr and Novapharm Inc. (another generic drug company) rights to produce AZT at lower prices. The court reasoned that Burroughs Wellcome should continue to possess sole rights to five of the six patents because the idea to use AZT on AIDS patients before the release of early test results originated with that company. A lower court will determine the status of the final patent after further investigation.

Despite the chance of ongoing resolution about this final patent, Barr president Bruce Downey was disappointed with the ruling.[17] Criticism mounted that this decision will negatively affect those patients who, as a result of Burroughs Wellcome's control of the AZT market, must continue to pay what some consider exorbitant prices for the drug. However, this situation need only continue until the 17-year exclusive patents expire in 2005. In February 1995, the Food and Drug Administration granted approval to Barr to create and market the generic form of AZT upon expiration of Burroughs Wellcome's patent rights.[18]

As the challenges to Burroughs Wellcome have progressed through the American legal system, other companies continue to manufacture potential AIDS vaccines. A recent three-year study of 1,749 HIV-infected adults has given drug companies as well as HIV-positive people even more reason to aggressively pursue treatment options other than AZT. Published in April 1994, the Anglo-French Concorde Trial demonstrated conclusively that AZT neither retards the progression of AIDS nor prolongs the lives of those who take the drug while symptom-free.[19] A study carried out at the Harvard School of Public Health revealed the following:

> Even for the patient who valued the time after a severe adverse event four times more than the time after the progression of disease, the quality-of-life-adjusted time gained with 500 mg of zidovudine [AZT] was less than 1 week during a period of 18 months.[20]

Another study, conducted by the National Institute of Allergy and Infectious Diseases and reported in September 1995, demonstrated that AZT used alone was less effective than DDI alone, a combination of DDI and AZT, or a combination of zalcitabine (DDC) and AZT. As compared to use of AZT alone, the other three treatments were more effective in preventing death, dramatic drops in CD4 count, and progression of HIV infection to full-blown AIDS.[21] This method of treating patients by combining AZT with other new drugs has also conferred positive results in the case of 3TC, a chemical cousin to AZT. This evidence suggests that AZT can no longer be considered the mainstay in the search for effective AIDS treatments.

Researchers continue to work feverishly to explore other approaches to AIDS therapy. For example, drugs called reverse transcriptase inhibitors that work like AZT are being tested in government-sponsored trials. Utilizing gene therapy in combination with these types of drugs may be a promising method of provoking the immune system to destroy the HIV virus. Another combination approach might involve the anti-herpes drug acyclovir that, according to a July 1994 study, prolonged the lives of those patients already taking AZT.[22]

One new advance that holds particular promise for AIDS treatment is the development, testing, and marketing of a class of drugs called protease or proteinase inhibitors, which work by disabling an enzyme crucial to the flourishing of the HIV virus.[23] Several pharmaceutical companies have been working on the manufacture of the drug under pressure from physicians and AIDS activist groups to offer the treatment to desperate patients even during early stages of testing. By initiating a lottery system in June 1995, Hoffmann-La Roche became the first manufacturer to offer free their version of the inhibitor, known as Invirase or sequinivir, to 2,280 AIDS patients. The lottery was expanded to include 2,000 additional patients in November. Merck & Co. followed suit by making the drug Crixivan available to 1,400 people. Abbott Laboratories also offered such a gateway program, promising to provide its experimental drug to 1,400 people by early 1996.

These developments have the potential to greatly improve the lives of those suffering with AIDS. Many argue that providing the experimental drugs to desperate patients before the full testing protocol has been completed manifests compassion, concern, and respect for the rights of those patients whose lives are at stake. Many expect that this trend of improved access to new drugs will continue. However, the majority of AIDS sufferers still face barriers in obtaining treatment. For example, within the first month of the announcement of the Hoffmann-La Roche lottery, the manufacturer received 10,000 registration requests from AIDS patients, many of whom eventually had to be turned away. Despite the compassion of these companies, the time-consuming and difficult process of manufacturing the drugs excludes many desperate patients from the programs. In addition, those who do gain access to the drugs may develop resistance in a phenomenon similar to that which occurs with AZT recipients. Although protease inhibitors appear to lower HIV levels while raising CD4 counts when used in combination with AZT, researchers admit that the development of resistance is most likely unavoidable.

Even generosity on the part of drug companies cannot solve all the financial and allocation problems associated with the AIDS epidemic, either. Although Barr plans to begin production of a generic AZT product in 2005 (which would considerably reduce the government's AZT purchase costs), the federal government has not addressed the issues surrounding AIDS treatment costs. The costs of some of the newer drugs, when marketed for widespread sale, could be just as high or higher than AZT. The federal government still does not recognize a social obligation to control the allocation of AIDS-effective drugs by fixing or lowering the market price, or to establish primary need groups among those afflicted. Each state has established priorities in categories (for example, the blind, aged, permanently and totally disabled, and the like) and financial tests (for income and assets) that applicants must meet in order to receive Medicaid assistance for purchasing AZT. As a result, many AIDS patients are still economically ineligible for public assistance and financially unable to purchase the drug. Even if the promising developments in AIDS treatment research and development come to fruition, many who suffer from the disease will likely lack the resources and support necessary to take advantage of the new drugs.

NOTES

1. The following sources were used to develop the early history of the problems presented in this case study: "AIDS Drug Is Raising Host of Thorny Issues," *The New York Times*, September 28, 1986, Section 1, p. 38; M. A. Fischl, D. D. Richman, M. H. Grieco et al., "The Efficacy of Azidothymidine (AZT) in the Treatment of Patients with AIDS and AIDS-Related Complex: A Double-Blind, Placebo-Controlled Trial," *New England Journal of Medicine* 317 (1987), pp. 185–91; D. D. Richman et al., "The Toxicity of Azidothymidine (AZT) in the Treatment of Patients with AIDS and AIDS-Related Complex: A Double-Blind, Placebo-Controlled Trial," *New England Journal of Medicine* 317 (1987), pp. 192–97; Robin Levin Penslar and Richard D. Lamm, "Who Pays for AZT?" *Hastings Center Report* (September–October 1989), pp. 30–32; Philip J. Hilts, "AZT to Be Widely Given Out to Children with AIDS Virus," *The New York Times*, October 26, 1989, pp. A1, A22; Philip J. Hilts, "F.D.A., in Big Shift, Will Permit Use of Experimental AIDS Drug," *The New York Times*, September 29, 1989, pp. A1, A16; Martin Delaney, "The Case for Patient Access to Experimental Therapy," *Journal of Infectious Diseases* 159 (1989), pp. 412–15.
2. Anne Rochell, "'AZT Isn't Whole Ballgame Anymore,'" *Atlanta Journal and Atlanta Constitution*, July 23, 1994, p. E1.
3. *HS News* 4, Department of Health and Human Services press release, October 9, 1991.
4. *Ibid.*
5. The Wellcome Group, *Annual Report 1990*, p. 17.
6. T. E. Haigler, Jr., president and CEO, Burroughs Wellcome, in testimony before the Subcommittee on Health and the Environment of the House Committee on Energy and Commerce, March 10, 1987, p. 12.
7. *Ibid.*, p. 13.
8. David Kramer and Diana LeBas, "Barr Files Application to Manufacture Generic AZT," Barr Laboratories, Inc. press release, April 18, 1991.
9. Malcolm Gladwell, "Lawsuit on AIDS-Drug Patent Seeks to End Firm's Monopoly," *The Washington Post*, March 20, 1991, p. A2.
10. *Ibid.*
11. Malcolm Gladwell, "NIH May Seek to Void Firm's Patent on AZT," *The Washington Post*, May 29, 1991, p. A1.
12. Public statement of Bernadine Healy, director, National Institutes of Health, July 17, 1991.
13. *Ibid.*
14. *Scrip*, No. 1637 (July 26, 1991), p. 9.
15. Robin Goldwyn Blumenthal, "Barr Labs Granted Conditional License for AZT; Patent Fight Remains a Hurdle," *The Wall Street Journal*, July 18, 1991, p. 1.
16. Lourdes Lee Valeriano, "Barr Laboratories Applies to the FDA for Approval to Make an AIDS Drug," *The Wall Street Journal*, April 19, 1991, p. 4.
17. Wade Lambert, "Legal Beat: AZT Patent Ruling," *The Wall Street Journal*, November 23, 1994, p. B4. See also *Burroughs Wellcome v. Barr Laboratories, Inc.*, 93–1503, U.S. Court of Appeals for the Federal Circuit, Washington, DC.
18. "Barr Laboratories Wins F.D.A. Approval for Generic AZT," *The New York Times*, February 28, 1995, p. D4.
19. Concorde Coordinating Committee, "Concorde: MRC/ANRS Randomised Double-Blind Controlled Trial of Immediate and Deferred Zidovudine in Symptom-Free HIV Infection," *The Lancet* 343 (April 9, 1994), pp. 871–81.
20. William R. Lenderking, Richard D. Gelber, Deborah J. Cotton et al., "Evaluation of the Quality of Life Associated with Zidovudine Treatment in Asymptomatic Human Immunodeficiency Virus Infection," *The New England Journal of Medicine* 330 (March 17, 1994), p. 742.

21. Lawrence K. Altman, "Experts to Review AZT Role as the Chief Drug for H.I.V.," *The New York Times*, September 17, 1995, pp. 1, 38.

23. Rochell, "'AZT Isn't Whole Ballgame Anymore.'"

23. See the following articles for background on this section: "AIDS Drug to Be Given Away," *The New York Times*, June 22, 1995, p. A17; Justin Gillis, "Merck to Provide New AIDS Drug," *The Washington Post*, July 17, 1995, p. A7; Justin Gillis, "Two Firms Will Offer Wider Access to Experimental AIDS Drugs," *The Washington Post*, September 21, 1995, p. A3; "Lottery for AIDS Drug," *The New York Times*, July 18, 1995, p. C3; "Lottery for New AIDS Drug Expands," *The New York Times*, September 19, 1995, p. C12; "New AIDS Drug to Be Offered Via Lottery," *The Los Angeles Times*, June 22, 1995, p. D2; "Roche Holding Ltd," *The Wall Street Journal*, September 18, 1995, p. B9; Michael Waldholz, "Unit of Roche Sets Up Lottery for AIDS Drug," *The Wall Street Journal*, June 21, 1995, p. A5; Michael Waldholz, "Merck Joins Roche in Offering Test Drug Free to Some AIDS Patients," *The Wall Street Journal*, July 17, 1995, p. B3.

AN ACCOUNTANT'S SMALL-TIME INSIDER TRADING

Donald Davidson is a young accountant who recently went into practice for himself. He literally placed a CPA shingle on a mantel post outside a basement office that he rented in a reconstructed part of downtown Frederick, Maryland. He chose this location because of its extremely low overhead, which was about all he could afford as he got his practice underway. Although he had only two clients in Frederick, Washington, DC, with its inexhaustible need for accountants, is only 40 miles away. Donald had made a number of contacts in Washington during a previous job that he briefly held at an accounting firm. Donald's father is a lawyer/accountant with a solid practice in Washington and is positioned to send some business Donald's way.

In fact, his father has already sent him one important client, Mr. Warner Wolff, the president of the medium-sized First National Bank of Beltsville, located in the Maryland suburbs of Washington. Donald had been working on the president's personal accounts, including his income taxes and two Keogh Pension Accounts the president had amassed for himself and his wife through a consulting business managed by his wife. Donald has often talked with Mr. Wolff about the bank's plans and programs, and he hopes there might be some contract work to be done for the bank in the future.

One day while going over the books on the pension accounts, Donald noticed that Mr. Wolff had sold the entire diversified portfolio of stocks in his wife's pension account, which he had traded for a value of just over $249,000. Mr. Wolff had then bought $248,982 of stock in the First National Bank of Beltsville for his wife's pension account. Upon seeing the record of these trades, Donald jokingly commented to Mr. Wolff that he must have supreme confidence in his managerial abilities to put all of his wife's pension money in the stock of his own bank.

Mr. Wolff, a sober and forthright person, took Donald's comment as a serious inquiry into the reason for the trades and gave a serious answer: "Although it won't be announced for three months and is top secret," he said, "we have signed a merger agreement with the largest bank in Maryland, and our stock price should rise dramatically on the announcement date." Donald was surprised at being let in on the secret, but he presumed that Mr. Wolff

This case was prepared by Tom L. Beauchamp. The case is factual, but some names and locations have been changed. Not to be duplicated without permission of the holder of the copyright, © 1992, 1996 Tom L. Beauchamp.

took the disclosure to be protected by normal accountant/client confidentiality. He thought nothing more of it and concluded his work on the records.

However, on the drive home he began to mull over his client's timely purchase and quickly saw that the same opportunity presented itself to him. He had no cash and only an IRA (individual retirement account) worth $10,000 at this stage of his young career, but the bank certificate of deposit in which he had invested his IRA was coming due in three weeks, and so he needed to reinvest this money anyway. Why not, he thought, put all $10,000 in the stock of the First National Bank of Beltsville?

As a student at the Wharton School, Donald had studied insider trading and the regulations governing it that were issued by the Securities and Exchange Commission. He vaguely remembered that the principle behind the SEC regulations is that it is illegal to trade on nonpublic, financially useful information that has been misappropriated or secured by a breach of fiduciary duty. Donald felt a need to bone up on his rusty understanding. He consulted a textbook he had studied as a graduate student and read the following description:

> The practice of insider trading has long been banned in the United States. The Securities and Exchange Commission (SEC) has actively sought rules against such trading since the enactment of the Securities Exchange Act of 1934. Under the terms of this law, a trader is forbidden to use information obtained on the inside to buy or sell securities or to pass the information on to others so that they may benefit. In the important precedent case of *S.E.C. v. Texas Gulf Sulphur*, a court held, "Anyone in possession of material inside information must either disclose it to the investing public, or, if he is disabled from disclosing it in order to protect a corporate confidence, or [if] he chooses not to, must abstain from trading in or recommending the securities concerned while such inside information remains undisclosed."
>
> Insider trading has proven difficult to define. An inside trader is someone who trades in the stock of a corporation based upon material nonpublic information he has obtained by virtue of his relationship with the corporation. Some believe that the information should be relevant to the price and to the purchase of the stock. For example, one might have confidential information that could not be disclosed and yet would not likely affect the stock's price even if it were known. The SEC has said that the nonpublic information must be misappropriated by the trader, but a definition of the term misappropriate has likewise proven difficult.
>
> There is considerable moral ambiguity surrounding insider trading. The SEC believes that the insider trading laws serve a moral purpose: preserving the fairness and integrity of the nation's securities market. Investors who have nonpublic inside information are thought to be unfairly advantaged. The underlying principles of these laws are that all investors in a free market should have equal access to relevant information, that securities markets must operate on faith and trust, and that

insider trading undermines public confidence in the marketplace. The United States Supreme Court has stressed a different moral purpose. The Court has held that an inside trader is one who violates a fiduciary duty to retain confidential information; insider trading is, therefore, like stealing from an employer. Insider trading is also believed to obstruct the market in capital formation.

Other authorities do not consider insider trading unfair. Several scholars have argued that permitting insider trades would make the securities market more efficient. The activity of the traders would be spotted and the market would respond more quickly to essential information. Ben R. Murphy, a partner in a merchant banking firm in Dallas, argues as follows: "My theory is that if we didn't have [insider trading laws] the market would eventually discount all the leaks and rumors and become more efficient. People would have to take a risk on believing the rumors or not." It is noteworthy that over $50 billion of securities trades daily on American exchanges, and no one is prepared to argue that even as much as 1 percent involves insider trading or any form of illegal transactions.

Jonathan Macey, Professor of Law at Emory University, has argued that a person who locates undervalued shares in a company through inside information can provide a valuable service to the market by the discovery, whether insider trading occurs or not. But in order to encourage such discovery the person or institution must be allowed to profit. This is basically what stock analysts do; they all try to get information not yet public before their rivals do in order to reward clients who pay for their activities. The amateur investing public has no chance against such professional knowledge and can only hope that the market price already reflects insider information. Macey concludes that "a complete ban on trading by those with confidential information about a company would be disastrous to the efficiency of the capital markets. If such a rule were enforced, nobody would have an incentive to engage in a search for undervalued firms, stock prices would not accurately reflect company values, and, perhaps worst of all, investment capital would not flow to its most highly valued users. Thus, we would all be better off if the SEC would de-escalate its war on insider trading."

Donald realized that the laws regulating insider trading were often inconsistent. There were no federal securities laws explicitly prohibiting insider trading as such. Rather, the laws had developed gradually from SEC and judicial decisions. Donald could see that the term *misappropriated* was too vague to be meaningful, except in a highly subjective way or on a case-by-case basis. He did not think that he would be engaging in a breach of fiduciary duty by trading in the bank stock, because he had no relevant fiduciary duty. As he saw it, he had a fiduciary duty not to disclose the secret that his client had revealed, but that was not his intent. In his judgment, he no more obtained the information through a breach of fiduciary duty than does a bartender who overhears information at the bar about a merger of two companies. Donald asked himself, what fiduciary duty could I possibly have not to buy this stock?

Moreover, Donald also knew that the Justice Department had traditionally construed insider trading to apply exclusively to an insider with a fiduciary duty to a corporation not to use confidential information obtained in their relationship. He could not see that he had any corporate connection. Such insiders were almost always Wall Street professionals. He also knew that in one of the few cases to reach the U.S. Supreme Court, the Court had dismissed charges of insider trading against a printer who had traded stocks based on the reading of confidential information he had been given to print. The Court held that the printer had no legal obligation not to use the confidential information. Donald saw himself as in much the same situation as the printer.

Donald had read about the insider trading cases that had made the headlines in recent months. In fact, his current copy of *Business Week* magazine had a cover story that examined the recent history of insider trading. He reached for the article and began to read the historical parts about two notorious insider trading scandals, both of which had previously escaped his attention. The first case involved a reporter, R. Foster Winans of *The Wall Street Journal,* who had taken advantage of his position as a reporter for personal financial gain (not very effectively) and had also helped his friends and associates gain financially (very effectively). The Winans case was not easy for Wall Street to dismiss, but Winans was an outsider looking in. The excesses of a juvenile journalist did not seem to directly attack the staid atmosphere of the Wall Street investment firms on which Winans reported.

However, shortly after Winans's dealings, a more consequential case erupted. Dennis Levine, a managing director who specialized in mergers and acquisitions at Drexel Burnham Lambert, was arrested for allegedly trading the securities of 54 companies (including major companies such as Nabisco and McGraw-Edison) on insider information in order to earn over $12.6 million. Levine was one of Wall Street's most successful figures and had taken home $3 million in salary and bonuses during the previous year. He had also just pulled off a major deal by advising Pantry Pride in its takeover of Revlon.

Levine's walk on the wrong side of Wall Street evidently began on a trip to the Bahamas in 1980, where he deposited $170,000 at secret branches of a Swiss bank. Using code names, he ultimately set up two dummy Panamanian corporations that traded through the Bahamian bank. On or about March 22, 1984, Levine bought 75,000 shares of Jewell Companies stock. He sold them on June 5, 1984. In 1985 he bought 145,000 shares of American Natural Resources Company stock on February 14 and sold them March 4. The continuous pattern of such trading netted Levine the $12.6 million in a short period of time. The SEC launched an investigation after noting a pattern of suspiciously well-timed stock trading at the Swiss Bank's U.S. trading accounts.

The Levine conviction reinforced a view that is strongly held at the SEC: Insider trading is rampant on Wall Street. The stock of a takeover target will repeatedly jump in price immediately before a takeover offer is announced to the public. For example, just before Levine's arrest, General Electric acquired

RCA. Immediately prior to the announcement, the stock had jumped a dramatic 16 points. The SEC's massive investigation made it clear that the agency is dedicated to major policing efforts in the attempt to contain insider trading. Since Levine's arrest, several other famous Wall Street figures had been arrested and successfully prosecuted.

The SEC discovered that insider trading was not confined to corporate insiders, but that many Wall Street outsiders were actively involved. In reporting on the Winans case, *Business Week* pointed out that

> Executives do it. Bankers do it. Accountants, secretaries, and messengers do it. And so do printers, cabdrivers, waiters, housewives, hairdressers—and mistresses. Some do it on their own. Others work in rings with connections as far away as Switzerland and Hong Kong. But they all work the shadowy side of Wall Street by trading on inside information to make money in the stock market.

The SEC and the Congress have been working together to crack down on insider trading. They recently took a hard look at the role that accountants play when insider trading by institutional investors occurs in markets for high-yield bonds. The trading typically occurs after consultation with attorneys or accountants a few days before favorable information is released about companies that had formerly been considered to be in financial difficulty. The preferred accountants are often those who sit on creditors' committees of companies that are undergoing bankruptcy proceedings. Nonetheless, ambiguities and inconsistencies in the laws that regulate insider trading have prevented effective enforcement, and prosecutors have often had difficulty in convicting offenders, especially in bond markets where insider trading is less clearly delineated than in stock markets. Donald read, in *The Wall Street Journal*, that government prosecutions for insider trading also might now be delayed for as much as a year, pending a new Supreme Court decision expected to set a precedent for the courts.

Both the SEC and the Congress have also been considering statutory definitions of insider trading. The congressional legislation introduced by senators from Michigan and New York and the SEC proposal would both toughen penalties for insider trading. The proposals would define it as the "possession of material, nonpublic information" obtained "wrongfully, whether knowingly or recklessly." The information is obtained wrongfully "only if it has been obtained by, or its use would constitute, directly or indirectly, theft, conversion, misappropriation or a breach of any fiduciary, contractual, employment, personal or other relationship of trust and confidence." According to the SEC proposal, the prohibition would apply to anyone with a "regular nexus to the operation of the nation's securities markets."

Donald could see that he had obtained his information in confidence, but, again he could not see that he was violating that confidence or that he had either directly or indirectly stolen his information. Although the new congressional definition was disquieting to him, Donald was buoyed to read a quotation taken from the leading investment journal, *Barron's*, which maintained that the SEC is "riding roughshod over due process of law," drying up the free flow of information and harming the interest of those it is sworn to protect. In discussing the Winans case, the *Barron's* article adamantly insisted that Winans had done no legal wrong and that the SEC had twisted the idea of "misappropriation" of information to the breaking point in getting a conviction of Winans. Winans's only wrong, said *Barron's*, was the moral wrong of violating *The Wall Street Journal's* rules of ethics. But this was clearly just a matter of journalism ethics, not business ethics, as far as Donald could see.

Donald had been involved in accounting long enough to know that government rules, especially Internal Revenue Service rules, had multiple interpretations and borderline case situations. He recognized that he might be in a borderline situation morally, but he could not see that he would be violating any clear legal principle by purchasing the bank stock. After considerable thought, he decided that he would buy the stock in three weeks, unless he saw new reasons not to do so. However, he felt uneasy about his decision. He was not worried about the law, although any new laws were likely to be more restrictive. Donald's two deepest concerns were his IRA and his integrity.

Chapter Six

THE MULTINATIONAL

INTRODUCTION

Multinational corporations often find themselves perplexed by the laws, rules, and customs of a host country in which they conduct business or have subsidiaries. They wonder whether they should do as the locals do or conform to the different and even conflicting cultural guidelines of their home states. For example, should a Canadian firm follow the rules of financial disclosure required in Canada or the rules in certain Arab countries in which it has subsidiaries? Should a U.S. firm that does business in Japan sanction payments for services that are encouraged in Japan but legally prohibited in the United States? Should a company liquidate its stock of artificially sweetened fruit by selling to customers in West Germany, Spain, or Third World countries when the product has been declared hazardous and outlawed in the home country?

No international body has answered these questions authoritatively, and there is at present no uniform agreement about the measure of control that governments and corporations should introduce for circumstances in which standards or expectations vary. The multinational setting presents a new level of complexity that compounds the ethical complexities encountered in the cases in previous chapters. In this chapter, the cases cover three broad problematic areas that multinationals confront: (1) differences in the treatment of employees and consultants, (2) different products and practices for consumers and clients, and (3) different government expectations and types of government-industry relationships.

In the first area, an employer engaged in manufacturing or marketing in a foreign culture cannot simply assume that workers should be governed by the same salary standards, grounds for dismissal, workplace standards, requirements of company loyalty, and promotional standards as those prevalent back home. An example of this problem of fair and equal treatment involves the use in a foreign workplace of hazardous chemicals such as benzene (see Chapter 5) that would not be permitted in the workplaces of a corporation's home country. If a foreign state does not require masks to be worn by workers or does not stipulate permissible chemical dose levels in the workplace, should a multinational adopt more stringent standards than those required locally?

Several different issues are presented in this chapter by the cases "Sexual Harassment at Mitsubishi Motors" and "Polaroid In and Out of South Africa." The Mitsubishi case focuses on the issue of fairness to employees who perceive the actions of others in the workplace as intimidating and sexually abusive. The case raises questions about the need for training programs in sexual harassment. The Polaroid case raises questions about the responsibilities to employees in a country with extraordinarily different race relation policies than those found in the multinational's home country. This case explores problems of alleged exploitation of workers and questions whether a multinational corporation can develop and maintain adherence to policies in a country whose own policies are radically different.

The latter problem has led some to argue that morality has no place in a country that demands that a business participate in immoral actions to survive, but others take the position that some moral values transcend any policy imposed by another country and that these values may not be ignored. This problem is examined in deep, but also sometimes amusing, ways in "Italian Tax Mores."

In the second area of multinational dilemmas, the consumer of a company's product in a foreign country or a client from a foreign country may not be subject to the same government requirements or have the same concerns about a product or policy that persons in the home nation have. "Confidentiality at Swiss Bank Corporation" illustrates the problems in an international market for wealthy clients who prefer to keep their investments in the confidential and sophisticated financial climate of a country such as Switzerland.

Regulatory controls on foods, drugs, and financial markets in the United States are probably more stringent than those found in any other country. These rules are framed for a culture with established views about acceptable risk, adequate testing, and fairness that do not exist in some countries in which multinationals operate. A product that is banned in the United States may be welcomed by authorities in another country; there is nothing illegal about marketing these items. These authorities may be ignorant or too loose in formulating standards, but nevertheless, the existence of these variations presents the multinational corporation with both a ready market and a conflict about whether it is right to satisfy that market.

American companies that market on an international level commonly believe that the requirements of the FDA and other government agencies are too cautious, necessitate too much testing, and are too strict when applied to other cultures. American government officials, however, tend to see these standards as reasonable protections for all consumers, irrespective of their cultural affiliation. The implicit view seems to be that if there are good reasons for banning a product or restricting sales in the United States, then it would be immoral not to conform to these standards when marketing elsewhere. This is another example of the principle that some values transcend territorial and statutory boundaries.

Sometimes risks are worth taking, and the same risks can be judged acceptable in some cultures and unacceptable in others. One possibility in handling different perceptions or regulations about risk is to warn consumers about possible harms when they purchase a product. According to principles of adequate disclosure and comprehension, a company cannot be faulted for marketing a product with accompanying risks and consequences as long as all parties understand the terms of the transaction and act freely. However, warnings have proved no less controversial than marketing bans.

In the third area previously mentioned, if moral standards, professional codes, and criteria of acceptable prudential judgments in dealing with a government vary from society to society, which system of values, if any, regulates the multinational? Perhaps the best-known problem of this type is the facilitation of business transactions through so-called "grease payments" and special "consulting contractors," either for government officials or for influential members of a society. Some corporations have defended these payments on the grounds that they are not illegal (often in either the host or the home country), are in the corporation's best interests, are harmless, provide new employment opportunities for persons at home and abroad, and provide stimulation to the economies and to technological development in both states.

Opponents have viewed grease payments, special consulting money, and the like as simple bribery or influence peddling—as we see illustrated in this chapter in the case "Consulting for Jones and Jones Pharmaceutical." These critics are not content to cite laws and moral views about the unacceptability of bribery and special payments. They look to a broader set of social consequences they believe will result from the practice of special payments and consulting contracts. For example, bribes promote government mismanagement; those who take the money attain a more favorable economic position than other members of their society who have no source of special payments; quality products become less important to manufacturers and government officials; competing firms with quality products may be ignored; and competition is weakened.

"Consulting for Jones and Jones Pharmaceutical" presents a situation that involves a practice regarded as acceptable in Switzerland but not acceptable in the United States. The problem is that of establishing consulting contracts with government representatives who regulate an industry's affairs, a straightforward problem of conflict of interest in the United States. Such conflicts arise when an employee (or employer) has a personal interest that is at variance with the interests of a firm or another party such as a government agency with which the individual is associated. Usually, the conflict is found in contexts in which reasonable objectivity and impartiality are expected. Thus, for example, a manager who wants to promote his daughter instead of a more experienced and more senior employee has two interests that at least potentially conflict: his interest in his family's welfare (including his own pride and satisfaction) and his company's welfare.

Similar problems about government-industry relationships surround other practices such as the understated tax reports involved in the "Italian Tax Mores" case. For example, if tax understatement is condoned or is a "way of life" in another country, does this practice persist because it is approved or consented to in that culture, or only because those in power have institutionalized the practice? Even if it has become customary, would it be regarded as scandalous if it resulted in public attention in the foreign state?

SEXUAL HARASSMENT AT MITSUBISHI MOTORS

The automobile assembly plant in Normal, Illinois, owned and operated by Japanese industrial giant Mitsubishi Motors, is that company's sole production facility located in the United States. It employs 4,233 people, including 894 women. Mitsubishi auto workers are considered among the best paid in the auto industry. Most are members of the United Auto Workers Union (UAW). The Japanese-owned company is the second-largest private employer in Normal, and pays higher wages than any other employer in town.

I.

In April, 1996, the United States Equal Employment Opportunity Commission (EEOC) filed a class-action suit against Mitsubishi Motor Manufacturing of America, Inc. in the federal district court of Peoria, Illinois. The suit followed a fifteen-month investigation of allegations of sexual harassment at Mitsubishi's Illinois facility, including interviews with more than 100 female employees, their alleged harassers, and other witnesses. The EEOC alleges that between 300 and 500 female employees have been subjected to various violations of both the Quid Pro Quo and Hostile Environment tenets of Title VII of the Civil Rights Act of 1964. According to John Rowe, Director of the EEOC regional office in Chicago, "the EEOC is seeking back pay for the women, as well as compensatory and punitive damages, which could equal more than $150 million."[1] The size of the potential settlements would make this the largest sexual harassment case in the nation's history. Paul Igasaki, Vice Chairman of the EEOC, commented that "this case is going to show that sexual harassment in the workplace is bad for the bottom line."[2]

A complicated portrait of the alleged harassment emerged from the testimony of numerous witnesses. Many women claimed that they were repeatedly subjected to violent, abusive, and intimidating behavior by male employees: their genitals, breasts, and buttocks were frequently grabbed, and they were routinely addressed by male co-workers on the assembly lines as "bitch" or "whore" instead of their proper name. Some of the female plaintiffs claimed even further that they had been threatened with loss of their job unless they

This case was prepared by Jonathan Larkin, Jennifer Esposito, and George R. Lucas, Jr. Not to be duplicated without permission of the authors.

consented to unwanted sexual advances by male colleagues. Several plaintiffs described how male employees drew pictures of female genitalia, titled the pictures with female co-workers' names, and taped these drawings to cars as they proceeded down the assembly line. Others described the circulation in company dining facilities of graphic photographs depicting male employees having sex with women while other males watched. Still others claimed that men wrote female co-worker's names and phone numbers on bathroom walls, listing men who had allegedly had sex with them. One worker who was eventually fired confessed that he had etched a picture of a woman with her legs open on his female co-worker's plastic face shield so that she would be forced to wear the picture over her face while she worked. He also confessed to being among those who had scrawled graphic and insulting graffiti on bathroom walls. He described his behavior as simply "joking around" and denied any malicious intent. "Easing into it, you don't recognize it [as sexual harassment]," he said. "You don't realize it's as bad as it is until you step back." He added that he had never been warned or reprimanded by company officials for these actions.[3]

Most of the alleged harassment involved line workers, their immediate supervisors, and lower-level management. Some male witnesses contend that they tried to report the offenses and denounce their fellow employees' behavior to senior management and were ostracized or even punished as a result. One male witness described how a desperate female co-worker had come to him for assistance in dissuading the man's friend from pressuring her to have sex. When the witness intervened, his erstwhile friend not only continued the offensive behavior, but turned most of the other members of their work team against him. Eventually, this witness reported the problem to officials in Mitsubishi's human resources department, but no action was taken for over a year.[4] The EEOC's broader charge is that Mitsubishi company officials appear to have had extensive knowledge of the offensive behavior but took no action to eliminate or prohibit it.

A number of observers cite such testimony and charges as evidence that this episode in middle America is actually a bizarre instance of an international cultural problem. In this instance, they allege, the rough and abusive behavior of Midwestern American blue-collar workers was tolerated, excused—and, most shockingly, perhaps even encouraged and reinforced—by Japanese managers who themselves hold women in the workplace in low esteem.

Several workers reported, for example, on routine "training trips" to company headquarters in Nagoya, Japan that were offered new male workers after only a few months on the job. Shortly after his arrival in Nagoya, one man testified, his Japanese hosts escorted him and several other co-workers to an "audience participation bar." Described by their Japanese hosts as routine local entertainment, the bar featured nude Filipino women who had sex on stage with members of the audience. Patrons were even invited to rent Polaroid cameras and photograph one another engaging in sex with the women.[5] Allegedly, these are among the pictures that subsequently circulated in the dining facility at the Normal, Illinois plant. Witnesses and participants allege that such training "perks" are customary rewards offered to male employees for loyal corporate behavior in Japan, and that, in these instances, Japanese plant managers in the U.S. were attempting to integrate American male workers fully into a "Japanese" industrial and corporate culture in order to promote harmony, loyalty, productivity, and good morale.

Another cultural factor often cited as a source of problems in this scandal is the tradition of unwavering loyalty of Japanese employees at all levels to their employer. Employees cited longstanding efforts to instill and to foster such attitudes at all levels of management in the Illinois plant, in order to counter the American "tradition" or customary problem of confrontation between management and union employees. In this instance, the cultural strategy may have backfired by encouraging managers to respond unsympathetically and defensively to the filing of complaints about sexual harassment. A computer programmer at the plant (who left in disgust to pursue a law career in 1993) explained, for example, that there was little that sympathetic bystanders could do to protect women from abuse. Management, he claimed, did not appear to be concerned about the reports of offensive and intimidating behavior. He testified that Japanese management officials informed people who dared to complain of the inappropriate behavior that "the nail that sticks up gets beaten down."[6]

Press reports in Japan have taken sharply divergent views of the American scandal. The majority opinion seems to be that this entire affair is overblown, and that the cultural criticisms represent simply another instance of "Japan bashing" in the United States. Other Japanese citizens, including younger workers and females, take a different view. A young female management trainee at a rival Japanese automaker who had also studied in the United States, for example, expressed disdain for the behavior of Mitsubishi workers and for the defensive response of the Japanese press. The issues, she and many of her co-workers felt, were generational and gender-based rather than cultural. Younger Japanese workers, especially those who had worked and traveled abroad, recognize (she claimed) that the abuse and subjugation of women in the workplace was unacceptable and counterproductive in any culture, and they did not share the views of preceding generations in Japan that women did not belong in the workplace, or were fit only to dress in uniform and serve tea to male workers in the afternoon.[7]

II.

Mitsubishi Motors Vice President and General Counsel, Gary Schultz, issued a statement to the press in response to the formal filing of the EEOC suit, stating "discrimination of any kind will never [be]—and has never been—tolerated at this plant." Though he criticized the filing of the suit as politically motivated during an election year, Schultz later admitted that the company had documented 89 incidents of sexual harassment over the past ten years—a rate (he hastened to add) far below that claimed in the current litigation.[8]

Immediately following the announcement of formal charges, the plant management sent a letter to its employees maintaining that the company "cannot allow allegations of political and monetary motivation to dampen our morale and efforts."[9] At the suggestion of Sheila Randolph, a procurement branch manager, the company organized a rally for workers near the Chicago regional office of the EEOC. Schultz himself announced to employees in a company-wide meeting:

> "We've got to win the media by parading thousands-strong in Chicago. . . [The suit make the company look like] a band of sex maniacs. . . We can't tell you what to do because if we do it comes across as so biased that it losses its effect. . . You are all clever people. . . I ask you to think of things that might help us get through this. . . I want to see a backlash"[10]

Nearly 3,000 workers attended the Chicago rally. The company shut down production at the Illinois plant for a full day and paid employees their full salary, as well as providing lunch and round-trip transportation, chartering altogether some 59 busses to transport volunteer participants to Chicago. One worker explained at the rally: "We're here because right now we're worried about our jobs, and that the publicity will hurt our products."[11]

Sign-up sheets for the rally were posted in advance throughout the plant, clearly indicating the names of those employees who supported the plant and singling out those who did not. Those who chose not to participate in the rally were expected to work their normal plant shift, and were required to submit written explanations for this choice to their supervisors. The company also set up phone banks in the plant and encouraged workers to telephone their congressional representatives, the White House, and representatives of the media (on company time and at company expense) in order to defend the integrity of the company. Anna Rogers, a technical coordinator in the plant, was quoted as having described the EEOC suit as "just a blatant case of slander. . . We didn't deserve it and we resent it. [The EEOC filed this lawsuit] just to justify its existence."[12]

Some employees subsequently reported that the company-sponsored responses to the pending suit created an extremely tense working environment within the plant. Many women who had not initially complained of harassment later charged that they were pressured to support the plant publicly, and that the pressure inflamed gender-based hostilities in the plant. One man reportedly scrawled a message in a men's bathroom in what was described as "harshly crude language," threatening "that if a woman caused him to lose his job, he would 'go hunting' for women."[13] Local townspeople dependent upon wage income generated by the plant were likewise threatened by the prospects of closure or layoffs should Mitsubishi be found liable for payment of large punitive damage claims arising from the EEOC suit. Many residents of the town of Normal spoke out in favor of the plant, and against the veracity of the women plaintiffs. Local female restaurant employees interviewed by a reporter from *The Washington Post*, for example, described the EEOC's action as "a bucket of hogwash," claiming that the male auto workers' actions were "all in good fun." "Why ruin something that's good for the town?" wondered another.[14]

Not all executives in the Mitsubishi international conglomerate (or *keiretsu*), however, agreed with the strategy of retaliation pursued by the Mitsubishi Motors division. "I think it's a terrible idea. It sounds like pressuring someone rather than going through the judicial process," said James Brumm, the General Counsel at Mitsubishi International Corporation, a New York-based trading company. Another public relations official in the conglomerate added: "I'm totally mystified. I'm not so concerned about being branded the discrimination company any more, but being branded the incompetence company."[15]

III.

In addition to the aggressive response to the EEOC, Mitsubishi Motors is pursuing legal counter-action against twenty-eight female workers who independently filed a private sexual harassment suit. The company's lawyers have asked for the plaintiffs' gynecological and psychological records. "One of the plaintiffs has a pattern of promiscuous sexual behavior involving male workers at the plant," said Roy David, a lawyer for Mitsubishi.[16] For several weeks following the formal filing of charges, the company steadfastly refused to cooperate with the EEOC on investigation of the sexual harassment allegations. The company maintained it would like to settle the case promptly, but not on the government's terms. Mitsubishi acknowledged that some acts of sexual harassment may have taken place in the plant, but not nearly to the extent portrayed by the EEOC.

Then abruptly, on July 16, 1996, Mitsubishi Motors announced that it would begin what the company described as "a comprehensive training program on sexual harassment for all of the more than 4,000 employees at the plant, beginning with managers. Senior executives will participate annually in a two-day workshop entitled 'Men and Women as Colleagues'," the company reported. The company had earlier retained former U.S. labor secretary Lynn Martin to review its policies, and it was she who recommended the proposed changes. In addition, Mitsubishi announced that it would hire an employee to serve as ombudsman for complaints concerning sexual and racial discrimination, and would seek to increase the number of its car dealerships owned by women and minorities. Tsuneo Ohinouye, Mitsubishi's chairman and CEO, called a news conference to announce the innovations and stated that he hoped to settle the EEOC lawsuit in the near future. EEOC Chairman Gilbert F. Casellas responded with praise for Mitsubishi's efforts to improve the Illinois workplace through such training, but stated that the company's actions "in no way affect the EEOC's ongoing litigation against Mitsubishi." An attorney representing the women who had filed a separate lawsuit against the company denounced the new program as "window dressing," noting that the company had thus far done nothing to compensate women who experienced severe sexual harassment.[17]

NOTES

1. Korsten Downey Grimsley, "EEOC Says Hundreds of Women Harassed at Auto Plant," *The Washington Post*, 10 April 1996, p. A13.
2. "EEOC Sues Mitsubishi Unit for Harassment," *The Wall Street Journal*, 10 April 1996, p. B1.
3. "Why Men stay Silent: Fear of Retaliation Fostered Abusive Atmosphere, Mitsubishi Workers Say," *The Washington Post*, 26 May 1996, p. H7.
4. *Ibid.*, p. H1.
5. *Ibid.*, p. H7.
6. *Ibid.*, p. H7.
7. Privileged correspondence, discussing the news reports and public reaction to the U.S. Mitsubishi case in Japan; name withheld by request.
8. *The Washington Post*, 10 April 1996, p. A13.
9. "Fighting Back: A Mitsubishi U.S. Unit is Taking a Hard Line in Harassment Battle," *The Wall Street Journal*, 22 April 1996, p. A1.
10. *Ibid.*
11. "Mitsubishi Workers March on EEOC," *The Washington Post*, 23 April 1996, p. A9.
12. "Mitsubishi Organizes Rallies to Protest Sex-Harassment Suit," *The Wall Street Journal*, 18 April 1996, p. B12.
13. "Auto Plant Sexual Harassment Case Divides Community," *The Washington Post*, 24 April 1996, p. A17.
14. *Ibid.*
15. "Fighting Back: A Mitsubishi U.S. Unit is Taking a Hard Line in Harassment Battle," *The Wall Street Journal*, 22 April 1996, p. A1.
16. "Lawsuit Distracts Mitsubishi Motors from Repair Effort," *The Wall Street Journal*, 29 April 1996, p. A19.
17. "Mitsubishi Takes Steps to Reshape Workplace," *The Washington Post*, 17 July 1996, p. D1, D8.

DRUG TESTING AT COLLEGE INTERNATIONAL

Dick Bowie, president of College International Publishing Company of Austin, Texas, faces a difficult decision about the control and monitoring of his employees. Increasing theft, employee absenteeism, sloppy follow-up on assignments, lethargy, and morale problems—complicated by declining sales and profits in the international college textbook market—now threaten the publishing business that he had founded as an independent subsidiary of a major publisher located in the eastern United States. Interviews with employees have confirmed to his satisfaction what Bowie has long suspected: Drugs have become a major factor in reduced employee performance, morale, and overall productivity. Pivotal in Bowie's thinking is that his company's finances are now so shaky that the parent company is considering absorbing it into an international editorial and marketing division.

College International was established in 1963 as an international science textbook company. Its market was then rapidly expanding for both top-flight English language texts and translations of texts. Bowie was the first president of the new satellite. Under his management the company had grown from a four-editor, one-sales-manager operation to an international company with an editorial and sales staff spread throughout North, Central, and South America. College International today employs approximately 1,500 translators, editors, salespersons, technical and clerical assistants, and secretaries.

Bowie had been a superb editor at the parent company before becoming College International's president. He had built up several fields through long hours of patient training of new editors. He taught them all the skills of manuscript acquisition and sales needed to get ahead. He had tried to do the same at College International, and in the first decade he had been successful. But in the last 15 years, many editors left for larger companies as soon as they had gained experience and could learn nothing further from Bowie. He at first shrugged off these losses as the industry's new way, but the general lack of employee loyalty—a far cry from his early years with the parent company— also shocked him. Corporate and personal loyalties had been institutionalized in those days, and an employee typically concentrated on attaining higher

This case was prepared by Tom L. Beauchamp, and revised by John Cuddihy. The case is based on a history of a publishing company, but is a composite of several different cases involving the use of drug tests. All names of actual persons and companies have been changed. Not to be duplicated without permission of the holder of the copyright, © 1992, 1996 Tom L. Beauchamp.

management positions in the company. Over the years Bowie has gradually and reluctantly come to the conclusion that the declining level of commitment to the job and to the company is related to an increased reliance on drugs, especially by his editors. Several editors reported to Bowie that they accept this view themselves—although they always talked only about other editors, not about themselves.

The major management challenge in textbook publishing has always been to attract and develop promising editors with strong individual initiative and the ability to work with the sales staff in the field. This staff includes a number of company representatives or "travelers" who "work" various science departments in their home region's universities and colleges. "Working" involves calling on professors to promote books, searching for manuscripts in preparation, making phone calls to encourage the adoption of texts, and in some cases gathering data for direct-mail campaigns. The sales force cannot be supervised on a day-to-day basis because its members work independently in distant cities. They also tend to move from company to company even more frequently than do editors.

During his early years as president, Bowie developed an efficient and effective system of managing editors and sales staff of which he was justifiably proud, but the lack of commitment among his present editors has caused the whole system to fall into serious disarray. Bowie has discovered that members of the sales force have developed a pattern of "cheating on company time." The La Jolla, California, representative, for example, had become the apartment manager for the 190-unit apartment house in which he lived. Allegedly only taking on a "weekend job," the employee in fact spent over 80 percent of his time managing the apartment house, where he frequently held drug parties. The employee had cleverly concealed the deception, although a first-rate editor would long ago have detected how sloppy the salesman's record had become.

While Bowie was trying to discover the solution to this problem, he was confronted with the apparent embezzlement of over $15,000 by his highly trusted sales manager, Bennie Jett. Because Jett was married to the company's accountant, Bowie was unsure how aggressively to pursue the matter and how much proof he could muster. He knew from his auditors' examination of the company's finances only that the company had inexplicably lost $15,000. Jett, but not his wife, had been arrested recently on a minor drug charge. After later interviewing the sales manager to determine whether he had a drug problem, Bowie was sure there was some connection between the $15,000 loss and the man's apparent drug habit, but he had no real evidence. During the interview he was disquieted by Jett's insistence that several editors held regular Friday night parties in which they used "designer drugs"—synthetically produced narcotics that are sometimes hundreds of times stronger than plant-manufactured narcotics. Jett denied participation himself.

This discouraging series of events has convinced Bowie that he has to protect the company through new initiatives. He is now angry and depressed about the company's future. He has always keenly felt a sense of responsibility to his employees, but now he feels betrayed by them.

In order to combat employee lethargy and declining job performance, Bowie is considering requiring drug testing for all employees. The test is relatively simple and works as follows: An employee's donated body specimen is tested for the presence of drugs and metabolites (a drug's inert byproducts) through a variety of chemical tests. Urine remains the most commonly used workplace specimen, but some companies also test breath, hair, saliva, and blood samples for prior drug exposure. If the first test reveals a drug's presence, the company or its testing agent will run a confirmatory, second test to verify that drugs have indeed been used. Drug tests detect drug use, but they do not accurately determine recency of use, history of use, or the user's impairment levels. Drug testing has spread throughout much of the nation's public and private sectors. Corporate drug testing has skyrocketed since the early 1980s, and approximately 50 percent of Fortune 500 companies had instituted some type of drug testing program by late 1987 (up from approximately 20 percent in 1982).

College International had never implemented any form of employee inspection program in its offices in the United States. However, the company had long used both polygraph (lie detector) tests and drug testing at its other, smaller offices in Latin America. Bowie had personally authorized the tests at these locations several years ago, after they were requested at an international staff meeting by his ten office managers, each of whom was a citizen of the country in which the local office was located. Bowie had never been worried about either the ethics or the effectiveness of these employee inspection programs, because they were widely used techniques in each of these countries and had been proven effective. Unlike in the United States, polygraph testing is legal in these countries; U.S. companies typically follow the practices widely used in these countries for testing employees, even though they may not use the same practices in the home office.

The success of these methods of testing in decreasing corporate costs has been documented to Bowie's satisfaction in each of the ten offices south of the border. Nonetheless, Bowie still resists introducing drug testing into the workplace in Austin. He finds himself paradoxically horrified at the idea and attracted to its benefits. He recently watched a television documentary on "the new era" of industrial spying and snooping that examined the new wave of drug tests and so-called "monitoring devices," which are principally wiretaps placed on office phones. The documentary was very convincing in expressing the scope of the problem of drugs in the workplace. It noted that approximately 25 million Americans are currently using some form of illegal substance that affects cognitive and sometimes physical function. In the previous ten years there had been a 200 percent increase in cocaine-related deaths. The documentary made the point that except for alcohol, no problem in American society so deeply affects job performance.

Bowie sat up and took notice when the documentary pointed out that in his area of industry roughly 11 percent of all employees use drugs *on the job*. This figure was exceeded only by the construction and entertainment industries. Bowie took notice a second time when the documentary reported that insurance costs double or triple in firms hit hard by drug and alcohol abuse. This part of the documentary also showed a segment in which President Ronald Reagan's Commission on Organized Crime strongly recommended both public and private sector drug testing in its 1986 report. The U.S. Department of Defense had used the kind of program recommended and praised it as highly successful in decreasing drug use on the job. The federal government had now authorized the testing of over 50 percent of all federal employees.

The next segment of the documentary showed supervisors helping with urine samples, which must be collected by someone of the same sex who is personally familiar with the employee. The collection must occur in a room with one tester and one company employee, so that urine samples are not switched or contaminated and proper identification occurs. The camera zoomed in on the faces of the employees while they were urinating in a testing facility in the presence of two observers. Although the eyes of the employees were obliterated by a camera bar that made identification impossible, Bowie could nonetheless detect the acute embarrassment, humiliation, and sense of affront present on the mouths and foreheads of several employees.

He imagined that his employees would feel the same way. It did not occur to him to think of the employees in Mexico City who had already undergone both drug and polygraph testing. He did reflect on how unpleasant he would find it to be in the position of his Latin American managers, who had to both administer and take the tests. But he was able to cast this thought aside because the managers themselves had requested the testing. No one in Austin had ever requested such testing.

Employees who were interviewed in the documentary expressed strong reservations about drug testing on grounds that the testing invades their privacy and challenges their personal integrity without cause. The executives interviewed, all of whom had instituted drug testing in their workplaces, denied that they were authorizing unjustifiable invasions of privacy. They reasoned that *company* resources, not *private* resources, were at stake. Employees also raised issues about confidentiality. Although in medical testing there is a standard expectation of privacy of information when testing bodily fluids, the executives confirmed that drug testing realistically cannot carry such a guarantee in their firms.

The powerful feelings displayed by employees and management struck Bowie. The documentary made an excellent case that corporate drug testing raised productivity, cut costs, and reduced waste. Also, to date, no one has shown that the tests lower employee morale, as long as executives and employees at all levels receive similar treatment. Still, employees *complain* of lower morale and of decreased loyalty to the company.

Part of Bowie's discomfort at the thought of instituting drug testing is caused by the problem of "false positive" results. Drug tests look for drugs' metabolites, not the drugs themselves. Consequently, a standard test can mistake the metabolites of over-the-counter pharmaceuticals for illicit drug metabolites. For example, standard decongestants and diet pills may closely resemble amphetamines in drug test results. In a more extreme case, herbal teas can be mistaken for trace elements of cocaine. The "false positive" danger typifies the problems and complications associated with drug testing.

Bowie has searched for other solutions and has already conducted an extensive series of interviews with his senior editors. But he believes that the alternatives cannot correct the problems that now threaten the company's existence as an independent firm. He has hired two consultants, both of whom support his hypothesis that the drug tests would likely be successful both in identifying and eliminating untrustworthy employees and in screening new employees. Another publishing company executive has told him that his firm has enjoyed a large cost reduction since the institution of drug tests. He also said there had been no complaints from employees once the examinations had become routine. The very *threat* of possible drug detection, he argued, deters most employees from active protest and opposition.

Bowie also hired a management consultant from New York who proposed a scheme under which College International would use preemployment, periodic, and upon-return-to-work drug tests—as well as immediate testing for all employees involved in an office accident that requires medical attention. All urine collection would be done in the presence of two observers of the same sex. Consent would be required and confidentiality would be assured (although Bowie would himself be given all results), but testing would also be an essential condition of employment.

However, current employees would not be tested for the next three months. No questions would be asked about any drug use that might have occurred prior to the time of the tests. Bowie would therefore never learn about past drug use, and employees would not have to worry about surprising disclosures or test results. Employees would also not be asked about the behavior of other employees unless there existed some legitimate suspicion about a specific employee. The tests would be administered to potential employees prior to employment and annually to all employees, including Bowie. If the tests discovered evidence of drug use, Bowie would ask the employee to enter an employee assistance program (EAP) to rehabilitate herself or himself. Employees who voluntarily entered an EAP would not lose their positions with the company. Only those employees who refused to seek treatment or who failed to rehabilitate themselves would be asked to leave the firm.

Bowie was strongly attracted to this consultant's program, which had worked effectively elsewhere, but he still shivered when he thought about personally taking urine samples from his editors. He wondered if specimen collection might be done without observers.

CONFIDENTIALITY AT SWISS BANK CORPORATION

Alan Adler is an investment advisor in Zurich, Switzerland. Educated at the London School of Economics, he established his practice in Zurich because he saw an international market for wealthy clients who prefer to keep their financial transactions in Switzerland's confidential and sophisticated financial network. Alan trades in international currency, bonds, and stocks for his clients, each of whom keeps at least $1.5 million in his or her personal account. Most of his clients are from Germany and the United States, with some from Britain and South Africa. He has no clients from Switzerland but often trades in Swiss currency.

Alan prefers the freedom with which investment counselors can deal with their clients in Switzerland, and he has always liked being able to assure his clients of absolute confidentiality. His official client records are maintained by number rather than name. He makes annual reports to his customers by their numbers only, and his clients use only their numbers in correspondence. He keeps the decoding system for names and numbers in a Swiss Bank Corporation (SBC) safe-deposit box. He does not file a report with the government and is not legally required to do so.

The Swiss Bank Corporation is crucial to Alan's client relationships. All clients keep their money and securities in their own names in SBC accounts. Alan has obtained written authorization from each client allowing him to use the client's money to buy stocks, bonds, or foreign currency to be placed in their account. Although all transactions are at his discretion, he cannot himself withdraw anything from a customer's bank account. Only the customer can request or make a withdrawal, and he or she must make any request directly to the bank. Alan receives no fees per transaction. His fees come only from a percentage of the annual net *gains* he makes for his customers.

Alan has become concerned about the extent to which his promises to clients of confidentiality can be sustained. Swiss banks seem to be shifting from their previously secretive policies. The Swiss government has become more interested in prosecuting local tax abuses, and foreign governments have been pressing for additional revisions in financial regulations. Jean-Paul Chapuis, the Swiss Bankers' Association's managing director, has said, "There is no guarantee of secrecy if you are dishonest." As the bankers view their situation, Swiss

This case was prepared by Tom L. Beauchamp and revised by Jeff Greene. Not to be duplicated without permission of the holder of the copyright, © 1992, 1996 Tom L. Beauchamp.

banks can no longer remain aloof from international financial restrictions because their expanded operations have made them vulnerable and responsive to international pressures. Local law applies in the countries in which Swiss bank branches conduct their business.

Alan typically hands his customers a booklet entitled *Profile*, published by the Swiss Bank Corporation as an annual report and explanation of bank services. He urges his customers to read the section entitled "Switzerland's Advantages as a Financial Centre," which guarantees a "safeguarding of privacy." Two of the sections follow:

7. Tax Morality
Switzerland is one of the few countries in which voters can directly determine how heavy their tax burden should be. This prevents prohibitive tax rates and is an important precondition for tax morality. The principle of self-assessment is yet another reflection of the special relationship between the Swiss and their government. The safeguarding of privacy vis-a-vis the tax authorities is guaranteed by banking secrecy.

The state concentrates its efforts on combatting the abuse of this relationship. In recent years, the measures to hinder tax evasion and tax flight have been substantially strengthened. Parliament, and secondarily the people, may mend existing fiscal disadvantages (Stamp Duty Act, double taxation of corporate earnings) at any time within the framework provided for statutory revisions.

8. Responsibility of the Individual
In contrast to countries with a centralist political structure, Switzerland places great emphasis on the individual citizen's responsibility for himself. The State's role is to guarantee the impartial administration of justice as well as an environment propitious to economic activity.

Until recently Alan simply asked his clients to read these sections and told them that his data and the bank's data were strictly secret, protected by a pledge of confidentiality. However, recent events have convinced him that the Swiss government and banks are modifying their methods of cooperating with foreign requests. For example, the government recently froze the Swiss bank assets of two former foreign dictators, Ferdinand Marcos and Jean-Claude Duvalier, at the request of the respective Filipino and Haitian governments. Previously, Swiss banks had consistently refused to confirm even whether they held a deposed ruler's account. The U.S. government had tried for nearly 20 years to locate suspected Nazis' bank accounts, but it could not penetrate Swiss confidentiality regulations.

But Swiss banks have recently cooperated with the U.S. Securities and Exchange Commission in prosecuting inside trader Dennis B. Levine. In a worrisome development for Alan and his clients, the Bank Leu Limited divulged the name and records of Levine in return for immunity from prosecution. The Swiss government shortly thereafter announced that it was helping the U.S. government investigate three cases of tax fraud. Later, in August 1990, Swiss government officials (for the first time) outlawed money laundering. Shortly thereafter, in March 1991, the government announced that it would ease its formerly strict rules on secrecy in banking and would investigate alleged money laundering. The Swiss Parliament immediately thereafter announced formal debates on appropriate legislation.

In 1992 the Swiss Federal Banking Commission followed up on its 1990 law that made money laundering illegal with guidelines and tips on how to recognize dirty money. In 1994, Switzerland's lower house of Parliament approved legislation that allowed banks to report suspected illegal activities without fear of breaking bank secrecy laws. Finally, in 1995, several years after the accounts of Ferdinand Marcos were frozen, it appears that those who were victimized by Marcos's financial activities will collect at least part of the balance of his accounts. Permitting these victims to obtain money from Marcos's Swiss bank accounts sets a significant precedent. However, there is concern among Swiss government officials, who believe that these developments challenge their banking secrecy laws and sovereignty. In response, they delivered two diplomatic letters of protest to Secretary of State Warren Christopher. One of the letters stressed that the Swiss courts froze all Swiss assets of the Marcos family in response to a request by the Filipino government. The purpose of this freeze was to permit the "repatriation of those assets to the Philippines" if a Swiss court ruled that the assets were stolen property.[1] These examples seem to indicate a further and perhaps fatal weakening of the maintenance of secrecy and confidentiality within the Swiss banking industry.

Two U.S. court cases have also badly shaken Alan's confidence. In a Tampa, Florida, case, U.S. District Court Judge Ben Krentzman threatened two Swiss lawyers with contempt citations unless they ceased to resist efforts to obtain financial information about U.S. criminal suspects with Swiss bank accounts. The contempt threat successfully intimidated the lawyers into stopping a legal maneuver by defending their client. In another U.S. case, federal Judge Milton Pollack threatened Banco della Svizzera Italiana—a Swiss bank—with a daily $50,000 fine unless it disclosed the identities of traders in the common stock of St. Joe Minerals. Faced with the seizure of its U.S. assets, the bank "persuaded" one of its customers to waive his secrecy rights and then identified him.

The Swiss Parliament had earlier (on December 18, 1987) passed an insider trading bill that made illegal the exploitation of confidential facts for personal or third-party gain. Alan now realizes that the Swiss government, under international pressure especially from the United States, will help prosecute bank clients involved in illegal financial transactions, money laundering, and many transactions that it formerly placed under the category of legitimate secrecy.

Disconcerted by these developments, Alan requested further information from the Swiss Bank Corporation. He noticed that the SBC's most recent edition of the *Profile* booklet had been revised, with the sections concerning banking secrecy omitted. Another SBC booklet published by the bank entitled

Secrecy in Swiss Banking explained banking policies in new and unnerving detail. The bank affirmed the premium placed on individual liberty and privacy in Switzerland, but it forthrightly recognized that banking secrecy is not absolute. Alan read a section entitled "Limitation of Banking Secrecy under Swiss Law":

> Where stipulated in the law, banks are required to furnish to public authorities pertinent information on clients' accounts. Such disclosures are mandatory in actions involving inheritance, bankruptcy and debt collection as well as in all criminal cases, but not in ordinary tax matters and when violating foreign exchange regulations.
>
> Switzerland is party to many bilateral and multilateral conventions for legal assistance with other countries. Where such treaties exist, Swiss authorities assist foreign countries in criminal cases under conditions provided by these treaties. To be prosecuted as a crime, however, the alleged offense must always be considered a crime under Swiss law, too.[2]

Alan concluded that the legal shelter of secrecy in Switzerland still rivaled any world competitor—for example, the Bahamas' banking system—but nonetheless was shrinking in scope and reliability.

He wondered what responsibility he had to his customers to alert them to these changes. Should he warn them of new risks? He did not know whether his customers reported the status of their accounts to their respective governments, and he did not wish to know. However, he had given his customers an absolute guarantee of secrecy and confidentiality. He knew that he would never violate confidentiality himself. Yet his safe-deposit box did contain his clients' names, addresses, and account numbers.

Alan sat down before his word processor and drafted a letter to inform his clients of the new developments. But when he read his words on the screen, the changes that he announced sounded ominous, as if the clients' names and accounts might not be secret at all. He decided to try another draft the next day to see if his words sounded less alarming. At that moment his eyes landed on a story in *The Wall Street Journal* that was on his desk. According to this story, a private detective in New York, Jules B. Kroll, had been successfully hired by the Kuwaiti government to trace the hidden assets of Iraqi dictator Saddam Hussein. Mr. Kroll had managed in just a few days to use giant computerized data bases and private contacts to trace Hussein's hidden wealth to over 40 "secret" bank accounts throughout the world. As he scanned the story Alan had even less of an idea of what to say in his letter to his clients.

NOTES

1. Henry Weinstein, "Victims of Marcos May Finally Reap Millions," *Los Angeles Times*, November 27, 1995, p. A1.
2. *Secrecy in Swiss Banking: Separating Fact from Myth* (Swiss Bankers' Association, 1995), p. 6.

CONSULTING FOR JONES AND JONES PHARMACEUTICAL

Ricardo D'Amato is a high-salaried executive who for four years has been on the payroll of a large international pharmaceutical company, the Jones and Jones Company. Located at the European headquarters in Sweden, D'Amato is in charge of certifying that new products are ready for the approval and registration process and for subsequent marketing. His office is responsible for sending new products to the relevant government authorities in European countries, each of which has an organization similar to the U.S. Food and Drug Administration (FDA), where drugs are tested for safety and effectiveness.

Although D'Amato's relations with his peers have been without significant strain, he now suddenly finds himself enmeshed in controversy and crisis. He has refused to authorize a $15,000 payment on a contract the company has with a consultant in Switzerland. The contract calls for the company to pay the specified fee to a distinguished pharmacologist, Dr. Helmut Koenig, for giving advice on how to obtain approval from the Swiss regulatory authorities. Dr. Koenig is uniquely qualified for this work because he is also employed by the Swiss Drug Regulatory Agency, the same agency that is responsible for approving all Swiss drug products for marketing.

Sitting on D'Amato's desk is an internal memo written by the most powerful vice-president at Jones and Jones, who arranged and then signed the contract with Dr. Koenig. The memo has a section on credentials that says, "Dr. Koenig is a vital influence and creator of opinion in the approval of drug applications in Switzerland."

D'Amato was alarmed when he discovered Dr. Koenig's position of influence and his contractual arrangement with Jones and Jones. He believes that it is unethical to make such payments to a man who is currently involved with the approval of five to ten pending product registrations for Jones and Jones. He has written Dr. Koenig to this effect. In particular, Dr. Koenig is involved with the application for Lotriprox, a drug that those who have tested it for the company believe to be more effective in the treatment of psoriasis than its main competitors. Jones and Jones had submitted the original application for approval of this drug twice; the Swiss Drug Regulatory Agency rejected both attempts. On each occasion the agency said there was a lack of evidence of the drug's effectiveness. Jones and Jones officials view the receipt of Swiss

This case was prepared by Kelley MacDougall and Tom L. Beauchamp. Not to be duplicated without permission of the holder of the copyright, © 1992, 1996 Tom L. Beauchamp.

approval as vital because regulatory agencies in other countries often follow the Swiss lead.

D'Amato is an American working in Europe, but most of his fellow executives in Sweden come from various European countries. Almost all have given him their opinion on the matter. They all concur that the practice of hiring regulators as consultants is a common and accepted practice in Switzerland. They point out, correctly, that other companies that market similar products have been hiring these consultants for years. They deny that this practice involves the use of devious or special influence to get applications approved, and they emphasize Dr. Koenig's ability to properly advise pharmaceutical companies on how to proceed.

Dr. Koenig has responded in a terse letter directly to D'Amato that he knows as well as anyone how to keep his consulting work separate from his work at the regulatory agency. He notes in the letter that he has many times been in this position and that there are clear advantages to be enjoyed by both the company and the regulatory agency in his dual role. For example, he is able to keep on top of every aspect of a drug and of the approval system. He points out that the reason Jones and Jones has not previously obtained approval for Lotriprox is the company's "terrible testing" of the drug, which is precisely his professional domain.

Nonetheless, D'Amato does not accept these arguments, which he views as rationalizations prompted by a corrupt system. However, he has tried to make it clear to those with whom he has discussed his views that he is not disputing the history of the Swiss consulting process. His concern is with the practices of his company, Jones and Jones. He sees the contract with Dr. Koenig as a willing and in fact devious violation of practices that are unacceptable in the United States—and in his company, which is, after all, American.

Three weeks ago, on his own authority and without anyone's advice or approval, D'Amato wrote the Intercantonal Office of Medicaments in Switzerland to ask for an investigation. To his surprise he received a detailed and carefully crafted response. The investigators said that they did find that Jones and Jones pharmaceutical products and the products of many other companies had been consistently approved for marketing after the hiring of well-placed consultants, but they found no indication that these approvals were made under fraudulent circumstances. Unless D'Amato could submit additional evidence to the contrary, the investigators concluded there was no reason why an educated and experienced adviser could not separately render his or her services to an outside company. In fact, they advised him that it makes good practical sense for Jones and Jones to obtain evaluations prior to submitting products for approval. As they see it, this process facilitates the production of a safer and more effective product, and it spares both the company and the regulatory agency time that would otherwise be wasted considering inferior products.

D'Amato still maintains that, even if these payments do not openly constitute bribery, Jones and Jones has abused its position of influence. Furthermore, he believes that Dr. Koenig is locked in an untenable conflict of interest.

D'Amato is adamant in his view that under the Swiss system any corporation of sufficient size and financial backing could wield unfair advantage over less powerful companies.

D'Amato's supervisor, Raymond Freymaster, has now intervened in a process that he believes cannot be allowed to stalemate any longer. He has told D'Amato that the contract with Dr. Koenig is proper and therefore must be paid. Freymaster has increased the pressure by saying that if D'Amato does not authorize payment within ten days he will be fired, and Freymaster will then authorize it himself. D'Amato now sees no way to maintain both his integrity and his job.

ITALIAN TAX MORES

The Italian federal corporate tax system has an official, legal tax structure and tax rates just as the U.S. system does. However, all similarity between the two systems ends there.

The Italian tax authorities assume that no Italian corporation would ever submit a tax return which shows its true profits but rather would submit a return which understates actual profits by anywhere between 30 percent and 70 percent; their assumption is essentially correct. Therefore, about six months after the annual deadline for filing corporate tax returns, the tax authorities issue to each corporation an "invitation to discuss" its tax return. The purpose of this notice is to arrange a personal meeting between them and representatives of the corporation. At this meeting, the Italian revenue service states the amount of corporate income tax which it believes is due. Its position is developed from both prior years' taxes actually paid and the current year's return; the amount which the tax authorities claim is due is generally several times that shown on the corporation's return for the current year. In short, the corporation's tax return and the revenue service's stated position are the operating offers for the several rounds of bargaining which will follow.

The Italian corporation is typically represented in such negotiations by its *commercialista,* a function which exists in Italian society for the primary purpose of negotiating corporate (and individual) tax payments with the Italian tax authorities; thus, the management of an Italian corporation seldom, if ever, has to meet directly with the Italian revenue service and probably has a minimum awareness of the details of the negotiation other than the final settlement.

Both the final settlement and the negotiation are extremely important to the corporation, the tax authorities, and the *commercialista.* Since the tax authorities assume that a corporation *always* earned more money this year than last year and *never* has a loss, the amount of the final settlement—that is, corporate taxes which will actually be paid—becomes, for all practical purposes, the floor for the start of next year's negotiations. The final settlement also represents the amount of revenue the Italian government will collect in taxes to help finance the cost of running the country. However, since large amounts of money are involved and two individuals having vested personal interests are conducting the negotiations, the amount of *bustarella*—typically a substantial cash payment "requested" by the Italian revenue agent from the *commercialista*—usually determines whether the final settlement is closer to the corporation's original tax return or to the fiscal authority's original negotiating position.

Whatever *bustarella* is paid during the negotiation is usually included by the *commercialista* in his lump-sum fee "for services rendered" to his corporate client. If the final settlement is favorable to the corporation, and it is the *commercialista*'s job to see that it is, then the corporation is not likely to complain about the amount of its *commercialista*'s fee, nor will it ever know how much of that fee was represented by *bustarella* and how much remained for the *commercialista* as payment for his negotiating services. In any case, the tax authorities will recognize the full amount of the fee as a tax-deductible expense on the corporation's tax return for the following year.

About ten years ago, a leading American bank opened a banking subsidiary in a major Italian city. At the end of its first year of operation, the bank was advised by its local lawyers and tax accountants, both from branches of U.S. companies, to file its tax return "Italian-style", that is, to understate its actual profits by a significant amount. The American general manager of the bank, who was on his first overseas assignment, refused to do so both because he considered it dishonest and because it was inconsistent with the practices of his parent company in the United States.

About six months after filing its "American-style" tax return, the bank received an "invitation to discuss" notice from the Italian tax authorities. The bank's general manager consulted with his lawyers and tax accountants who suggested he hire a *commercialista*. He rejected this advice and instead wrote a letter to the Italian revenue service not only stating that his firm's corporate return was correct as filed but also requesting that they inform him of any specific items about which they had questions. His letter was never answered.

About 60 days after receiving the initial "invitation to discuss" notice, the bank received a formal tax assessment notice calling for a tax of approximately three times that shown on the bank's corporate tax return; the tax authorities simply assumed that the bank's original return had been based on generally accepted Italian practices, and they reacted accordingly. The bank's general manager again consulted with his lawyers and tax accountants who again suggested he hire a *commercialista* who knew how to handle these matters. Upon learning that the *commercialista* would probably have to pay *bustarella* to his revenue service counterpart in order to reach a settlement, the general manager again chose to ignore his advisers. Instead, he responded by sending the Italian revenue service a check for the full amount of taxes due according to the bank's American-style tax return, even though the due date for the payment was almost six months hence; he made no reference to the amount of corporate taxes shown on the formal tax assessment notice.

Ninety days after paying its taxes, the bank received a third notice from the fiscal authorities. This one contained the statement, "We have reviewed your corporate tax return for 19___ and have determined the [the lira equiv-

alent of] $6,000,000 of interest paid on deposits is not an allowable expense for federal purposes. Accordingly, the total tax due for 19____ is lira ____."
Since interest paid on deposits is any bank's largest single expense item, the new tax assessment was for an amount many times larger than that shown in the initial tax assessment notice and almost 15 times larger than the taxes which the bank had actually paid.

The bank's general manager was understandably very upset. He immediately arranged an appointment to meet personally with the manager of the Italian revenue service's local office. Shortly after the start of their meeting the conversation went something like this:

GENERAL MANAGER: You can't really be serious about disallowing interest paid on deposits as a tax deductible expense.

ITALIAN REVENUE SERVICE: Perhaps. However, we thought it would get your attention. Now that you're here, shall we begin our negotiations.[1]

NOTE

1. For readers interested in what happened subsequently, the bank was forced to pay the taxes shown on the initial tax assessment, and the American manager was recalled to the United States and replaced.

POLAROID IN AND OUT OF SOUTH AFRICA

American companies operating in South Africa have become increasingly sensitive to charges that their activities bolster a regime that practices apartheid, a legal system of racial segregation and oppression. Although rapid improvements have occurred in South Africa during recent years, many corporations in the West continue to view the system in South Africa as fundamentally conforming to the axioms of apartheid. Polaroid is a company that fits this description.

Apartheid is an Afrikaans term meaning *apartness,* in this case racial apartness. Until recently, this policy of white domination had been the cornerstone of social policy in South Africa since the beginning of the Union of South Africa in 1910. According to the classification scheme that was prevalent at the time that this policy was implemented, South Africa's population was 17 percent white, 70 percent African, 10 percent Colored (mixed descent), and 3 percent Asian. Until 1994, whites alone could be members of Parliament and the cabinet, and only whites could possess firearms or be arms-carrying members of the police and military forces. Organizations doctrinally opposed to apartheid were banned. There has also been a history of political involvement by indigenous industrialists that seek to promote apartheid in the interest of keeping labor both cheap and unorganized.

Despite enforced segregation, most nonwhites reside in white-owned urban territory or on white-owned farms whose economies depend on their labor. In this system, blacks are allowed to own only 13 percent of the land surface. These lands are designated as "native reserves." Though whites constitute 17 percent of the population, they control 87 percent of the land. Whites also control all major business activities, and the system is constructed so that black workers are paid less than white workers for comparable work.

AMERICAN INVESTMENT

Many American corporations do business in South Africa because it is a financially attractive country for investment. Profits are substantial, labor is remarkably cheap, and, until recently, capital has not been threatened by the political

This case was prepared by Tom L. Beauchamp, with assistance from R. Jay Wallace, and Barbara Humes, and revised by Joanne L. Jurmu, Jenny Givens, and Jeff Greene. Not to be duplicated without permission of the holder of the copyright, © 1992, 1996 Tom L. Beauchamp.

insecurity created by unstable governments. Overall, the market is thriving. Currency is hard and convertible, and South Africa is rich in natural resources, especially minerals. The United States is the second largest direct foreign investor in South Africa, a nation of 30 million people, 5 million of whom are whites. U.S. investments in South Africa were approximately $1.3 billion in 1986, down from $1.7 billion in 1976.[1] U.S. companies control substantial portions of South Africa's petroleum, auto, and computer markets and are the main suppliers of many major consumer products. Thus, the U.S. presence in South Africa is a significant factor in the country's economic health.[2]

U.S. corporations began to trade in South Africa around 1880, when only the white South African community was involved in commerce and employment. Whites at that time held all available jobs, even in factories. There were no black employees. Gradually the South African economy became so spectacularly successful that there were not enough whites to fill the available positions, and blacks began to move into factory work and other low-paying jobs. Although their salaries have always been low, blacks have made enough money to purchase goods and thus to become a factor in the South African economy. The more they interacted in the economy, the more repressive apartheid laws became, and this in turn presented dilemmas for U.S. corporations about compliance with the regulations that the South African government had established.

U.S. corporations have become increasingly sensitive to charges of exploitation and opportunism. Between 1984 and 1986 over 60 companies took the initiative to withdraw from South Africa, including General Motors, IBM, Coca-Cola, AT&T, Procter & Gamble, and General Electric.[3] They pulled out for several reasons, ranging from declining market share to political pressure imposed by shareholders. However, Polaroid was one of the leaders in withdrawing operations from South Africa as an expression of corporate social responsibility. Polaroid has had a long history of sharply criticizing the South African government and has withdrawn completely from all entanglement in South Africa.

Polaroid was one of the first U.S. firms to condemn apartheid publicly and to assume responsibility for the uses the South African government had made of Polaroid technology. Polaroid views itself as a "corporation with a conscience" and has been a pace setter in both race relations policies and community relations programs in the United States.[4] In February 1987 Polaroid was given a special award by the Council on Economic Priorities for exhibiting social responsibility by "its decision to pull out of South Africa a decade before it was chic" for businesses to withdraw.[5] Underlying this decision, however, was a history of frustration and disappointment.

POLAROID IN SOUTH AFRICA

In 1970 Polaroid found itself embroiled in a controversy over its involvement in South Africa. The events in this controversy began when a few of Polaroid's black

American employees formed a group called Polaroid Revolutionary Workers Movement (PRWM). They were outraged because they believed Polaroid products were being used in South Africa's repressive pass book system. The South African government designed the hated pass laws, abandoned in the early 1990s, to control the movement of blacks in urban areas. Bishop Desmond Tutu, head of the South African Council of Churches, has described this practice as "among the most humiliating of the dehumanizing laws and regulations applied to this country."[6] In brief, these laws required that (1) all African citizens over 16 carry a pass book that gives such details as where the person is permitted to be and personal information such as the person's place of work and payment of taxes, and (2) Africans may not remain in a white urban area longer than 72 hours without a permit unless special permission has been granted or the person has a long history of approved residence and work in the area.[7]

PRWM employees at Polaroid in the United States distributed leaflets entitled "Polaroid Imprisons Black People in 60 Seconds." They also placed these leaflets on company bulletin boards. This campaign intensified and came to a point of confrontation in October 1970. The employees made the general charge that Polaroid was (like other U.S. companies) exploiting cheap black labor in South Africa and (unlike most other U.S. corporations) was having its technology used to support the more repressive aspects of the apartheid system.[8] The previously mentioned pamphlet and this last charge refer to the use of film and cameras to implement the South African government's pass book system. At least one Polaroid executive (Tom Wyman, vice-president of sales) acknowledged that Polaroid products were being used in early 1970 in the pass book identification program. The supply source was Frank and Hirsch, Polaroid's (independent) South African distributor.[9]

On October 27, 1970, some large demonstrations organized by PRWM were held in Boston, and the more activist-minded members of PRWM called for a worldwide boycott of Polaroid products. In this same month Polaroid officials denied that the company's equipment was at that point being used in the pass law program. Polaroid's director of community relations was authorized to make the following statement in response to PRWM charges: "We have a responsibility for the ultimate use of our product. . . . In response to the charge we articulated a very strict policy of refusing to do business directly with the South African government. . . . We as a corporation will not sell our products in instances where its use constitutes a potential abridgement of human freedom."[10] Mr. Edwin Land, then owner and manager of the corporation, also reiterated his "personal ban" on the sale of Polaroid products to the South African government, a ban originally instituted in 1948, but less than diligently enforced in some years.[11]

Instead of yielding to PRWM demands to have Polaroid put an end to all activities in South Africa, Polaroid management determined that it would rather investigate less radical alternatives. Management at Polaroid then formed a committee of 14 employees, representing a cross section of the company's workforce. This group was mandated to make a final withdraw-or-stay decision. The committee recommended

1. That a four-member fact finding group be sent to South Africa to review the feeling of blacks in South Africa firsthand. The four-person team was to report on the use of Polaroid products in South Africa, conditions at Frank and Hirsch, and the use of Polaroid film in the Pass Book Program, and was to give recommendations on the engagement-disengagement decision.
2. That the committee would consult outside experts in economics, African history, politics, and other fields in order to assist them in making recommendations about Polaroid's future in South Africa and Polaroid's future business in "free Black Africa."[12]

THE POLAROID EXPERIMENT

This four-person team had a reasonably free hand to assemble data and conduct interviews while in South Africa. Its final recommendation was that Polaroid should not pull out of South African operations but should instead initiate a program that would come to be known as "The Polaroid Experiment." The program had four main provisions:

1. Sales to the South African government were to be discontinued.
2. Polaroid's local distributor and its suppliers were to improve salaries and other benefits for black employees.
3. The company's South African associates were to start a training program for blacks to enable them to take up more important posts.
4. A proportion of Polaroid's South African profits was to be devoted to the support of education for black students.[13]

The South African government agreed to permit these employment practices by a U.S. company as long as no law was violated. The government specified, however, that any promotion of nonwhites into positions of authority over whites would not be permitted.

One year later Polaroid evaluated the effects of this experiment and found that significant improvements had been made in the salaries, advancement, and benefits of its nonwhite employees. The average monthly salary for blacks had increased 22 percent (including a "bonus" for black employees). Polaroid had accepted and implemented the principle of the same pay for the same job. In fact, the company promoted eight black employees to supervisory positions. Polaroid designed three programs to improve the education of black employees' children, to establish a foundation to support black students and teachers, and to promote black leadership. Polaroid also contributed $75,000 in grants to black educational groups in South Africa.[14]

This program continued successfully for six years. However, the actual measure of "success" is debatable. Frank and Hirsch noted at the time, and Polaroid knew, that it would be extremely difficult to enforce a complete ban on the sale of all products to the South African government. It was easy to stop direct sales, but it would be difficult to stop indirect sales through private photographers and retailers in other countries. Thus, there was considerable doubt about the effectiveness of the ban on the sale of Polaroid products during these years. Nonetheless, for six years both Polaroid and Frank and Hirsch expressed virtually complete satisfaction with the program. Frank and Hirsch's managing director noted that it was a period when racial discrimination was attacked and virtually eliminated at Frank and Hirsch. Blacks and whites came to share the same offices and have the same working hours. The racial balance of Frank and Hirsch employees grew to be almost 50 percent black and 50 percent white, and the company donated money to upgrade the education of black African children.[15]

"Experiment" Discontinued.   In November 1977 a dramatic new development occurred in Polaroid's "Experiment." On November 21 *The Boston Globe* ran a front-page story claiming that Frank and Hirsch had been clandestinely selling Polaroid products to the South African government in violation of its 1971 standing agreement not to permit such sales. This story emerged through the whistle-blowing efforts of a former employee in the shipping department, a South African Indian named Indrus Naidoo. He had made photostatic copies of invoices documenting the delivery of Polaroid products to the Bantu Reference Bureau on September 22, 1975. This agency issues pass books for nonwhites. Naidoo passed on this photostatic copy and other information to Paul Irish, a staff member of the American Committee on Africa in New York. Irish then released the copy to *The Boston Globe* when Naidoo was able to leave South Africa (as an exile, after discharge from his job). Naidoo's documentation showed that Frank and Hirsch had for years billed all its shipments to the South African government through a drugstore in Johannesburg. These shipments of film and cameras were packed in unmarked cartons. Deliveries had also been made to the military, including a large shipment of Polaroid sunglasses. Since all billing was done through the pharmacy, there was no record of direct sales.[16]

Polaroid had been informed by *The Boston Globe* of these charges five days prior to the appearance of the story in the newspaper. The company immediately sent its export sales manager to South Africa to investigate the charges. The sales manager was able to document several deliveries to the South African government and to interview Mr. Hirsch (the owner of Frank and Hirsch), who expressed shock and complete ignorance of these sales. Polaroid officials indicated at the time that they had long been suspicious of Frank and Hirsch and had periodically attempted investigations, but all were unsuccessful.

Polaroid announced on the day the story appeared in *The Boston Globe* that it was terminating its distributorship and all involvement in South Africa. Polaroid issued an official public statement saying it "abhorred" the policy of apartheid and that it was largely the recommendations of black Africans that had led to continued sales in 1971. The statement also mentioned that Polaroid's contributions to black African scholarships during this period amounted to approximately half a million dollars, that there was considerable evidence that Polaroid had had a positive effect on black employees and on foreign investors, and that it would not establish a new distributorship in South Africa.[17] Polaroid's South African annual sales were then between $3 million and $4 million. The company's universal 1977 sales were over $1 billion.[18]

According to Harry Johnson, manager of public relations, all contracts in South Africa expired five weeks after the announcement of Polaroid's withdrawal, and no new business was done in South Africa for the next 17 years. He stated emphatically in 1987 that "our practice is our policy."[19] Until 1992 Polaroid's policy was essentially the same as it was in 1977, despite the massive changes that occurred in South Africa during that time. In 1993, plans were underway for multiracial elections to be held in 1994. In light of these plans, Nelson Mandela requested that sanctions against South Africa be lifted. Polaroid decided at this point to review the situation. In the fall of 1993, a team of Polaroid employees from the United States and the United Kingdom were chosen to visit South Africa and to evaluate the situation. Upon their return, they recommended that Polaroid resume business in South Africa. The company began its reentry process in April 1994 after the U.S. sanctions were lifted. Polaroid currently has an office in Johannesburg with four employees who manage the five South African distributors of sunglasses, disposable cameras, and film. Polaroid has adopted the code of ethics established by the South African Council of Churches, which advocates commitment to equal opportunity, education, workers' rights, environmental protection, and social programs.[20]

NOTES

1. "U.S. Stake: $1.3 B," *U.S. News and World Report* 100 (June 30, 1986), p. 29.
2. See Richard DeGeorge, "U.S. Firms in South Africa," in his *Business Ethics* (New York: Macmillan Publishing Co., 1982), pp. 253–55; and Dharmendra T. Verma, "Polaroid in South Africa" (Bentley College, 1978), distributed by Harvard Business School, HBS Case Services, p. 6.
3. Harry Anderson, "Big Business Pulls Out," *Newsweek* 108 (November 3, 1986), p. 44.
4. C. L. Suzman, "Polaroid Experiment in South Africa" (Johannesburg, South Africa: Graduate School of Business Administration, University of Witwatersrand, 1974, revised 1977), distributed by Harvard Business School, HBS Case Services, p. 2.
5. Janice E. Simpson, "Here's the Newest Top 10: Companies with a Conscience," *The Wall Street Journal*, March 3, 1987, p. 18.
6. Marjorie Chan and John Steiner, "Corporate America Confronts the Apartheid System," in George A. Steiner and John F. Steiner, eds., *Casebook for Business, Government, and Society*, 2d ed. (New York: Random House, 1980), pp. 86f.
7. See Muriel Horrel, *South Africa: Basic Facts and Figures* (South African Institute of Race Relations, 1973).
8. David Vogel, *Lobbying the Corporation: Citizen Challenges to Business Authority* (New York: Basic Books, 1978), p. 173; Chan and Steiner, "Corporate America Confronts," pp. 86f; and Suzman, "Polaroid Experiment," p. 6.
9. See accounts in *The Boston Globe*, October 18, 1964, p. 64, and Suzman, "Polaroid Experiment," p. 7.
10. As quoted in Vogel, *Lobbying the Corporation*, p. 173.

11. H. Landis Gabel, "Polaroid Experiment in South Africa" (Charlottesville, VA: Colgate Darden School of Business Administration, University of Virginia, 1981), distributed by Harvard Business School, HBS Case Services, p. 1; and Suzman, "Polaroid Experiment," p. 7. See also *Business Week* (November 14, 1970), p. 32.
12. Suzman, "Polaroid Experiment," p. 10.
13. *Ibid.*, p. 12; see also Gabel, "Polaroid Experiment," p. 2.
14. Chad and Steiner, "Corporate America Confronts," p. 89.
15. Suzman, "Polaroid Experiment," p. 14.
16. George M. Houser, "Polaroid's Dramatic Withdrawal from South Africa," *Christian Century* (April 12, 1978), p. 392. Mr. Houser was then executive director of the American Committee on Africa, located in New York. See also Verma, "Polaroid in South Africa," p. 3; Vogel, *Lobbying the Corporation*, p. 173; and Gabel, "Polaroid Experiment," p. 1.
17. Polaroid Corporation, public statement, November 21, 1977.
18. Verma, "Polaroid in South Africa," p. 104; and Houser, "Polaroid's Dramatic Withdrawal," p. 392.
19. Telephone conversation between Joanne Jurmu and Harry Johnson, manager of public relations, Polaroid Corporation, Cambridge, MA, March 18, 1987.
20. From information supplied by the Office of Public Relations, Polaroid, April 1995.